Alabama Getaway

To Naomi –
With affection
and admiration –
Best wishes at
Duke!   Allen
March 21, 2011

Alabama Getaway

 *The Political Imaginary
and the Heart of Dixie*

ALLEN TULLOS

The University of Georgia Press
Athens & London

© 2011 by the University of Georgia Press
Athens, Georgia 30602
www.ugapress.org
All rights reserved
Designed by Walton Harris
Set in 10/14 Minion Pro
Printed and bound by Thomson-Shore
The paper in this book meets the guidelines for permanence
and durability of the Committee on Production Guidelines
for Book Longevity of the Council on Library Resources.

Printed in the United States of America

15   14   13   12   11   P   5   4   3   2   1

Library of Congress Cataloging-in-Publication Data

Tullos, Allen, 1950–
Alabama getaway : the political imaginary and the
Heart of Dixie / Allen Tullos.
       p.   cm. — (Politics and culture in the
twentieth-century South)
Includes bibliographical references and index.
ISBN-13: 978-0-8203-3048-8 (hardcover : alk. paper)
ISBN-10: 0-8203-3048-5 (hardcover : alk. paper)
ISBN-13: 978-0-8203-3049-5 (pbk. : alk. paper)
ISBN-10: 0-8203-3049-3 (pbk. : alk. paper)
1. Alabama—Politics and government—1951–
2. Political culture—Alabama. I. Title.
F330.T85 2010
976.1′063—dc22   2010027930

British Library Cataloging-in-Publication Data available

For Cynthia and Hannah Rose

How perilous is it to choose
not to love the life we're shown?

— SEAMUS HEANEY, "Badgers"

CONTENTS

ACKNOWLEDGMENTS   *xi*

INTRODUCTION   *1*

PART ONE   Habits of Judgment

CHAPTER ONE The Sez-you State   *21*

CHAPTER TWO The Punitive Habit   *65*

PART TWO   Public Figures of Speech

CHAPTER THREE In the Ditch with Wallace   *109*

CHAPTER FOUR Oafs of Office   *125*

CHAPTER FIVE The One-trick Pony and the Man
on the Horse   *145*

PART THREE   Stakes in the Heart of Dixie

CHAPTER SIX Black Alabamas   *183*

CHAPTER SEVEN Baghdad as Birmingham   *213*

CHAPTER EIGHT Invasions of Normalcy   *233*

EPILOGUE   *273*

NOTES   *279*

SELECTED BIBLIOGRAPHY   *337*

INDEX   *347*

ACKNOWLEDGMENTS

This book has its origins in my Alabama childhood and education, and the writing of it has been the work of many years. Conversations with dozens of people contributed to its making, and both Emory University and the National Endowment for the Humanities provided me with valuable fellowships and sabbatical time to support my research and writing. I have relied not only on the work of scholars and historians but also on that of dogged and intrepid newspaper reporters and editors, many of whom exemplify through the quality and persistence of their work a fierce commitment to the well-being of all of Alabama's citizens.

The advice and enthusiasm of Derek Krissoff, my editor at the University of Georgia Press, as well as the energies of project editor John Joerschke, copyeditor Daniel Simon, and indexer Valerie Jones made the shepherding of this manuscript to press a remarkably seamless process.

Many thanks in particular to the following, and to any I may have neglected to mention: Alvin Benn, Shirley Blakeley, Lakin Boyd, Joey Brackner, Ed Bridges, Jim Carnes, Rosie Carpenter, Dan T. Carter, David Carter, Mark Childress, Bill and Sandy Christenberry, Joseph Crespino, Dorothy Dix, Jack Drake, Deborah Ellis, Alston Fitts, John Fleming, Wayne Flynt, Brett Gadsden, Paul Gaston, Elliott Gorn, Randy Gue, Susan Pace Hamill, Craig Hines, Phil Holladay, Patty Horn, Peter Horn, Randolph Horn, John Howard, Harriet Jones, Rodney Jones, Ralph Knowles, Susannah Koerber, Howard R. Lamar, Jay Lamar, Cris Levenduski, Charles McNair, Michael Moon, Donna Waid Murray, Jeff Norrell, Wendell Paris, Daniel W. Patterson, Robert Paul, Jack Pendarvis, Minnie Bruce Pratt, Tom Rankin, Patricia Saik, Hank Sanders, Ellen Spears, Nick Spitzer, Theresa Starkey, Wanda Suitts, Natasha Trethewey, Dorothy Tullos, Rolf Tullos, Albert Turner, Tim Tyson, Donald Waid, Francis X. Walter, John Ward, Susan Ward, Deb Watts, Jim Williams, Randall Williams, Alex Willingham, Charles Reagan Wilson, Jake Adam York, and John Zippert.

Candace Waid's stories, generosity, and deep ties to our home state have informed and inspired me since our first conversations at the University of Alabama.

Special acknowledgment goes to Steve Suitts, whose friendship and insights on Alabama politics have proven invaluable. Steve read and offered helpful comments on successive drafts of this book.

To Cynthia Blakeley, my wife, closest reader, and getaway partner, my deepest appreciation and love.

Alabama Getaway

Introduction

It is the place, promised, that has not yet been.
— MINNIE BRUCE PRATT, "No Place"

All he had when he left one bitterly cold morning was enough cash for
gas and oil and occasional snacks, a thermos full of coffee, sandwiches
Mama had made and wrapped, a road map, a bill of lading, several army
blankets, and a kerosene heater on the floorboard. He would be back, he
told us, when he got back. And off he went.
— PAUL HEMPHILL, *Leaving Birmingham*

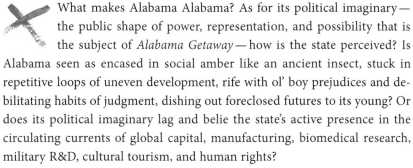 What makes Alabama Alabama? As for its political imaginary—
the public shape of power, representation, and possibility that is
the subject of *Alabama Getaway*—how is the state perceived? Is
Alabama seen as encased in social amber like an ancient insect, stuck in
repetitive loops of uneven development, rife with ol' boy prejudices and debilitating habits of judgment, dishing out foreclosed futures to its young? Or
does its political imaginary lag and belie the state's active presence in the
circulating currents of global capital, manufacturing, biomedical research,
military R&D, cultural tourism, and human rights?

A turn through modern Alabama history evokes tumultuous memories for an aging generation while introducing the young, via archives of
vivid images and sounds, to scenes of rage and murderous white reaction
against the African American struggles of the 1950s and 1960s. Tuskegee,
Montgomery, Selma, Anniston, Birmingham drew international attention.
Notoriety descended upon white political leaders and bloodied the state's
public face. During these years of upheaval, Alabama stridently proclaimed
itself the "Heart of Dixie," a phrase I use throughout *Alabama Getaway* to
designate a retrograde political imaginary, mapped by a constellation of
pernicious habits, that remains tenacious, dynamic, at odds with efforts to

1

extend social justice, and subject to wincing reconfirmation with any morning's headlines.

During the closing decades of the twentieth century, the Heart of Dixie held official Alabama in thrall, reasserting states' rights interposition, parading religious self-righteousness and intolerance, defeating efforts at desperately needed tax and constitutional reform, refusing to adequately and equitably fund public education, fouling air and water, and enforcing a punitive regime of criminal justice. The campaign slogan for the successful reelection in 1990 of Primitive Baptist, Republican, preacher-governor Guy Hunt — "Alabama is doing just fine" — became the motto for a state of neglect.[1]

Against this ingrown retrenchment, black Alabamians pressed a sustained movement for social justice and democratic inclusion — as measured by the impact of civil rights and voting rights legislation, by the number and cumulative effect of black elected and appointed officials in local and state government, and by the displacement of the racist *terrortory* of violence and intimidation that once haunted everyday life in Alabama and throughout the Deep South.[2]

Many Alabamians, white and black, have wearied of the state's reputation as Alabamastan, a proving ground for theocrats, creationists, abortion clinic terrorists, the pistol-packing and trigger-happy, and the punitive hearted.[3] Many, but how many? Perhaps the pulse of a new generation will yet beat out of time with the Heart of Dixie, but a 2009 Gallup Poll of political ideology found Alabama the most conservative U.S. state.[4]

"The old images of Alabama are fading," touts the *Mobile Press Register*. "Alabama is a global player." State officials and business leaders crow over their recruitment of German, Japanese, and Korean auto and steel factories, thanks to hundreds of millions of dollars in Alabama incentives. Investments of other millions by the Retirement Systems of Alabama have reinvigorated the downtowns of Mobile and Montgomery with world-class hotels and office buildings. "The state once known for racial intolerance and rural poverty is gaining recognition as a leader for globalization and free trade."[5]

As one of its narrative threads, *Alabama Getaway* takes notice of the eager imagineering (the strategic marshaling of hype and publicity) of the state as a "global player." Newly enticed manufacturing outposts soak up Alabama giveaways, but the state's median income stagnates or loses ground.[6] The hourly wages are good for those who can get them, but industry decision-making takes place elsewhere. In Alabama, as Wanda Rushing has observed about capitalist globalization in Memphis, "each new wave of development strategies tends to reproduce old patterns of inequality, generating wealth and power for a few and maintaining the structure of poverty and inequality for many."[7] In the state's Black Belt region, neither the boondoggle construction of the Army Corps of Engineers' Tennessee-Tombigbee Waterway nor the vast holdings of transnational timber and paper companies have done much to raise the quality of life for local residents. When recession comes calling, the Black Belt unemployment rate easily doubles that for the hard-hit state as a whole.

"A goal of social justice is social equality," insists Iris Marion Young, whose critical justice theory informs *Alabama Getaway*. For Young, social equality "refers not primarily to the distribution of social goods . . . [but] to the full participation and inclusion of everyone in a society's major institutions, and the socially supported substantive opportunity for all to develop and exercise their capacities and realize their choices."[8] By these measures, social equality in Alabama remains a vision on a distant horizon. Will the state ever become known more for equity and inclusion than for inequalities, intolerance, and disparities? More appreciated for child care and health care than shamed by high dropout rates, diabetes, obesity, poverty, gun-related deaths, environmental degradation, and out-migration of talent? Will its members of Congress one day replace the state's dependency on military largesse with advocacy for health care, education, and environmental protection?

And how to remedy the clogged plumbing of governance jammed by the world's lengthiest constitution, perpetrated upon the state in 1901 by an alliance between vote-stealing planters and Big Mules (corporate and industrial elites centered around Birmingham) determined to remove all blacks, and many poor whites, from electoral participation and cripple state government? Because the revenue-raising restrictions upon income and property taxes fixed by the constitution are so hobbling, movements for tax reform and constitutional revision are inextricably entwined. "Alabama's constitution," observes Susan Hamill, author of the most extensive study of the state's tax structure, "resembles a broken down air conditioner in the middle of a long, hot Alabama summer: both allow a highly oppressive environment to obstruct the business of day-to-day life."[9] Hamill's 2002 critique echoes that made by Horace Mann

Bond in the 1930s: "The Constitutional limitations on taxation in Alabama are held to have 'distorted and warped' the development of the entire revenue system of the State."[10]

Following a failed statewide vote in 2004 that would have removed lingering Jim Crow language from the constitution and repealed a 1956 amendment declaring that the state's children have no right to public education, *Birmingham News* columnist Eddie Lard, African American and a native of the Black Belt, reminded readers that in 1996 "Alabama voters approved a silly constitutional amendment protecting our freedom to hunt and fish — by an 84 to 16 percent margin. Think about that: Hunting and fishing are constitutional rights, but not education."[11]

Leading the opposition was the Christian Coalition of Alabama, which claimed that removing racist language from the constitution would open the door to activist judges' ordering equitable funding of public schools and result in that most evil outcome of all — higher taxes. Thanks to such habits of judgment, white and black students in low-income school districts are denied an education in any way commensurate with that of students in affluent districts. Alabama's high school dropout rate, approximately 40 percent, ranks consistently among the bottommost states.[12]

How many ways can you say "disparity" so that the injustice becomes clear? Alabama collects the nation's lowest per capita combined state and local property taxes. The state has the largest inequality gap in taxation. The poor in Alabama pay a larger percentage of their income in state taxes than the wealthy, and they begin paying those taxes at one of the lowest income thresholds in the United States.[13] A family of four in Alabama that subsists at the federal poverty line owes the nation's highest state income tax.[14]

Alabama's tax structure, the 1901 constitution that produced it, and long-held habits of constructing entrenched fiefdoms of political power point backward to the era of white-supremacist, planter–Big Mule rule as well as forward to the narrow interests of a business-first, trickle-down political economy. "Alabama ranked throughout the twentieth century at or near the bottom among all states in three interrelated categories: property taxes, public services, and quality of life," observes historian Wayne Flynt. "This circumstance was no accident."[15]

Realistic assessments of property values accompanied by progressive taxation of property and income (for instance, of the highest earners whose incomes increased fourfold between 1979 and 2005 while their tax rates declined) would go a long way toward adequately funding education and public services.[16] Alabama will remain more a hostage to the nineteenth century than an actor in the twenty-first until a constitution expressive of inclusive democracy, economic justice, and public transparency shifts power from privileged insiders, lobbyists, political action committees, and favored legislators while allowing for new streams of state and local revenue to meet the obligations of government.[17]

HEART OF DIXIE

Across the range of public discourse and figurative expression, *Alabama Getaway* explores the political imaginary of my native state. An affective terrain rather than a sovereign polity, a political imaginary configures possibilities and outlines limits, suggests the boundaries of the legitimate and the outrageous, limns the contours of power. Political imaginaries take shape through popular narratives as much as by legislative acts; in the words and deeds of public figures of speech; through rumor, jokes, statistics, journalistic ascriptions, blog entries, art, and music.[18] Certainly, features that make up the Alabama imaginary appear in the profiles of other states, and in that still dissolving, still compelling configuration of former Confederate nationalism known as the South. But my major concern is with representations of Alabama and especially with debilitating habits of judgment and feeling that shape the state's reputation and pile stones in its path. In *Alabama Getaway*, I aggregate these atavistic, persistent habits into a political imaginary called the "Heart of Dixie."

According to the Alabama Department of Archives and History website, the Heart of Dixie slogan was dreamed up in the late 1940s and early 1950s as "a public relations tool":

> It was first promoted by the Alabama Chamber of Commerce. It was to give Alabama a distinctive motto and replace a commonly used motto of the "cotton state" (which could also be used to describe many other states). The Chamber noted that "Alabama is geographically the Heart of Dixie, Alabama is industrially the Heart of Dixie, Alabama is, in fact, the Heart of Dixie." The Chamber of Commerce advocated its use on state license plates and a bill was passed in 1951 to add it to license plates.[19]

The Chamber knew but didn't note that Alabama was also, segregation-
ally, the Heart of Dixie. That came with the terrortory, the heart of whiteness. The Chamber denied living nightmares, but thunder was in the thicket.
The post–World War II years witnessed rising African American pressure
for justice, inclusion, and democracy in Alabama. Montgomery and the bus
boycott, Tuskegee and the *Gomillion* disenfranchisement case. The Heart
of Dixie highway led backward through the black and white waiting rooms
of Jim Crow to the secular religion of the Lost Cause, the Confederacy, the
rise of southern sectionalism, the enslaved society that made the Black Belt
of Alabama among the richest regions of the U.S. in the 1850s, and the land-
grabbing and expulsion of Native Alabamians in the 1830s that unsettled the
state.

"Montgomery was the first capital of the Confederacy. I suspect that it will
also be the last," wrote North Carolina journalist Jonathan Daniels in 1938.[20]
Alvin Holmes, an African American state legislator from Montgomery known
for tackling symbolic dirty work — leading the fight to remove the Confederate
battle flag from atop the state capitol where it flew from 1963 to 1993 and spon-
soring the legislation that led to repealing Alabama's constitutional ban on
interracial marriage — has argued year after year to have the phrase "Heart
of Dixie" stricken from Alabama license plates.[21] The heart-shaped logo remains, shrinking in size until it has become a barely visible scarlet thumb-
print. Perhaps, passé, it will one day disappear and drivers won't be ticketed
and fined for covering it with duct tape.[22] In 2002 the heart-shaped Dixie
logo ceded a portion of its space to "Stars Fell on Alabama," and in 2008 to
Lynyrd Skynyrd's "Sweet Home Alabama" and to the slogans of multiplying
specialty license plates extolling colleges and causes from Ducks Unlimited to
the Alabama Shakespeare Festival to Alabamians opposing abortion rights.[23]
As for "Dixie," attached to businesses and persons, it dwindles away from advertisements and phone listings.

From its inception, "Heart of Dixie" was a false-hearted slogan, meant to
distract from the crisis of Jim Crow that dwelled in the heart of whiteness,
"a fairy land where no one else could enter," as go the lyrics to the 1934 song
"Stars Fell on Alabama":

> We lived our little drama
> We kissed in a field of white.[24]

Heart of Dixie imagined as heraldry draws a bloody valentine on fields of snowy white, as did what it replaced: the "Cotton State," a moniker denoting the oppressive sovereign of an era too long in passing, its generations entrapped by fleecy staple.

Although called the Sez-you State throughout this book, Alabama has no official nickname. The state archives and history website does designate an amphibian, the Red Hills Salamander; an alcoholic spirit (Conecuh Ridge Alabama Fine Whiskey, made from water transported to Kentucky where it can be legally distilled, then transported back to Alabama where it can't); and a fossil (*basilosaurus cetoides*, an extinct whale).[25] Old-timers remember when the image of a crowing rooster and the words "White Supremacy for the Right" appeared on election ballots as the symbol of the state Democratic Party. "'The white cock,' some of us used to call it," writes Alabamian John Lewis in his memoir, recalling the starkly oppositional choice of the black panther as the emblem of the Lowndes County Freedom Organization.[26]

If Alabama shares in a broader southern movement of change, as Gary Younge suggests for Mississippi, "these changes have come about not because most white Southerners wanted them to but because many black people and a handful of whites forced them to."[27] Many African Americans affirm southernness and Alabama roots, but rare are those who claim to be from "Dixie." Over the long haul of social justice, black Alabamians have sharpened a political imaginary that drives a stake in the Heart of Dixie. They have challenged the persistent institutions and received structures of inequality, and they have taken their stands at such sites of resistance as Kelly Ingram Park, the Edmund Pettus Bridge, Dexter Avenue, in scores of municipal and county governing bodies, and in the Alabama legislature.

IMAGINING ALABAMA

What is the public face of Alabama in the twenty-first century? How is the state regarded in the minds of residents, visitors, and observers near and far? Semblances of Alabama take multimedia form in journalism, advertising, television, and the Internet's infinite hall of mirrors.

Following the success of the television show *Survivor*, an Internet jokester suggested an Alabama version. "Contestants are given [a] pink car to drive from Dothan, to Birmingham, on to Decatur, and back to Dothan. On each car is a bumper sticker that says, 'I'm gay, I'm a Yankee, and I'm here to steal your guns!' First one back wins."[28]

In 2009 the state's Alcoholic Beverage Control Board banned the Cycles Gladiator pinot noir wine from Alabama liquor stores because the bottle's label featured an art-nouveau female nude with flying bicycle, in violation of ABC rules against showing "a person posed in an immoral or sensuous manner."[29] That same year, the Alabama Supreme Court upheld a ban on the sale of sex toys. Back in 2003, when he had tried to get the legislature to repeal the sex toy prohibition, Birmingham representative John Rogers won the "Shroud Award" for the most dead-on-arrival bill. "I get tired of Alabama being the laughing-stock of the country," said Rogers.[30]

In the late spring and summer of 2007 "Alabama Senate Fight" was a YouTube favorite: on the floor of the state legislature, a senator lands a fist upside the head of a political enemy before other senators can intervene. "The first images I saw were on a local TV station," said an outraged Senator Hank Sanders. "The next images were on CNN, already all over the country. I heard someone had seen it in Spain. Another saw it in Istanbul, Turkey. In a few hours, it was all over the world, reinforcing the worst stereotypes of Alabama."[31]

Alabama's political imaginary appears differently to a white, suburban, Shelby County Republican than to an African American, rural, Greene County Democrat, and different still to a London journalist. Unlike the stars that fell on Alabama, imaginaries don't rain from the sky but coalesce and take expressive form in the social world. Long-standing habits of judgment and feeling are hard to shake. "Alabama" does not mean what it did a half-century ago, but antidemocratic privileges and practices still impede the unfolding of what Alabama can become. Many white Alabamians declare hostility toward government at every level—as if government weren't the essential vehicle of democracy-in-progress.

Early in *Alabama Getaway*, I consider how the state's prevailing political imaginary remains saddled with debilitating habits of judgment—a concept adapted from philosopher Judith Butler. Habits of judgment take hold with the formation of subjectivity, through a mutual structuring of cultural values and strong emotions. Habits of judgment, and of feeling, that characterize the Heart of Dixie cluster around reflexive fundamentalisms of religion, race, gender, economics, and sexuality. Expressions of these fundamentalisms rely upon the punitive, upon male prerogative, defensiveness against criticism, antigovernment animus, knee-jerk patriotism, and "free-market" capitalism. If, as Slavoj Žižek writes, "You should tell the truth, *even if it helps you*," then help comes from calling out habits of judgment that have stigmatized Alabama by wreaking social mischief and mayhem yet continue to provide a perverse satisfaction that is hard to turn loose.[32]

Habits of judgment grow from location, historical practices, institutional affirmation, and cultural repetition. How much of the animus against nonwhite peoples and the joy in militarism took hold long ago in the encounter with and displacement of Native Americans (including the namesakes of the state) during the eras of exploration and "settlement"? How much of the offhand dismissal of ecological stewardship (the once-rich Black Belt eroded away in mere generations) stems from taken-for-granted exploitive and erosive agricultural practices, legitimized by the biblically sanctioned charge to subdue nature? How much of a legacy still lingers from the world the slaveholders ruled, belligerently seceded for, and ruinously and bitterly lost? What portion of Alabama's inadequate support of education, health care, cultural institutions, and social services derives from anti-egalitarian attitudes stamped generations ago by selfish and self-protective elites (planters, Big Mules, got-rocks)[33] upon the state's political institutions and its taxing powers? Among the hardest habits to shake are cynicism, defeatism, and the habit of doing without.

Nowhere do persistent habits of judgment express themselves more destructively in Alabama — and stand starkly convicted — than in the punitive treatment of the jailed and imprisoned. More than a reminder of the state's racist past, the disproportionate incarceration of young African American men testifies to a failure to provide educational and occupational opportunity. The state's prevailing attitude toward crime, punishment, and livelihood seems closer to the early nineteenth century's: "He questioned himself if human society could have the right alike to crush its members," wrote Victor Hugo of Jean Valjean, "and to keep a poor man for ever between a lack of work, and excess of punishment."[34] Hardened in its habits, the Alabama imaginary can't escape the shame of a system of "corrections" punitively enmeshed in a chronically starved public sector.

"Public Figures of Speech," Part Two of *Alabama Getaway*, features a procession of the state's most visible political actors since the upheaval of the 1960s: governors, members of Congress, state legislators, and judges — sequential oafs of office whose outrageous behavior has sustained the Heart of Dixie. For his base of supporters among the rural and urban white working class, George Wallace modeled a public demeanor, performative style, and executive disengagement that stunted and still haunts Alabama. After Wallace, politicians ambitious for statewide office often imitated The Guvner's style and posturings, flailing against modernity like upturned turtles in the Alabama sun.[35] This was an era of high risibility, spotlighting such scenes of national chagrin as the return of the convict lease system, official disavowals of evolution, and heraldings of Christian nationalism, alongside battles over public display of the Confederate flag and the Ten Commandments. There were the spectacles of Alabama's chief justice being removed from office, one governor resigning under threat of removal, and another being led off to federal prison.

Contention over the Alabama imaginary assumed old as well as new forms throughout the 1990s and into the new century. In high-priced electoral contests, corporate interests wrested the state supreme court from "send them a message" plaintiffs' lawyers. Pressing for responsive state government and increased inclusion in the institutions that affected their lives, the state's black citizenry, complemented by a minority of whites, sought to widen the horizon of democracy. Angered that Christ-on-their-sleeve politicians were scaring away migrating companies and sustaining the state's reputation for intolerance, business-first Republicans threw their heft and money into the watershed election of Bob Riley as governor in 2002 and his reelection in 2006.

Part Three begins by reviewing recent efforts of black Alabamians to shape a political imaginary in opposition to the Heart of Dixie and moves on to interpret skirmishes over public memory and memorialization — as in the shifting meaning of the Edmund Pettus Bridge at Selma. The use that former U.S. Secretary of State Condoleezza Rice makes of her 1960s Alabama childhood is the subject of "Imagining Baghdad as Birmingham." The book's concluding chapter assesses battles lost, won, and still unfolding in the struggle for social justice, and the effects these conflicts have had upon resolving the state's knotty dilemmas and changing Alabama's political imaginary.

"HAD ENOUGH?"

"I'm tired of being first in things that are bad and last in things that are good," complained Governor Riley in the summer of 2003, early in his first term, assuming the voice of benighted Alabama and intent on improving the state's reputation.[36] Riley brought an end to some of the worst acting out — the decades-long court orders and consent decrees gone unsettled, the use of the governor's office to enrich self, family, and cronies. He stayed out of jail, avoided indictment, served up no humiliating viral videos, never threatened a federal judge with a barbed-wire enema, and worked to lure foreign manufacturers. Facing revenue shortfalls, he urged legislators not to cut a successful early reading program (found in all public elementary schools) as well as math and science initiatives (in over half of elementary and middle schools).[37]

On the opposite side of the ledger, calamitous habits of judgment had consequences. Early in Riley's first term, intent on overcoming voters' ingrained distrust of government initiatives and a "Vote No!" publicity campaign bankrolled by large landowners and right-wing business forces, he was unable to enact even modest tax reform for the support of education. Then, in actions of his own choosing, the Christian governor signed execution orders, championed (along with all of the state's Republican congressmen) the squanderous Iraq War, buddied with Dick Cheney for political fundraising among the wealthiest, did little to expand the role of women in leadership positions of state government, and was frequently at odds with concerns pressed by the 27 percent of Alabama's population that is African American. In one of the few measures of social betterment where Alabama stood out nationally — providing health care to low-income children — Riley opposed lowering the income eligibility level so that more children could participate.[38] During the last year of his second term, lacerated by his own moral strictures, Governor Riley went "bonkers over bingo."[39] Riley threw away much accumulated goodwill and temperate reputation by ordering trooper raids to squelch electronic bingo halls that were mushrooming around the state. Religiously opposed to gambling, Riley's timing and tactics couldn't have been clumsier as he battled cash-starved jurisdictions (bingo operations were untaxed), wealthy entrepreneurs, the state attorney general, and piecemeal laws in testing the definition of a slot machine. Federal investigators conducting their own bingo probe exposed the shadowy world of Alabama lobbyist-legislator dealings in a state without effective ethics standards.[40]

Well into the new century, Alabama has made little movement up the lists of the bottommost in terms of income disparity, tax fairness, overall health, high school graduation rates, and improved opportunities for the next generation. The Great Recession brought bleeding rounds of budgetary cutbacks and proration, undoing recent increments and modicums of betterment. And paradoxically, the rescue by the federal government of U.S. banks and deregulated financial institutions devastated by their escapades in high-stakes gambling touched off a right-wing, faux-populist reaction nowhere felt more strongly than, nor as poorly understood as, in undereducated Alabama.

"Had enough?" chafes longtime Mobile newspaper columnist Frances Coleman. "Tired of the drip, drip, drip of surveys and reports" consigning Alabama and Mississippi to the bottommost "on the basis of appearance, economic issues and/or quality of life? Me too. . . . It's enough to make a person wonder why anyone lives here." Provoked and annoyed, Coleman seems unable to sort the disastrous from the merely unpleasant, scenery from substance, forest from trees. "The woods are thick with trees," she writes, trying to counter the dismal social statistics. "The Mobile Delta provides spawning and nesting grounds for an incredible variety of game, birds and fish. . . . The color and texture of the Gulf beaches rival shorelines anywhere." But trumping even Alabama's natural wonders (so long as they survive gushing oil spills and developers' designs) are the selectively chosen rituals of personal relations:

> Most of all, it's the people who make Alabama and, yes, good old Mississippi what they are. If too many of us are overweight and plagued with other health-and-beauty issues, so be it.
>
> If our incomes aren't as high as we'd wish and our schools aren't as good as education gurus would wish, well, those things are what they are.
>
> Our accents are gentle and our people are kind. I do not believe you will find friendlier folks anywhere in the country.[41]

The gracious plenties are tangible and tasty, whether folded into a confection called "Sweet Home Alabama" or stirred into the lyrics of a dozen songs by the country-rock band Alabama during its heyday. Down-home Samaritans rush to the roadside rescue of broken-down Yankee travelers. Handy Alabamians cultivate house and garden, gun and story, humor and food. They chase after sports and the wild outdoors. They take pride in hard work and self-sufficiency. But for far too many, the grim indices of health, education, income, and opportunity are just as real, of a greater order of magnitude than cushioning manners and gentle accents, and shameful for their long-tolerated persistence and fatalistic dismissal.

In its newly celebrated global presence, Alabama shows contradictory faces, represented through the glad-handing eagerly extended by development officials and in labor practices reminiscent of an earlier era. Effusive in offering infrastructure improvements, tax breaks, and promises of compliant labor, state officials hop from industrial recruiting trips abroad to meetings in Montgomery with representatives of governments to discuss trading relationships.[42] Meanwhile, the Birmingham-based Drummond Company faces repeated charges of union busting, failure to protect labor leaders from murder, payments to paramilitary terrorists, and exploitation of workers in unsafe conditions at its vast, open-pit coal mining operations near La Loma in Colombia, South America.[43] Alabama's late-nineteenth-century industrial beginnings in coal and iron were founded upon the forced labor of state prisoners, almost all of them African American. The enormous wealth of Alabama's antebellum planters rested upon an earlier capitalist globalization featuring slavery, the cotton trade, and textile manufacturing. Will the state's latest incarnation as a "global player" deliver broadly shared benefits or record another sorry set of entries in the account book of haves and have-nots?

ALABAMA GETAWAY

The notion of an "Alabama getaway" poses language's difficulty going and coming. In the Grateful Dead's "Alabama Getaway," the singer wants to be rid of a vain, overbearing character named Alabama, one way or the other. Not so long ago some might have wished for Alabama to change its name, so mired was it in the miscreant and sullied. Now, to offer one visible difference, the battlegrounds of Alabama's freedom struggle have come to represent places where an oppressive regime was challenged and rolled back, so that the state itself became hearth to a movement and to one of the largest concentrations of black elected officials in the U.S.

Can Alabama give the slip to the Heart of Dixie?

Somewhere an ad campaign teases: "Give Yourself an Alabama Getaway!"

Glossy magazines and website pop-up ads tout golfing Alabama from north to south on the eleven courses and adjoining hotels and residential developments of the world-class Robert Trent Jones Golf Trail, conceived as both a money-maker and a work of positive imagineering by David Bronner, long-reigning chief of the Retirement Systems of Alabama.[44] Alabama getaway tourism is a multibillion-dollar-a-year business that includes the U.S. Space and Rocket Center in Huntsville, the Civil Rights cultural district in Birmingham, antebellum mansions of the Black Belt, the white sands of Gulf Shores, and innumerable barbecue and biscuit stops in between.[45] The guileless Everyman, Forrest Gump, offers you a rocking chair on his front porch, good buddy.

On each corner where Rosa Parks crosses Jeff Davis, there's money and irony to be made of tourism that feeds upon the Alabama imaginary. "To me, the Civil War and civil rights are not separate stories," says a recent director of the state office of tourism and travel. "They are bookends of the same conflict." But the unnamed "same conflict" defies containment and keeps spilling off the shelf — in the resegregation of Alabama's urban and suburban spaces, in the racial disparities of wealth, education, and social services. Slavery existed before the Civil War, and racism remained after the 1960s. Simplistic history and evasive advertising bend to silver-lining hyperbole. "No other state has the quality or quantity of destinations of what was once a battlefield in the '60s."[46] A bloodied list where Alabama grapples for top spot.

Alabama can also be a getaway for runaway shops. "It's all about cost," explains Ron Harbour of Harbour and Associates, a Troy, Michigan, management and manufacturing firm, explaining why the auto industry is drawn to Alabama tax and land giveaways and the anti-union climate. In 1993 Mercedes announced it would build an assembly plant near Birmingham. "That put us on the map internationally and did away with a lot of negative images," says Alabama Power Company's Ted Levi, who later helped the state lure Hyundai and chase other automakers with hundreds of millions of dollars in subsidies and tax breaks. "Today," writes Jay Reeves, "a state once viewed by many as a racist backwater gets a hearing when site selection specialists begin compiling lists of potential plant locations."[47] The Sunbelt boosterism of legislators, governors, and development officials may have polished Alabama's "backwater" image, but at an unknown price. The extent to which bountiful tax credits and giveaways to migrating manufacturers result in widespread and lasting benefits remains difficult to assess.

The verdict on automobile chasing was far from rendered when the Great Recession arrived in late 2007. By 2010 Alabama unemployment had risen to over 11 percent — its highest rate in over twenty-five years — to place it on the list of most-affected states.[48] Due in part to the slowdown in auto manufacturing — the sector of the national economy that suffered the largest percentage of employment losses during the recession — economists predicted that it would take the state years to recover the vanished jobs.[49]

What if, the next time a car maker comes calling, a goodly portion of the hundreds of millions of dollars in industry enticements went instead to early childhood education, child care, the reduction of class sizes in public schools, dropout prevention, and health care? In a generation, the life chances of children of low- and middle-income Alabamians would markedly improve. The history of the convict lease, of New York–based U.S. Steel's takeover of Birmingham's coal mines and steel mills, of textile factories shuttered and abandoned by manufacturers gone to Mexico or the Philippines, hardly makes the case for again selling Alabama workers on the cheap to the latest iteration of cyclical industries. "Human dignity, in a global economy, is just one more cost to cut," laments Rick Bragg in his portrait of the 2001 closing of the cotton mill in his hometown of Jacksonville.[50]

"The process of democratic struggle," writes Iris Young, "is an attempt to engage others in debate about social problems and proposed solutions, engage them in a project of explaining and justifying their positions."[51] The shifting Alabama imaginary represents the visible, public shape of an ongoing debate about the prospects for greater democracy and opportunity in the state. Many actors tussle over this figurative terrain: hundreds of black officials win election in counties and municipalities where voting-rights activists were killed, beaten, and jailed not so many years ago; black Selma activists topple a monument to Confederate general and Klan patriarch Nathan Bedford Forrest; a law professor and her team of students produce an unprecedented study calling to Christian conscience the iniquities of Alabama's tax code; writers, historians, musicians, and visual artists, unflinching in their synopses, reshape the imaginary.

Alabama Getaway does not offer up the state as an American exception, no matter the Grateful Dead ("Forty-nine sister states all had Alabama in their eyes") or Neil Young ("You've got the rest of the union to help you along"). But while Alabama shares features with other U.S. states, even more with the

South, it also has a distinctive constellation of historical tragedies, perversities, ideological blinders, parochialisms, and pitfalls that constructs habits of feeling and judgment both public and personal. Joan Didion, seeking the origins and the ideological shadings of her California consciousness, confessed that *Where I Was From* (2003) "represents an exploration into my own confusions about the place and the way in which I grew up . . . misapprehensions and misunderstandings so much a part of who I became that I can still to this day confront them only obliquely."[52]

In *Carry Me Home* (2001), the acclaimed chronicle that leads up to and revolves around the civil rights struggle during the "national turning point known in history as the Year of Birmingham, 1963," Diane McWhorter writes of a long personal transformation accompanying her quest for knowledge about her home city and about her father, suggestive of Didion's lifelong search for the meaning of California and her uneasy inheritance of location.[53] Both Didion and McWhorter sprang from families of privilege, gifted, articulate children headed for conventional promise. Both eventually broke from their expected trajectories to question where they were from and what history and location had to do with the making and undoing of their subjectivities. "Indeed, I was very much a part of my place," writes McWhorter. "Sometimes, for a city as well as a person, growing up means becoming what one will unbecome."[54]

McWhorter made a getaway to New York, as many talented Alabamians have done. But she remained bound to Alabama, taking some twenty years to uncover and assemble the pieces of *Carry Me Home*, making vivid the white-supremacist mayhem of Birmingham-area Klansmen as well as the African American insurgency that overthrew the city's oppressive regime.

The poet Jake Adam York grew up in north Alabama near the blue-collar, Klan-haunted city of Gadsden, where his father worked as a steelworker and his mother taught history. York studied architecture and English at Auburn before heading to Cornell for graduate school. From a perch at the University of Colorado in Denver, he published *Murder Ballads* (2005) and *A Murmuration of Starlings* (2008), books of poems that delve into Alabama history, memorialize civil rights martyrs, and constitute a personal truth-and-reconciliation commission.[55] "If you're from a Southern family as I am," writes York, " — my family is six, seven generations in Alabama and before that further up the Appalachian chain — you're already implicated in the history in so many ways that you can't know specifically."[56] York describes his Alabama getaway to Ithaca in 1994, an undoing necessary to becoming:

Think of everything you hate — librarians' eyebrows, Baptist deacons' hair, a bookshelf of Bibles and nothing else. Walk through your room once again, checking under the bed, the desk, in all the dresser drawers. . . .

Don't think how everything you own fits in this one little car. How your whole life could be erased if you wrecked in just the right place. . . .

Look straight ahead. Adjust the rearview mirror. Adjust the rearview mirror. Feel it warm beneath your hand, its box of river and sun and steel and shadow. Ignore your heart rising to your throat, this terrible relapse.

Think of everything you hate. Everything. Then pull the mirror down.[57]

Such is the dilemma of the Alabama getaway for the native son or daughter — whether staying, leaving, or returning: how to get clear of the Heart of Dixie. For many of us who "come from Alabama," the political imaginary seems as natural as an old banjo song and as compelling as habits formed in childhood.

PART ONE

Habits of Judgment

Who will be a subject here and what will count as a life,
a moment of ethical questioning which requires that we
break the habits of judgment.

    —JUDITH BUTLER, "What Is Critique?"

When they aggravate her she wants to pinch their habits
off like potato bugs off the leaf.

    —MINNIE BRUCE PRATT, "My Mother Loves Women"

CHAPTER ONE

The Sez-you State

"They can't do that, can they?"
"This is Alabama," I said. "Who's going to say they can't?"
    —JOEY MANLEY, *The Death of Donna-May Dean*

By the time I became aware of the concept of Alabama, it sickened and shamed me, for it seemed a place where knowledgeable people colluded with buffoons to promulgate an intolerable society based on racism and narrow, xenophobic interpretations of Scripture.
    —RODNEY JONES, "A Half Mile of Road in North Alabama"

It's easy to make fun of a place where you can find *To Kill a Mockingbird* on the library's how-to shelves. Across the years, Alabama dependably delivers headlines and punch lines that fade into the next boldfaced outrage or televised fiasco. A reputation so constructed out of historical predicaments becomes easier to sustain than dismantle. Humiliations, obsessions, and grim revelations pile up, rendering a long list of bunglings, neglect, everyday iniquities, malfeasances, and atrocities: Jim Crow and the convict lease, lynchings, racist bombings and beatings, killings of homosexuals, church burnings, book bannings, the Tuskegee syphilis experiment, interpositions, laughingstock politicians, whipping posts and chain gangs, toxic dumps, Ten Commandment judges, abortion clinic terrorists, governors impeached and imprisoned. In a perverse balance of trade, the state pays in reputation for one of its leading exports — laughs at its expense — a dependable source of disdain for many beyond its borders.

"For Georgians," clucks the *Christian Science Monitor*, "Alabama is the big tom at the turkey shoot."[1] "Can't we just go back to picking on Alabama?" ask Atlantans, bored with the latest celebrity scandal.[2]

During the 2008 Pennsylvania Democratic presidential primary, residents of the Keystone State resented political strategist James Carville's recycled characterization, first made in 1986: "Between Paoli [a Philly suburb] and Penn Hills [a Pittsburgh suburb], everything else is Alabama."[3]

"Like so many frontier locations," complains a Canadian newspaper, "the natural beauty of Alaska is sensational; what man has added is mostly ugly. Think redneck Alabama with permafrost."[4] An Australian journalist writes of his country's taxpayers being as easy to bilk by politicians as "an Alabama redneck at a Las Vegas blackjack table."[5]

Worse than the jokes are the no-jokes.

"Birmingham resident Bernard Jones remained in guarded condition as of Monday after suffering a gunshot wound to his abdomen. . . . According to his cousin and barber Alex Jones, the victim was shot outside a barber shop after arguing unsuccessfully with another patron about 'what opossums eat.'"[6] Except they would have said "possums." They would have agreed on that.

A full-page, back-cover ad in the *Nation* magazine for Working Assets, a long-distance service that donates 1 percent of customers' phone bills to nonprofit groups such as the Children's Defense Fund and Planned Parenthood, recruited customers in the 1990s by pitching, "Phone your narrow-minded, self-righteous, abortion clinic picketing sister in Alabama and thank her for helping you support a woman's right to choose."[7]

How many years' wandering in the wilderness is enough? Jokes about Alabama crash into that mythical-historical mashup called the "South," now more than ever an entropic imaginative terrain. "The South," wrote Adrienne Rich in the mid-1980s, "has heavily borne the shame of the omnipresent racism of this country." It has served as "the scapegoat of white supremacism and terrorism." The South, "Dixie," and Alabama — when it is perceived (and when it behaves) as the Heart of Dixie — function as dumping grounds for abject imaginaries, toxic sites of the gullible, disenfranchised, redneck, dumb-assed, feckless, soiled, and toothless. "When we allow a piece of the world to remain exotic in our imaginations," adds Rich, whose childhood runs to Georgia and Alabama, "we dehumanize its people and collaborate in our own ignorance."[8] Playing upon Alabama as a designated reservoir of racism can conveniently shift self-scrutiny away from other places with their own egregious habits. "When it comes to racial disparities, and how to correct them," observes the *Economist*, "America remains closer than it thinks to the Alabama it still affects to despise."[9]

In *South of Haunted Dreams* (1993), African American writer Eddy L. Harris comes to question his received impressions of blacks in the South only after a slow motorcycle journey below the Mason-Dixon Line. "It seems very often that blacks in the North feel themselves superior to blacks in the South," writes Harris, "because they think blacks in the South were simple-minded enough to stay and suffer the worst of the horrors and indignities. Southern blacks too often are called 'Bamas' and country niggers, and are seen as backward and uneducated."[10] A glance at the *Urban Dictionary* turns up entries like "That girl looks like a straight-up bama in those shoes" or "Man, he is such a bama."[11]

"That's why it was called Bama Day," complained the *Montgomery Advertiser* in 2000, "when students at a junior high school in Washington, D.C., walked the halls wearing plaid pants, mismatched socks, goofy ties and silly hairstyles."[12]

Being a soft target for ridicule instills stiff-necked, in-your-face, sez-you resistance down home. Captioned "I Have a Dream," a bumper sticker on the streets of Montgomery shows the Confederate battle flag flying atop the Alabama capitol.[13] Shifting the way Alabama is imagined requires dislodging the Heart of Dixie from pride of place. What price for renaming rights to "Alabama"?

After the May 2007 announcement that German conglomerate Thyssen-Krupp planned to build a $3.7 billion foundry for the production of stainless steel near Mobile, the director of the Alabama Department of Economic and Community Affairs (ADECA) suggested that it was time to quit paying attention to late-night TV jokesters' humiliation of Alabama and Mississippi: "It's interesting that international business people view our states as hot places to be, yet they still make fun of us on Jay Leno and David Letterman."[14] No matter that Birmingham is home to a medical center of international reputation, or that Huntsville (where *Wikipedia* founder Jimbo Wales played with computers as a child) practices aerospace science and hatches tech startups in its four-thousand-acre Cummings Research Park. In some ways, reputation hasn't caught up with reality.

WHERE ALABAMA IS

If, during the early nineteenth century, all that was about to become Alabama had taken "Sez-You" as its official motto, honest cards would have been laid on the barrelhead. It was the springtime of patriarchs and brides, brothers, sisters, children, and cousins, conveying the forced entourages of the enslaved from the Carolinas, Georgia, and Virginia to claim riverine acres they would turn to cotton. It was the springtime presaged by Indian fighters and strongman patriarchs eliminating, removing, or enclosing Natives in the name of tillage and Christian civilization, and opening millions of acres for the in-pouring. In 1819 the winners took the place name of the disappeared.

By the 1830s, Ol' Hickory, now President Jackson, found himself on the belligerent end of Alabama governor John Gayle's claims of state sovereignty. Gayle, Presbyterian, slaveholder, prohibitionist, and veteran of the Creek War, took the side of land-grabbers against treaty-protected Creeks. It was a formative moment in Alabama's political imaginary, with Gayle initiating scenes that would be imitated for generations to come. Decrying his onetime friend Jackson's deployment of federal troops to Alabama soil to protect a tenuous remnant of Native landholdings, Gayle created a state militia and claimed authority over the intruders.

So began the opening act in Alabama's long-running, tragic theatricality of states' rights extremism. Springing from a disdain for the lives and legitimacy of othered peoples and from its belligerent attitude toward the federal government and outside opinion, Alabama's polity instituted precedents that stemmed from and begat habits of judgment. The 1833 crisis ended without shooting between U.S. troops and Alabama militia, but Native rights withered along with Native landholdings.[15] In the antebellum era, historical tragedy followed from the shrill and righteous rigidity of its leadership with their claims of states' rights, and then from the humiliation and bitterness of Confederate defeat.

Conceived by state archivist Marie Bankhead Owen in 1923, Alabama's official motto, *Audemus Jura Nostra Defendere* ("We Dare Defend Our Rights"), complements the sez-you ethos.[16] "Just try and make me" is the translation. Sez-you can apply whether resisting federal voting-rights laws or not wearing a motorcycle helmet. "I must place my grandchild in a booster seat in the car — I have no choice, I must," gripes a 2004 letter to the *Montgomery Advertiser*.[17] Sez-you snarls at protections of people from themselves, assumes no responsibility for consequent social costs.

Whether fire-breathing, secessionist nullifiers like William Lowndes Yancey, or fire-breathing, blue-collar, white-resentment opportunists epitomized by George Wallace, a fractious procession of Alabama politicians has promoted slavery and segregation, domination and exclusion, from underneath the states' rights shell. As they demonized the feds, Alabama governors, admits Albert Brewer, the forty-seventh, "have found it politically useful to position themselves as protectors of the state's citizenry from the actions of those in Washington." These chiefs-of-state have demonstrated an "unfortunate willingness to subordinate discussion about the real issues that affect our lives — education, roads, prisons, public health — to appeals to fear and emotionalism for the purpose of political gain."[18] Brewer's euphemistic "unfortunate" covers a range of myopic and repressive actions across Alabama's history.

Writing in the 1990s, an Atlanta journalist who grew up in Alabama found that the "studied disregard for the opinions of outsiders," this "nose-thumbing, show-the-world tendency," was a creature of mid-nineteenth-century caricature, evident in an exchange between a worldly-wise traveler and a hair-trigger Alabamian in Herman Melville's *The Confidence Man.*

> "I do hope now, my dear fellow," said the cosmopolitan with an air of bland protest, "that, in my presence at least, you will throw out nothing to the prejudice of the sons of the Puritans."
>
> "Hey-day and high times indeed," exclaimed the other, nettled, "sons of the Puritans forsooth! And who be Puritans, that I, an Alabamaian, must do them reverence?"[19]

The Heart of Dixie's modern-day, sez-you cultural hero was the snarling Wallace. A press conference excerpt from May 1963 reveals The Guvner's circumscribed horizon. As the world's media showed the fire hoses and police dogs directed by Bull Connor against black Birmingham youth, a reporter asked Wallace if he was worried about how the world perceived Alabama. "It seems that other parts of the world ought to be concerned about what we think of them instead of what they think of us," answered The Guvner. "After all, we're feeding most of 'em. . . . In the first place, the average man in Africa and Asia doesn't even know where he is, much less where Alabama is."[20] And so the world came to perceive Alabama as an archive of damning images and sounds.

On a 1978 road trip, black journalist Chet Fuller had to fight "the long-held fear I had of Alabama in general. I had grown up in Georgia in mortal fear of Alabama. During my childhood, friends and neighbors and the radio and television sets in our home told horror stories daily. . . . In my young mind,

Alabama — the state that called itself the Heart of Dixie — came to symbolize the evil of the world."[21]

When, in the 1980s and 1990s, Alabama's Bible-thumping governor Fob James fought with federal judges to keep prayer in public schools and the Ten Commandments affixed to the courtroom wall of circuit judge Roy Moore, when he reintroduced the prison chain gang and whipping post, and when he acted like an ape at a state board of education meeting to ridicule the teaching of evolution, Thumper performed Wallace in the sez-you role expected of Alabama governors. "To a large extent," commented historian Jeff Norrell at the time, "a majority of Alabamians are indifferent to what national opinion thinks about the state."[22]

In the first decade of the twenty-first century, Alabama's senior U.S. senator, Richard Shelby, the state's most popular politician, became nationally known as "Senator No" for his opposition to progressive legislation. During the most severe economic crisis since the 1930s, Shelby led unsuccessful Senate resistance to federal stimulus funds that would help states make up shortfalls and mitigate the hardships of recession. "It's the road to socialism," he admonished.[23] He fought against the creation of a consumer protection agency that would guard against duplicitous mortgage lenders and deceptive credit card issuers. "The nanny state at its worst," he protested.[24] Shelby, whose road to continual reelection was paved as befitted the ranking Republican on the Senate Banking Committee, was frequently joined in "no" votes by the state's junior senator, Jeff Sessions.[25] Both senators urged the Iraq invasion. Both opposed extending health care for the poor and uninsurable, even though, as with consumer protection legislation, Alabamians would benefit more than residents of almost any other state.[26] Shelby and Sessions refueled the association between Alabama drawls, militarism, and hard-shell conservative political gospel sprinkled with racist code words.

HABITS OF JUDGMENT

Neither bigger nor smaller than life, habit embodies the everyday. One in front of another, habits of judgment turn childhood steps into second nature. Absent the unaware practice, without habit and its confirming emotions, the quotidian would loom unnavigable, maddening, every effort a bewildering first one. Oft-told narratives and reflexive expressions domesticate the repeating days and nights, help to shape perception and feeling, channel and foreclose expectations. Earliest, formative relations and habits of selfhood are lost to memory.

"Moments of unknowingness about oneself tend to emerge in the context of relations to others," writes Judith Butler. "If we are formed in the context of relations that become partially irrecoverable to us, then that opacity seems built into our formation and follows from our status as beings who are formed in relations of dependency."[27] Social creatures, we interdepend through habits, conventions, and innovations, in accustomed affective fields with buried origins beyond our ability to fully recall or understand. To break with a culture's deep forms, its formative affective structures, and the repertory of daily routines risks loss of social identity, loss of the subjectivity of self.

Habits of judgment sustain the everyday conventions, patrol the borderlands of expectation, shepherd the trails of personal satisfaction and disdain. If the idea of the political imaginary is helpful for understanding the broader public shape of power, representation, and possibility, habits of judgment reveal a culture's hearts and minds. If the political imaginary traces the realm of social ideation and figurative speech, habits of judgment animate the political in the personal.

Breaking habits of judgment leads to a reckoning of individual subjectivity with the socially expected and to a reassessment of the making of feelings and allegiances. Without an altering jolt, some reason to disbelieve, habits bind their hosts. Before the shattering of Jim Crow, the constrictions of segregation shaped black and white Alabamians from the inside out. In retrospect, the legal and habitual structures of segregation now seem unreal. On a 2005 segment of Alabama Public Television's weeknight state news program *For the Record*, host Tim Lennox read from *Inside Alabama: A Personal History of My State* by his studio guest, historian Harvey Jackson:

> It is hard to explain, even now, after thinking about it so many years, just why segregation worked. Not how it worked — rules, regulations, customs, conventions, laws, and legalisms can accomplish all sorts of injustices — but why? Why so many good white people, church-going decent people, moral middle-class people who would give to the poor, visit the sick and shut-ins, comfort the afflicted, and bring hope to the hopeless, would allow it. But they did.[28]

Born during World War II, Professor Jackson grew up in small-town southwest Alabama, the descendant of families who had come into the state in the

1830s "to farm and fight and finally settle, calm and almost civilized." He talked about the sentences that Lennox had read:

> That was the hardest paragraph in the book. I wrote that paragraph maybe twenty-five or thirty times. Set it down. Decided I wadn't going to put it in there. Came back again. And then one evening, it wrote itself. Those are my people. That's what I grew up with. I grew up among decent, God-fearing, white, middle-class people who would do anything for people, black and white. I've seen it over and over again. Yet segregation, somehow or another, transcended all that. And I'm still struggling with that.
>
> Why did they do it? Was it fear? Was it just this basic conservatism in Alabama that change is bad? Change is always going to work against us? I don't know. I just know it happened.[29]

In *Inside Alabama*, Jackson wrote of the pervasive, habitual structure of segregation. White Alabamians "assumed it would never end."[30] Having no reason to give up entrenched habits of judgment, they fought the reactionary fight before eventually ceding the end of de jure segregation and abandoning the political party of their fathers and grandfathers. "Support in the South for the national Democratic Party crumbled in the quarter-century from 1948 to 1972 for several reasons," observes Kevin Phillips; "racial anger, religious alienation, small-town values, pro-military sentiment and growing pro-business and entrepreneurial self-identification produced by the region's economic boom. But the single most important reason was that the national Democratic Party abandoned its longtime role as the voice of Southern white supremacy."[31] The GOP became the latest white people's party.

Across generations of childhood, habits of judgment, which enforced the regime of white supremacy, reproduced delusions. When the African American justice struggle broke through in the 1950s and '60s, whites resisted bitterly, noisily, silently, some murderously, making few admissions of complicity, then or into their graves. Many of Harvey Jackson's "decent, God-fearing, white, middle-class people who would do anything for people, black and white" moved on to form the next line of intransigence, built houses amid the elephants in the cotton-fields-turned-burbs, unwound racial animus into the code words of "freedom of choice," "freedom of association," "states' rights," "no new taxes," "neighborhood schools," in opposition to "busing," "welfare," "quotas," "affirmative action," "liberals." Snarling over paying the taxes necessary to sustain modern civil society, they sought another sort of secession — from city limits, government in general, and black people.

"Sadly, we do what we always did," concedes Birmingham columnist John Archibald. "We retreat, and blame those different from us." Archibald writes askance at renewed talk of secession: that the heavily white municipalities of Hoover, Mountain Brook, Homewood, and Vestavia Hills might turn their backs on nearly bankrupt Jefferson County and aggregate into a new entity, "where nine of ten people would be white and median income would triple that of Birmingham." As the name of this jurisdiction, Archibald proposes "Jim Crow County." "The cradle of civil rights won't return to separate water fountains for black and white," he adds. "It'll have separate counties instead."[32]

IMPRINTING THE RAMMER JAMMER

One way to think about the formation of habits of judgment in Alabama in relation to the political imaginary is to consider the reliable life lessons of football, the state's secular religion since Bear Bryant went around mumbling, "Sacrifice. Work. Self-discipline. I teach these things, and my boys don't forget them when they leave."[33] What else gets taught and becomes equally hard to forget?

In *Rammer Jammer Yellow Hammer*, Birmingham-born Warren St. John's quest to understand his lifelong obsession with Crimson Tide football, St. John determines that his deep allegiance arose in childhood through a latching-on of feeling, a visceral bond, animal in origins. "I chose Alabama," he decides, "the way a baby bird chooses its mother; it was the first thing I saw. I liked the feeling of belonging to it. The imprinting was complete, and here I am." As a thirteenth birthday present in 1982, St. John's father arranged for Warren to shake hands with the Bear on the set of his Sunday morning TV show. "I became an Alabama fan and Bryant fan," concludes St. John, "the way most people come to their teams and their heroes — because my father liked Alabama."[34]

During the 1999 season, when St. John took a leave from his New York magazine job to hit the road with Bama fans traveling in their RVs and Airstreams from game to game, stadium to stadium, he learned that race remained a powerful subject of Bama nation chit-chat. He cringed when he heard the Tide faithful slide into racist slurs — "the brazen expression of such hatefulness is as jarring as it is depressing" — and wondered how deep and wide it ran, how much the intense camaraderie thrived on whiteness. Would he have to abandon Alabama football, the moveable feast of the fan caravans, the spectacle of Saturday crowds?[35] "Can enough bad people project enough bad ideas onto your mental screen," St. John wonders, "to blur out your own beliefs and spoil it for you? . . . It strikes me as a miniature version of the dilemma citizens face when their governments do terrible things." He explains:

> You can either renounce your citizenship on the spot — pick a new team, as it were — or else you make as loud and as convincing a case as possible that your government is wrong and hope to persuade others to your side. For better or worse, most people choose the second option. . . . It's as though once we've joined a group, we're hardwired to stick with it, no matter how flawed the group turns out to be. Maybe that's because leaving something just creates the problem of figuring out where to go next. . . . We make allowances. We hang around, and hope our being there brings the averages up.[36]

In troubling over his attachment to the Tide, St. John's "miniature version of the dilemma citizens face when their governments do terrible things" suggests how habits of judgment, deep feeling, and the political imaginary shape and run interference for each other.

You would expect a state so overinflated with football to provide many life lessons from the sport. The Bear always maintained it did. In *The Death of Donna-May Dean*, Joey Manley's remarkable novel of queer youth in 1980s small-town, north Alabama, the narrator, in the process of moving out of the trailer park where he lives with his mother and moving in with newfound gay friends, revisits his own meanings of Bama football:

> I stood on the bed, took down the Roll Tide pennant from the wall. Mostly so Keller wouldn't see, get the wrong idea about who I was. It hadn't even been mine, or my idea. Dad had put it up there. It had been in his room when he was a boy. "What any boy's room should have," he said.[37]
>
> I'd always been afraid of it, for just that reason. And even more afraid to take it down. A small victory, then: I rolled it up, put it in my back pocket.

From such small victories over formidable and conforming pressures of gender identity, habits of judgment come into question and life-changing possibilities appear.

A TERRIBLE PAROCHIALISM

Among white Alabamians who have recorded their break with white supremacy and fatherly authority, one of the most cited autobiographies remains that of Virginia Foster Durr. Daughter of an elite Alabama family in decline, Virginia in 1922, having "the time of [her] life" as a sophomore at Wellesley College, had to choose between eating her meals at an assigned table with an African American student or being sent home. "This was," she writes, "the first time that my values had ever been challenged. . . . It was terrible for me, because I knew if my father ever heard of it, he would be furious. . . . I had been taught that if I ate at the table of a Negro girl I would be committing a terrible sin against society." After a sleepless night, she chose to stay and eat.

The "tremendous effect" of that New England experience spun the high-spirited Virginia onto a trajectory that would take her "outside the magic circle" of customary society and into a life of interracial political activism.[38] The effort to make a new social self draws courage from such breaks with habits of judgment. Durr's story, as Fred Hobson has noted, belongs as well to a group of autobiographical, white southern daughters' writings in which these women "experience their greatest racial conflicts with their fathers."[39] Questioning the father and white cultural obligation required doubt and revelation. Habits of judgment form through the confluence of strong affective streams among family, friends, religious affiliations — the full range of social ties, beliefs, and structures. These formative and sustaining bonds become ties that bind and blind. Against such powerful affective fields, the remaking of self proves frightening and daunting.

Moments of unmaking lie at the core of Anne Rivers Siddons's first novel, *Heartbreak Hotel* (1976), set in a thinly disguised Auburn University of the 1950s amid the stirrings of Deep South desegregation. In breaking, even gingerly, with habits of judgment instilled since childhood, Siddons's main character, coed Maggie Deloach, writes a column for the campus newspaper that makes an empathetic argument for the humanity of southern Negroes, based on an incident she witnessed while visiting her fiancé's hometown in the Mississippi Delta. A young black man, part of a group who've just made a break from a county jail, finds himself quickly in the hands and at the mercy of two white captors, one of them Maggie's beau.

The Negro raised his head and looked full into Maggie's face. His face was closed and still, but his eyes were alive. . . . They held hers. Across six feet of heavy, swimming Delta air, Maggie read pure, naked fear, and dull hate, and something else. She read, as if it were limned on the air, a humble desire to please, to placate, to avoid punishment from the two captors who held him. Please, said the eyes through hate. I will do anything.

In a dome of still vibrating shock, Maggie thought very clearly and precisely. That's me.[40]

When Maggie writes her campus newspaper column about the shared "country of the human heart," her few words are enough to land her outside the circles of whiteness that have given meaning to her life — family, college sorority, pending marriage to the Delta scion she'd met at the KA's Old South Ball — and to throw her into unreality and unbecoming.[41] *Heartbreak Hotel* ends with Maggie's Alabama getaway to alterity's roomy mecca, New York City.

In another grappling with habits of judgment, as Alabama teen Mab Segrest witnessed attempts at school desegregation in Tuskegee, her estrangement from white culture and "flash of identification" with black youth became integral to the undoing and re-formation of her subjectivity.

As racial conflict increased in Alabama in the 1960s, I also knew deep inside me that what I heard people saying about Black people had somehow to do with me. This knowledge crystallizes around one image: I am thirteen, lying on my stomach beneath some bushes across from the public high school that was to have been integrated that morning. It is ringed with two hundred Alabama Highway Patrol troopers at two-yard intervals, their hips slung with pistols. Inside that terrible circle are twelve Black children, the only students allowed in. There is a stir in the crowd as two of the Black kids walk across the breezeway where I usually play. I have a tremendous flash of empathy, of identification, with their vulnerability and their aloneness inside that circle of force. Their separation is mine. And I know from now on that everything people have told me is "right" has to be reexamined. I am on my own.[42]

Other recent narratives — autobiographical, fictional, musical — raise white Alabama writers' disquiet over the making of self and subject, questioning the boundaries of family, the meanings of gender, the habits of judgment, the rigidities of fatherly authority. In her 1988 novel *Gathering Home*, Vicki Covington tells a modern, white Birmingham family's story from the point of view of a dutiful daughter performing her expected role. Covington lays out structures of feeling, bound-in-blood ties, traps of repetition:

> Afterward, she put on a boring dress — white with oval buttons. "Sweet" is what some people might have said about this dress. But Whitney was going to dinner with her parents. And, being Cal's daughter, she had learned to play the part. If there was one thing she could do well, it was play the part. It was something she'd learned from Cal and Mary Ellen. Whitney knew from the real acting she'd done over the years — she was on fire for drama — that the ties you developed being in a play with someone were deep and strong. So, in this way, she believed her family was very close.[43]

The performance of family can become a parochial theater for emotions circumscribed by kinship. But not playing along can lead to one's undoing. "We feel that we know the answers," writes Butler. "We know what family is, we know what desire is, we know what a human subject is, we know what speech is, we know what is comprehensible, we know its limits. And I think that this feeling of certainty leads to a terrible parochialism."[44]

And when doubts intrude upon family theater's tragedy? When well-trafficked hatreds stop making sense? In Alabama native Jason Isbell's song "Decoration Day," the singer is haunted by a compulsion typifying the emotional bind of Butler's "terrible parochialism." Isbell exhumes the blood-bonds underlying Decoration Day, perhaps the most venerable family-based tradition that continues in the rural Deep South, a Sunday when churchyard cemeteries fill with kin, flowers, and dinner on the grounds. Isbell's "Decoration Day" bares the resentment of a son obliged to his murdered father to carry on a blood feud between two families that keeps claiming brothers and sons, who have no idea how or why the feud began.

> It's Decoration Day.
> And I've a mind to roll a stone on his grave.
> But what would he say.
> "Keeping me down, boy, won't keep me away."[45]

Trailing an aura of timeless doom through old strands of Appalachian balladry, the voice of "Decoration Day" wrestles the death hold of a spectral Daddy and the paternal social compulsions figured by the image of the feud. "And I've got a mind to go spit on his grave." How difficult to break with habits of judgment and feeling.

"I think it's possible sometimes to undergo an undoing," insists Judith Butler, "to submit to an undoing by virtue of what spectrally threatens the subject, in order to reinstate the subject on a new and different ground." The acts of repetition, of iteration, of all the Decoration Days, of all the paternal coercions, produce the possibility of alteration, of chasing away the haintly threat. "I am also trying to say," Butler concludes, "that while we are constituted socially in limited ways and through certain kinds of limitations, exclusions and foreclosures, we are not constituted for all time in that way; it is possible to undergo an alteration of the subject that permits new possibilities that would have been thought psychotic or 'too dangerous' in an earlier phase of life."[46] To arrive at new possibilities requires the courage of making a break, a getaway.

As parsed in the introduction to *Alabama Getaway*, Diane McWhorter's *Carry Me Home* acknowledges a lengthy unmaking of self, an "alteration of the subject" that the author took for granted while growing up in the Heart of Dixie. The interconnections of McWhorter's family history with that of Birmingham, and her quest for knowledge about her father's ties to violent right-wing extremists and the Klan, reveal reciprocal ties of terror across many decades between the white working class and the elite to which her family circle was joined. The personal and the social shape each other. "I did not understand my father," she writes, "but because of that I learned to see the world in a new way. For in order to define him, I had to invoke the history of a race, of two races, and of a place."[47] Through the writing of *Carry Me Home*, McWhorter rejected the imaginary of the city's white fathers for the "magnificent nonviolent revolution" led by blacks such as Fred Shuttlesworth, fearless point man for the Birmingham movement. "This is my monument to the Movement," she writes near the book's end, "but it is a monument to my father too: another enemy disarmed by nonviolence, another lost soul, now consecrated to history."[48] McWhorter's children's book, *A Dream of Freedom* (2004), offers a new generation an alternate Alabama imaginary and a meaning of human kinship beyond the bonds of blood and the enveloping habits of judgment.

UNDOINGS

There is no deeper, confounding, present threat to the constellation of Alabama habits of judgment than the expression of sexual difference. Down-home gayness fundamentally questions and undermines prevailing gender and affective arrangements. Whether mobilizing hostility or stirring introspection, efforts to reconfigure sexuality have the power to transform personal subjectivity and reshape the political imaginary. The dangers, however, remain real. Warns Butler, "I cannot come in close proximity to that which threatens to undo me fundamentally."[49]

It was an evening during the political primary season of 2006, and just another low-key Alabama Public Television interview with an obscure candidate. Host Tim Lennox asked Democratic gubernatorial long shot Nathan Mathis how he planned to vote on a proposed state constitutional amendment that would ban same-sex marriages. With his Wiregrass drawl and self-effacing demeanor, Mathis, son of sharecropper parents who had become a wealthy landowner, agribusinessman, and state legislator, seemed the least likely person to answer as he did.

NATHAN MATHIS: Well, I got a unusual situation. I'll just be straight with you. My daughter in 1995, she committed suicide because she was gay. She came to me and said, "Daddy, I don't want to be gay. Will you help me get some help?"

And I told her yeah, because I'd always been taught the Sodom and Gomorrah story. But it's not exactly like I was taught. I took my daughter to medical doctors and I took her to a psychiatrist. And they every one told my daughter, "You can't help the way you are."

What I would do for gay people, I would treat them with respect like the Constitution calls for. It says all men are created equal. They are endowed by their creator with certain inalienable rights. And among these are life, liberty, and the pursuit of happiness. We need to quit letting the Republicans use gays as a whipping post. Like they say, "We believe in family values . . . [but] people need to look at . . . and realize we are all human beings and they need to treat gay people just like they are human beings too.

TIM LENNOX: I'm sorry. I didn't know about your daughter. I apologize.

MATHIS: Look, that's fine. That's fine. It's a bad part of my life. I miss my daughter terribly. I wish she was still here. But this trying to use gay folks as a way to get elected, we need to stop that. We need to realize we got some people here in Alabama who are gay and they deserve to be treated just like anybody else.[50]

A couple of weeks after Mathis's *For the Record* interview, the state's voters gave over 80 percent approval to the gay marriage ban. Piling on, the Christian Coalition blamed voter confusion that the victory was not larger, pointing out that some Alabamians might have voted "no," thinking they were voting against gay marriage, when a "yes" vote signaled approval of the amendment.[51]

"Homosexuality violates the intended purposes of sex," pronounced Alabama's Southern Baptists in a resolution of 1992. "Homosexuality is not a viable alternate lifestyle for Christians. . . . We deplore homosexuality as a perversion of divine standards and as a violation of nature and natural affections."[52] In 1995 Alabama attorney general Jeff Sessions, soon to become the state's junior senator, went out of his way to sign on as a friend of the court in a case before the U.S. Supreme Court that sought to strike down Colorado municipalities' anti-homosexual discrimination ordinances.[53] "It's a states' rights argument," said Colorado's solicitor general, not weighing the reactionary resonance of that phrase throughout Alabama history.

Scenes of empathy and separation, and the narratives of undoing, reveal structures of class, gender, and sexuality. Mab Segrest and Minnie Bruce Pratt are two white Alabama writers whose identification with the African American freedom struggle prompted their own challenges to sexual orthodoxy. For both, "racial integration and homosexuality," writes Fred Hobson in *But Now I See* (1999), "constituted threats to established roles of race and gender that the South, even more than most societies, held sacred."[54]

Segrest's *Memoir of a Race Traitor* (1994) breaks with the Heart of Dixie's racial and sexual habits of judgment. Growing up in the 1950s and 1960s, Segrest is shaken by what is happening around her: her father organizes a network of segregation academies in Alabama; her distant cousin, Marvin Segrest, slays a black student activist, Sammy Younger; her Methodist church in Tuskegee turns away African Americans trying to integrate. But her narrative takes in more than racism. Writing in the 1990s, Segrest speaks from the unspoken dimension of the South's tangled web of exclusions and segregations that writers such as Lillian Smith and Katharine Du Pre Lumpkin, bold as they were a half-century earlier, did not address in a direct, personal manner. She "breaks the silence that Smith and Lumpkin could never break."[55]

"A decade after Marvin shot Sammy at the Tuskegee Greyhound station," writes Segrest,

> I recognized I was lesbian, a self that I first fled and only later came to celebrate. Two decades after Younger's murder, I heard a call, clear as a bell, to oppose the white supremacist forces that kill both "niggers" and "queers." As I did that work, I re-read the biography of Sammy Younger's life in my hometown, finding in his angers, fears and resolves a deeper understanding of my own outcast self.[56]

Reflecting on her "breaches in identity," Segrest clarifies, "it's not my people, it's the *idea* of race I am betraying."[57] The bonds of blood kin strain against and foreclose a fuller human possibility. For it's also the *idea* — the habits — of gender and sexuality that Segrest betrays.

In *Rebellion: Essays, 1980–1991*, Minnie Bruce Pratt, from a venerable Bibb County family, also connects racism and homophobia. "Pratt writes that her love for another woman, and the disapproval she felt from society because of that love, 'led me directly . . . to work against racism and anti-Semitism,'" comments Hobson.[58] Pratt's poem "No Place" evokes the spatial and emotional disorientation, the almost unbearable isolation, of unbecoming. "One night before I left," she is forced by her husband to choose:

> Man or woman, her or him,
> me or the children. There was no place to be
> simultaneous or in between.[59]

As Tara McPherson examines in eloquent detail, Pratt's *Rebellion* charts a journey out of an entrapping emotional and spatial Alabama landscape, mapping "the transit route from guilt to mobility," and the ongoing creation of a new subjectivity.[60] "The path Pratt narrates is not an easy one to tread," writes McPherson; neither are the "psychological maneuvers" necessary in reconfiguring racial and sexual possibility.[61] The public culture of Alabama, having taken its time to awaken to discussions of historical racism, has moved even more circumspectly in questioning gender hierarchy and gendered judgments.

"Sometimes," writes Judith Butler, "a normative conception of gender can undo one's personhood, undermining the capacity to persevere in a livable life." Such was the dilemma of Nathan Mathis's daughter in the Heart of Dixie. "Other times," Butler continues, "the experience of a normative restriction becoming undone can undo a prior conception of who one is only to inaugurate a relatively newer one that has greater livability as its aim."[62] Such were the experiences of Segrest and Pratt, who managed, for complex reasons, to escape a repressive normativity and reinvent themselves.

The political imaginary of Alabama makes very little room to challenge sexual orthodoxy. Wary of audience reaction, the state's public television network refused to air the BBC's *Great Performances* production of *The Lost Language of Cranes* (1992), a drama based on David Leavitt's novel about a gay father and son.[63] Five years later, Birmingham television station WBMA was the only ABC affiliate in the nation refusing to broadcast the "coming out" episode of the sitcom *Ellen*, claiming it was inappropriate for family viewing and replacing it with a locally produced, innocuous feature.[64]

In a one-sided 1996 roll call (342–67) in the U.S. House of Representatives, all seven members of the Alabama delegation, including African American Democrat Earl Hilliard from Birmingham, voted to define marriage under federal law as the legal union of a man and a woman. By contrast, in neighboring Georgia, both of that state's black representatives, including Alabama native John Lewis, voted against the majority.[65] The week of the congressional vote, the Alabama coordinator for the American Family Association — "Either get your lives straight or get back in the closet where you came from" — organized an anti-homosexuality rally outside the Gadsden courtroom of Roy Moore. Inside, Judge Moore refused to recuse himself from a divorce and custody case in which a lesbian mother had an extramarital affair. In giving custody of the couple's two children solely to the father, Moore ruled that "the minor children will be detrimentally affected by the present lifestyle" of the mother, "who has engaged in a homosexual relationship during her marriage forbidden both by the laws of the state of Alabama and the laws of nature."[66] In 1997 the state supreme court removed Moore from a case in which he had barred a lesbian from contact with her own child. The popularity of his prejudices, however, soon won Moore a seat on the state's highest court.[67]

In a 2002 child custody opinion, Moore, by now Alabama's chief justice, wrote that homosexuality was "abhorrent, immoral, detestable, a crime against nature and a violation of the laws of nature and of nature's God." By being in a lesbian relationship, a child's mother was assumed to be violating the anti-sodomy law and was therefore a criminal and unfit to have custody. Moore proclaimed homosexuality to be an "inherent evil against which children must be protected," and homosexuals were "presumptively unfit to have custody of minor children under the established laws of this state."[68] Below the public discourse sanctioned by jurists, attorney generals, and Baptists, acts of intolerance and terror await their places and times.

ALABAMA BURNING

On the night of February 19, 1999, "on a dark road in Alabama, Billy Jack Gaither was brutally killed and set on fire because he was gay."[69] So begins an episode of Public Broadcasting's *Frontline*, framed to raise questions about the motivation of crimes against gays in the U.S. Gaither's death on Peckerwood Creek in rural Coosa County is neither as well remembered nor as well commemorated as that of Matthew Shepard, which took place under similar circumstances in Wyoming six months earlier. Elton John, interviewed in late 1999 by David Frost about the progress of the gay rights movement, points out that "awful things [still] happen, like the Matthew Shepard incident" — and "the guy in Alabama." Writing in the *Advocate*, Michelangelo Signorile chafes at the reasons why the death of Shepard — younger, cuter, "angelic-appearing," more traveled — was more likely to be remembered than that of Gaither, a thirty-nine-year-old employee of an athletic apparel company who lived with his parents. "The news media know that young, beautiful people cut down in their prime resonate with the public," writes Signorile. "But every death is an equally brutal reminder to us all of the enormous work we still have ahead."[70]

As the news ran its course, the Gaither murder and subsequent charging of two men with the crime attracted wide attention. President Clinton expressed his "grief and outrage" and linked Gaither's death as a hate crime with that of Shepard and with James Byrd's vicious killing in Texas, also during the preceding year.[71] Journalists considered the murder in light of Alabama's history of racist violence. "Arguably, this part of the world may be a better place now for people of color," commented ABC TV's John Quiñones, "but when it comes to those who are different because of their sexual preferences, there are many here who say very little has changed."[72]

Airing a year after Gaither's death, *Frontline*'s "Assault on Gay America" combined a chilling narrative of the crime with interviews of Gaither's friends and family members, comments by the imprisoned murderers, and discussions with psychological researchers about "homosexual panic" killings. The documentary suggests how small-town Alabama and its gay residents sometimes find space for each other; how parents can deny knowledge of, while making room for, a gay son; and how close to the surface loom violence and murder.

In the statement made to police following his arrest, part-time construction worker and small-time repeat offender Steve Mullins, age twenty-five, admitted to killing Billy Jack Gaither because he was homosexual. Mullins alleged that Gaither had approached him for sex but that he had rejected his advances. "I tried to brush it off and act like it really didn't happen," he told ABC News. "It started eating at me and bothering me a lot."[73] Deciding he would kill Gaither, Mullins claimed he recruited a friend, Charles Butler, twenty-one, to help. "I thought I could trust him," he said about Butler, "and I knew he didn't like queers either."[74]

On the night of his death, the three men were drinking and riding in Gaither's car. While stopped in the countryside, Mullins attacked Gaither, slashed his throat, stabbed him, and put him in the trunk. Butler and Mullins drove to remote Peckerwood Creek to dispose of the body. Gaither, still alive, emerged from the trunk, knocked Mullins down an embankment, and tried to escape.

"I drug him to the back of the car and got the axe handle," Mullins admitted, "and started to beat him. I beat him until I couldn't do it anymore, until, you know, all the adrenaline was gone."[75] Mullins and Butler then burned Gaither's body in a fire started with old tires and kerosene.

Family members and friends rejected the idea that Billy Jack would have approached Mullins for sex. They knew that over the course of many months, Gaither had given car rides and bought food and beer for the perennially cash-strapped Mullins. "Billy Jack didn't proposition people," said his brother Ricky. "You know, they may come up and talk to Billy, and — because Billy wouldn't approach anybody that didn't approach him. He didn't push hisself on people. He didn't push the gay life on people."

In June 1999 Steve Mullins pleaded guilty to murder. Butler, who had come forward in March to tell police about the crime, turned down a plea agreement and his case went to trial. Butler's lawyer argued that his client had not known of Mullins's intention to kill Gaither but was intimidated into going along by the physically larger and tougher man. Mullins, over six feet tall and weighing two hundred pounds, with a troublemaker's reputation and what he called a "skinhead tattoo" on one hand, had served time for burglary.[76]

Butler's trial took a surprising turn when witnesses placed Steve Mullins at a gay party in Anniston and testified that he had a secret homosexual life. One man swore to dancing and having oral sex with Mullins.

"I suspect this guy [Mullins] was sexually aroused to his victim," University of Georgia psychologist Dr. Henry Adams told *Frontline*. "What he was doing was essentially punishing the victim for the impulses that he had himself."

"The level of hatred these men have for themselves can be staggering," said Arthur Ciaramicoli, a clinical psychologist at Harvard Medical School, in a 2000 *Advocate* interview about gay killings. "They take what they don't want to see and can't accept in their own self-image and project it onto someone else. Then they can hate it because they've divorced it from who they are. Essentially, they're beating out in others what they are scared of in themselves."[77]

"It's too early for sweeping generalizations," cautioned Gregory Herek of the University of California, Davis. "Sexual identity is very complex and little understood. . . . In American society, being 'a man' is often a difficult undertaking. It's more defined by what you are not supposed to be than what you are supposed to be. But one thing is clear: You're not supposed to be a sissy or a queer. That social pressure can have a huge impact on men who have sex with men and then bash gays. As much as what's going on inside his head, he may be trying to prove to other guys he's not a queer."[78]

In August 1999 Mullins and Butler were sentenced to life without parole. Billy Jack Gaither's family had asked the judge to spare them the death penalty. "I can't see taking another human being's life, no matter what," said Marion Gaither, who called Billy Jack "one of the finest sons a man could want."[79]

"God forgives for everything," Steve Mullins told an interviewer in prison. "If you ask, you shall receive. And I asked for forgiveness, and that's what I got. I repented. He's in hell because he's a homosexual and it tells you in the New Testament that that's wrong."

"I got engaged at one time," says Kathy Gaither, Billy Jack's sister, a lesbian who had been a close confidante of her brother. "He got engaged. But we weren't true to our hearts, you know? You know, we wanted the family's respect. We'd do anything we could to make sure that they knew, 'Hey, we love you.'

"It was very hard living a lie. You know, Billy tried several times. I didn't. I tried once, and I said, 'I can't do it,' because I knew for years, you know, this is me. 'I love you all, but I just — I've got to be me.'"[80]

ALABAMASTAN?

Speaking to the Childersburg Kiwanis during his successful 2000 campaign to become Alabama's chief justice, Roy Moore ranted against the growing prospect of legalized gay unions as well as abortion rights. For Moore, reported the *Times'* Kevin Sack, "without a moral and legal standard based on Scripture . . . the logical extension will be laws allowing unions between 'two men and four women,' or between 'a sheep and a man.'"

"Let me ask you this," Moore said. "Are you going to pay your tax money to support a man and a sheep on welfare?"[81]

Patriarch Moore's heart beat to a stony higher law, leading outsiders and Alabamians in exile to talk of "Alabamastan." "Now some of you are going to call this 'Christian bashing,'" declared Atlanta radio personality and libertarian Neil Boortz, "but this guy sounds like a theocrat to me. While listening to him I got the impression that he would be all too willing to take his religious beliefs and have them made law so that others could be compelled by the state to live as he thinks God wants them to. If you closed your eyes you could easily imagine him standing there before those news cameras with a double-fistful of snakes. If you gave this man the power he would shut every retail store in Alabamastan on Sunday."[82]

Theocratic currencies come in several denominations. President George W. Bush's appointment of federal judges with records of religious opposition to homosexual rights included the May 2003 nomination of Alabama attorney general and Catholic fundamentalist William Pryor for the U.S. Court of Appeals for the Eleventh Circuit, based in Atlanta. That February, Pryor had submitted an amicus brief with the U.S. Supreme Court siding with Texas's criminalization of homosexual acts. Alabama's sodomy law resembled that of the Lone Star State, but the attorney general (like his predecessor Jeff Sessions) was in no way obliged to join the case. Professor Bryan Fair of the UA School of Law complained of Pryor's running his office "more as a personal law firm than as the state's lawyer," involving Alabama "in litigation across the country even when Alabamians had no interest."[83] Pryor's eager participation signaled a hostile intolerance not lost on observers. His brief for the Texas case, editorialized the *New York Times*, "puts sexual relations between gays in the same category as necrophilia, bestiality and pedophilia, and argues that states have the right to punish people who engage in gay sex as criminals."[84] In the summer of 2003, the U.S. Supreme Court, in a six-to-three ruling, rejected the Texas "homosexual conduct" law that had been used in arresting a male couple in their home.[85] The youthful Pryor took his appellate seat in Atlanta.

On July 22, 2004, the "beaten, strangled, stabbed, cut and burned" body of gay teenager Scotty Joe Weaver was discovered decomposing in the woods of Baldwin County, Alabama. "We think the manner and degree of assault may be related to his lifestyle more than the need to rob him," said the district attorney upon the arrest of Weaver's roommates, who were later sentenced for the killing.[86]

Less than a week after Weaver's body was found, Roderick George, age forty, was sitting in his car in Montgomery when he was shot in the head and killed. The man arrested for his murder told police that George had made "inappropriate sexual advances and lunged at him."

"I grew up in the rural part of Montgomery [County] in the 1950s," said state representative Alvin Holmes following the deaths of Weaver and George, "and I saw people shot and killed and lynched just because they were black, not because they had done anything. They do the same thing towards gay people."[87] As he had for several years, Holmes would introduce legislation to add a sexual orientation provision to Alabama's hate crimes statute. Reintroduced annually, Holmes's bill has not yet passed.

At a small rally on the capitol steps marking the sixth anniversary of Billy Jack Gaither's death, Cheryl Sabel, acting president of Montgomery's chapter of the National Organization for Women, voiced the anger of gay-rights supporters: "Every member of the House who voted against Representative Holmes' amendment has encouraged homophobia in Alabama and has bloodied their hands when future hate crimes are perpetrated here."[88]

In 2007 Patricia Todd, a Birmingham Democrat who had recently won election as the first openly homosexual member of the state legislature, took her turn in support of Holmes's legislation: "It will just take a couple of people drinking beer on a Saturday night after listening to some hate talk deciding that they want to go and kill a queer. And believe me, they know where I live. I'm asking you as my friends and my peers to take this issue seriously, to stand with me and say we will no longer tolerate hate in Alabama."[89]

"Sez-you," answered the legislature.

THE SAME OL' SAME OL' SAME OL' BOYS

"Why," a reporter asks the state's first female lieutenant governor, "have so few women made it around the Cabinet tables of governors?"

"Well, shoot, honey," Lucy Baxley answers, "look who's appointing cabinet members. Governors, and last time I looked, they've all been men with the exception of Mrs. [Lurleen] Wallace, and she was a stand-in for her husband."[90]

Only one woman could be found in the cabinet of Guy Hunt in 1988, and the situation has only marginally improved since.[91] When Alabama governors make appointments, they look first to other white men of influence, businessmen, campaign strategists, major contributors. In a state thick with the briar patches of male fiefdoms, governors come and go, legislators accrue seniority, and well-greased lobbyists and lawyers roll along like the toxic Alabama River.[92]

Alabama stubbornly records some of the lowest percentages of women in the legislature and women in appointed positions of executive authority. A few upward ticks registered in the mid-1970s with the election of two or three women to the 140 seats in the Alabama house and senate. Not until the twenty-first century, however, did women, primarily Democrats, break the 10 percent barrier. Nationally, by 2010, women held nearly a quarter of state legislative seats, and in several state legislatures outside the South, more than a third of the representatives were female. "I don't think we've turned the corner yet because the numbers are still so low," asserts Auburn political scientist Anne Permaloff.[93] Alabama, Oklahoma, and South Carolina vie for the lowest percentages of women in their legislatures, with Alabama at 12 percent.[94]

In 2010, Democrat Terri Sewall and Republican Martha Roby won election to the U.S. House, marking the first time since 1978 that Alabama counted even one woman in its congressional delegation. Sewall, who took the seat abandoned by Artur Davis in his delusional run for governor, became Alabama's first black congresswoman.[95] But with a few rule-proving exceptions, including the unsinkable Sue Bell Cobb's ascendance through the judicial ranks to become the first female chief justice of the state supreme court, women remain vastly underrepresented as judges in the state and federal courts of Alabama. Women in Alabama hold fewer than half of the major policy-making positions that one would expect in proportion to population.[96] Of thirty appointed policy leaders in Alabama in 2003, twenty-two were white men, four were white women, three were black men, and one was a black woman; no members of other minorities were included.[97] Only three women could be found on a list of twenty-five members of Governor Riley's cabinet in 2007, when the national average was 31 percent. "We do look for women to fill important roles and serve in the Cabinet," Riley's communications director claimed. "It's not for lack of looking."[98]

Perhaps a good woman *is* hard to find. When, for instance, Governor Riley did appoint an African American woman, Anita Archie, as head of the commission that supervises the state's Department of Environmental Management (whose authority includes issuing pollution permits to businesses), Archie subsequently accepted a second job as lead lobbyist for the Business Council of Alabama. She perceived no inherent conflict of interest despite the requirement by the federal Clean Water Act that excludes any person from holding a state environmental agency position who receives "a significant portion of income directly or indirectly from permit holders or applicants for a permit."[99]

It wasn't until 1946, the year Big Jim Folsom became governor and Sibyl Poole treasurer, that Alabamians elected their first woman to statewide office. In 1950 Poole was reelected and Agnes Baggett became secretary of state. In 1954 Baggett won the state auditor's job and Mary Texas Hurt Garner became secretary of state. These three women are still remembered in Alabama for piling up large majorities into the 1970s. As of 2010, women held all the seats on Alabama's three-person public service commission. Save for the anomalous Lurleen, however, the governor's office remains a male bastion.[100]

Ol' boy governance has debilitating consequences. Where women lack significant political power, the results are tangible, measurable, across the range of human services. "There is certainly ample evidence linking the percentage of women in a legislative body and the passage of laws benefiting women and children," concludes Ann Crittenden in *The Price of Motherhood* (2001). "And it is even more obvious that when women have little or no political power, things are very, very bad for most people." Crittenden pointed to Alabama as a place with few women elected officials and "surprise, surprise — the state is near the bottom in most measures of the quality of life."[101] Recent reports by the National Women's Law Center awarded Alabama an F in women's health, weighing dozens of indicators such as rates of poverty, life expectancy, infant mortality, diabetes, arthritis, high blood pressure, rates of stroke, and access to health insurance.[102]

"I think it makes a difference in the kind of government the state gets," says Pam Baker, who was appointed Alabama's first commissioner of children's affairs during the administration of Don Siegelman. "Women are more willing to talk about problems, talk about various solutions and not lock onto just one or two ways of doing things. And I don't think women are as quick to get their egos all caught up in some discussion where somebody's got to win and somebody's got to lose. I think those are strengths that lead to better decisions."[103] Gains in the state legislature suggest the potential of women to shift the priorities of social policy.[104] "We're concerned about children and education and health care," adds Priscilla Dunn, an African American Democratic legislator from Bessemer.[105]

Now and then, pent-up grievances rising from within the ol' boy structures come to light, suggesting the sweep of the landscape. "The state's community colleges, junior colleges and technical colleges are major habitats for the beneficiaries of patronage," wrote U.S. magistrate Vanzetta P. McPherson in a 1997 ruling favoring three women community college administrators denied promotions because of their gender.[106]

In fields that have been predominantly filled by women, such as private and public health nursing, with fewer structures of exclusion to dismantle, women advance to supervisory and executive jobs. In 2004 three women, all former nurses with business degrees, served as chief executive officers of Birmingham hospitals, while Carol Garrison, the president of the University of Alabama at Birmingham, the city's largest employer and a major medical center, had graduate credentials and teaching experience in nursing and epidemiology. "I think nursing is one of the great unsung leadership opportunities," says Cathy Wright of the Alabama Women's Initiative. "It's no surprise that nursing, where women haven't had entry barriers, has produced leaders."[107]

When women do work their way into positions of responsibility for social services in Alabama, their sense of mission often contrasts with the auto industry chasers competing to out-largesse other bottom-tier states in tax forgiveness and resource giveaways. Consider Birmingham native Suzanne Watkins.

After more than two decades as a public health nurse and family health coordinator for six west Alabama counties, Watkins challenged state legislators and members of county commissions to "spend a block of time in their districts' health departments, and not just an hour or two." She prescribed home visits with the nurses, where

> they would see people who have lived in bad situations for so long that they think, "I've been put down, and put down, and put down. There's no way I am going to go anywhere in this world, no way my children are going to go anywhere."
>
> . . . In every part of this state when a person feels hopeless, they stop caring about their bodies. They say, "I might as well let my teeth rot and eat what I want to because, hey, so I have a heart attack and die when I'm 55, what's the big deal. I am not making any progress now."

Watkins's strategy for interrupting the fatalistic sense of life chances, the repetition of intergenerational habits, entails teaching children "how valuable they are." She is an advocate of health education in the schools to help children learn "how great bodies are and how well they work . . . [and] what they can do to keep their bodies in good health," arguing, "that's the foundation."

For low-income Alabamians, like many in Watkins's territory, the absence of health care means that even if there were money for testing and screening, acute and chronic illnesses take debilitating, deadly tolls. "Without access to clinics and doctors, testing for high blood pressure or diabetes can't be followed up with treatment, and patients end up going to the emergency room in a public hospital." In rural Black Belt counties, emergency rooms remain few and distant. "Most of the cars in people's yards don't run," adds Watkins; "there's not adequate public transportation for people living on country roads, and it's expensive to pay someone to take you somewhere several counties away to see a doctor. . . . We could make a real difference out here where a real difference needs to be made."[108]

Face-to-face with Alabama's wretched health statistics, a number of women have dedicated themselves to improving the odds. Sophia Bracy Harris of Montgomery launched the Federation of Child Care Centers of Alabama (FOCAL) in 1972. One of the first black graduates of an integrated school system in Wetumpka in the late 1960s — her family's house was bombed on New

Year's night in 1966 — Harris went on to Auburn University for a degree in family and child development. She began FOCAL to offer child care providers technical assistance, training, and advocacy skills for working with low-income black families. By 1991, when her work was acknowledged nationally by a MacArthur Fellowship, FOCAL was servicing more than one hundred day care centers, and Harris had secured over $40 million of state legislative support for her human services work.[109]

As the efforts of one generation build upon those before, Sophia Bracy Harris's mother, Mittie Marie Bracy, had cofounded the Willing Workers for Freedom and Unity during the school integration efforts of the 1960s in Wetumpka. Willing Workers supported black parents in signing Freedom of Choice forms in their successful effort to integrate the city's schools. "She was a real passionate woman about justice," Sophia Harris says about her mother, who died in 2005 at age eighty-four. "She was a staunch believer in community service and she was equally a staunch believer in the betterment of our race, so she talked to us a lot about how we needed to get a good education and we needed to serve."[110]

In 2009 Barack Obama recognized Dr. Rebecca Benjamin's accomplishments and contributions in her nearly two decades of family practice along the Alabama Gulf Coast by appointing her the U.S. surgeon general. Earlier that year, Dr. Benjamin, the youngest doctor and first black woman elected to the American Medical Association's board of trustees, received a MacArthur Fellowship to support work at the clinic she had founded in Bayou La Batre. A maid's daughter who paid for her medical education with a commitment to provide several years of care for the poor, she had gone into debt rebuilding her clinic after Hurricane Georges in 1998 and again after Katrina.

"It should not be this hard for doctors and other health care providers to care for their patients," Dr. Benjamin remarked in her White House nomination ceremony. "It shouldn't be this expensive for Americans to get health care in this country."[111] She pledged to advocate for patients, work for primary health care coverage, and advance preventive medicine. "Known for her unswerving determination and frank speech," wrote the LA Times, "Benjamin has the potential to be one of the strongest voices in public health in decades."[112] The habits of judgment and feeling sustained and encouraged by women such as Watkins, Harris, and Benjamin have helped reshape the Alabama political imaginary around conceptions of inclusion and equity.

TO LIVE AND DIET DIXIE

Just when the *New York Times* writes a front-page story about the Opelika public schools, where lunchrooms serve fresh turnip greens, peas, and lima beans from the local farmers market and nary a fried chicken finger, this salubrious Alabama moment is pushed aside in the public imagination by the Trust for America's Health annual list of the "fattest" states, with Mississippi and Alabama vying cheek by jowl for first place. Over 30 percent of Alabama adults are fat, and two-thirds are overweight. "This is not a cosmetic problem," warns Dr. Donald Williamson, Alabama's state health officer. "It's a major health problem." It's also a problem of mendacity, as Big Daddy might say, for Alabamians (and other Americans) lie to themselves and others about their eating and exercising. "People's memories are pretty faulty in that," says M. Cay Welsh, a University of South Alabama specialist in sports behavior.[113]

It's also a problem of poverty. But not all poor states are states of obesity. So mix in the fondness for fatty, fried, unhealthy foods. Fold in the fact that too many Alabamians are sedentary, drive everywhere, lack public transportation that they can walk to, and would rather not move around at all when it's ninety degrees in the shade. Like the Alabama imaginary itself, fat Alabama is a distinct conglomeration of ingredients.[114]

"As I browse the statistics, I am dumbfounded," reads a letter to the *Birmingham News*. "Alabama is statistically significantly higher in almost every area of concern, from rates of teen deaths, diabetes, infant mortality, teen birth, firearm deaths, occupational deaths, physical inactivity, gonorrhea and syphilis, to Medicaid-paid births."[115]

Alabama, the state with the highest rate of diabetes, is consistently next to the bottom in providing care for Medicare diabetes patients. (Sometimes there is still a Mississippi.) This means going without blood sugar tests, eye exams, and lipid profiles for victims of a devastating disease with complications that include heart disease, blindness, and amputations. One of every three children born in Alabama since 2002 will eventually develop diabetes, says the state health officer, raising the prospect that children's life expectancies could become shorter than their parents'.[116]

"If you cannot eat what you want in the South, life is not worth living," writes Rick Bragg, voicing the immeasurable bond between foodways and the meaning of existence.[117] Food fuses cultural loyalties and identity. Old habits die hardening. Political discourse in the sclerotic Heart of Dixie snorts at proposals to tax sugary soft drinks, fatty snacks, or junk food advertising — strategies that would reduce obesity and rates of diabetes while generating revenue.[118] Children whose eating habits are still in formation would be prime beneficiaries. No matter. As for grown-ups, what Big Brother would dare infringe upon the right to eat yourself to death? Who will lick the last of the caramelized, congealed, trans fat off the bottom of the deep fryer, just because, by god, some guv'ment agency says you might live longer if you didn't?

THE HABIT OF BREATHING

When, in 1991, the Institute for Southern Studies, publisher of the journal *Southern Exposure*, listed Alabama among the worst states for environmental conditions and policies, it was easy enough for dealers in chemical waste and defenders of major coal-burners TVA and Alabama Power Company (APC) to dismiss the institute's Green Index as a shrill, typical blast from socialistic whiners.[119] Likewise, when the Resource Renewal Institute (RRI) published the 2001 *State of the States* report, surveying some sixty-five measures pertaining to the "relative ability of states to pursue sustainable development using established principles of green planning as its basis," it ranked Alabama fiftieth. What would you expect from the eco-crazed, California-based RRI?[120]

But when the same criticism came from the self-advertised "capitalist tool" *Forbes* magazine in 2007, the facts and the embarrassment were harder to fend off. The *Forbes* survey found Alabama to be the third most polluting, energy-wasting state in the U.S., just where the Green Index had placed it more than fifteen years earlier. Weak environmental laws and lax enforcement by the Alabama Department of Environmental Management (ADEM), the particulate pollution spewed by Alabama Power's coal plants, the dumping of toxic waste, contaminated industrial sites, excessive commuter driving associated with ex-urban sprawl, and inadequate public transportation all contributed to the dismal assessment.[121]

As for water quality, a 2009 report by the Gulf Restoration Network and the Alabama Rivers Alliance gave the state a D+ grade, based largely upon the failure of ADEM to adopt statewide limits controlling the runoff of nitrogen and phosphorous (from fertilizers and organic waste) into the river systems. "Mobile Bay bears the brunt of all the pollution in Alabama's rivers," says

Mitch Reid of the Rivers Alliance. "It all flows into the bay before heading into the Gulf. The lack of statewide regulations as far north as Birmingham means [dead zones] in Mobile Bay. Fish can't breathe in their own water."[122]

A five-year study (1995–2000) by the U.S. Public Interest Research Group concluded that Alabama Power was the state's top polluter.[123] Alabama Power's coal-burning plant in Jefferson County pumped nearly a ton of mercury into the air in 2007, more than any other power plant in the U.S. An APC plant in nearby Shelby County ranked number eight on the mercury emissions list; another in Mobile made the top twenty-five. As it fought pollution regulations, the company was forced to construct smokestack scrubbers to remove sulfur dioxide from its Birmingham-area coal-fired generating plants.[124]

In its most recent annual surveys, the American Lung Association finds the air in the Birmingham metro area, extending north to Cullman and south to Hoover, among the most polluted in the U.S. Short-term particle pollutants, once called smoot, are the primary offenders churned out by Alabama Power coal burners.[125] These tiny particulates seep into the lungs, provoking and exacerbating asthma and chronic bronchitis. In addition, Alabama "adds more than its share of greenhouse gases to the atmosphere," reports Sean Reilly of the *Press-Register*. "Although medium-sized by territory and population, Alabama placed thirteenth nationally in per-person releases, according to 2005 estimates compiled by the World Resources Institute." The American Council for an Energy-Efficient Economy ranked Alabama forty-ninth in energy efficiency in 2008. The Southern Company, parent of Alabama Power, employed "sixty-three lobbyists seeking to influence climate change legislation, far more than any other U.S. business or interest group."[126] "They will do anything it takes to win," says former EPA enforcement official Eric V. Schaeffer. "Some companies facing lawsuits say, 'Let's settle this.' Some will joust with you over the law. And then you have Southern, who says, 'This is our business and we will do whatever it takes to keep you out of it, and if that means going to the White House and getting you rolled politically, we will do it.'"[127] Southern's executive vice president, Dwight Evans, raised more than $200,000 for George W. Bush's 2004 reelection campaign.[128]

"Just about everyone in Alabama's political circuit, however, considers Alabama Power a good citizen," writes the *New York Times*' Neela Banerjee.[129] With its effective monopoly on electricity for a service area that covers two-thirds of the state, Alabama Power has parlayed the deep pockets provided by its ratepayers into a loud and self-satisfied voice of antiprogressive corporate politics. It strategically contributes to charities and nonprofit groups and carries out government-funded research in "clean coal" capture and storage technology and mercury emissions. Its officials press company positions on issues of public interest and often serve as governors' advisers or appointees. Yet Alabama Power and its parent holding company, the Atlanta-based Southern Company, have a long record of relentlessly fighting environmental regulation, making concessions to public health only when compelled, and only after deploying a formidable army of lobbyists and lawyers and publicists. The Southern Company bitterly resisted the reduction of nitrogen oxide emissions, a key ingredient in smog and acid rain, even though it was a major contributor to Birmingham's air pollution. It spent upwards of $14 million preventing the passage of congressional legislation that would have required the United States to generate 15 percent of its electricity from renewable sources by 2020.[130]

A company is known by the companies it keeps and the common air they foul. The Southern Company and its employees have donated millions of dollars to national Republican campaigns since the early 1990s.[131] In state elections, Alabama Power consistently ranks among the top contributors, supporting selected Democrats and Republicans. In addition to its own in-house lobbyists, Southern retained right-wing Mississippian (later governor) Haley Barbour, whose D.C. firm earned several fortunes peddling influence for the tobacco industry. Barbour, who served as Republican National Committee chairman before returning to Mississippi for two terms as governor, had face-to-face access to Vice President Dick Cheney, head of the national energy task force. In an extensive array of public and private actions, the Bush administration rode to the rescue of Southern and other polluting coal powers.[132]

Rather than work to modernize and clean up its older coal-burning plants in the 1980s and 1990s, Alabama Power evaded the law and resisted in court, fighting the Environmental Protection Agency for over a decade until former Republican fundraiser and George W. Bush–appointed federal judge Virginia Hopkins ruled in the company's favor in 2006 and 2008.[133] In the meantime, all those campaign contributions were reaping dividends. The Bush administration systematically weakened regulations used in the past to force power companies to clean up their emissions. The decade-after-decade, antisocial behavior by Alabama Power, the most dominant of the state's industrial companies, has proven deleterious to public health and serves as a very visible reminder of Alabama's poor international reputation for environmental policy.[134]

As it works the home front, Alabama Power has pursued a what's-in-it-for-us strategy, recognizing that increased funding for education must be paid for by some minimal tax reform. The company's interest in an Alabama workforce that is adequately — if not broadly or critically — educated complements its vision of how the state should develop economically. "After all," comments historian Wayne Flynt, "new industry consumes more electricity, which generates higher profits for Alabama Power." Flynt has pointed to the company's "special interest in reversing the three tiers of property taxes that range from private houses/timberland, to businesses, to utilities, which pay the highest rate."[135] More than any other lobbying force in the state, Alabama Power, à la noblesse oblige, believes that it should shape the Alabama imaginary to represent its corporate mission and timetable. With every breath it takes. In a participatory democracy — where people would have a controlling say over the significant actions of major institutions affecting their lives — Alabama Power's historic presumptions would be understood as arrogance.

"KNEE-JERK PATRIOTISM"

Leaning on everlasting arms, early Alabama history is rife with do-it-yourself gun-toters and land squatters applying folk justice since before the formation of the state. What of "Alabama" itself and the Native tribe that first carried this name?[136] Fourth graders learn of the backwoods glories of Indian fighters, squatters, skirmishers, and militias that eliminated Native populations while making military habits and careers formative to Alabama male identity. Out of desire for land, the state came into being torn from the Mississippi Territory and indigenous people. Cherokee. Creek. Choctaw. Generations of twentieth-century schoolkids read of Andy Jackson and Sam Dale, heroes of Indian killing and removal. In the Great Canoe Fight of November 1813, Dale, "one of the bravest Indian fighters in the state," and two comrades battled hand-to-hand and canoe-to-canoe in the middle of the Alabama River against a larger force of Red Stick Creeks.

> It was an heroic conflict. The three Americans, in a life or death fight and at a great disadvantage in their small dugout, dispatched nine Indian warriors. That

the three men were not killed attests to the amazing prowess of our hardy fron-
tiersmen. Sam Dale and Jere Austill became heroes of the wide frontier.[137]

For his part, Andrew Jackson rode into legend as Ol' Hickory after the
Battle of Horseshoe Bend (1814), which destroyed Creek power in Alabama.[138]
More slaughter than battle, Jackson's well-armed forces "dispatched" between
eight hundred and a thousand Creeks, while losing fewer than fifty men. With
their resistance crushed, the Creeks ceded twenty-three million acres to the
U.S.; land that soon flooded with settlers.[139]

The religiously sanctioned, foundational violence of Native extermination
in Alabama and the Deep South was followed by church-sanctioned, proslavery sectionalism and code-of-honor, fire-eating secessionist rhetoric to feed
the doomed experiment of Confederate nationalism. In the wake of the Lost
Cause, generations of aspiring soldiers and enlistees sought military academies
and new foreign battlegrounds in which to prove their mettle and display their
realigned nationalism. "The South has compensated for its historic blunder,"
concludes longtime Selma civil rights attorney J. L. Chestnut, "with a knee-jerk
type patriotism that supports every ill-advised militaristic indulgence by the
United States since Appomattox."[140]

Military stints opened the world to provincial sons and daughters, black
and white, providing an escape from prolonged agrarian collapse, a means of
livelihood, a chance to learn skills, an Alabama getaway. But in a state where
white politicians rage against government welfare, saber-toothed congressmen thrive by buttressing military bases and delivering procurement contracts, expanding and entrenching Alabamians' reliance upon the fortunes
of war.

The new millennium has affirmed Alabama's eagerness to lead the salute-
to-war parade. The jingoism accompanying the startup of the 2003 Iraq War
easily carried the day. The "shock-and-awe" attack, invasion, and occupation
became the latest diversion from Alabama's endemic problems.

But not everyone fell in line.

"African-Americans are as patriotic as any other Americans," argued lawyer Chestnut as the war began. "Indeed, we have fought and died in every
American war while defending a democracy denied us, but we reject the knee-
jerk patriotism so prevalent in the white South. We reject the 'my country,
wrong or right' mentality, and because of what has happened and continues

to happen to us we are profoundly apprehensive about Washington bombing innocent women and children of color on the other side of the world."[141]

Early on and publicly, black Alabamians questioned the rush to war in Iraq, while white Alabama's elected officials egged on, then celebrated the aggression. The votes of the state's congressional delegation exposed the racial divide. The key roll call on October 10, 2002, for authorization of U.S. forces to overthrow Saddam Hussein's regime found Alabama's African American member of Congress, Earl Hilliard of Birmingham, solitary in opposition. Hilliard's Democratic colleague, Bud Cramer, from a district anchored by military R&D in Huntsville, voted yea. The state's other five representatives and both senators (Republicans all) enthusiastically supported the Iraq invasion and the Bush doctrine of preemption.[142]

A national poll in late 2002 showed only 19 percent of African Americans favoring the imminent war.[143] Elected black Alabamians likewise voiced opposition. "It is senseless. It is crazy," said state senator Vivian Figures of Mobile; "I do not support George Bush on this war." Senator Hank Sanders of Selma tied the impending war to U.S. military blunders of the recent past and to family history. "I have a brother who died in Vietnam," said Sanders, "and I don't want a war unnecessarily. Tens of thousands of troops ended up dying in Vietnam for no good reason." After Sanders blocked a resolution that would have praised President Bush's vigilance and wisdom in acting to "protect our citizens from weapons of mass destruction in Iraq," Republican Steve French of Birmingham announced, without apparent irony or awareness, "a black day on the blotter of the Alabama Senate."[144]

Endorsing the Bush administration's claim that Iraq posed an imminent threat to the U.S., Senator Shelby stirred up fear and circulated false information during the 2002 run-up. He urged a first strike. "Every month, every week, Saddam Hussein will have more weapons of mass destruction to use against us," Shelby blustered after meeting with Defense Secretary Rumsfeld. "Why put it off? . . . I believe it's not a question of if we invade Iraq. The question is do we wait until he continues to manufacture more weapons of mass destruction that can do us irreparable damage and our troops, or do we try to preempt some of this?" Shelby saw Iraq's request to have weapons inspectors return to the country as "playing the so-called U.N. card" (a traitorous act in talk radio nation) and "trying to delay the inevitable."[145]

"You are going for all the right reasons," Governor Riley pep-talked members of the Alabama National Guard in Mobile as they deployed.[146] If Alabama led the nation in per capita enlistees in the Guard, Riley's hilly home county of Clay — rocky, pine and scrub-oak forested, with next-to-no manufacturing base (a chicken processor and a few cabinetmaking shops) — led Alabama in production of Guard recruits and military reservists. During the 1990–91 Gulf War, "this area's rate of service was so high," reported the *Christian Science Monitor*, "that Alabama's legislature officially dubbed it the 'Volunteer County.'"[147]

"One minute you're playing in the sand box," the father of a nineteen-year-old Clay County marine stationed in Kuwait told a television crew from NBC, "the next minute they're over there in a big sand box."

"The United States is the only superpower left," added Josh Nelson of Ashland (pop. 2,000), the county seat. "We're the policemen of the world. You got a problem with that, you got a bad problem."[148]

Did Clay County pace the nation in per capita, knee-jerk patriotism? "None of us wants to go to war," declared Ashland mayor Norman McNatt, who seemed to visualize the scraggly countryside of east Alabama facing an incoming Iraqi missile. "But it's a duty to protect our country, it's a duty to protect our community." McNatt, a major in the National Guard, took the Bush administration's justification of the war without apparent second thoughts or questions. "Folks here know they have a job to do, and they're ready to go today. They don't like to sit and wait."[149]

Asking what gave Clay citizens such gung-ho habits, the *Birmingham News* sent its own reporter. The short answer: "duty and dollars." Family military traditions unite with enlistees' need to cover car payments, college tuition, and living expenses in a county where 17 percent of the population lives below the poverty line and the median household income falls well below the average in this near-the-bottom state.[150]

Even here, however, there were dissenters. "He's too aggressive," retired Clay County teacher Ruth Carmichael told the *Monitor*, meaning President Bush with his go-it-alone belligerence. "I don't think that's too smart."[151] Hers was a rare voice, but not a singular one. Up the highway a few miles from Ashland, John Fleming, editor of the *Anniston Star*, bristled at George Bush's "cowboy diplomacy," voicing his paper's opposition to the "inevitable" war. *Star* publisher Brandt Ayers wrote of the "coming war in Iraq" as "the first engagement of a new Imperialism, a wholly new and assertive American approach to world order designed by the Bush administration."[152]

"As a Christian, it's against everything I believe and everything I think Jesus taught," Diane Sosebee, librarian and peace activist in the south Alabama town of Evergreen, told a Mobile reporter. "This is all about oil, power and money."

While convinced that the U.S. would invade, University of Alabama political science professor Donald Snow dismissed Iraq as a serious threat to the U.S. More accurately than the state's white members of Congress and its governor, he foretold the spending of lives and resources as well as the occupation that would spark resentment within and beyond Iraq. "Even if the war itself goes well, the post-war will not," Snow predicted. "We will become the recruiting poster for al-Qaida and other terrorist organizations."[153] In his heyday, George Wallace would have ripped into critics like Snow as pointy-headed, treasonous intellectuals. In the new century, their warnings, while good for newspaper quotes, still went largely unheeded in Alabama.

Outraged over the imminent attack, Alabama native son, civil rights veteran, and Georgia member of Congress John Lewis spoke to a convocation at Howard University in September 2002. Lewis decried the shift of presidential attention away from "a worsening economy and growing national deficits" and from the "moral obligation" of national health care. Saddened by the president's "going from state to state, from city to city, beating the drums of war," he linked U.S. Iraq policy to domestic neglect:

> Bombing Baghdad may make us forget about our nation's poor schools, but it will not educate our children. Invading Iraq may distract us from corporate scandals, but it will do nothing to replenish the nest eggs of American workers.
>
> For every black man in college — for every black man with a college degree — there is a brother in jail. How will war solve this problem? How will war keep our youth from robbing, stealing, doping, and killing?[154]

Some nine months after the September 11, 2001, World Trade Center attack, polling suggested that fewer than 20 percent of Alabamians — well below the national average — felt favorably about Muslims. "More than one-third of the respondents," reported the *Mobile Register*, "said they believed that Islam's teachings encourage terrorism and violence — even though the overwhelming majority admitted they don't know much about those teachings." Two-thirds of those polled identified themselves as born-again Christians. At the 2002 meeting of the Southern Baptist Convention, former Mobile pastor and SBC past president Rev. Jerry Vines affirmed that the prophet Mohammed was a "demon-possessed pedophile."[155]

Repeatedly, Governor Riley endorsed the Bush rationale of war to preempt a trumped-up Iraqi threat. "It's certainly justified," he said. "What Americans have to remember is that after 9/11, today we have a moral right to remove a threat to this country wherever it exists. If we have an opportunity to preemptively remove a threat, it is much better than reacting afterward. I think that is what the president is doing tonight. This is not about oil. This is not about any kind of conquest of additional territory. This is about protecting America." Such simplistic, deep-seated expressions of knee-jerk patriotism arose from hardened habits of judgment that reaffirmed the worst in Alabama's political imaginary.

"Our planners and our commanders know exactly what they're doing," avowed Senator Shelby. "Saddam Hussein joins a long line of tyrants who doubted the resolve of America to act in self-defense," echoed Shelby's junior colleague, Jefferson Beauregard Sessions III, bearer of the names of two Confederate stalwarts who had tested U.S. resolve in an earlier skirmish.[156]

"The Bush Doctrine . . . plays well below the Mason-Dixon Line," wrote Michael Lind in late December 2002, "not least because it melds two Old Dixie traditions — militarism and Protestant fundamentalism." Reminding readers that "white Southerners are the most martial subculture in the United States," always "overrepresented in the U.S. military — and underrepresented in the diplomatic corps," Lind argued that the present moment of unilateralism nicely complemented the militarist culture of conservative southern whites, especially white males with no more than a high school education — one of Alabama's leading demographics.[157]

How to break with uncritical patriotism in a place where the culture, attitudes, and financial power of the military have an entrenched intergenerational hold? In Alabama, the Pentagon budget supports hundreds of thousands of personnel from the Gulf Coast port of Mobile, to training facilities at forts and air force bases scattered throughout the state, to the Tennessee Valley region centered around Huntsville. Adjoining Huntsville — the Rocket City — lies some 38,000 acres of the Redstone Arsenal, described on its website as "the heart of the Army's rocket and missile programs," with a "population served" of nearly 160,000 active and retired soldiers and their dependents as well as 28,000 civilians tied to military contract employment. Advanced weapons systems and missile defense R&D are among the tasks that keep Redstone scientists and engineers at the front of high-technology warfare projects. The Aviation and Missile Command manages the army's missile systems through their "life cycles" and also accounts for hefty sales of helicopters and missiles to foreign countries.[158] Huntsville's Marshall Space Flight Center received $2.5 billion — 15 percent of NASA's budget — in 2006.[159]

Military-dependent citizens of the Tennessee Valley expect their representatives in Congress to assert their interests. With the startup of the Iraq War, Democratic representative Bud Cramer of Huntsville, a former Army tank officer and military reservist, called the invasion a "clear and noble mission. . . . This is truly a war for our freedom, and we are grateful to the soldiers who are fighting for American liberty."[160] In September 2006, although support was slipping, a majority of polled Alabama voters still believed the U.S. "did the right thing" by invading Iraq. But racial differences were conspicuous. When it came to George Bush's handling of the war, 57 percent of polled white voters were in support, while 84 percent of blacks disapproved. "President Bush is very unpopular in the African-American community because of his policies," said Artur Davis of Birmingham, the only member of the Alabama congressional delegation to vote for an Iraq withdrawal.[161]

Not until 2007 did a majority of Alabamians come to believe the Iraq war was "not worth it." Popular conservative congressman Jo Bonner of Mobile conceded that his party could have been more skeptical about the invasion: "We as a Republican majority didn't do a good enough job asking the tough questions that should have been asked over the last few years, and perhaps we gave too much freedom to the administration without that intense oversight."[162] But three out of four Alabama Republicans still rated George Bush's job performance as good or excellent.[163]

Signs of dissatisfaction flickered among those who have traditionally heeded the military's call. In the early 1990s, Alabama received two presidential citations for being first in the nation to exceed recruitment goals. Yet each year between 2000 and 2004, the Army fell short of its target numbers in the state. Mack Bazzell, an Army public relations and advertising manager, told a Birmingham reporter that the usual "influencers," male relatives with Vietnam experience, weren't enthusiastic in recommending the military to younger family members.[164] As the Great Recession took hold, the military's attractiveness to Alabama's working-class youth again assured recruiters of their quotas.

In their knee-jerk support of the Iraq War, Alabama's white elected leadership — the state's governor, congressional representatives, and senators — failed their constituents simplistically and tragically, succumbing to reflexive judgments and acting against the interests of their state's citizens, especially of the men and women sent to carry out the invasion and occupation.

Across the post–World War II era, official Alabama opted for the wrong side of the African American freedom struggle; rushed into the disaster that was the Vietnam War; failed to achieve tax equity and constitutional reform, or to adequately fund health and education; and cheered a younger generation onto the battlefields of Iraq. In contrast, the public positions of Alabama's African American political organizations and leaders on major domestic and international issues since the end of the Civil War, far more often than not, have aligned with the historical trajectory of social justice, economic opportunity, and democratic inclusion. Hardly humbled or chastened, the state's ol' boy politicians seem to learn little from history and rarely examine the habits of judgment that steel their debilitating allegiances to the Heart of Dixie.

BEREFT

One of the most melodic and lyrically poignant songs to come from the Iraq War, Jason Isbell's "Dress Blues," recounts through minimal, forgone detail, a high school gymnasium memorial service for a young soldier. Alabama native Isbell, former member of the Drive-By Truckers, introduced the song to an Austin, Texas, audience in April 2006: "So this guy that I went to high school with, he decided when he was about eighteen, he would go into the military. And he went overseas to the Middle East and he didn't come home. And he's from Greenhill, Alabama, and his name was Matt Conley. This song's for him. He was a Marine."[165]

Addressed to the dead soldier killed by "bombs in the sand" while fighting "somebody's Hollywood war," "Dress Blues" locates the voice of its singer among "old legionnaires" and "silent old men from the corps," among "mamas and grandmamas" who provide unequivocal love but are depicted as sidelined from scenes of politics and power. Sung from inside the culture that produced both Isbell and Conley, anger seethes beneath the matter-of-fact melancholy of flags and signs bearing Bible verses along a north Alabama highway.

What can you see from your window?
I can't see anything from mine.[166]

Not a song celebrating patriotism, nor the Bush-Cheney obsession with Iraq, "Dress Blues" laments the death of a young husband and father one week before his twenty-second birthday and two weeks before the end of his tour.

Matt Conley died in February 2006 in Ramadi from an improvised explosive device that blew apart his Humvee. Conley's wife, Nicole, was expecting the couple's first child. Before he graduated from Rogers High School and enlisted in the Marines, Matt Conley had quarterbacked the football team. "He was proud to serve his country, and me and his mother were proud of him, and always will be," his father told a reporter. "They're over there so we can enjoy our freedoms," said Conley's widow. "I thank God for the men and women who are there to keep us safe."[167]

FUNDAMENTALIST STRIPES

"What is at stake in Alabama," observed Wendy Kaminer during politicians' efforts in the late 1990s to mandate school prayer, "is the right not to pray to Jesus or be subjected to religious indoctrination."[168]

"The reason that the prayer issue remains contentious," insists Wayne Flynt, an Alabama Baptist himself and one of the state's abiding voices of prophetic indignation, "is that politicians have found it a useful tool for avoiding the tough problems like wretched schools and poverty. It's marvelous for demagoguing, it's very opportunistic politics and a great way to get elected." Flynt made his comments when a 1997 public prayer rally in Montgomery featured Governor Fob James, right-wing attorney general Bill Pryor (soon to be a Bush-appointed appellate judge), Christian Coalition leader Ralph Reed (soon to be discredited for mixing Native American gambling money with politics), and ultraconservative Republican presidential candidate Alan Keyes.[169]

Earlier that year when Pryor, a proponent of government-sponsored prayer, was sworn in as Alabama's attorney general, he had announced, "With trust in

God, and his son, Jesus Christ, we will continue the American experiment of liberty in law." When Pryor talked this way in public, he would concede that the "American experiment is not a theocracy and does not establish an official religion" before going on to issue such theocratically situated statements as "the Declaration of Independence and the Constitution of the United States are rooted in a Christian perspective of the nature of government and the nature of man. The challenge of the next millennium will be to preserve the American experiment by restoring its Christian perspective." Pryor's version of Christianity stresses the punitive and intolerant, undergirding, for example, his arguments in favor of the execution of a convicted criminal who was severely mentally retarded. More than once he has said that *Roe v. Wade* was "the worst abomination in the history of constitutional law."[170]

"The acknowledgment of God is not a religion," insisted state chief justice Roy Moore on NBC TV's *Today Show* in the summer of 2003; "it's a responsibility under the Alabama Constitution [that says] our justice system is established upon God, and no judge, federal or otherwise, can tell the chief justice of the state of Alabama that they cannot acknowledge God. It's a sad day in Alabama when a federal judge enters into the state and tries to disestablish a justice system by saying you can't acknowledge the foundation of that system."[171] Federal judge Myron Thompson had ruled that Moore, through the prominent placing of a two-and-a-half-ton Ten Commandments monument, sought to establish the primacy of the Judeo-Christian god in state affairs. For refusing to remove his carved granite block from the rotunda of the state judiciary building in Montgomery, Moore himself was tossed off the supreme court by a panel of judicial peers.

Three years later, Roy Moore got nowhere in his 2006 run for the Republican nomination for governor against Baptist businessman incumbent Bob Riley. Then, amid the state's slide into double-digit unemployment, and white Alabama's Obama backlash, Moore briefly bobbed to the surface again in 2010. To a gathering of Wetumpka Tea Partiers, he railed that it was not too late for Christian nationalism to triumph. "God will again give us a heart to know him," preached Moore, "that we will be his people, and he will be our God, for we shall return to him with all our heart."[172] The recurrent appeal of an atavistic figure such as Roy Moore suggests the tenuous and shaky ground of Alabama political progress.

WE DARE DEFEND OUR RITES

Alabama and Mississippi consistently report the lowest percentages of foreign-born population in the Deep South. From 2000 to 2010, Alabama's U.S.-born population inched downward, from 98 to 97 percent.[173] But even with the arrival of Latino migrants, concentrated in low-wage work such as poultry processing, construction, and landscaping, the state remains a black and white society.[174]

Alabama's state-born population, which was 85 percent in 1960, declined to 71 percent by 2006, reflecting a rise of in-migration. By comparison, only 55 percent of Georgians in 2006 were born in Georgia, largely a testament to the magnet of metro Atlanta. In 2009 the Pew Research Center categorized Alabama as a leading "Low Magnet / High Sticky" state — a place that people weren't likely to migrate to, that tended to lose population to more dynamic states, but that also had a distinctive culture capable of anchoring natives.[175] Veteran reporter and Alabama native Tom Gordon wondered how long it might take before the slow influx of people born in other states would have a diversifying effect upon the way Alabama governs. "I hope it will in due time, but it's not right now," UA political scientist William Steward replied. "It's still pretty much the business of those people who've been here a long time, to run things."[176]

Being Alabama-bound means traveling less frequently and widely outside the U.S. It makes news when a Mercedes initiative sends thirteen German students into Alabama and a similar number of Alabama high school students to Germany for a two- to three-week exchange.[177] Alabamians remain more comfortable talking football X's and O's than languages other than English.

Along with anti-outsider predispositions comes a suspicion of "foreigners" by many white Alabamians, as well as of internationalism — including a visceral hatred of organizations such as the United Nations, fanned for decades by TV and radio preachers and talk-show hosts. As for immigration, Alabama's political leadership thinks more of barriers than entryways. Senator Jeff Sessions proposed erecting double-layered security fencing along the U.S. border from the Pacific Ocean to the Gulf of Mexico and making illegal entry a felony.[178]

In what should be a routine matter, the state is purposely slow in providing noncitizens with IDs.[179] When Alabama immigrants sued in 2004, the AP's Kyle Wingfield put the situation into cultural context:

> "The federal government has said these people are legal," said Ben Bruner, attorney for the immigrants. "The state of Alabama is trying to go back and determine which categories of legal persons they want to deal with, and we would allege that that's illegal."
>
> State employees were off Monday for the Confederate Memorial Day holiday.[180]

Pandering to the anti-immigrant mood of the state's Republican voters and demonstrating that he has his father Fob's talent for boosting Alabama's negative image, 2010 gubernatorial candidate Tim James won the *New York Times* "award for the best bottom-feeding campaigner," thanks to his statewide TV ad promising that, if elected, he would make sure the driver's license exam would be English-only. "This is Alabama," declared James. "We speak English. If you want to live here, learn it."[181]

Although Alabama welcomes thousands of international visitors and residents yearly — scientists, students, medical professionals in the tech-rich oases of UAB and Huntsville, managers of auto plants, tourists at civil rights sites in Birmingham, Montgomery, and Selma — the state is not yet home to more than a small sampling of the world's linguistic and cultural variety.[182] The habit of not knowing what's missing is one of the hardest to break. "Taking for granted one's own linguistic horizon as the ultimate linguistic horizon," writes Judith Butler, "leads to an enormous parochialism and keeps us from being open to radical difference and from undergoing the discomfort and the anxiety of realizing that the scheme of intelligibility on which we rely fundamentally is not adequate, is not common, and closes us off from the possibility of understanding others and ourselves in a more fundamentally capacious way."[183] The defensiveness provoked by linguistic parochialism suggests a spectrum of cultural constraints and prejudices in need of confrontation. When they come, breaks with parochialism invite breaks across the entire range of compulsive habits of judgment and feeling, allowing the reimagining of Alabama as a geography of expanding horizons.

CHAPTER TWO

The Punitive Habit

Astonishingly, many politicians seem to think that we should
lead the world in prisons, not in health care or education.
— NICHOLAS KRISTOF, "Priority Test: Health Care or Prisons?"

Shadowing Alabama's political imaginary is what Avery Gordon
calls the "fundamental sociality of haunting," the proposition that
"we are haunted by worldly contacts" that we'd rather step around
or over than acknowledge. The punitive habit wears blinders, dismisses criticism along with dissident signs and conflicting evidence embodied by the
unrecognized. Daily routine shuns these apparitions of the contrary, yet
they lurk, worldly evidence of judgment upon the polity. Unacknowledged,
shunted aside, these presences produce effects that invite comparison with
specters and haunting due to the way that "systematic compulsions work on
and through people in everyday life" — the way the habits of judgment and
feeling harden, bind, and take hold. A ghost, suggests Gordon, is "primarily a symptom of what is missing. It gives notice not only to itself but also
to what it represents. What it represents is usually a loss, sometimes of life,
sometimes of a path not taken."[1]

Alabama ghosts fill the ranks of the undeserving poor: if you are poor, it's
your own damn fault. Ghosts are consigned to marginalizing institutions for
the abject: homeless shelters, nursing homes, mental institutions. But nowhere
do Alabama's living ghosts clump more thickly as they indict the state's practice of justice than between prison walls, out of sight except for sensationalized
TV documentaries and YouTube clips spackled by stabbings with handmade
shivs, bloody shoeprints, cellblock shakedowns, inmate extractions, and run-
amuck incidents.[2] The living spirits who overfill and circulate in and out of

Alabama's prisons represent losses of every sort: forfeited lives, missing education and work skills, the lack of supportive social networks and institutions, and the absence of racial justice.

Down-home punishment only begins with conviction and sentencing. Prison in the Heart of Dixie brings the hammer down upon transgressors — individuals certainly, but socially predictable as to race, class, gender, age, geography, and education. Characteristic of the punitive habit in Alabama, Mississippi, and Georgia is the vastly disproportionate number of African Americans in these states' prisons and jails, as well as a white incarceration rate much higher than the national average.[3] "We're a state that's long on punishment, but frighteningly short on justice," concludes *Birmingham News* columnist Robin DeMonia, after years of reckoning the back of southern hospitality's hand.[4] In bearing down hardest upon young, uneducated, poor, black men, Alabama justice complemented the punitive national turn in the late twentieth century.

"Our criminal justice system would not be tolerable to the majority," observes David Cole, "if its impact were felt more broadly by the general population, and not concentrated on the most deprived among us."[5] In its prison practices, Alabama resembles other states, only more so. "Over the past three decades," writes Marie Gottschalk, "the country has built a carceral state that is unprecedented among Western countries and in U.S. history."[6] Early into the twenty-first century, one in every hundred adults was incarcerated in a nation distinguished for "the sheer size of its prison and jail population; its reliance on harsh, degrading sanctions; and the persistence and centrality of the death penalty." Whether measured by numbers or the rate of incarceration, the U.S. leads the world. Alabama consistently ranks among the five states with the nation's highest incarceration rates, at least 25 percent above the national average.[7]

Alabama prisoners take their punishment while trying not to fall off some forgotten map. The state's penal history, underwritten by a harsh criminal code, presents an extended narrative of racism, labor exploitation, brutality, isolation, political demagoguery, and official evasion sprinkled with moments of litigative resistance. Prior to 1860, despite an antigovernment ethos, the dominating regime of slavery, and the association of prison reform with Yankee abolitionists, all the southern states except the Carolinas and unsettled Florida built penitentiaries. As with incarceration, punitiveness has an enduring Alabama history. The last U.S. executions for robbery, burglary, theft, arson, and counterfeiting took place in the Heart of Dixie.[8]

If in the North the roads to the penitentiaries were paved with good intentions, down in Dixie, amid the ruins of the Civil War and Reconstruction, white Redeemers' drive to regain control over their states and over the labor of recently freed blacks led to wide adoption of the convict lease.[9] Introduced by the U.S. military governments put in place in the South, the convict lease, writes Vann Woodward, "fitted perfectly the program of retrenchment" imposed as white regimes regained political power.[10] During an era that extended from the late 1860s into the 1920s, the semislavery of state and county prisoners laboring in the mines made fortunes for the owners of such extractive industries as Tennessee Coal and Iron, Pratt Coal, and Sloss Iron and Steel; provided counties and the treasury of Alabama with a major stream of revenue; murderously enforced racial domination; undercut free labor and unionization efforts; established punitiveness as official practice; and set off an incarceration boom. "The degradation and brutality produced by this system," concludes Woodward, "would be incredible but for the amount of evidence from official sources."[11]

By 1920 convict labor had become the state's largest source of revenue.[12] "Governments and corporations," writes Mary Ellen Curtin, "willingly and knowingly traded prisoners' lives for profit."[13] By 1923 Alabama was the nation's leader in the value of prison goods produced, some $7.5 million.[14] For the several thousand black men who made up almost all of the convict labor force, working and living conditions were hellish, beatings and torture routine, death common. The rate of white imprisonment would increase in the coming decades, but black men, many of them dragooned and kidnapped into the new system of involuntary servitude by the flimsiest of vagrancy and debt laws, continued to make up the preponderance of the state's incarcerated.[15]

A feature of New South modernization, the convict lease complemented Jim Crow laws by allowing emerging industrial capitalists "to use the state to recruit and discipline a convict labor force," argues Alex Lichtenstein, enabling them "to develop their states' resources without creating a wage labor force and without undermining planters' control of black labor." Because convict labor "reinforced, rather than disrupted, the forms of social control necessary for extreme labor exploitation in the South's plantation districts, this was a form of 'modernization' acceptable to planter and industrialist alike."[16] The most petty property crimes, perceived disrespect, or law officer's caprice could turn into perishable offenses for black sharecroppers in the Black Belt or black laborers in Birmingham or Mobile, consigning them to years of involuntary labor.

In 1928 Alabama became the last state to abolish the convict lease, while continuing to exploit prisoners at its textile mills and farms and on road construction, a characteristically ironic feature of white, southern progressivism that would resurface from time to time in the decades ahead. This is the moment branded into Dixie's imaginary by the 1932 book and movie *I Am a Fugitive from a Georgia Chain Gang*.

On Alabama road gangs, blacks and whites labored together in brutal conditions, subject to whippings and beatings by despotic guards, denied opportunities for education or training. As in the era of slavery, it was go day, come night, God send Sunday. Inside the state's prisons, iron-skinned long-timers and quickly aging small fry occupied the same oppressive spaces. Dilapidated buildings had to catch fire before they were replaced, with wood construction eventually giving way to concrete structures and rudimentary plumbing. Not until the mid-1960s did Alabama have a facility for confining as many as a hundred young, male — and largely white — first offenders apart from the jail-scarred. Not until 1970 was Kilby Prison, a relic from the 1920s, closed and razed. The state's large, maximum-security prisons, built in rural Escambia County in 1949 and 1969, were situated about as far from public scrutiny as you could get without crossing into Florida. They remain much as a young writer described them in 1972, "man heaps in remote south Alabama."[17] Here, at Holman Prison, executions are carried out, and inmates, beyond public and family proximity, are enveloped in lost time-space, interrupted occasionally by scandals, lawsuits, or producers of television "Doc-Blocks."

REFORM AND REGRET

Encouraged by court rulings ordering humane treatment for inmates in Alabama mental institutions (especially *Wyatt v. Stickney*) and prison medical facilities (*Newman v. Alabama*), a contingent of reform-minded litigants in the 1970s pressed prison inmate complaints before sympathetic federal judges seeking, as the historian of this effort has written, "to end the horror in the state's penitentiaries" where conditions of confinement were "monstrous in the extreme."[18] The conditions uncovered by the lawsuits included negligent

deaths in prison hospitals; a chamber of disciplinary depravity called the dog-
house, where men were starved and crammed together for weeks at a time;
frequent rapes, stabbings, and beatings; and a climate of dread and hopeless-
ness. Twenty-seven Alabama prisoners were killed in 1972–73. A riot in early
1974 left a guard and an inmate dead, and forty other inmates beaten by guards
wielding pickax handles.

Perennially oppressive conditions had turned barbaric. In response, the
Alabama legislature called for more guns and riot gear for guards, more dog-
house-style cells for unruly prisoners. For their part, inmates continued to
raise complaints that the National Prison Project, the Southern Poverty Law
Center, Legal Defense Fund, and the Civil Liberties Union of Alabama turned
into lawsuits.[19] "Ultimately," writes Marie Gottschalk in her discussion of how
the civil rights movement critically influenced the prisoners' rights movement
in the United States, "federal judges issued comprehensive orders calling for
overhauls of the entire prison system or key pieces of the penal system in all
eleven Southern states."[20] Did the incarcerated have a constitutional right to
medical treatment? To rehabilitation? To safe and adequate living space? To a
classification system that distinguished between levels of risk and supervision?
The series of federal cases begun in the 1970s — *Newman v. Alabama, Pugh
v. Sullivan*, and *James v. Wallace* — sought to reform Alabama's prisons and
establish national precedents.

In 1976 Judge Frank M. Johnson, who four years earlier had ruled in
Newman that inmate medical care was willfully and intentionally inadequate,
now found the entire prison system guilty of "cruel and unusual punishment"
and ordered the Board of Corrections into receivership until Alabama could
satisfy court-ordered reforms to remedy overcrowding and inmate abuse.
Johnson pointed to the "rampant violence and jungle atmosphere existing
throughout Alabama's penal system" and determined that inmates had "no
chance of leaving the institution with a more positive or constructive attitude
than the one he or she brought in."[21] Johnson's order marked the first time a
federal judge had set specific minimum conditions for a state prison system.

"It was the result of neglect and mismanagement through all the years of
Governor George Wallace," concludes Roland Nachman, chair of the reform
commission put in place by Judge Johnson. "There was a lack of interest by
Wallace over a long period of time and I'm being kind in that assessment."[22]
Wallace, first elected governor in 1963, used the office to feed his bottomless

political ambition and extend his web of cronies. He had nothing to gain and much to lose among his constituents by coming to the rescue of a prison population that was predominantly black but, black or white, was both poor and disenfranchised. Within another decade, Wallace would channel white backlash into what Vesla Mae Weaver calls "frontlash," shifting the blatant but faltering attack on black civil rights into such code phrases as "law and order" and "getting tough on crime."[23] The punitive habit easily accommodated the racist slack.

Among the Department of Corrections' schemes in the 1970s was a throwback idea from a century earlier that would have prisoners pay the costs of the corrections system through menial agricultural work. "It was absurd," writes Larry Yackle about the latest self-sufficiency push, to insist "that inmates be required to work not to provide them[selves] with the chance for self-improvement, but to finance the prison system without an additional investment of tax dollars. . . . In the teeth of expert advice that agricultural lands should be leased to commercial operators or sold outright, state authorities insisted on sending inmates out to pick butterbeans by hand."[24]

A new "good time" program proposed by a prison task force and passed by the legislature in 1976 over a Wallace veto resulted in the early release of some six hundred inmates judged to be safe risks. This short-lived policy became political fodder not only for Wallace and resistant Attorney General Bill Baxley, but also for law 'n' order demagogues exemplified by Mobile district attorney Charles Graddick (no good-time Charlie he).[25] Opponents of new prison construction, such as Civil Liberties Union of Alabama executive director Steve Suitts, warned that unless a way could be found to comply with Judge Johnson's fundamental concerns, the state board of corrections would soon be mobilizing contractors and bulldozers.[26]

In Alabama, hope bleeds eternal. With Wallace prevented by state law from succeeding himself, new governor Fob James became the court-appointed receiver of the prison system in 1979. According to Ralph Knowles (whose Tuscaloosa law firm worked for years on *Newman* and other Alabama prison cases), businessman James, with his "simplistic, conservative views about government . . . did not function as a receiver. Instead, he hired a new — albeit more competent — commissioner of corrections and went about business as usual, assuming that his new commissioner would implement simple management principles and that the problems and the federal court would go away."[27]

The lot of prisoners did improve marginally. During the years under court order, several work-release centers opened, and the legislature, compelled by the alternative of having to free hundreds of inmates, authorized new prison construction.[28] Conditions, including medical care, ratcheted up a notch, perhaps, but the state's prisons remained what the *Economist* called "a persistent disgrace."[29] "Efforts to implement Johnson's order," writes Yackle, "faced a long and bitter campaign against myriad forces seeking to derive only political benefits from the tragedy at Alabama's penal institutions."[30]

As dramatic and unprecedented as the judge's orders were, he stopped short of requiring fundamental change in penal policy, seeking instead to improve prisoners' actual living conditions and life chances, much in the manner of the Christian injunction to minister unto the hungry, thirsty, or imprisoned — "the least of these."[31] When Judge Johnson accepted a seat on the Fifth Circuit Court of Appeals in Atlanta in 1979, he passed the prison cases on to federal judge Robert Varner, whose willingness to order the release of inmates butted against the sez-you posturings of Graddick, now the state attorney general.[32]

If the prison population declined a bit during these years, it was mainly due to the number of state inmates piling up in local lockups, the not-in-my-backyard resistance by municipalities and citizens to building prisons, and the abolition impulse of groups such as the Alabama Prison Project and the ACLU. By 1981, during the first James administration, the only available cell spaces for fourteen hundred of Alabama's six thousand prisoners were inside county jails — miserable spaces, reminiscent of premodern times and facing their own lawsuits for sorry conditions. Cartoonlike jail walls bulged and contracted with every breath taken by their sardine-can denizens. Desperate, the state launched a raft of new construction, first throwing together concrete-block warehouses aimed to meet the minimum court-ordered space, then opening new prisons in north Alabama. During the next ten years, the state's inmate population increased over 200 percent, the fastest growth of any southern state.[33]

The preceding century of Alabama penal practices had fused neglect with mean-spiritedness. The new groundswell for incarceration fed off of punitive ideology, a dearth of alternative sentencing possibilities, and a will for social control — aimed especially at young black men — churned by politicians such as Graddick. Swept up in the national three-strikes frenzy that accelerated through the fundamentalist, Reaganite 1980s, Alabama joined the tougher-than-thou states applying mandatory minimums to nonviolent repeaters.

Despite black caucus resistance, the legislature dished out the law 'n' order, putting felons away "for smaller crimes than previously, for longer terms and with less chance of parole."[34] A 1989 Clark Foundation survey found that only 4 percent of Alabamians believed sentences should be shorter, while 41 percent thought that the convicted should do even more time.[35]

"Rather than seeing the South's higher crime rate as reflected in her higher rates of functional illiteracy, teenage pregnancy, and impoverishment, or in her lower expenditures per capita on education, health care, and other essential services," wrote Gregg Barak, chair of the Department of Criminal Justice at Alabama State University, in 1986, "it is still politically preferable, at least in Alabama, to point fingers at the individual offenders rather than at the institutional arrangements of the old and new South alike, and at the same time, to call for stricter forms of punishment where severity is already the name of the game."[36]

Nor, following Wallace's final exit from office, did Guy Hunt, the Accidental Governor, concern himself with prisons. That it was Hunt and not Charles Graddick who sat behind the governor's desk owed something to the election challenge attorney Knowles and law partner Jack Drake had spearheaded following the twisted Democratic primary of 1986. "Graddick's defeat," Knowles acknowledges, "was probably my major contribution to the Alabama prison system."[37]

In December 1988, after sixteen years of litigation, Judge Varner dismissed the litigation that had sprung from *Newman v. Alabama*. Knowles surveyed the results: "A political climate demanding longer, sometimes mandatory sentences along with serious state budgetary problems caused the dream of the creation of a constitutional and humane prison system to cruelly and persistently elude us."[38] Larry Yackle, who had toured the prison system in 1976, returned in 1986 to compare a decade's change in conditions. He found improvements in cleanliness and basic public health standards. Four new prisons and several minimum-security facilities helped house a doubled inmate population. Dormitories were more open and more officers patrolled the floors. A classification system existed. Yackle saw many of the improvements as "housekeeping," however, and "could not share the view that the Alabama prison system was now affirmatively good as opposed to merely better. . . . The nature of the prisons was, moreover, unchanged. . . . Their very character denied the humanity of the inmates they confined." Prisons' isolating geography, dehumanizing concrete and steel construction, encircling razor wire, constant noise and crowding, deployment of small modular structures to house inmates, and ultimately "primitive" classification process cast an atmosphere of despair. "Something fundamental had not changed; men and women were still kept in cages, and long enough to ensure that they could never again function as ordinary citizens."[39]

THE LAND OF LITTLE FLACK

Following the years claimed by the ineffectual Guy Hunt, the world again witnessed the punitive tendencies of Alabama's political imaginary as Fob James, now a Republican, returned to office in 1995. Lest old times and institutions be forgotten, Governor James backed his prison commissioner Ron Jones's revival of the chain gang. Yellowed newspaper images and early Hollywood black-and-white films ripened into living color as prisoners outfitted in orange and white jump suits, legs linked together, labored on highway shoulders. "Like Confederate widows, Yellow Dog Democrats and faded signs that say 'See Ruby Falls,'" wrote Alabamian Rick Bragg for the *New York Times*, "the chain gang's era in Southern history seemed long gone."[40] Echoes of the Wallace heyday shouted that the Heart of Dixie beat on. "People say it's not humane," said Commissioner Jones, "but I don't get much flack in Alabama."[41]

Justifying the decision to put hundreds of men on chain gangs for twelve-hour days of hard labor, Governor James explained that "many convicted criminals found life in Alabama jails so comfortable that they chose to remain in prison at taxpayers' expense rather than be paroled!" James followed up his delusion with a defense of the punitive. "Critics call chain gangs cruel and unusual punishment," he wrote in an essay for *USA Today*. "What they forget is that prisons are for punishment. The chains we use are lightweight (less than two pounds) and impose no hardship upon the prisoner other than restricting his ability to escape."[42]

Supporting the governor's turn to chain gangs ("I think it's perfectly proper") was Attorney General Jeff Sessions, eyeing his successful run for the U.S. Senate.[43] "This is something . . . that is going to be here to stay," insisted the warden of the Limestone Correctional Facility.[44] It's "degrading," countered the executive director of the National Sheriffs Association. Putting men in chains tells them they are animals, argued Alvin Bronstein of the ACLU's

National Prison Project, who challenged James's and Jones's contention that the practice had deterrent effects. "You tell a person he's an animal, you get a self-fulfilling prophecy."[45]

While shackled convicts sledgehammered rocks into gravel and worked the roadsides, Commissioner Jones, reported the *Montgomery Advertiser*, also "cut back on amenities like coffee and stamps . . . and ended a low-cost treatment plan for sex offenders."[46] Celebrating the punitive while dismissing the rehabilitative, Jones paraded his "sez-you" stance, recalling George Wallace's fumings against judges and court orders, claiming that the state had budgeted sufficient money for prisons. "For twenty years we have been told if you would only invest some money, the problem would diminish," he griped.

> We have repeatedly done that and it has failed. We have been down that road for 20 years and we have 20 times the prison population, it is 15 times more expensive and there is failure in all directions.
>
> There was a mood in our state which was reflected in our election. We are not going to put any more money in.[47]

Ultimately, however, it was not Ron Jones's support for the caning of unruly inmates that led to Fob James's dismissing him as prison commissioner, nor Jones's attempt to deny HIV-infected inmates at Julia Tutwiler Prison a vegetable garden, nor his proposal to house inmates in tents, nor even his wish to cut the pay of guards as much as 20 percent — but his intention to put women on chain gangs.

Joe Hopper, who promised that the incarcerated would have more meaningful work to do than pounding big rocks into smaller ones, followed the obdurate Jones as commissioner. He put convicts to digging up stumps on prison land, claiming, "That's productive and, at the same time, it's a lot harder work than was being performed on the rock pile." Hopper's "solid ground" innovation was saluted by the *Montgomery Advertiser* as "a sensible approach to corrections," cementing institutional patterns of Alabama forced labor dating back to the late nineteenth century.[48]

RECIPE FOR CALAMITY

Bruce Western has tied the national prison boom to the waning of the 1960s civil rights movement. In his view, the turn to mass imprisonment "was produced by a historic collision between the political forces of racial conservatism and the collapse of urban labor markets." The disappearance of inner-city job prospects as economic opportunities moved to the suburbs, harsh penalties associated with crack cocaine convictions, the declining urban tax base accompanied by the nonsupport of public schools and services, rising dropout rates and attendant poverty — all these factors put severe pressure on black urban populations. "The basic brute fact of incarceration in the new era of mass imprisonment," writes Western, "is that African Americans are eight times more likely to be incarcerated than whites." If prisons are built with bricks of law, amid geographies of economic desperation, a good deal of the incarceration boom "was fueled by the poor job prospects of less-skilled blacks."[49] Crime, especially drug-related theft and dealing, became a survival option for black youth and young men trapped in declining city neighborhoods and projects.

"The problem in Alabama, but not just Alabama," notes Robert Sigler, professor of criminal justice at the UA law school, "is we decided to get tough on crime. That meant getting tough on minor offenders, who steal my lawnmower, but don't represent the threat to me like someone who assaults me. We do the opposite of what we should and put the petty thieves in prison."[50]

The get-tough animus helped feed the Republican rise to power in Alabama and other states of the old Confederacy.[51] White voters, whether in rural places, small towns, or the booming burbs of Birmingham, Montgomery, Mobile, and Huntsville, turned to candidates with an outspoken punitive bent.

Gottschalk would complicate Western's explanation for the national prison boom that began in the 1970s by tying law 'n' order ideology to the moment of political opportunism that allowed conservatives to stir and capitalize on the emerging victims' rights movement. Gottschalk's argument details how "legal wrangling around the death penalty bolstered . . . the expansion of the carceral state."[52] Out of the U.S. Supreme Court's rulings on two Georgia cases — the first (*Furman v. Georgia* in 1972), which suspended the death penalty, and the second (*Gregg v. Georgia* in 1976), which allowed executions to resume — came a mobilization of conservative public opinion. Death-penalty wrangling also "helped to embolden the deterrence argument — that is, the controversial contention that harsher sanctions greatly deter crime — which had been discredited in many other countries," as well as "enshrine a zero-sum view of victims and defendants in capital and noncapital cases." In Alabama, the dominant politics of the 1970s, fueled by Wallaceism's synergy of racism, law 'n' order, and resentment against social services for the undeserving poor, meant the table was set for punitive gruel.

Fourteen Alabama prison commissioners came and went between the early 1970s, when the first overcrowding lawsuit was filed, and Bob Riley's second term, beginning in 2006. Each commissioner seemed initially gung-ho in a job that offered no stolen moments while inmates stacked up like cordwood. In 1971 there were some 3,800 state prisoners; by 1992 the number had grown to 16,000. In 2002 an additional 10,000 stuffed the system's concrete and metal architecture to twice overflowing. Prisoners were squeezed into hallways, gyms, and chapels. Alabama's population, 4.4 million in 2002, had grown by less than a third in these thirty-odd years, while the number of prisoners increased sevenfold. Newspaper editorials in Alabama dailies across the decades arrived at the same verdict: "The state, going back several governors and legislatures, has shown itself incapable of dealing with the looming disaster."[53] The prison morass continues to serve as a ready target for editorial writers. More difficult is advocacy of necessary revenue increases to pay for a range of carceral alternatives.

"I have watched over the years the political arena in the state of Alabama in regard to the judicial system and the Department of Corrections," read a letter to the *Montgomery Advertiser*. "It is horrifying to watch the drama that is played about life and death. . . . We do not need to build more prisons. This is only a short-term solution to a consistent problem that has not ended and will not end until we have alternative programs that address social problems that we have created." Considering the large percentage of the incarcerated doing time for drug-related crimes, the letter writer, D. Miller of Fairfield, added, "We are in need of drug treatment programs that not only address the drug addiction, but the problems that the individual has that resulted in crime and addiction — poverty, unemployment, lack of education, domestic abuse, lack of decent housing, nutrition and health care."[54]

Where were the elected Alabama politicians, except an African American minority, who would admit in public that prisons were packed due to "social problems that we have created"? Unwilling to acknowledge the repercussions of generations of racism, exclusion, and inequality, or the consequences of large and increasing disparities of wealth and poverty, white legislators below the Mason-Dixon latched onto buzz-phrase rhetoric revelatory of the spreading panic, but habituated to the punitive.

"We're not smart on crime," said the Republican chair of the Alabama senate's prison oversight committee in 2003. "We're tough on crime."[55]

"Recipe for calamity," umpteenthed the *News*. "A state that wants to be both tough and cheap on crime "must be especially smart with its money or risk disaster, and Alabama has been anything but smart. Perhaps only by luck has Alabama, with its dangerously overcrowded and understaffed prisons, been spared a bloody prison uprising or breakout."[56] The state now had — and still has — one of the highest imprisonment rates in the world, one of the most punitive habitual-offender statutes in the U.S., and prisons that function primarily as living abacuses, totaling up the law 'n' order bodies.

The penal numbers and percentages grew. The U.S. rate of incarceration averaged 110 prisoners for every 100,000 citizens during the fifty years preceding the mid-1970s. By 2000 it had leaped fourfold, to 478. The punitive tone was bipartisan. "The two defining moments of Democratic crime politics in the 1990s," writes Chris Suellentrop, "were Clinton's decision as governor of Arkansas to allow the execution of the mentally impaired Ricky Ray Rector in 1992 and the passage of the 1994 crime bill; along with banning assault weapons and putting 100,000 cops on the street, the bill also prominently featured longer sentences for criminals and a federal three-strikes law."[57] Gottschalk points to the successful efforts of the victims' rights movement to undermine criticism of the growing carceral state, and the constricted situation in which liberal groups usually in opposition to the punitive mentality sometimes found themselves. "Being for victims and against offenders became a simple equation that helped knit together politically disparate groups," she writes.[58] The loudness and clout of these disparate groups' calls for punishment varied from group to group, and from state to state, but the effects helped feed the prison population boom.

Speaking to the 2003 graduating class at the Alabama Corrections Academy, a training school for guards, Selma police chief Robert Green conceded that the state's prisons were "dehumanizing, overcrowded monstrosities." That year, Alabama had some 2,700 correctional officers for its 27,000 prisoners, half the rate of Florida, Georgia, and Tennessee, and 2,000 short of the nationally recommended number.[59]

Prison commissioners have come and gone, some better intentioned than others, but all have found themselves trapped by the narrow range of resources, tactics, and tolerance demanded by punitive parsimony. The legislature has never appropriated anything close to sufficient money; no governor has made a transformative commitment. Having all but abandoned rehabilitation, Alabama logic continues to insist that prisons must never be mistaken for summer camps or military barracks. As uninhabitable and dangerous as some inner-city areas have become, prisons must remain even less desirable destinations, lest they be mistaken for gated communities.

INVISIBLE INEQUALITY

Is it irony, or something worse, that condemns reformers of humanity's grimmest institutions to have their names ever after affixed to them? Alabama's women's prison was named for the remarkable Julia Tutwiler (1841–1916), Tuscaloosa born and Vassar educated, who in the late nineteenth century, according to the Alabama Department of Corrections website, "traveled to the remote prison camps throughout Alabama ministering to the convicts and teaching them to read so they would be better citizens upon their eventual release." What would the "Angel of the Stockades" think of her namesake, built in 1942 to hold four hundred women, packed by century's end with a thousand prisoners, many of them nonviolent drug offenders and small-time thieves?[60] Julia Tutwiler Prison, where bad-check writers were bunked near murderers, where a woman awoke one unbearably sweaty summer night in 2002 drenched in blood from her razor-slit throat, had a higher rate of fights and assaults than any of the men's prisons. "The taxpayers don't want to pay to air condition prisons for inmates," said a state spokesman when Tutwiler prisoners sued to improve conditions.[61]

"It's too much tension," a former Tutwiler inmate told National Public Radio's Melanie Peeples, describing the pressure cooker. "You can walk by somebody and look at them wrong and they're like, 'Hey, what are you looking at me like that for? You got a beef with me?' and then it'll start from there. It'll start from something petty and it'll go to just — it will end up in a fight."[62]

"Politically, whatever the state is going to get away with is what the state is going to do," argued Lisa Kung, an attorney with the Southern Center for Human Rights (SCHR) representing the Tutwiler inmates in 2003.[63] Federal judge Myron Thompson agreed, declaring the women's prison a "ticking timebomb" and "unconstitutionally unsafe," warning Governor Riley and his legal advisor Troy King that "lack of money is not a defense." The state's answer was to hire more guards, to set up special dockets to speed some paroles, and to begin sending as many as three hundred Tutwiler inmates into a Louisiana for-profit prison run by LCS Corrections Services.[64]

Attorney Kung called the transfers tragic. "Sending them that far away destroys families. These are mothers with children. People struggled just to make it to visitation at Tutwiler."[65] Dispatching inmates out of state disrupted the already torturous access to medical care. And into what sorts of situations were they going? In 1995 a federal judge had found the LCS prison in Basile — the new home for displaced Tutwiler women — unsafe, poorly equipped, and understaffed. The company's facilities in Louisiana and Texas had experienced riots and escapes, and inmates had met with brutality and sexual exploitation.[66] Prison entrepreneur, architect, and LCS founder Patrick LeBlanc told the *News'* Crowder that conditions had changed: "Like I jokingly say, when I got in the business, we had no business being in the business. But you learn very fast."[67] Trends were good to LeBlanc. In the mid-1990s, Alabama was near the top of the list among nearly a dozen states cramming prisoners into the for-profit pipeline.[68]

At the turn of the new millennium, 2 million U.S. citizens lived behind bars, 4.5 million were on parole or probation, and another 3 million were ex-convicts.[69] In 2006, according to Department of Justice data, one out of every thirty-one U.S. adults was in prison, jail, or on supervised release.[70] As the nation became the "world's leading jailer," incarcerating more people per capita than any other country, Alabama imprisoned its adult citizens at a rate one-third higher than the fifty-state average. The Heart of Dixie banded with the usual suspects: Louisiana, Texas, Mississippi, Oklahoma. With overcrowding, understaffing, poorly paid corrections officers, and negligible funding for education, counseling, health care, or training in meaningful work, Alabama has consistently, by a large margin and for decades, ranked last in spending per inmate — usually less than half the national average.[71]

U.S. mass imprisonment, insists Western, is "race-making, attaching the marker of moral failure to the collective experience of an entire social group."[72] For the nation as a whole, African Americans make up around 13 percent of the population but constitute over half of its prisoners.[73] The ignominy borne by African American prisoners and ex-cons resides in the readiness of white society to blame group failure rather than take the measure of the differential racial effects, the contours of power, structured into existing social arrangements and institutions, and the wide economic disparities between rich and poor. "Alas," comments Stephen L. Carter, "the structure of our politics makes it increasingly difficult to address the plight of those for whom race and poverty have become inexorably intertwined."[74] Easier for punitive Alabama logic to dismiss the whole lot as failures due to their own bad habits and bad choices rather than embrace a transformative empathy intent on redressing social, educational, and economic inequities.

"Invisible inequality," concludes Western, "was the unintended consequence of a mass imprisonment produced by a combustible mixture of elevated crime rates, a political upheaval in race relations, and a chronic shortage of jobs in poor inner-city communities. . . . Chronic joblessness is as much a political as an economic fact. Missing, perhaps, some social supports of the European kind, violence, disorder and idleness flourished in America's ghettos, creating for government not just an economic problem, but a problem of social control."[75] Western's conclusion, however, does not mean penal history can be reduced to an ahistorical narrative of social control or of race. As Gottschalk points out, slavery, convict lease, Jim Crow laws, and the "unprecedented" prison boom of the last quarter of the twentieth century must all be understood in their own social-geographical contexts. "Today's incarceration rate," she writes, "of nearly 7,000 per 100,000 African-American males dwarfs the number of blacks imprisoned in the South under convict leasing. Although today's policies of mass imprisonment are undeniably about race and social control, it is important to look more specifically at the political and institutional context that sustains them."[76]

How many legislators, while in office, ever visit a prison? Who inside the gated burbs of Shelby County, or playing the fairways of the Robert Trent Jones Golf Trail, worries over the underfunded schools or the wrecked neighborhoods that give rise to Alabama's youngest offenders? Among children committed to the Department of Youth Services, the recidivism rate runs at more than 70 percent, with eleven- and twelve-year-olds, hardening through the experience, as the most likely to return to juvenile prison. Teens sent into Youth Services come, as one director put it, "from backgrounds that often include poverty, broken homes, and alcohol and drug abuse, and all too often go home from DYS programs to this same environment with little or no aftercare supervision."[77] Absent care, youthful offenders become older prisoners, if they live long enough. Studies of the U.S. dropout population show that nearly one in four black male dropouts are incarcerated. The estimated cost to society over the working life of each dropout approaches $300,000.[78] Since there are few more accurate predictors of doing time than dropping out, some argue it would make sense to pay at-risk students to finish high school and community college.[79]

Who, in their everyday work and routine, learns of the myriad obstacles thwarting those released from Alabama prisons? Outside the efforts of a handful of advocacy and family-support groups, and the quickly dismissed journalistic alarms offered across the years, inmates, probationers, and parolees remain a constituency not only without clout, but one that attracts denigration.[80]

IN THE JAILHOUSE NOW

With the prison population climbing beyond the ability of journalists' adjectives to keep pace, Alabama's county jails, packed to the razor wire with local denizens, became extended-stay holding pens for hundreds of inmates awaiting transfer to state custody. A contentious history of complaints and litigation since the early 1990s by the Association of County Commissions of Alabama led, in 2002, to Montgomery County circuit judge William Shashy's fining the state $2.16 million and threatening to lock up Governor Siegelman's prison commissioner for failing to reduce the backlog of the convicted from the jails. "If sheriffs were allowed to do what the commissioner is doing," Judge Shashy observed, "then the administration of justice would cease to exist in this state." Although county sheriffs were holding 1,700 state prisoners, Siegelman claimed his administration was making "great progress."[81] The governor's legal adviser considered a tent city for inmates: "It has not been ruled in or out. It would be a large set of tents, and that would be viewed as a last-resort situation."[82]

Back in the 1920s, the Alabama legislature authorized payment to sheriffs to feed county prisoners at the rate of $1.75 a day per person. The sheriffs could pocket any unspent money. For some, squeezing pennies out of turnip soup became a coveted second income. The legislature has yet to end this tawdry practice, and into the twenty-first century, fifty-five of Alabama's sixty-seven counties still participated in the feeding-allowance system, unique in the nation.[83] The daily rate, $1.75, had not changed in nearly a hundred years. "A sheriff does have to be rather creative to feed for that amount," said Siegelman's corrections commissioner Michael Haley.[84] Do you want your Kool-Aid with stale vegetables and chips, or alongside scoops of powdered food? "It's a bad system," agreed Buddy Sharpless, executive director of the state's county commissioners association, "and it ought not be that way."[85]

Profiting from inmate hunger was just the sort of Heart of Dixie scandal waiting for national notoriety. In early 2009 a parade of Morgan County jail inmates testified before federal judge U. W. Clemon that they had lost significant weight from being underfed by Sheriff Greg Bartlett. The sheriff had managed to squirrel away $212,000 of state food allowance in just three years at the $1.75 per inmate rate. For violating a federal consent decree regarding inmate living conditions, Judge Clemon ordered Sheriff Bartlett jailed until, as the *Times'* Adam Nossiter wrote, "he came up with a plan to adequately feed prisoners more, anyway, than a few spoonfuls of grits, part of an egg and a piece of toast at breakfast, and bits of undercooked, bloody chicken at supper."

It took Sheriff Bartlett a night behind bars to decide to put all the inmate food allowance toward inmate food. Bobby Timmons, the head of the Alabama Sheriffs Association, opted for the defensive sez-you: "You're never going to satisfy any incarcerated individual . . . an inmate is not in jail for singing too loud in choir on Sunday."[86] George Wallace couldn't have said it better.

SICK FOR JUSTICE

Testimony in lawsuits on behalf of sick and dying Alabama inmates indicts the prison system's perennial failure to provide humane care. An audit by a Chicago medical consultant in 2002 showed the death rate at the medium-security Limestone Correctional Center, a drafty, leaky, former warehouse near the northern boundary of the state where three hundred HIV- and AIDS-infected inmates were kept in rows of beds, was twice the national prison average. "Alabama," wrote the *New York Times* in the too-familiar story that sustains the Heart of Dixie, "is the only state to keep inmates with HIV or AIDS isolated from other prisoners — not only in its cells, but in all prison programs."[87] While courts in Alabama were persuaded that segregation of HIV patients lowered the risk of spreading infection, advocates for inmates argued that the resulting lack of care for the segregated sick resulted in misery and preventable death from treatable diseases. The *News'* Crowder summarized the findings of a report on conditions at Limestone prepared in 2003 by Dr. Stephen Tabet, an infectious disease specialist from the University of Washington:

> It's a place where sick men beg for food, then die from starvation. . . . Where pneumonia goes untreated and men drown in their own respiratory fluids. Where HIV-weakened patients stand in long lines in the middle of the night for pills they take on empty stomachs; then they vomit.
>
> "The most egregious medical failure at Limestone," concluded Dr. Tabet, "is the number of preventable deaths."[88]

Throughout the Alabama system, the prison death rate has consistently exceeded that of most other states.[89] Private companies have profited from the state that ranks last in money spent on inmate medical care. "We're not advocating for fancy medical care, for plastic surgery, for tooth-whitening treatments," argued the legal director of the Southern Poverty Law Center in 2003, representing one contingent of inmates. "We're advocating for cancer patients to get chemotherapy, for kidney dialysis patients to get proper dialysis, basic care that any person with any shred of decency would provide to another fellow human being."[90]

"I saw toes rotted off of feet of diabetics," a former St. Clair Correctional Facility nurse told National Public Radio's Debbie Elliott. "Nothing was being done about it. . . . I saw people that had cancers that had grown back that weren't being treated. I saw people that needed better pain control and that there were no processes in place to give them better pain control."[91] Two days after joining with other inmates in a lawsuit alleging that the St. Clair facility denied him necessary treatment, inmate Jerry Baker, age sixty-three, died from severe breathing problems.[92]

Bradley v. Haley, initiated in 1992 by the Southern Poverty Law Center, offered a glimpse into forgotten sites of despair and immiseration. "The lead plaintiff . . . Tommy Bradley, spent most of his adult life medicated and isolated in a cell for 22 hours a day. Instead of receiving therapeutic treatment and counseling for his paranoid schizophrenia, Bradley and other seriously mentally ill prison inmates in Alabama were simply warehoused in segregation cells and left in the care of inadequately trained staff." This is the SPLC's description of Bradley's situation, but other mentally ill prisoners were confined in equally abysmal conditions.[93] Eight years later the Department of Corrections settled this lawsuit with an agreement to improve care. A follow-up report in 2003 found "remarkable" progress in the Department of Corrections' mental health services. Yet, given the state's history, what is the likelihood for continued improvement in care for sick and mentally ill inmates? For the improvement in the life chances for Alabama's jailed and imprisoned? "How many times," wondered the *Birmingham News* in 2003, "have Alabama leaders recognized a problem and fixed it without courts forcing them to? . . . There are reasonable suspicions that some Alabama department heads have silently welcomed lawsuits as a way to get their agencies' funding needs addressed."[94]

Adequate care and attention for imprisoned and institutionalized populations remains a distant prospect when even emergency funding depends upon lawsuits revelatory of state negligence and criminality. If Alabama has perennially failed to adequately educate its children, particularly its poorest and its African American children, how likely is it that lawbreakers will melt the punitive heart? As Larry Yackle concludes from his study of pioneering federal lawsuits — *Pugh v. Sullivan* and *James v. Wallace* — that sought to improve conditions for the state's inmates, prison reform necessarily engages with "an intricate web of political arrangements that [have] to be altered, and altered significantly, if public resources [are] to be channeled away from more popular uses and toward a prison system housing the most despised and least politically influential of all citizens."[95]

Almost certainly, the future promises more of the cruel and myopic. Inmate lawsuits will challenge scandalous treatment, overcrowding, and insufficient funding. A tenacious minority will press for alternative sentencing, drug courts, decriminalization of marijuana, community corrections, and reentry programs.

In the throes and aftermath of the Great Recession, vast shortfalls have appeared in the state's general fund, the source of money for most of Alabama's non-education obligations. Perhaps legislators and public officials will return to the days of menial, forced prison labor. Or, will the state join a growing national reaction to the punitive turn? While a Bureau of Justice Statistics report for 2008 suggests that for the first time in nearly four decades the national prison population is on the verge of declining, with some states already showing significant decreases, Alabama is still adding to its year-over-year numbers.[96]

LIMITS OF THE PUNITIVE?

In September 2002 Judge William Shashy called a prison "summit" with selected state elected and appointed officials as well as a representative of the county commissioners. "The system is broken from one end to the other," said Rosa Davis of the attorney general's office. And how to pay for a fix? House speaker Seth Hammett left the meeting after making a rare commitment for an Alabama leader: increase taxes to fund prison alternatives. The punitive habit would prevail, however, as voiced by Lieutenant Governor Steve Windom: "Not only would the legislature be unlikely to support necessary taxes for the corrections programs needed for nonviolent substance abuse offenders, the people in Alabama are conservative. . . . If this is seen as soft on crime, there is zero chance the Legislature will pass it. You'll have to sell people on the idea that community corrections is serious punishment."[97]

Before there was time to pitch a last-resort tent city populated by prisoners, Governor Siegelman, failing in his reelection bid, folded his own tent. Soon he himself would join the ranks of the convicted, shuffling in and out of prison, albeit the preferable digs of the federal system rather than the state facilities. Hardly among the forgotten, Siegelman sought to tie his conviction for taking money in exchange for the appointment of HealthSouth executive Richard Scrushy to a state hospital board to the machinations of Republican political opponents tied to George W. Bush operative Karl Rove. Both Scrushy and Siegelman were dispatched to prison, and while Scrushy was deemed a flight risk, Siegelman managed to gain temporary release while his appeals wound through the courts. His loyalists mounted an unsuccessful national campaign to argue that his prosecution had been purely political. Would the former governor yet emerge as a corrections reformer? A campaigner for ex-felons' right to vote?

Judge Shashy's prison overcrowding order carried over into the Riley administration. Although the state supreme court ultimately disallowed the accumulated millions of dollars in contempt-of-court fines against the prison commissioner, it ruled that counties could send as many as a hundred state inmates weekly to the prison system, shifting the onus back up the line. "If we ever have a [prison] commissioner in the future who says the state is not going to pick up inmates," commented the director of the county commissioners association, "we now have a court order that says we can deliver the inmates to the state anyway."[98]

"I wanted to see it, feel it and taste it," Bob Riley said, becoming the first governor in memory to tour Holman and Fountain prisons in remote south Alabama, talking with inmates and eating fried fish and scalloped potatoes on a two-hour walk-through soon after he took office in 2003. It was a visit that lent a moment of hope to those promising early months of the Riley administration, before his tax reform amendment, which would have sent more money to schools and to corrections, went down in defeat. "We can't sustain this level of incarceration," the governor said, amid rows of three-tiered bunks in these two facilities that held over eighteen thousand prisoners.[99]

That places such as Holman and Fountain, where inmates far exceeded the minimally required number of corrections officers, had not exploded in mayhem during any number of un-air-conditioned summer afternoons testified to what? The largely benign disposition of the incarcerated population? The futility of revolt? Underreporting of incidents? "Most of the inmates don't want trouble," vouched Donal Campbell, Riley's first corrections commissioner. Two-thirds of new prisoners were now nonviolent offenders, up from 56 percent at the beginning of the Siegelman term.[100] "We need new beds, we need new maximum security beds, and it's still my goal to bring new beds on line," said Campbell, who at the time believed he was dealing with possibility.[101]

As it had in response to Judge Thompson's court order for the women's prison, Alabama in the summer of 2003 prepared to send fourteen hundred male prisoners to a for-profit prison for multimonth stays until cells could be found in-state. The destination was a new Corrections Corporation of America $35 million facility situated at the margins of visitation and public scrutiny in the Mississippi Delta.[102] Publicly traded CCA charged $25.50 per day per prisoner.[103] "The expansion of the 'prison industrial complex,'" observes Alex Lichtenstein, "provides jobs for the rural unemployed even while it siphons off the urban 'underclass.'"[104] This arrangement feeds the punitive habit while evading, as Gottschalk puts it, "prevention, rehabilitation, services for victims, fundamental economic and social changes, and yes, social justice."[105] Into the new century, with the state's prisons overflowing, even some Alabama politicians pondered the limits of punitiveness and expediency and began to gesture at remedy.

In 2004 the Riley administration settled three lawsuits — at Tutwiler, the St.

Clair prison, and the Limestone HIV facility — each centering on inmate care, overcrowding, and unsafe conditions, and each mandating an outside monitor to assure the hiring of additional guards and medical staff. Rather than battle judges and the lawyers of the SCHR, the Riley administration opted for negotiation and compliance.[106] It was one measure of this governor's difference from his predecessors. In relations with courts, Riley recognized the futility of the sez-you posturing of Wallace and Fob James. Acutely conscious of Alabama's image as he pursued foreign business investment, the governor sought to reshape external perceptions of the state. Riley chose not to rage against the forces of the devil or Washington. He avoided judicial confrontations. For their part, judges at state and federal levels, often conservative Republicans and new federalists amenable to the punitive, balked at issuing court orders for costly, lengthy institutional overhauls.

The state's prisons remained mired and starved, the legal climate harsh and vengeful. When Riley's corrections commissioner Campbell, a twenty-five-year veteran of the Tennessee prison system, began sending inmates out of state in response to federal judge Thompson's overcrowding order, he acknowledged the overwhelming numbers and his boxed-in situation: "You're probably not going to find any other state with some of the laws on the books that will get you life and life without [parole] than you'll find in Alabama."[107]

Stymied after repeated efforts to secure minimal increases in operating, repair, and construction funds from the legislature (Tennessee was spending over twice as much per prisoner as Alabama), prison commissioner Campbell resigned in early 2006. "So much is so much and you can only beat your head against the wall so long before it becomes unbearable," the president of the DOC employees' organization said at Campbell's departure.[108] During Campbell's three years, the DOC budget approached $300 million a year for a system holding 28,000 prisoners (about $10,700 annually per inmate). By contrast, New Jersey, with a similar number of inmates, had a corrections budget of nearly a billion dollars; North Carolina spent nearly $950 million on its prison population of 33,500; and Arkansas allocated almost two-thirds more per inmate than Alabama.[109]

"I don't believe we need to build another prison," insisted state senator Earl Hilliard in 1992 as he unsuccessfully opposed a $25 million prison construction bond issue. Representing the Black Belt, the state's former plantation heartland, Hilliard would soon become Alabama's first African American member of Congress since Reconstruction. His priorities represented his constituents' more fundamental concerns. "I think we need to put that money into education and early childhood programs so that we don't have this problem later on. . . . Every time they build a prison it's filled immediately — there's no end to it."[110] Hilliard's point of view has yet to prevail.

By his second term, Governor Riley, like his predecessors, faced the dilemma of where to store a steady stream of the newly convicted, the strange fruition of years of get-tough legislation. Because the "state system remains at 200 percent capacity," he insisted, it was "not physically possible" to move any faster in making transfers from the county jails.

"People want to lock up criminals and throw the key away," chided the presiding judge of Jefferson County, "but no one wants to pay the price that it takes."[111]

When the key gets thrown away, so do prisoners. Those released at the end of their sentences take away ten dollars and a bus ticket, plus accumulated baggage.[112] A social group characterized by low literacy, poor self-esteem, and few occupational skills, ex-felons reenter society largely on their own, receiving next to no help in recovering their lives and livelihoods. "They suffer civic excommunication," writes Glenn Loury, who insists that "we need to ask whether we as a society have fulfilled our collective responsibility to ensure fair conditions for each person." Encountering fear and prejudice, but no paycheck, ex-felons find insurmountable obstacles, cold hearts, and a greased slope leading back inside the wire. Almost two-thirds of Alabama inmates have been there before, the same fraction of employers who say they wouldn't consider hiring an ex-con.[113] From undeserving poor, they transform into unredeemable lawbreakers, throwaways, consigned to the underclass, written off for having created their own predicaments. Pressed into ghostly invisibility, released prisoners are all but lost to social support networks and neighborhoods, stuck without educational opportunities, eyed suspiciously by employers.

Estimates of the number of persons currently disenfranchised in Alabama due to past criminal convictions run to 250,000. As much as a third of the state's adult, black male population has lost the right to vote.[114] Alabama remains among a dozen or so states that do not automatically restore the voting rights of released prisoners, but insists upon an interminable petition process. Following sustained pressure from black legislators and civil rights activists, the legislature passed a law speeding up, but not making automatic, the process for reclaiming voting rights. Governor Riley first vetoed the law before ultimately signing it in 2003. While a few thousand former prisoners pursued and regained the franchise in the following couple of years, this represented a small fraction of those eligible. The white people's party fought the restoration law. "There's no more anti-Republican bill than this," said Marty Connors, the state GOP chair. "As frank as I can be, we're opposed to it because felons don't tend to vote Republican."[115] With some 60 percent of Alabama's prison population being African American in a state where 90 percent of black voters were voting Democratic, the roadblocks to regaining voting rights has diluted African American political clout.

As a Christian activist, former inmate Kenneth Glasgow of Dothan has sought to help other ex-felons with a variety of reentry programs offered by his Ordinary People Society ministry. His agenda includes the reclaiming of voting rights. "The men and women who have redeemed themselves by serving their time in prison should be embraced and welcomed home," insists Glasgow, half-brother to New York's Rev. Al Sharpton. "Restoring their right to vote is a crucial part of giving them a second chance. As a person who has been previously incarcerated, I know that voting connects you to your community by building responsibility for your neighbors and advancing common goals of democracy."[116] Glasgow seized upon a loophole in Alabama law that allowed felons convicted of crimes not classified as acts of "moral turpitude" to remain eligible to vote even while imprisoned. As state officials scrambled to clarify what crimes were turpitudinous (drug possession? drunk driving? receiving stolen property?), Rev. Glasgow registered hundreds of county jail inmates and former state prisoners for the 2008 election.[117]

SLAP 'EM BACK IN JAIL

Bruce Western's analysis of the U.S. prison boom concludes that while "crime rates increased significantly in the 1960s and 1970s and street violence became a serious problem for poor communities, policy makers could have responded in many ways. By building more prisons, severely criminalizing drug-related activity, mandating prison time, and lengthening sentences, lawmakers chose a punitive course."[118] Marie Gottschalk agrees: "Building more prisons in reaction to the disturbances of the 1960s only looks like a foreordained outcome now, decades after the fact." What if, she asks, instead of expanding the "carceral state," resources had gone to support the human services network, including child care and education?[119]

In Alabama, editorialized the *Montgomery Advertiser* in 2003, because there has "never been any significant political pressure from the citizenry for dealing with prison problems . . . a long string of governors and legislators could get away with doing little about the steadily increasing problems of the Department of Corrections." In "the dereliction of the past," lawmakers were abetted by elected judges and attorneys general trying to out-tough their competition for office.[120] "One Alabama judge," reported the Southern Center for Human Rights, "who was in a closely contested election, set a capital trial for the week before the election to benefit from the publicity that came from presiding over it. The judge ran advertisements in the newspapers proclaiming, 'It doesn't matter whether a judge is a Democrat or a Republican, so long as he will hand down a death sentence.'"[121] Allowed by state law to override jury verdicts in capital cases, Alabama judges, as Anthony Lewis pointed out in a mid-1990s commentary, "have rejected 47 jury recommendations for life sentences, imposing death instead, while reducing jury death sentences to life only 5 times."[122]

"In this state we have one of the harshest and most backward habitual-offender laws in the country," raged Selma attorney J. L. Chestnut in 2006.[123] The state's three-strikes law did not consider the time between convictions or even the seriousness of earlier offenses. A couple of forgery convictions, years apart, could result in a life sentence. "If you have three nonviolent crimes," explained a prison spokesman, "you could still get the same sentence as someone who has committed three violent crimes."[124] By the late 1990s, more than six thousand Alabama inmates had no hope of ever emerging from prison as a result of the draconian habitual-offender law, which, since its enactment in 1980, produced little effect upon property or violent crimes while burying alive youthful lawbreakers.[125]

Whenever journalists, such as the *Birmingham News*' Carla Crowder, gathered the life stories of Alabama's locked-up population, the gratuitous cruelty of get-tough laws take unsettling, familiar form. In 1989 Vietnam vet Douglas Lamar Gray, owner of a roofing business in Moulton, bought $900 of marijuana and was charged with trafficking. That Gray, who had a wife and son, was lured to a motel by a police informant with a criminal record counted for less than the several months of jail time he had served for burglaries in his teens and early twenties. The habitual-offender law kicked in, stamping Gray's ticket for mandatory life without parole. Then there was Michael Peek, a small-time, occasional marijuana seller from Macon County who "grew up hunting, fishing and smoking pot." In 1998 Peek was caught with friends and 4.75 pounds. Because of three prior drug convictions, he merited Alabama's mandatory life without parole. Doubtless a pattern of stupid decisions, but deserving of a lifetime lockup? With no record of violent offenses?

In 1979 twenty-two-year-old Terry McLester, as smashed as his marriage and the mall windows he plundered, was arrested by Dothan police. "He was drunk in a prison work-release program two years later," writes Crowder, "when he threatened a convenience store cashier, was convicted of robbery, then sent to prison for the rest of his life."[126] By 2004 McLester, still locked up, was trusted to counsel and mentor other inmates. "I'd have no problem seeing Terry get out," said the Houston County district attorney who had prosecuted McLester. The problem lay with the inflexible law. Larry Gibson of Brookside received mandatory life without parole in 1992 due to three teenage theft convictions and, some twenty-two years later, a bullet he fired through a pickup truck window following a beer-joint fight.[127]

For an accumulation of alcohol, marijuana, and small-theft offenses, Brian Knighten, a sixth-grade dropout, found himself in Fountain Correctional Center in 1991 ineligible for parole until 1999.

Getting caught in the wrong place can also send a person to a worse place for far longer than expected. Randy Reid, a thirty-six-year-old roofer who had never been to jail, sold an undercover officer less than a half-gram of crack and lost twelve years of freedom. Reid "didn't have a weapon on him when he was arrested and didn't have a violent criminal history. He made the serious mistake of selling drugs on Birmingham's First Avenue North, just a few miles from at least seven public schools and two public housing complexes." Location added ten years to Reid's sentence.[128]

Punitive judgment demands incarceration on the cheap, not resources to take account of personal histories or underlying conditions that give rise to crime. Across the Deep South, prisons swallowed larger bites of state budgets, with little but prolonged misery to show for it. Then slowly, into the new century, half of the states across the country began to abandon some of the worst mandatory minimum laws they had zealously passed during the preceding twenty-five years. Early release and the chance to earn "good time" for good behavior returned as options. In some states, nonviolent drug offenders increasingly received parole, treatment, and counseling instead of lockup. The project of "re-entry," initiated by the National Institute of Justice toward the end of the Clinton administration, pressed for a pragmatic shift of emphasis, "from the criminal to the community," on how to ready larger numbers of prisoners for safe release. It was a movement complemented by a shift among conservatives — including figures such as Chuck Colson ("Watergate crook turned Christian evangelist") and former Virginia Republican legislator Mark Earley, a Colson convert — to, as a *New York Times* writer put it, "save lives, to save souls and also to save money."[129]

Seeking relief from the escalating costs of escalating imprisonment, reality-bitten Alabama officials, citizens' groups, and legislators sought to slow the inflow without seeming "soft on crime," an offense carrying a sure political death penalty. There had been tentative efforts at corrections options in the early 1990s, such as a poorly funded Birmingham program of alternative sentencing.[130] Prompted by a 1998 study committee begun by Attorney General Bill Pryor and Perry Hooper, chief justice of the Alabama Supreme Court, the legislature in 2000 created the Alabama Sentencing Commission, an appointed agency of criminal justice officials and victims' rights advocates, to make recommendations that addressed overcrowding, sentencing disparities for similar crimes, and incarceration alternatives.[131] Gathering data and floating proposals, the commission also provided a self-protective way for elected officials to gauge public reaction to possible legislation before putting themselves on the line.

As in so many areas of social justice, Alabama trailed all but a handful of states in moving toward sentencing guidelines.[132] "This is the first set of major reforms," trumpeted Pryor on the appearance of the commission's timid recommendations in late winter 2003. Petty matters turned into stumbling blocks, including the resistance of the Alabama Retail Association to raising the monetary threshold (from $250 to $500) for prosecuting first-time property crimes as felonies. After several rounds the legislature succeeded in making the change, which the Sentencing Commission claimed could result in three thousand fewer prisoners over five years.

Many prosecutors, from the attorney general down to local DAs, were willing to trade the release of some nonviolent property offenders for "truth in sentencing" laws that doled out mandatory, irrevocable time for persons convicted of violent acts, sex offenses, and drug trafficking. But just who constituted "nonviolent offenders" or "repeat offenders"? Where to draw the line between possession and dealing? How to address the vastly different social class and racially significant mandatories between cocaine and crack offenders? The state remained fixed upon punitive habits rather than willing to join the movement for compassionate reentry. Reform appeared to be driven by the functional need to free up prison beds. "There are many low-risk, nonviolent inmates occupying expensive beds in maximum and medium security prisons in Alabama," reported the commission, "beds that could be used to incapacitate dangerous violent offenders."[133] When the legislature passed a version of the "community corrections" approach to work-release programs and home confinement as alternatives for very low-risk offenders, these were tentative concessions, already widely in place across the U.S.[134]

"I would like for citizens to recognize that we're coming to a point in the very near future that we won't have room in the prison for rapists because we're putting too many shoplifters in," warned chief assistant attorney general Rosa Davis, a commission member. "I've been in the attorney general's office 30 years, and we've been the 'lock them up and throw away the key' office." Davis tried out the new vocabulary: "We're now learning the difference between being tough on crime and smart on crime."[135]

But even modest attempts by the Sentencing Commission to move drug criminalization more in line with the rest of the nation met habituated resistance. A first marijuana possession in Alabama was a misdemeanor; the second was a felony that sent some four hundred people a year to prison for ten years. And woe to a parolee busted for a joint.

In contrast, "I can't remember anybody going to jail for pot in the last 15 years," said the attorney for Arlington County, Virginia, talking about the Old Dominion's handling of marijuana possession.

"If you go toward the idea of legalizing marijuana," objected Shelby County, Alabama, district attorney Robby Owens, "you're going to put more and more kids in harm's way, because we as a society are telling them go ahead and do this because we're not going to do anything to you, and I am opposed to that course of conduct."[136] Although liberalizing state drug laws would be an achievement, no one on the Sentencing Commission had suggested decriminalization, a suggestion that would instantly place its proponent beyond the boundaries of acceptable political discourse.

"I think it's going to be a learning process," suggested Circuit Judge David Rains, a commission member, when a few voluntary sentencing guidelines trickled out of the legislature in 2006. "The whole purpose is to save bed space for the violent and repeat cases that are incorrigible."[137]

Like "bed space," the language of "reentry" required practice, lest a lapse of the punitive tongue become a slippery slope. A *Decatur Daily* editorial expressed the moment's contradictions out loud:

> It costs a lot to keep these people jailed. It's far less expensive for the state to hire extra parole officers and pay their benefits than to keep all of these people in jail. Whatever the outcome, it's a chance we should take.
>
> If they can't lead the type of life society expects of them, then slap them back in jail.[138]

As if the conditions, opportunities, and life chances that will allow young offenders to "lead the type of life society expects" can be addressed by the hiring of parole officers.

Sentencing guidelines for property and drug crimes remained so unreformed that on the day the commission approved them in April 2004, one of its most valued and experienced members resigned in frustration. "When I came on this commission, I thought we were really going to make an impact and start doing the right thing," protested state district judge Pete Johnson. "We're sentencing people too long for offenses that are not serious, and using that history to guide what we're going to do. And it's bad history." Judge Johnson's Jefferson County drug court had drawn rare national praise to Alabama through his meting out of treatment and rehab, jobs and community service. In eleven years Johnson's court had moved four thousand drug offenders into a treatment-alternatives program overseen by UAB, with a success rate better than the national average. "In our political situation in this state, there will still be judges who will feel compelled within the range to give the maximum," he complained, "and it won't be the right thing to do. They love to play on the fear of the public."[139] In a roundabout way, through efforts at standardizing and rationalizing sentencing, the legislature and a succession of attorneys general engaged in an expansion of state power that their antigovernment rhetoric belied.[140]

The creation of a second parole panel — which, due to the insistence of Alabama's Black Legislative Caucus, included African American representation in proportion to the state's population and the panel's first African American woman — speeded the release of as many as three thousand nonviolent offenders in 2003 and 2004. A year later, however, the number of eligibles had shrunk and the prison population resumed its climb.[141] In 2005 the Alabama Senate filibustered ten modest proposals from the Sentencing Commission that the House had passed. Ratcheting the moral machinery, DAs sought tighter limits on who could be released. Predictable voices of outrage chimed in, depicting the incarcerated as incorrigibles, as throwaways. "We are talking about convicted felons here," James Harrison, citizen of Prattville, told an *Advertiser* reporter. "They have been found guilty. You think they are all of a sudden going to straighten up just because they get paroled? I say put up tents and fence them in. Tents and latrines are good enough for our soldiers in Iraq and Afghanistan. Are you telling me we should treat convicted felons better than our military people?"[142] Harrison's rant served up the punitive nutshell.

In 2007 Governor Riley's keen-to-punish attorney general, Troy King, stood outside the doors of the state parole board and publicly advocated the abolition of parole. Convicted criminals, he said, should serve their full sentences with no option for parole or good time (i.e., reduction for being well behaved). "Our sentences are meaningless right now," argued King. "People should know that if I commit this crime, this is the punishment I'm going to get and when I get it, I'm going to serve the sentence I got. All this talk about rehabilitation. We build prisons, yes to rehabilitate, but we also build prisons to punish."[143] Just how far removed the Alabama attorney general stood from the rehabilitative tradition can be measured against the words of mid-twentieth-century English prison commissioner Alexander Paterson: "Men come to prison as a punishment, not for punishment. It is the sentence of imprisonment, and not the treatment accorded in prison, that constitutes the punishment."[144] Rather than admit the barbarism of its prison system and own up to the necessary reallocation of human, institutional, and fiscal resources, politicians such as King stoked the incarceral appetite.

During his second term, as the state's incarcerated population pushed past thirty thousand, Governor Riley puffed a small breath of life into the Community Partnership for Recovery and Reentry initiative, calling upon "faith-based organizations and community groups" — which he described as "among the most trusted and effective institutions when it comes to helping those in need" — to work with state agencies in prerelease and parolee strategies. Among the 7,000–11,000 inmates released in Alabama each year, well over a third would return to prison.[145] Riley took his language nearly verbatim from the guidelines of the Bush administration's grant-scattering Compassion in Action (CIA) initiative.[146] As with his 2003 "Amendment One" tax-reform campaign, Riley was responding to genuine need and to the fundamental obligations of a state to its citizens. But if voters couldn't be moved to approve new revenues for the education of Alabama's children, how likely would Riley be to find money so that "more ex-prisoners have a successful transition back into society"? Acknowledging that need far exceeded resources, the Community Partnership selected for reentry support 1,000 inmates from the more than 10,000–12,000 released each year whom it thought had the best prospects of avoiding a return to prison. Riley prayed that churches and charities would take up the state's job.[147]

"Encouraging churches to get involved with prison and after-prison care should be applauded," concludes the author of the most thorough study of reentry, "but it cannot and should not replace the primary governmental responsibility."[148] Goodwilled, euphemistically named reentry programs and halfway houses — Renascence, Celebrate Recovery, Return to Reality, Lovelady Center, New Beginnings Foundation — make critical differences in the lives they reach, but these initiatives of volunteerism, boosted by small donations and uncertain grants, can't approach the enormity of need for housing, education, counseling, health care, social resources, and livelihood to released prisoners. The punitive habit teaches that the poor and near-poor get along without adequate social services and safety nets, so why should ex-cons receive public support?

In April 2008 five years of bipartisan effort in Congress produced the Second Chance Act, which "for the first time in decades" sought "to make the lives of prisoners and ex-prisoners easier, not more difficult." While Democrats offered their expected support, significant to legislative passage were Republican Christian conservatives professing a newfound concern for the plight of ex-prisoners. Second Chance backers envisioned federal grants to nonprofits (including religious groups) and to local governments in support of a variety of needs and services for released offenders. But where was the money?[149]

As he announced his retirement after more than twenty-eight years on the bench, U. W. Clemon, Alabama's first black federal judge, decried the descent into punitiveness. "The advancement of civil liberties is no longer a primary direction of the federal courts," concluded Clemon. "When that is coupled

with the mandatory minimum sentences and the unduly long sentences required by the sentencing guidelines, I feel that my life could be better spent in
other pursuits."[150]

DEATH'S DOOR

Few things are more certain in the Heart of Dixie than politicians' love of the
death penalty and pledges of no new taxes. "It's been drummed into people
through the years," attests state senator Hank Sanders, a consistent sponsor of
anti–capital punishment legislation. "The death penalty, the death penalty, just
like no new taxes, so people react viscerally on it."[151] As the twentieth century
became the twenty-first, Alabama was sentencing more people to death for the
size of its state population than any other state. It was also consistently failing to provide competent death-penalty defense lawyers and failing to provide
them with adequate support to represent their clients.[152] "Few states allow the
death penalty in so many situations," writes the *News'* Robin DeMonia, "and
few states do less to try to ensure proper legal representation. . . . Our system of capital defense is considered one of the worst, if not the worst, in the
country.

> We were one of the last states to abandon the electric chair. We're the only state
> that allows elected judges to regularly sentence defendants to death even when a
> jury recommends life. Until the U.S. Supreme Court declared it unconstitutional,
> we executed the mentally retarded. We have also executed the clearly psychotic,
> and we will execute people for crimes they committed as young as 16, the lowest
> age allowed by the U.S. Supreme Court.[153]

As with civil rights litigation, Alabama death-penalty cases addressed by
the U.S. Supreme Court have brought wide public notice to the state's archaic
practices, while testing emerging legal strategies. In a widely cited dissenting
opinion in a 1963 case that the court refused to hear, Justice Arthur Goldberg
was joined by Justices Douglas and Brennan in challenging the imposition of
the death penalty for a rape conviction. What became known as the "Goldberg
dissent" argued for "evolving standards of decency that mark the progress of
[our] maturing society," standards that are "more or less universally accepted"
and avoid excessive punishment and "unnecessary cruelty."[154] "In this way,"
notes Gottschalk, "Goldberg inserted public opinion considerations into the

national debate over capital punishment." The Legal Defense Fund (LDF) built upon Goldberg's opinion to press a growing number of death-penalty challenges during the moment when, in 1964, a Gallup poll counted only 42 percent of the public in favor of capital punishment, a historic low.[155]

In another LDF case from Alabama in the mid-1960s, *Maxwell v. Bishop*, a federal district court and a U.S. appeals court upheld the death penalty for a black man convicted of rape despite overwhelming statistical evidence of racially discriminatory sentencing patterns. Gottschalk writes that the LDF strategy of taking on as many death-penalty cases as possible in the hope of mobilizing public opinion for the abolition of capital punishment had the unforeseen consequence of "defending numerous marginal, violent members of society," a significant number of whom came with white racist orientations, while the violent crimes committed by some African American defendants "reinforced white stereotypes about black criminality."[156] Between 1968 and 1977, no executions took place in any state. Yet, as Gottschalk points out, liberal groups and academic organizations were slow in mounting a broad campaign against capital punishment.

While litigation had become the principal strategy of anti–death penalty advocates, public sentiment began to reverse course. Supreme Court rulings presented setbacks. Lacking a vigorous national political effort and public opinion campaign, the death-penalty abolition movement became restricted by the limits of litigation even as it now found itself on the losing side of public sentiment. Despite many state and local affiliate efforts, it was not until the 1980s, Gottschalk argues, that the ACLU, for instance, mobilized nationally as "a leading foe of capital punishment and the new punitive politics."[157] Executions resumed, gathering slow speed at first, then escalating as the end of the century approached.

"Administration of the death penalty," wrote Michael S. Greco of the American Bar Association, as it pressed for a moratorium on executions in 1997, "is neither fair nor consistent, and can fairly be described as a haphazard maze of unfair practices, a maze that tolerates injustice in case after case."[158] By 2002 Alabama, for the size of its population, had the largest number of residents on death row of any state, yet it lacked a statewide system to oversee and fund the delivery of indigent defense; was unable to ensure fair trials, competent defenses, or adequate appeals; and showed a general unwillingness to review old convictions in light of DNA evidence.

That Alabama attorneys general have so tenaciously defended the state's death machinery confirms for many inside and outside the state that the Heart of Dixie is alive and thumping. In a 2000 interview, Attorney General Bill Pryor expressed no reservations about the adequacy of capital case defenses: "My judgment is that at both the trial and appellate level we face very experienced and competent opponents." A staunch right-winger, Pryor would become, in 2003, one of George W. Bush's federal judges. Contrary to Pryor's (and his successor's) contentions, the evidence has long argued that Alabama's support for capital defense lawyers is extremely inadequate. "Basically," observes Kevin Doyle, a former defender of capital cases in Alabama who went on to similar work in New York, "these folks are sent into battle underequipped, undertrained and undercompensated."[159] At least two innocent people were dispatched to Alabama's death row between the late 1970s and the century's turn. Who knows how many others were executed? "Alabama provides the worst representation to people facing the death penalty of any of the states that have capital punishment," observes Stephen Bright, SCHR president.[160] "People get the death penalty not for committing the worst crime but for the misfortune of having the worst lawyer."[161]

In the summer of 2008 Philip Alston, a human rights investigator for the United Nations, visited Alabama, home to the nation's highest per capita execution rate, and Texas, the state with the highest number of executions and prisoners on death row. Alston, an Australian and a professor of law at New York University, concluded that Alabama officials "seem strikingly indifferent to the risk of executing innocent people and have a range of standard responses, most of which are characterized by a refusal to engage with the facts. The reality is that the system is simply not designed to turn up cases of innocence, however compelling they might be. Almost certainly Alabama has executed innocent people, but officials would rather deny than confront flaws in the criminal justice system."[162]

In a blast reminiscent of George Wallace's screeds against out-of-state critics (what Howell Raines calls "that vintage Alabama rhetorical trick, the excuse-by-comparison"), Attorney General King dismissed Alston's report with a sez-you: "The United Nations has grievous injustices in its own building that it ought to address before it begins worrying about a speck in the eye of a state like Alabama."[163]

Alabama's insistence on capital punishment suggests that if the new federalism (or the old "states' rights") ever wins the day, drawing and quartering will be ripe for a comeback. Shrill, prevailing voices still sound, like those of the advocacy group Victims of Crime and Leniency, which regrets the state's abandoning its electric chair (nicknamed Yellow Mama and in service since 1927) for lethal injection as of July 2002. "I don't think the chair is inhumane," insisted Vocal's co-founder Miriam Sheehan, when only Nebraska and Alabama continued to use electrocution as the sole method of execution. "There is no way the state will allow you to do away with them as horribly as they killed their victims," said Sheehan, a member of the standards committee of the Alabama Sentencing Commission. While a college student in Birmingham, Sheehan's daughter was raped and murdered in 1976. Of the three men convicted for these crimes, one was executed in 1990.[164] This remains the abiding dilemma, the dramatization of evildoer and victim in a culture where the personal figures so centrally in social relations and where popular opinion elects judges. Vengeance and punitiveness buttressed by genuinely heart-wrenching narratives foreclose a broader discourse about justice and how to alter the social and institutional conditions that, very predictably, produce most criminality and incarceration.

Against the punitive, grisly grain, some Alabamians, even among those who might lay claim to payback, do oppose the death penalty, demonstrating another kind of Christian practice than that trumpeted by the righteous right and politically ambitious prosecutors. "I'd like to think I could be like the family of Bettie Long," writes Robin DeMonia:

> Mrs. Long was robbed and gunned down in 1995 in front of her teenage daughter at their Kingston laundry. The killer, Taurus Carroll, just 17 at the time, said the gun went off in a moment of nervousness.
>
> A jury recommended life. A judge sentenced Carroll to death. The Alabama Supreme Court later overturned the sentence, calling it "excessive."
>
> What makes the case memorable, though, was the sentence recommended by the victim's husband, Raymond Long, and her mother.
>
> "It's the life that I live, and the God that I serve, [that] will not let me hate this young man," Katie Wright said at Carroll's sentencing hearing. "I, as a mother of a child of a life that he took, do not want to see him dead."[165]

In *The Prince of Frogtown*, a book written to come to terms with his father's wrecked life, which included much time inside bars and some behind them, son of Alabama Rick Bragg writes that he has known "a lot of men in prisons, men who will spend their eternity paying for their worst minute on earth."

> It came when they caught their wife cheating on them and thumbed back the hammer on a gun they bought to shoot rats and snakes, or got cross-eyed drunk in some fish camp bar and pulled a dime-store knife, just because they imagined a funny look or a suspicious smile. You do not have to forgive such men, ever, that minute. You can lock them away for it, put them to death for it, and spend your eternity cursing their name. It is not all they are.[166]

The punitive heart drums loudest in the telltale chambers occupied by prototypical Alabama attorneys general such as Charles Graddick, William Pryor, and Troy King. In 2004 King filed an amicus brief with the U.S. Supreme Court to support Missouri's right to execute sixteen- and seventeen-year-olds. "It strains the imagination and breaks the heart to see what diabolical cruelty teenage murderers can be capable of," King said. "A teenager who plots like an adult, kills like an adult, and covers up like an adult, should be responsible for his choices like an adult."[167]

Was King speaking as an adult whose Alabama education failed to include lessons about the physiological and social dimensions of juvenile immaturity? Exceptions are often made for juveniles in many areas of the law, observes Patricia Williams, because "we know that the prefrontal cortex, which governs executive function, does not fully develop until the early 20s. We know that juveniles are impulsive and not sufficiently forward-thinking to calculate all the consequences of their behavior."[168] Contrary to the mechanistic thinking of these attorneys general, treating juveniles differently from adults does not make excuses for tragic criminal acts but acknowledges psychological and neurological immaturity as a mitigating factor. In Alabama, as of 2008, eighty-nine juveniles were serving life without parole. That seventy-five of these youths were black, and that the state leads the nation in the percentage of black juveniles serving life sentences, attests to the racial bias at the historic heart of Alabama's criminal justice system.[169]

The disappointment within Alabama's executive branch was palpable when the U.S. Supreme Court agreed in 2007 to hear a challenge to Kentucky's cocktail injection death penalty. Governor Riley reluctantly postponed a scheduled execution while a new, painless chemical concoction was sought. Attorney General King chafed that he couldn't care less about the suffering of a convicted murderer: "In this arena we take our eye off the ball and that ball is the criminal, and we forget about the people who suffered at his hands. I don't think it's the obligation of the state to remove any pain from the death penalty." King's sez-you, the sort of pronouncement that reconfirms Alabama's reputation for cruelty and barbarism, was noted as far away as the *Irish Times*, which reported that Texas, Ohio, and Alabama had executed the most people that year, and while two out of three Americans favored capital punishment, a majority of blacks did not. "There may be little that citizens in other countries can do to stop the U.S. from killing its own people," the *Times* wrote, taking note of anti–death penalty activists "putting pressure on EU companies that invest in states that carry out most executions."[170]

Impatient for a ruling on the Kentucky challenge, Alabama tried three times to break the informal national execution moratorium. The high court issued stays while it mulled. On the day in April 2008 when the justices, seven to two, voted to allow a resumption of executions, Attorney General King seemed eager to send the backlog of two hundred men and four women on the ultimate Alabama getaway. "Today's decision has removed the barrier that has impeded justice for the past year," he announced. "There can be no greater call than to once again diligently seek enforcement of death sentences that have lingered far too long."[171] "No greater call" for the state's chief legal officer than the unleashing of executions.

A third certainty is the legacy of historical racism as it unfolds in death-penalty prosecutions. "In Alabama, 60 percent of homicide victims are typically black," commented DeMonia in a column about the 2006 PBS documentary *Race to Execution*. "But 75 percent of cases that have ended up on Death Row in the past three decades involve victims who are white. In a *News* editorial page series last year, we couldn't find justification for this."[172] DeMonia revisited the case of Robert Tarver, featured in *Race to Execution*.

Hugh Kite, a white man, general store owner, and mainstay of his rural Alabama community, was murdered during the course of a robbery on September 15, 1984. Less than four months after Kite's murder, Robert Tarver, a black man, was arrested, tried, and sentenced to die. The prosecutor at Tarver's trial rejected all but one of the African Americans qualified for jury service. Eleven white Alabamians and one African American constituted Tarver's jury of his peers.[173]

The illegal practice of keeping blacks off capital juries didn't result in Tarver's conviction being reversed on appeal or prevent his execution in 2000. His law-yer hadn't raised the racial composition of the jury as an issue at the time of his trial. DeMonia summarizes the arguments of attorney Bryan Stevenson of the Equal Justice Initiative (EJI) that trials such as Tarver's "must be judged in the context of Alabama's atrocious past of oppressing, terrorizing and lynch-ing blacks."[174] A 2010 EJI study revealed that "the practice of excluding blacks and other minorities from Southern juries remains widespread and largely un-checked. . . . In Alabama, courts have found racially discriminatory jury selec-tion in 25 death penalty cases since 1987, and there are counties where more than 75 percent of black jury pool members have been struck in death penalty cases."[175]

THE BIG PAYBACK

Many have argued that the incarceration boom of the 1980s and 1990s dramat-ically reduced violent crime. Bruce Western, while not denying that the 1990s crime drop was "a real and significant social trend that improved the quality of life among the rich and poor alike," challenged those who claimed that a third or more of the crime reduction was due to the expanding prison system. His review of state-by-state statistics "indicated that the 66 percent increase in the state imprisonment rate between 1993 and 2001 reduced the rate of serious crime by 2 to 5 percent, about one-tenth of the 1990s crime drop. The remain-ing nine-tenths would likely have happened anyway, as a result of other factors like the growth in urban police forces and the pacification of the drug trade following the crack-related violence of the early 1990s."[176]

The rising incarceration rates of the 1980s and 1990s fell heaviest on un-educated black men born between 1965 and 1975, particularly those segregated in cities with the greatest inequality in income between races.[177] This included areas of Birmingham and Mobile, where blacks who had given up the search for work were not recorded in official unemployment statistics. "Our society," writes Glenn C. Loury, "creates criminogenic conditions in our sprawling ur-ban ghettos, and then acts out rituals of punishment against them as some aw-ful form of human sacrifice."[178] In Alabama's black urban neighborhoods and in the rural Black Belt, where opportunity is bleak, labor markets scarcely ex-ist, and drug trafficking flourishes, the state's criminal justice system functions as a means of racial and social control. "Mass imprisonment," adds Western, is "a key component in a system of inequality—a social structure in which social inequalities are self-sustaining and those at the bottom have few prospects for upward mobility."[179] Insisting that "mass imprisonment" or "mass incarceration" is a mischaracterization, sociologist Loïc Wacquant argues that the "expansion and intensification of the activities of the police, courts, and prison over the past quarter-century have been finely targeted by class, ethnicity, and place, leading to what is better referred to as the *hyper*-incarceration of one particular category"—young, lower-class, black men, primarily in urban locations of high unemployment and low educational opportunity.[180]

In a state where a couple of hundred parole officers are assigned to keep track of more than forty thousand probationers and parolees, when a newly paroled individual disappears, goes off his meds and runs amuck, assaults or kills someone (drawing sensational press coverage), the clamor rises for payback; rancor takes aim at bleeding hearts.[181] In Alabama, public discussion of prisons seldom gets beyond variations of the punitive and a recurring acknowledgment of the enormous monetary costs. "In refusing to adequately fund state corrections," editorializes the *Mobile Register*, "Alabama's financial bind is a prison of its own making."[182] Such is the contradiction of ideologues who oppose institutions of big government and the bureaucratization of life but support prison construction, warehousing larger populations, and maintaining capital punishment.

DEVIL'S PLAYGROUND

"I wanted to see it, feel it and taste it," Bob Riley said when he visited two Alabama prisons at the beginning of his first term and promised a revised chapter in the state's horrific penal history. Yet the growth rate of the prison population in the Riley years slowed only slightly. The state remained among the leaders in locking up its residents. It ran the nation's most crowded prisons. It had the highest ratio of inmates to corrections officers and spent the least upon corrections of any state. The few alternatives to incarceration seemed token, often dependent upon unfunded, religiously based projects. Only $6.1 million of a corrections budget of $360 million was going to supervised release programs during the last year of Riley's governorship.[183]

"I'm here today to tell you as an officer who works inside a correctional facility each and every day, our prisons are an absolute time bomb waiting to explode," Captain Lloyd Wallace, president of the Alabama Correctional Organization, told the press in early 2009. "The fuse is clearly lit and moving fast." As they filed documents in support of a prisoners' lawsuit charging that Donaldson Correctional Facility near Bessemer was unconstitutionally crowded and dangerous, the corrections officers contended the governor had not delivered on campaign pledges to reform the system, relieve overcrowding, and improve pay.[184] An analysis of the prison system's internal incident reports by the Southern Center for Human Rights revealed that the Department of Corrections "repeatedly released inaccurate information to the public, significantly underreporting the number of persons assaulted in state custody."[185] The SCHR cited stabbings, sexual assaults, and suicides, as well as attacks against Donaldson corrections officers, that went underreported. Would scrutiny of other Alabama prisons turn up similar omissions?

One early cost of the Great Recession fell upon the work-release program that had allowed nearly 1,700 inmates in 2008 to take day jobs — as welders, auto mechanics, assemblers of mobile homes, day laborers — earning money for themselves and for the corrections system in a sixty-forty split. A year later the number of participating inmates had dropped by a fourth.[186] In 2009 lawmakers authorized $4 million less for corrections than the governor requested. "The money for prisons," wrote the AP's Bob Johnson, "was replaced with funding for special projects in legislators' districts. Those projects include festivals like the Ider Mule Day, Winfield Mule Day, Fyffe UFO Days, the Chocolate Festival in Rainbow City and the Franklin County Watermelon Festival."[187] Unlike mules or UFOs, inmates and disenfranchised ex-prisoners lack legislative clout. There is no reason to think things will change for the better. Perhaps a judge will again declare the prisons unconstitutionally cruel and overcrowded. But "corrections" in Alabama waited out even Frank Johnson. If jammed-together inmates eventually set the penitentiaries on fire, they can expect little empathy from the Heart of Dixie, and only a short, sensational flash of headlines.

"Idle hands is the devil's playground," Holman inmate Robert Tedder told the documentary crew of MSNBC TV's *Lockup* in 2006, as he pieced together one more electric guitar from plastic model boat kits.[188] Tedder, inside since the 1980s, had hit upon an approved craft for timelessness. With the high technologies of surveillance and control and the near-impossibility of escape, even without air conditioning the lid might stay on. Or not. Who can say? The persisting human tragedy, and the state's enduring deficiencies, take a deadening, brutalizing toll.

Historical studies of incarceration often wend their way to the same summation: "The way prisons are run and their inmates treated," writes the dissident Milovan Djilas, who experienced years of Yugoslavian captivity, "gives a faithful picture of a society, especially of the ideas and the methods of those who dominate that society."[189] In the Heart of Dixie's jails and prisons, home to the state's most invisible ghosts, punishment rules an atmosphere of bitterness, dread, and abandonment. "Down in the Valley of the Shadow," sing the Grateful Dead, "just you, Alabama, and me."[190]

PART TWO

Public Figures of Speech

Alabama's . . . lack of progress can be linked directly
to its penchant for electing buffoons.
— HOWELL RAINES, "The Politics of Embarrassment
in Alabama"

CHAPTER THREE

In the Ditch with Wallace

I was sitting in the bar of the Cotton Lounge,
railing against George Wallace, when the fist
rang in my stomach and I looked up
to a truck driver shouting down at me,
"Talk too much!"

　　— RODNEY JONES, "A History of Speech"

"I love it here," an Alabamian told British journalist Gary Younge during one of the trumped-up crises in which a governor, this time Fob James, threatened to call out the state troopers and the National Guard to fight a federal judge's ruling. "But when I think that people will look at that idiot and think that he represents us I just want to move."[1] Stretching beyond memory's horizon, trainloads of elected officials — governors foremost, but also senators, congressmen, and state legislators — have again and again hauled the freight of the bigoted and the dining cars of the privileged along a parochial track. While most state government workers have jostled along dutifully in penny-pinched public service, the state's governors — highly visible representatives of Alabama polity — have projected the "personality, character, political philosophy, programs, and policies" (to quote an uncommon insight from among their ranks) in keeping with the state's reputation for political dysfunction.[2]

During vivid moments when they have showcased varying degrees of intolerance, criminality, buffoonery, arrogance, and parochialism, recent public figures of speech such as George "The Guvner" Wallace, Brother Guy Hunt, Fob "Thumper" James, Roy "Ten Commandments" Moore, Richard "Senator No" Shelby, Don "Fratman" Siegelman, and Jefferson Beauregard Sessions III have reminded the nation and the wider world that the beat goes on in the Heart of Dixie.

Where to begin? With the good ol' boys. There was a time, Rick Bragg recalls, when "the bumper stickers on their trucks read WALLACE or nothing at all."[3] That time seemed an eon for anyone who lived through it. First elected in 1962, The Guvner officially exited the South Perry Street mansion for the last time in January 1987. He or his wife, Lurleen, had served all but a half-dozen of those years as the state's chief executive. The consequences were devastating and long lasting for the real as well as the imagined Alabama.

In his first phase, across the 1960s and into the early 1970s, George Wallace, Alabama's pit bull, modeled snarling, confrontational stances for the world to witness, cheered on by the white majority. The Little Fightin' Judge (so-called for his youthful exploits as a bantamweight boxer and his stint as a circuit judge) used his popularity to bully the legislature into making committee appointments that strengthened a new Black Belt–rural county partnership, "effectively dulling the impact of reapportionment," and extending the power of "the more reactionary elements" of the old planter–Big Mule alliance "years beyond what otherwise could have been expected."[4] Wallace's last two terms in office were lost to the physically and emotionally debilitating effects of Arthur Bremer's 1972 assassination attempt. Even now, to understand Alabama's contemporary problems and its political imaginary requires revisiting the years The Guvner stole.

As Wallace himself affirmed in *Crisis*, the schoolhouse-door television documentary made for ABC News in 1963, the trail of Alabama's bellicose leading men leads at least as far back as one of his personal heroes, secessionist fire-eater William Lowndes Yancey.[5] Dousing critics with ridicule and disdain, refusing to acknowledge generations of racial injustice, Wallace mesmerized the down-home gallery and marshaled the bogeymen. This was easier than tackling his state's structural predicaments.

Atop Montgomery's Goat Hill, the long-ago pasture where the state capitol now sits and lobbyists graze upon legislators, more than a century of Alabama governors have found themselves entangled in knots tied by the men who perpetrated the 1901 constitution. This antidemocratic document concentrated power in legislative and special-interest fiefdoms, strangled the fiscal potential and flexibility of state government, and encumbered the autonomy of counties, towns, and cities.

Largely unrestrained by ethics laws, and experienced in moving large amounts of money by means of untraceable transfers from one political action committee to another, lobbyists, fewer than a dozen in the early 1970s, numbered over five hundred by the early twenty-first century.[6] The state's ethics commission, among the weakest in the U.S., lacks subpoena power and the authority to issue court-enforceable orders. Cronies, special counsels on retainers, and favored kin chow down with PAC-men at the boodle trough of payoffs, kickbacks, sweetheart consulting deals, seats on governing boards, and administrative appointments — all part of doing the public's work.[7]

Alabama's constitution has grown to gargantuan proportions thanks to the legislature's suturing-on of hundreds and hundreds of amendments necessary to enable county and municipal actions ranging from sales tax increases to economic development initiatives. The amending strategy came about because the 1901 constitution had so severely restricted local governments from doing much of anything on their own. As decades came and went, instead of summoning the political will to write a new, democratically inclusive constitution (and thereby giving up their marketable power), state legislators took the path of tacking on amendments, as well as some thirty-five thousand hard-to-find local acts by 2009 — what PARCA's Jim Williams calls the "secret laws of the Legislature." "Rather than setting basic standards for everyone to follow, our constitution," observes Williams, "does little to establish common rules." The result is piecemeal, mutual backscratching between county delegations in which the constitution "just catalogs the results of the local deals made in Montgomery."[8]

When these county-by-county constitutional fixes go awry, whether in pursuit of economic development or infrastructure improvements or determining the legality of bingo in a particular jurisdiction, the results can be catastrophic — as the city of Birmingham and surrounding Jefferson County discovered in a plague of sewer mismanagement, corruption, and multi-billion-dollar financing swindles involving New York financiers that began to run amuck in the mid-1990s. A decade later numerous local officials landed in jail and the county's credit rating sank lower than that of any other municipality in the country. "Outside of the city of Detroit," concluded a managing director with Moody's Investors Service, "it's fair to say we haven't seen any place in America with the severity of problems that they're experiencing in Jefferson County."[9]

Given the thicket of statewide ungovernability as well as the paralysis that continually hobbles localities, Alabama governors have generally opted to make their reputations symbolically rather than substantively, fighting the reliable chimeras that threaten the Heart of Dixie.

"SPIRITUALLY DEFORMED"

Alabama governors, who until 1968 were not allowed to succeed themselves, have now and then pressed against the state constitution's structural restraints, sometimes winning a few palatable initiatives — provided they accommodated the legislative kingpins and major lobbyists. Unable to redress fundamental problems of governance, even when they wanted to, it's no wonder that Alabama's chief executives have put considerable energy into achieving national notoriety, bolstering their down-home popularity by railing against federal judges, instigators of affirmative action, feminists, ungodly schemers who try to steal prayer out of the mouths of schoolchildren, welfare mothers, freeloaders, homosexual teachers, drug-addled recidivists, environmental wackos, et al.

Through his defiant resistance to desegregation and his complicity in lawlessness and violence in the 1960s, The Guvner, George Wallace, became the international face and voice of official Alabama. Between his 1958 loss to John Patterson, after which he vowed never to be "outniggered" again, until 1987, when a wrecked and haunted man finally ceded the field, a generation of Alabamians grew up and raised voting-age children. Wallace's railings and posturings set a public tone and performative style that traumatized and stunted white Alabama politics into the twenty-first century.

The Guvner's longevity as Alabama's leading man, hopscotching in and out of the state's major elective office for two and a half decades, exacerbated the preexisting, tit-for-tat, money-for-favors environment of state government. Atop the roiling surface of his campaigns for governor and president, George Wallace floated his political boat on a sea of financial corruption, scheme making, bribe taking, and influence peddling carried on by close advisers and his ghoulish brother Gerald.[10] The office of the governor of Alabama was a right-wing soapbox set atop a strategic crossroads for looting.

"Shakedowns were a favorite ploy of the Wallace crowd," wrote Howell Raines in a 1990 retrospective, "although Alabamians insist that the Governor was too busy with national politics to pay attention to what was being done in his name." How did it work? A common strategy involved a Wallace crony who "would get a friendly legislator to draft a bill that would hurt a given economic interest — say dog tracks, or coal miners, or electric utilities — and then offer to have the bill killed in exchange for a fee." Not until 1990 was brother Gerald nailed by the IRS for tax evasion. Nor, Raines could add, had any Alabama prosecutor "ever initiated any comprehensive sting operation in Birmingham or Montgomery, the major transfer points of political money."[11]

As sure as there were backrooms filled with cardboard boxes of red and blue block-letter WALLACE bumper stickers, good for the next presidential or gubernatorial campaign, there were coat pockets, safes, and bank accounts chock full of political chips. The rhetoric of white racial resentment and blue-collar blues mesmerized Wallace followers even as it smokescreened a multitude of fiscal sins and distracted from what wasn't getting done to improve the life chances and possibilities for the state's people. To cite one example, The Guvner's self-trumpeted setting up of "scores of redundant junior colleges, trade schools and faux universities," writes Raines, sapped the education budget and functioned primarily as a network of "patronage mills."[12]

After a disappointing second run for president in 1968, winning only five Deep South states as an Independent, George Wallace in 1972 tapped more deeply into the politics of rage, especially the national antibusing backlash. Campaigning as a Democrat, the Little Fightin' Judge easily won the Florida primary that March, throwing fear into the national party leadership while delighting the Nixon reelection camp who saw Wallace as both beatable and divisive. In taking almost 60 percent of nonblack voters in Florida, The Guvner, writes Dan Carter in his important book *The Politics of Rage*, "understood and voiced the longing of millions of white middle-class and working-class voters for a stable world in which work was rewarded, laziness punished, blacks knew their place, men headed the household, women were men's loyal helpmates, and children were safe from vulgar language."[13] Building upon his "Send Them a Message" momentum, Wallace won both the Maryland and Michigan primaries on May 15, the day that he took three close-range bullets from Arthur Bremer in a suburban shopping strip near Laurel.

Wallace barely escaped assassination. Paralyzed below the waist, he also endured chronic pain from the effects of spinal and abdominal wounds that would require constant medical monitoring and repeated surgeries for the remaining years of his life. Knocked out of the presidential campaign, the former high school boxer and war veteran became a vulnerable, sometimes pitied figure, attracting well-wishers, including some of his old political enemies, from across the U.S. to Montgomery. On every front, all was far from well with Wallace. Once a political kingfish, he was now a fish out of water. Once a prancing rooster, he became a suspicious, bedridden husband in a bitter divorce.

In a 1979 interview with Birmingham native and *Washington Post* journalist Dale Russakoff, Wallace sought to recast his political past and deny that race was ever his central rallying issue — he was only standing up for Alabama citizens being bullied by the feds. "But," countered Russakoff, "the federal government wasn't the only force asking Alabama to change. Weren't large numbers of Alabama Blacks asking the same things?" Wallace's reply and the subsequent exchange are fascinating:

> There was a pause. "Did you say you grew up in Alabama?" Wallace asked.
>
> "Yes, sir."
>
> "Turn it off for a minute," he said, motioning toward the tape recorder. If this was an Alabaman he was talking to, it would be a personal talk.
>
> The tape recorder was duly turned off, but the following exchange was committed to memory:
>
> "I honestly said [in the 1960s] that I was for the existing order," he said. "Of course many people were then, and I was one and the same. Your own parents were probably the same. You say you're from Alabama. They probably supported me." He folded his hands as if the point had been made.
>
> "No, governor, they didn't support you."
>
> "They didn't?" He seemed deeply troubled.
>
> "No, sir."
>
> "Well, then, they were ultra-liberals," he said, with a decisive nod of his head. His voice got deep and spooky, the way it did in his television speeches when he'd warn in ominous tones about those "u-u-u-ultra liberals" in the North and in Washington, D.C. Once again, the point seemed to be made.
>
> "No, sir, they were just normal people to me."[14]

The popular sympathy that flowed to Wallace after his shooting meant that no serious candidate challenged his run for a third gubernatorial term in 1974. Ensconced for four more years in the South Perry Street governor's mansion,

The Guvner drew on the millions of dollars raised by right-wing, direct-mail fundraiser Richard Viguerie to launch what would be his last campaign for the White House. This time, Alabama rage did not translate into significant national support, and Wallace's bicentennial-year presidential bandwagon ran into a ditch. Subject to the curiosity and scrutiny of television news cameras, the wheelchair-bound Guvner was a pale, grotesque shadow in a post-Watergate moment that belonged to fresh-faced southern outsider Jimmy Carter, whom Wallace ultimately endorsed.

NEW DAY?

When in 1978 state law prevented a third successive term, it seemed that Alabama might emerge from under the Wallace spell. Pent-up, contending forces fought a gubernatorial campaign that led to what old-hand politico Bob Ingram called the "biggest upset in the past 50 years."[15] As the Democratic primary season began, it seemed a safe bet that one of the "three Bs" would prevail: Attorney General Bill Baxley, Lieutenant Governor Jere Beasley, or one-time, temporary governor Albert Brewer.

To set the scene requires shifting ten years earlier, to May 1968, when the amiable Brewer, a conservative Baptist, stepped up from the lieutenant governor's job to serve the nearly half-term remaining of Lurleen Burns Wallace. The state's only woman governor had died of cancer while standing in for husband George when Alabama law didn't permit succession. A legislative veteran and former house speaker, Brewer used his brevity as the state's chief executive to step back from The Guvner's racist, confrontational rhetoric and to work with the legislature on education initiatives, including increases in school district funding and teachers' pay. In 1970 Brewer appeared to have earned his own full term but for Wallace's last-minute breaking of a pledge not to run against his former ally. That year's contest remains notorious for the Wallace camp's race baiting and macho posturing. In an onslaught of scabrous speechmaking and slanderous leafleting, Wallace and his entourage depicted Brewer as a "sissy britches" propped up by black militants, while maligning Brewer's family as "sexual deviants, alcoholics and miscegenists" and sabotaging campaign appearances by Brewer's wife.[16] Wallace's victory in 1970, observed Wayne Flynt, "left Alabama politics spiritually deformed."[17] Coming at the end of an era in which black citizens' demands for broader inclusion in American life had brought repressive violence as well as breakthrough victories, Alabama entered the 1970s, as it had the 1960s, with an elected leader who reconfirmed for the wider world the worst of the Alabama political imaginary.

Betrayed and defeated by Wallace a decade earlier, but having come so close to election, Albert Brewer hoped his moment had come at last in 1978.

The second of the three Bs in that year's field for governor was Bill Baxley, a progressive bright light. As boy-wonder attorney general, Baxley had made two reputations: one for prosecuting air and water polluters and reopening civil rights cold cases from the sixties, and another for treading upon the habits of judgment of buttoned-up Alabamians. Rumors trailed the dark-haired, ruddy-cheeked politician as a married man too fond of drink, women, and flying to Vegas where, lore had it, Baxley's gambling skills had led to the posting of his photo at more than one casino.

Back in 1971, personally committed to redressing one of the most heinous crimes of the long freedom struggle, Attorney General Baxley had revisited Birmingham's 1963 Sixteenth Street Church bombing, which killed four black girls but for which no one had been convicted. As the prosecution's evidence-gathering dragged on, Baxley later told Howell Raines, "the timing of it was very damaging to me politically because if we had been able to wrap it up in '73 or '74, like we should have, instead of trying it a year before I ran for Governor, I think I might have won. . . . Every day, every town, every plant gate, a dozen people a day, at least, would not shake hands or would say, 'I would have voted for you, I liked you, I thought you were my kind, but you put that old man ["Dynamite Bob" Chambliss] in jail.'"[18] On the hustings, Baxley paid a political price among white voters for prosecuting a murderous Klansman.

Jere Beasley, 1978's third B, had served two terms as lieutenant governor while fellow Barbour County native Wallace dominated the state in the 1970s. As the Democratic primary battle lines took shape, Beasley lost out to Baxley in garnering key endorsements. He would ultimately give up running for office and turn to full-time lawyering, becoming one of the nation's best-known and wealthiest plaintiff attorneys as he won unprecedented judgments in Alabama courtrooms against a variety of out-of-state and out-of-the-country corporations for wrongful deaths and shoddy products. Parlaying his good-ol'-boy theatricality and smarts, Jere Beasley would take Wallace's "send them a message" slogan in an original direction, transforming Alabamians' sez-you distrust of outsiders into motivation for juries to make megamillion-dollar awards. A few more years and Beasley became, as *Forbes* put it, "the Sam Walton of litigation," provoking business groups' apoplectic demands for tort reform.[19]

But there was still one more candidate for governor in 1978, the rank underdog, Forrest Hood "Fob" James Jr. That he was named for two Confederate generals should have flashed a warning to the trio of Bs. An Auburn football star of the early 1950s, James had eloped with the university's homecoming queen before graduating with a civil engineering degree. He hit it big in his late twenties manufacturing plastic-coated weightlifting dumbbells. Politically ambitious, utilitarian, and newly wealthy, Fob James had served as a GOP fundraiser for a list of candidates that included Richard Nixon and had been a member of the state party's executive committee. He sold his business in 1977 and, preparing to enter the race for governor in a land still populated by many yellow dogs, became a Democrat.

James hired cagey media adviser Deloss Walker of Memphis, whose "It's time for a new beginning in Alabama" slogan pitched the candidate to voters who were uninspired by any of the Bs and weary of Wallace cronyism and Montgomery influence peddling.[20] His campaign played to white voters' love of a successful good ol' boy who hadn't risen above his raising, as well as their rejection of Baxley for his too-familiar ties to, and sympathies for, black Alabamians. The strategic, folksy, and well-financed New Beginning onslaught swept James into the governor's mansion.

With no experience in government, the impulsive Fob careened into serial disasters. He had promised education improvement and a rewriting of the 1901 constitution, but these initiatives died early deaths in a legislature that met regularly in the pockets of anti-tax-reform lobbyists. He bulldozed the tenuous borderland between church and state. "Not since 1946," complained native son Raines, revealing his own hopes, "had Alabamians voted so clearly for clean government, fair taxes and good schools. But James, a religious fundamentalist, devoted his term to a feckless crusade for school prayer."[21] The governor's zealous religiosity was egged on by his wife, Bobbie. Speaking to a gathering of the National Association of Evangelicals and the National Religious Broadcasters following the election of Ronald Reagan, Mrs. James, who took her fundamentalism sweetened with numerology, claimed, "It was Jesus that gave us this victory in November. God in his mercy heard the prayers of Christians all over this country . . . perhaps all over the world." Alabama's first lady told Marjorie Hyer of the *Washington Post* that she passed "most of my time in the prayer closet, which is where women belong," adding that the release of U.S. hostages after 444 days of Iranian captivity was, like her husband's election, a sign of God's hand: "I looked up what 444 means . . . a new beginning. So I believe God has intervened in American history."[22]

Democrat James dutifully appointed several black Alabamians to positions in his administration, including, in 1980, SCLC attorney Oscar Adams, the first African American to serve on the state supreme court, but the governor could hardly be counted among civil rights stalwarts. Bumptious and inflexible, he met frustration with helmet-headedness. When a worsening national economy led to a state revenue crisis triggering across-the-board proration of government budgets, disgruntlement reigned. Surely God was testing Fob, fallen from his New Beginning popularity, throttled in his battle for school prayer, and perplexed that state government could not be managed, as he would later say, like a dependable Waffle House. His only real gubernatorial success came in designating the unexpected proceeds from gas and oil leases into a state trust fund. When Governor James kept his 1978 campaign promise not to stand for reelection, taking his football and going home, no one imagined it was only halftime.[23]

It was 1982 and George Wallace, disregarding the warnings of family and failing body, campaigned for his fourth governorship. Neither officeholding nor claims of kin stirred Wallace more than the defibrillations of politicking. In and out of hospitals for nearly a decade, often bed bound, he ran this time as much to distract himself as he did for the visibility of the office. His publicized quest in the mid-1970s for Christian redemption and his attempts at reconciliation with former targets of persecution persuaded many Alabamians, including some African Americans, that Wallace had experienced transformation through a catharsis of pain, paralysis, religion, and medication.

Others were not so sure, or so forgiving. "If he had been really converted from his racist past," wrote Frank Morrer of Alabama State University, "he would have used the time he had left to mount as vigorous a campaign for racial justice as he had done for segregation. He did not do that."[24]

Acknowledging current realities of legal desegregation and the clout of significant numbers of new black voters, Wallace, like so many white southerners who grew up with Jim Crow, dismissed his 1960s behavior in an offhanded, unreflective manner. "I'm not apologizing for anything," he told *Washington Post* writer Art Harris on the stump in the Wiregrass city of Dothan. "I stood for what I stood for because I believed, like most white people of Alabama at the time, that segregation was right."[25] To say there was no further use in talking about segregation, its history, and its legacy made an Alabama truth and reconciliation commission unlikely. Unexamined, Heart of Dixie hostility found expression in opposition to affirmative action plans, in the persistence of segregated academies and poorly funded public schools, in the refusal of white voters to cast ballots for black candidates, and in the segregated residential patterns of sprawling new Republican suburbs in places like Shelby County, "over the Mountain," south of Birmingham.[26]

For all his years in office and his charismatic presence, Wallace did very little to help Alabama's economy move from its extractive natural resource and smokestack moorings. Workers were more likely to find new-technology jobs in neighboring states such as Georgia, Florida, and North Carolina. As Alabama's unemployment rate rose into the mid-teens in the early 1980s and its per capita income fell to the second lowest in the U.S., Wallace blamed the Reagan administration, recasting himself yet again, this time as an empathetic, colorblind populist. "Regardless of your color, we're all in the same fix," he proclaimed with rhetoric that might have made a difference had he said it twenty years earlier. "We can't pay our bills, so we must join together and see all black and white Alabamians have opportunities in schools and jobs."[27]

Wallace's major Democratic opponent in 1982 was Lieutenant Governor George McMillan, less tested than Bill Baxley but another of the potential New South governors that white Alabamians never seemed to get around to electing while they chased iterations of Wallace. McMillan counted on a coalition weary of The Guvner, including substantial black support such as that represented by powerbroker Joe Reed's Alabama Democratic Conference, and endorsements by figures such as native Alabamian Coretta Scott King. The new-model Wallace, however, was able to win over a third of the black voters in the first primary and ultimately took the September runoff by a 2 percent margin out of a million votes cast.[28]

In winning this time, George Wallace relied on a blue-collar, friends-and-neighbors pitch at a time of economic insecurity. Through rumor and innuendo, McMillan also fell victim to campaign tactics of gay baiting. "Much was made in a quiet way of Mr. McMillan's lisp," wrote Roy Reed of the *Times*.[29] Wallace had used this tactic before, campaigning in 1970 against "sissy britches" Albert Brewer.

African American voters who turned out for the 1982 general election concluded that a tortured, born-again Wallace seemed a more sympathetic human and posed a lesser evil than the pistol-packing, gung-ho, head-butting Republican mayor of Montgomery, Emory Folmar.[30] Wallace won with some 650,000 votes to Folmar's 440,000, taking perhaps as much as 90 percent of black ballots.[31] Folmar, observed Rick Bragg, who interviewed him during the campaign, "was so conservative that he compelled black people to vote in droves for George Wallace."[32]

During his final term, The Guvner suffered from near deafness and slurred speech, depended heavily upon pain medication, cycled in and out of hospitals, and appeared less and less frequently before a public that was more and more skeptical he could perform any duties. At his healthiest, Wallace had cared little for governing. By early April of 1986, slipping badly in the polls, he opted not to run again.[33]

In 1990, nearly two years after Wallace's death, in a *New York Times Magazine* essay that Dan Carter assessed as "a damning account of the governor's legacy in Alabama," Howell Raines castigated the Little Fightin' Judge for marching the state to the front ranks of racism and holding it there for the world to see, for enhancing Montgomery's political culture of corruption and chronic cronyism, and for failing to confront Alabama's tax inequities.[34] "Everyone agrees," wrote Raines, that "Wallace went into office after his election in 1962 with the intention — inherited from Folsom, his political mentor — of breaking the power of the corporations and the Black Belt planters. But when Potomac fever struck him, he found he needed two things — large amounts of money and an obedient Legislature. So he lined up with the old grandees in the Legislature."

Raines described an interview with George Wallace Jr., a diffident heir whose only chip on the shoulder seemed to be an animus against his father's detractors. "I don't know why Dad has difficulty being rehabilitated when he finally said, 'I was wrong and I'm sorry.' What more can a man do?" he wondered. "Hugo Black is considered this great progressive liberal, yet he was a member of the Klan and made some of the most outlandish statements about black people that have ever been made."[35] The younger Wallace's comment, noted Raines, was one of those reflexive Alabama evasions, "excuse by comparison."

George Jr. "told of riding away from the State Capitol on the day in 1986 when his father announced his retirement from politics: 'With tears in his eyes, he turned to me and said, "Son, I hope they will not let the rich and powerful take over."'"

"Was this," wondered Raines, "real regret for a career blighted by dema- gogy or just more Wallace bloviation? It is impossible to know. But if 'Little George' had been in an argumentative mood, he might have pointed out to his father that he had 23 years to tackle the retrograde forces that have kept Alabama in the ditch. When George Wallace pledged to preserve 'segregation forever,' he was a little off the mark. It was poverty and tax breaks for pine trees that he preserved."[36] During his final years as governor, Wallace appointed dozens of African Americans to a variety of state jobs and advisory groups, somewhat altering his in-state image. Beyond Alabama, he remained a white, sez-you icon.

"Wallaceism in all its forms never challenged the prevailing culture in Montgomery," writes Jeff Frederick, author of the most comprehensive study of The Guvner as governor. "Nothing was ever done to make an Alabama edu- cation at least as good as elsewhere in the South, and the regressive tax code was left alone, free to strangle the social mobility of another generation of poor Alabamians."[37] When you've never had much, you learn the habit of do- ing without. To choose only one telling measure, in Wallace's last year in office Alabama had the nation's highest infant mortality rate.[38] Were it possible to set aside the racial politics, George Wallace's "greatest and most troubling legacy," concludes Frederick, "is that he left Alabama in the same place that he found it in 1963." Like a specter, The Guvner provides a modern meaning to the an- cient notion of haunting. "Until the state addresses the core issues it faced in 1963 — issues that remain in the twenty-first century — Alabama will never be able to turn the page on the Wallace years."[39]

The 1986 governor's campaign offered the best hope in three decades for the dawning of a new day in Alabama and a major reshaping of the state's politi- cal imaginary. As Wallace stood down without endorsing a successor, a bitter gubernatorial primary broke out. Ronald Reagan had swept the state in 1984, but Alabamians were certain that their new governor would emerge from the intraparty contest for some 2.2 million registered Democrats, far fewer than half of whom would ultimately turn out.

As the primary campaign developed, two major contenders emerged: the presumptive favorite, Lieutenant Governor Bill Baxley (loser to Fob James in 1978) — with a coalition base in the Democratic leadership, the Alabama Education Association, public employees, union officialdom, trial lawyers, and both of the state's black political organizations — versus white-hope, tough-guy Charles Graddick ("I'll fry them until their eyeballs pop out and you can smell their flesh burn"). A former Republican district attorney in Mobile, Graddick (Charcoal-Charlie, Electric-Chair Charlie) had served two terms as a Democratic attorney general, a "man of convictions," punitive dispenser of hard time and celebrant of capital punishment.[40] "Graddick is the New version of the Old Wallace," wrote Randall Williams at the time. "Many who remember only the extremities of the past find it hard to call Graddick a racist because he actually does nothing overtly against blacks; his popularity with racists is due to the fact that he largely ignores the quarter of the state's citizens who are black, and that he is a demagogue for the Eighties, a subtle master of euphemisms and code phrases that communicate racial meaning without the blatantly nasty words of the previous generation."[41] Graddick claimed to ride the currents of "change," but his was an ill, back-blowing wind.

In the June 3 primary, Baxley led a five-person field but failed to win a majority of votes. Forced into a runoff with Graddick, he worked to rally his constituencies while trying to attract the followers of defeated candidates. Graddick harped on revelations about Baxley's personal life, made clear his own opposition to abortion, called for the firing of homosexual teachers, urged Republicans to cross over and vote in the Democratic runoff, and dangled race in front of rural and suburban whites in television ads complaining that "black politicians" had too much influence on Baxley. "In the old days, they used to cry 'nigger, nigger,'" countered Joe Reed of the Alabama Democratic Conference. "Now they just say 'black politician,' but everyone knows that's a code word that means the same thing."[42]

While he disavowed an endorsement from the Ku Klux Klan, Graddick also wrote off black voters, now a fourth of the state's electorate but a steadily increasing proportion of Democrats. "Graddick," praised the Grand Wizard in a letter to statewide followers, "was the only gubernatorial candidate who did not seek the endorsement of black organizations."[43]

With the June 24, 1986, runoff looming, charges escalated between camps: Baxley's unfiled federal income taxes and late penalties, his use of state cars and state employees for personal purposes, Graddick's alleged payoffs for political support. Baxley's calling Graddick a coward and daring him to take a lie detector test prompted the attorney general to fire back: "I wouldn't mind going right out here by the swimming pool in the grass and getting it on with him."[44] How damaging, in the buckle of the Bible Belt, for the married Baxley's candidacy were photos published by the *Birmingham News* showing a female Associated Press reporter emerging from his apartment where she had spent the night and was about to get into a campaign car?[45]

In a turnout of over 930,000, Graddick won the Democratic primary by fewer than 9,000 votes. In the closing weeks of the campaign, he had seized the momentum and mobilized conservative, white voters.

Refusing to concede, Baxley supporters argued that as many as 20,000 Republicans had crossed over and voted illegally at Graddick's open invitation.[46] Within weeks, Baxley's lawyers successfully challenged the election before a three-judge federal panel, arguing that Alabama had violated the 1965 Voting Rights Act through Graddick's soliciting and, in his office as attorney general, illegally permitting Republicans who had participated in their party's primary to vote in the Democratic runoff. The judges ruled that Graddick had behaved unlawfully and ordered the party to declare Baxley the winner or hold a new election.[47]

When Democratic officials chose to award Baxley the nomination without a second runoff, they infuriated many white voters who knew little and cared less about preclearance provisions of the Voting Rights Act. To them, it appeared that the man with the most votes was denied victory by a handful of party elites. Polling at the time showed that a vast majority of Alabama voters favored a new runoff.[48] Raging that the maneuverings of lawyers, insiders, and those familiar nemeses, federal judges, had trampled the popular will, white Alabamians had a sez-you excuse to rush into the GOP. "A lot of people would vote for Che Guevara if he showed up on the Republican ticket right now," fumed the thwarted Graddick as he exhausted his legal remedies, "because they're sick of what is happening among the Democrats." The national party sensed the potential in the new moment. "Doesn't Alabama deserve a Governor who believes in fair play?" asked Ronald Reagan at a presidential stopover in Montgomery.[49]

Back in June the *New York Times* had written that the runoff winner "is all but assured victory in the November election over Guy Hunt, a fifty-two-year-old farmer and businessman."[50] Things had changed. In the aftermath of the Democratic brawl, statewide polling revealed that potential voters had turned viscerally negative on both Baxley and Graddick, and now saw Republican Hunt, the all-but-unknown GOP placeholder nominee, as viable.[51] A Korean War veteran, Primitive Baptist preacher, former Cullman County probate judge, and Amway products salesman from the town of Holly Pond, Guy Hunt had been a perennial north Alabama Republican candidate for one office or another since 1962. His support of a victorious Reagan in 1980 was rewarded with a federal patronage position that he held until stepping into the 1986 governor's race. Although the GOP primary had drawn little attention and only 33,000 voters, Brother Guy, journeyman loyalist who kept his lamps trimmed and burning, made hay from the Democrats' implosion. On November 4, Hunt won 56 percent of the vote to Baxley's 44 percent and became the Accidental Governor. The state's first Republican chief executive since 1872, Hunt's election catalyzed a string of GOP victories signifying the party's new competitive position in Alabama. To anyone hoping for a progressive turn out of the Heart of Dixie, Baxley's loss was a miserably squandered moment.

CHAPTER FOUR

Oafs of Office

Being a conservative can be cool and, as Mitchell puts it,
not "just something that wacko people in Alabama do."
— JOHN COLAPINTO quoting CHARLES MITCHELL,
"Armies of the Right"

O God, we painfully recognize that all too often the only list
which Alabama heads is the alphabetical one.
— REV. HUGH TOBIAS, Trinity Baptist Church, Madison, Alabama

In January 1987, as the administration of Elder Guy Hunt began, Circuit Judge Charles Price, an African American Democrat appointed during the final Wallace term, considered the new makeup of the state's executive and legislative branches: "They're all in bed together. The Democratic Legislature now is controlled by the Business Council and the Farm Bureau and your very conservative pro-business elements. There's not going to be any concern about minorities."[1] For his part, Governor Hunt made only one black appointment out of some two-dozen cabinet-level positions.[2] As Price anticipated, thanks to Jimmy Clark, the conservative Democrat who was elected as new house speaker, no African Americans were to be found on important committees in the legislature, or as committee chairs. "I think it is time we talk about racism in Alabama politics," complained Senator Michael Figures of Mobile. "We need to really start pointing the finger in this state because black people are not going anywhere here."[3]

Hunt and the legislature quickly passed a tort reform package that would cap liability awards. The state supreme court, not yet under the sway of Republican justices supported by the Business Council of Alabama, struck down the legislation. Things grew testier. The governor's taxation and educational reform commissions offered recommendations, including increasing revenues for education, that were at odds with what legislators would accept. Several poor counties sued the state for failing to provide public education funding equivalent to that of wealthy counties.[4] Hunt fiercely opposed, and appealed, a state circuit court decision against flying the Confederate battle flag atop the state capitol where George Wallace had placed it in 1963 in defiance of school desegregation efforts.[5]

In his inaugural address, Hunt had pledged to "leave no stone unturned to make it clear that the business climate is second to none."[6] In practice, Hunt's search under rocks tempted industry with paleoeconomic incentives such as giveaways of site locations and development, tax breaks, exemptions, deferments, and cheap, non-union labor. As rural Alabama became sited as the nation's chemical septic tank, the ineffectual Hunt failed in efforts to stop incoming shipments of toxic waste and in his attempt to levy higher out-of-state than in-state taxes for toxics hauled to the vast ChemWaste site — known as the "toxic waste Cadillac" — near Emelle in the Selma Chalk at the western edge of the Black Belt.[7]

When the gubernatorial season loomed again in 1990, Republican strategist and state chairman John E. Grenier, a right-wing zealot since the 1964 Goldwater campaign, worked openly to establish "racial separation of the parties." The Republicans would become the white people's party, and "racial antagonisms," observed Howell Raines, "will enable Hunt to withstand the Democrats' charge that he is the puppet of the banks and insurance, oil, steel and forest-products companies represented by Grenier's Birmingham law firm."[8]

The Democrats' hopes for recapturing the governor's office from Guy Hunt lay with fifty-four-year-old Paul Hubbert, former teacher and school administrator who, over two decades, had built the Alabama Education Association (AEA) into one of the state's most powerful lobbying forces. Through its political action arm, A-VOTE, the AEA's seventy thousand members, primarily teachers but also janitors and bus drivers, provided millions of dollars in support of endorsed candidates. Political tactician Hubbert was said to sit in the balcony of the state house or senate and signal thumbs up or down to a bevy of legislators on the floor. Across racial lines, Hubbert worked with a variety of Democratic loyalists and organizations. The state Sierra Club, for instance, hoped a Hubbert administration would help get the Alabama Department of Environmental Management (ADEM) out from under the heavy-metal thumb of water and air polluters.[9]

In his first campaign for statewide office, Hubbert dared to suggest that George Wallace might have led the state astray. "The Democratic campaign," wrote Raines, "has an inescapable theme that Wallace's most enduring damage to the state was not the harm he did to its reputation for race relations, but the poor schools, bad health care and low wages of its people." As he scouted Alabama politics that spring of 1990, Raines also suggested that Hubbert was introducing "a new tactic . . . by driving a wedge into the business community." In the Hunt camp were the "extractive industries — timber, mining, petroleum," secure in their "favored tax status." But a growing number of "bankers, retailers and service corporations headquartered in Birmingham are tired of having prospective employees and investors shun them because of the state's poor schools, hospitals and cultural facilities and its troglodyte reputation. For the first time there is a chance that a few members of Birmingham's white-collar establishment could play the progressive political role played by their counterparts in Atlanta, Charlotte and Miami for the past two decades."[10] Under the dominion of U.S. Steel and local minions throughout much of the twentieth century, Birmingham had experienced old-fashioned extractive colonialism with the raw materials of coal, iron ore, and limestone transformed into iron and steel that left the region along with the industry's vast profits. The newer Birmingham was oriented around the University of Alabama's medical center as it grew into the city's largest employer. Because the obvious source for increased support of education and health care would be the undertaxed timberland that occupied a vast portion of Alabama, the state's large landowners and the wood-harvesting interests strongly opposed Hubbert.

"Alabama is to the rest of the nation almost as this country was to England 200 or 250 years ago," Hubbert argued. "We are a supplier of raw products. The gas coming out of Mobile Bay will be piped to Chesapeake Bay to turn the wheels of other people's industry. We'll buy back the finished product from them, and then to add insult to injury, they'll pay us 22 bucks a ton and they'll ship poison in here and bury it in our soil. And I think that makes us the equivalent of a third world nation."[11] All true enough, but not the sort of rhetoric any serious Alabama politician had used since the Depression, or before that, since the crushing of the Populist revolt of the 1890s.

After leading six candidates in the June primary, Paul Hubbert won the Democratic nomination in a runoff with Attorney General Don Siegelman, a man who would eventually fill a greater variety of statewide elected offices than anyone in Alabama history, as well as a federal prison cell. "I think the nightmare of 1986 is over," Hubbert said as Siegelman conceded, pledged party loyalty, and prophesied again the coming of the long-heralded: "We will bring Alabama into the New South with a Democratic progressive governor in office."[12] By now, the "New South" imaginary had become so shopworn and sunnyside-up, it could be put to any number of pliable, feel-good meanings.

The Business Council of Alabama led the opposition to Hubbert. Editorially, the *Montgomery Advertiser* called him a "hired gun to labor." In its endorsement of the Accidental Governor for a second term, the *Advertiser* confessed that Hunt was not "in our opinion, the most dynamic . . . in the land, nor the most visionary, charismatic and progressive," but he was still preferred over teacher lobbyist Hubbert as "an unpolished ripe apple is more palatable than a polished bitter-green one." An honest comparison would not have been apples to apples, but Hubbert's tree-shaking abilities against Hunt's having landed on a thick limb of ripe persimmons. The *Advertiser* claimed Hunt had brought "high-quality leadership to run various state agencies and departments" and that he had proven "dynamic in going after jobs and business, visionary in seeking a new regional airport, charismatic in unifying various Alabama constituencies . . . and progressive in certain social welfare programs such as foster parent, child care and infant mortality matters."[13] Backing the candidate least likely to shake the tree meant some serious straining of credulity.

"KANSAS AIN'T NO ALABAMA"

"Alabama is doing just fine," trumpeted Hunt's campaign ads, despite the state's perennial position among the nation's bottommost by measures of health, well-being, and median income. Guy was "Getting Us Moving" and "Making Us Proud." In fact, Hunt seemed a man out of time, trapped in a miserly vision of state government in both its taxing and its service powers. Bedrocked in the formative race relations of the Heart of Dixie, the governor declined an invitation to the unveiling of artist Maya Lin's civil rights memorial in downtown Montgomery.[14]

The gray-pated, neatly suited Guy came across as an avuncular north

Alabama patriarch, the sort of fellow who offered the opening prayer at shape-note singings and practiced a self-deprecating, folksy humor. "There's a lot of people who see him as a decent man," said UA history professor Bill Barnard. "And in some circles, simply not to have the state embarrassed over the past three years is an achievement."[15] Soon enough, Hunt would make up for lost time.

In an Auburn speech during the week in September 1990 in which the International Olympic Committee awarded Atlanta the 1996 games, Hubbert probed a chronic wound, how Alabama and Birmingham had only themselves to blame for losing out to their Georgia neighbors. "While Birmingham was worried about whether they had enough firehose," he said, "Atlanta was negotiating with Delta Airlines." Hubbert repeated his theme that Alabama had not elected a "New South kind of governor," such as Tennessee's Lamar Alexander, Florida's Bob Graham, or Arkansas's Bill Clinton, who had been able to market Alabama "the way they've been able to market theirs." Could Hubbert, best known to Alabamians as the "teachers' union leader," win voters as a salesman?

The 1990 campaign wore on. "Let us change the image of Alabama by changing the image of its officeholders," Governor Hunt proposed, between guest sermons and Amway pitches.[16] Yet two of his TV ads, appearing as voting day drew near, pitched straight from the Heart of Dixie imaginary. One featured a young woman challenging AEA leader Hubbert's supposed tolerance of homosexual teachers in the state's public schools. The second ad, evocative of the race-baiting used by George Wallace in his bitter 1970 campaign against Albert Brewer, showed Hubbert with several black and white political leaders labeled as "liberal." "They put Jesse Jackson's picture in an ad," fumed Joe Reed, Hubbert ally and the state's most powerful black politico. "What does Jesse have to do with the governor's race? . . . None of that had anything to do with prenatal care and infant mortality, old folks losing their homes, children getting a good education or having a good image for the state," added Reed, calling Hunt's campaign racist.[17]

Alabamians had stumbled across their Republican governor in 1986, but they acted with eyes open four years later as Hunt was reelected with 52 percent of the vote. For his part, Hubbert accepted a new contract running the AEA, where he continued being "the shrewdest politician in Alabama even though he never held elective office."[18] In another four years he would try a more conservative tack, unconvincingly selling himself as a species of good ol' boy, and fail to get the Democratic nomination.

Analysts chewed the election's aftermath. Perhaps as many as 20 percent fewer blacks turned out in 1990 than in the 1986 governor's race, and while Hunt got more than 60 percent of the white vote, he won a significant number of black voters while benefiting from those who stayed away. Chasing white voters, Democrat Hubbert seemed to have taken African Americans for granted.[19] Longtime political activist Gwendolyn Patton, frustrated with the Hubbert campaign, charged that while Hunt "never took a strong position on any issue" except for flying the Confederate flag on the capitol dome, Hubbert made a confusion of issues, ranging from his unclear position on the flag to his lack of clarity about welfare-workfare, tax reform, teacher testing, abortion rights, and a state lottery. "African-American voters saw very little difference," Patton concluded, "between Hunt's non-verbal positions and Hubbert's 'waltzing around the issues.' As a SNCC kid, I appreciated the intelligence of black people, and I still do. Black Alabamians . . . saw through the duplicity of Hubbert."

Patton also pointed to growing sentiment among black voters that Joe Reed, a key Hubbert ally, was autocratic and out of touch with younger blacks. Born in 1938, the legendary Reed, who wore simultaneous hats as associate executive secretary of the Alabama Education Association, president of Alabama State University's board of trustees, a Montgomery city councilman, and chairman of the Alabama Democratic Conference, resembled an old-line boss. "Reed's recalcitrance to share power with other black political figures," insisted Patton, "has angered and severed relationships with blacks throughout the state who no doubt could not stand the thought of having Reed so close to the throne of power." Not so much as an inclusive democrat, Patton wrote, "many of us think of Reed as an individualist, conservatist-opportunist."[20]

Preacher Hunt's second term found him immersed in increasingly deeper, hotter water. The Alabama Ethics Commission followed up news accounts that the governor had used official airplanes for travel to Primitive Baptist preaching appearances in and outside of the state, where he took up several thousand dollars in love offerings. Many citizens seemed not to be bothered by Brother Guy's mixing of church and state. "If he's a Christian man serving his God and the people at the same time, what's the problem?" asked Raleigh Pratt, a retired textile worker from Opelika.[21] Hunt stopped his fly-in preaching gigs and paid back the state for prior expenses, but his troubles were just beginning.

Declines in tax revenue meant that the governor had to make a second consecutive year's worth of cuts in the education budget in 1991. Serious talk about shortening the school year ultimately withered under public pressure.[22] After a $424 million proposal offered by a legislatively created tax reform commission intent upon establishing more tax equity and on modestly increasing property taxes to pay for education failed to become law, the chancellor of the University of Alabama system lamented that "we are just about out of time." Failure to pass tax reform would "condemn a significant portion of the next generation of Alabamians to poverty, joblessness, welfare and prisons."[23] For his part, Governor Hunt was having none of it, charging instead that the state was getting a bad rap from its major newspapers. Pointing to front-page stories showing the results of a Kansas-based study that put Alabama in its usual place at the bottom of national rankings, Hunt complained, "I lived in Kansas for almost two years and Kansas ain't no Alabama. . . . It's not moving like Alabama."[24]

In what direction Alabama was moving could be measured by the activities of its oafs of office. With the governor at his side, gun-toting Montgomery mayor Emory Folmar kicked off a rally for the reelection of President George H. W. Bush with an I-had-a-bad-dream speech.

"I dreamed that Bill Clinton — 'Slick Willy' — was president," Folmar agonized as the GOP crowd yukked it up. "Vice President Jesse Jackson had just been named to head the search committee to select federal judges."

Folmar conjured a list of potential Clinton cabinet members frightening to most white Alabamians — Patricia Schroeder for Defense, Jerry Brown at Treasury — and finished his dream with the specter of a Democratically ruled House and Senate increasing taxes by $500 billion "to buy everybody below the poverty level two Cadillacs." Just "a bad dream?" asked the mayor, in his parody of Martin Luther King Jr. "No. Reality if we don't do our job."[25]

Ron Brown, African American chair of the National Democratic Party, found Mayor Folmar's speech "blatantly offensive" and called for his resignation as head of the president's Alabama campaign. Folmar's use of the welfare-Cadillac image, charged Senator John Breaux of Louisiana, was "clearly a racial remark designed to pit blacks against whites, rich against poor."[26] The national

Bush campaign claimed that Folmar "was speaking to Governor Clinton's economic policy and not to racial issues." It was all in jest, joshed the mayor.[27]

Late in 1992, a thirteen-count corruption indictment clung like day-old manna to Governor Hunt. He was ultimately convicted of violating state ethics laws by making personal use of $200,000 taken from a tax-exempt 1987 inauguration fund primarily to pay himself back for a loan to his unsuccessful 1978 gubernatorial race. In April 1993 Hunt became the first Alabama governor to be removed from office by means of a felony conviction. He was sentenced to five years' probation and a thousand hours of community service, and ordered to repay the money. The well-groomed Democratic lieutenant governor, Jim Folsom Jr., stepped up to serve the less than two years remaining of Hunt's term.[28]

LITTLE JIM'S BIG ADVENTURE

Guy Hunt's predicament seemed more the bumblings of a novice than the premeditated hoodwinkings of a Goat Hill professional. "Whatever his offenses," wrote an Atlanta columnist, "they were committed completely outside the circles of corruption that have given Alabama its reputation for chicanery. No one taught him how to break the law in a skillful way; instead he improvised, like some primitive artist making figurines out of pop bottle caps. Whether it was right or wrong, Guy Hunt did what he did with all the openness and sincerity of a newborn pig."[29]

The London *Independent* reported that Hunt had "the lowest popular support of any governor in the nation and has become an object of ridicule." "Let there be an end to it," pleaded Wayne Flynt, Alabama's resident prophet Amos. "We're pretty much sucking wind down here. We're not going anywhere compared to any other Southern states. Truth of the matter is, this state has been rudderless for as long a I can remember — and this trial doesn't help."[30]

"But if Alabama's leaders have scarcely evolved," observed the *Economist* in 1993, "its problems are increasingly urgent. Like other states in the south, notably Texas, Alabama is bound by a recent court order to equalize school financing among local districts. This, in turn, means tax reform." Shouldn't the tough-minded British journal have known that in Alabama "this" hardly meant tax reform, but recalcitrance and evasion? Beyond that bit of naiveté lay a well-traveled dirt road leading to the familiar dead end. "Any serious

overhaul of Alabama tax codes, however, will require a look at the state's constitution. It is there, in a bizarre document with over 500 amendments, that
the state's low pro-business property taxes have been enshrined since the turn
of the twentieth century, guarded by crowds of lobbyists."[31]

Stymied, the *Economist* sought the Heart of Dixie's relief in mythical deliver-
ance. "Alabama must hope that somehow, some day, fate will throw up a candidate like Georgia's Zell Miller or Arkansas' Bill Clinton. Until then, the state
will continue to trail its southern neighbors, and the rest of the country, in its
rankings for income per head, productivity and pollution: keeping Alabama,
as one resident put it, 'suckin' on the hind teat of poverty.'"[32]

What Fate threw up was Alabama's next accidental governor, James Folsom
Jr., son of one of Dixie's most legendary post–World War II figures. During two
staggered gubernatorial terms — 1947–51 and 1955–59 — atavistic populist Big
Jim had lumbered forth. A towering hunk of a man who recognized the devastating scourge of white racism, Folsom Sr. urged reform of segregated institutions from juries to the legislature. Wildly popular among the farming class,
he began a network of paved, farm-to-market roads for a largely premodern
state. Ultimately, Kissin' Jim was toppled by the plutocrats — the got-rocks and
Big Mules — by the rising seg chorus, by his outsized fleshly appetites, and by
stories like the one about the time Big Jim lent Adam Clayton Powell the state
Cadillac when the Harlem congressman visited the governor's mansion.

It was the fate of six-foot, three-inch Little Jim, like other juniors sired by
Alabama legends such as Hank Williams, George Wallace, and Bear Bryant,
to wrestle with long, irascible shadows. But perhaps it *was* southern hospitality learned at daddy's knee and not the hundreds of millions of dollars worth
of incentives from state and business interests that convinced German automakers to build their first American assembly plant in the countryside near
Tuscaloosa in the mid-1990s.

"Twenty miles east of the university town where Wallace made his stand for
segregation," wrote Atlanta reporter Mike Williams, "a giant swath has been
cleared in the deep forest, and a gleaming glass and metal building has been
erected. It is a Mercedes-Benz factory, and its giant circular logo, a symbol
of luxury around the world, towers over the futuristic plant on a pedestal. If
Wallace is a symbol of Alabama's past, boosters argue that this building is the
symbol of Alabama's future."[33] If Williams put the plant on a pedestal, it was
because that's where he found it. "The economic impact the Mercedes-Benz

plant will have on Alabama is beyond measure," predicted political veteran Bob Ingram. "But scarcely less significant is the impact this prize will have on state politics, and most especially the 1994 race for governor."[34] The Benz plant was going to turn on the lights in Little Jim's attic, butter his biscuit, grease his rails. Desperate Alabama had out-wrangled South Carolina, North Carolina, Tennessee, and Georgia—all told, some twenty states contended seriously for Mercedes—in giveaways, site acquisition and preparation, bottomless tax and water tables, utility breaks, and auction blocks of non-union labor.[35]

Landing the Mercedes plant seemed to transform Little Jim into man-in-full-James headed for a four-year term of his own. It surely stirred to life a new iteration of the Alabama imaginary. "Because of our image problems," argued Governor Folsom, "we were continually being written off when people were looking for factory sites. Mercedes' decision to come to Alabama is worth billions of dollars in public relations to us. Now I think we'll be looked at in a different light." In persuading the Germans, Folsom said, "We tried to tell them that Alabama is no more the state it was in the 1950s and 1960s . . . than Germany is the same country it was in the days of the Hitler regime. They kind of nodded their heads when I said that."[36]

Perhaps Folsom's narrative strategy "kind of" helped open the door, but the Mercedes deal came down to which state anted up the most boodle. Celebratory Alabama media failed to do their homework until caught short by a story in the *Wall Street Journal* reporting that the state "wound up promising Mercedes well over $300 million in incentives, which economic-development experts call a record package for a foreign company." Among the dealmakers, no other state would match Alabama's agreement to pay the new plant's 1,500 workers' salaries for their first year on the job, a total of $45 million. This on top of the legislature's granting millions in tax exemptions, and the payment of further millions of tax credits to Mercedes as an in-advance, interest-free loan.

"We never realized how much 'free' there could be in free enterprise," the *Montgomery Advertiser* groaned. "With Alabama taxpayers guaranteeing to pay to build its plant, to train its workers, to pay those workers for a year or more, to pay the company's taxes, to give its workers refunds on taxes the company gets to keep, and even to buy many of its utility trucks, anyone should be able to make a profit."[37]

As he lauded Little Jim's role in the Mercedes recruitment, pundit Ingram, who'd observed forty years of Alabama gubernatorial campaigns, reminded readers of his weekly column that the 1994 election was not about to be called off and replaced with a coronation.[38] He ferreted out the strategy that Republicans would use in trying to deny Folsom a victory lap with the state seal changed into a German hood ornament.

"A GOP victory," an elder from the Goldwater days made clear at a Mobile meeting of the like-minded, "has to be won with the rural vote." Pitted against what Republicans publicly called the "bloc vote" (the black vote), the rural vote, wrote Ingram, "translates as the 'white vote.'"[39] To win against Folsom in the fall, the Republicans would have to sweep the white counties, which now included the metastasizing burbs, and hope that black Democratic support did not show up in its full strength of 25 percent of the state's registered voters.

As debate continued about the hidden costs and projected benefits of Mercedes, what else did Folsom have to show for his brief moment in office? For one thing, against a hornet's nest of Lost Cause diehards, "Fergit, hell!" on their lips, he had dropped Guy Hunt's legal appeal to return the Confederate battle flag to the capitol dome. At what cost of the "rural vote"? Education reform died its usual death, unfunded in the legislature. Another season passed without tax reform. A power grab by Folsom appointees to take over investment in the state's retirement system collapsed in spite and embarrassment. Angering David Bronner, the rooster of the Retirement Systems of Alabama, was never wise. Since his recruitment from Minnesota in the early 1970s, Bronner had transformed the RSA into a financial powerhouse worth tens of billions of dollars.

A special session to deal with ethics went nowhere as rumors grew about Folsom confidants and appointees, a half-dozen of whom would eventually be indicted or plead guilty to public corruption. "You say other governors have friends, but you always say that I have 'cronies,'" George Wallace had repeatedly griped to journalists.[40] Cronyism had not begun with Wallace, nor would it end after Folsom's payrolling of relatives and pals, and pals' pals, in sinecures at the Emergency Management Agency and in something called Technology Plus ("formerly known as the Alabama Center for Quality and Productivity, and more appropriately known as the Pork Palace"). "'Little Jim,'" editorialized the *Advertiser*, "has shown himself easily his father's equal when it comes to giving jobs to unqualified political hacks and buddies." Governor Folsom's campaign for a term of his own was further damaged by heading off for a family vacation in the Cayman Islands aboard gambling kingfish Milton McGregor's airplane. His special counsel headed to jail.[41] Given the gathering clouds and the GOP's targeting of the "rural vote," Folsom's election no longer seemed a sure thing.

FOBBED AGAIN

Folsom's ripening vulnerability stirred the Republican contenders of 1994 into a face-off. Winton M. Blount III was a wealthy GOP loyalist, owner of automobile dealerships, and former executive in the vastly successful construction company cofounded after World War II by his father, Red Blount. The elder Blount, a longtime Republican and a grand patron of Alabama fine arts, had served as Richard Nixon's postmaster general.[42] Opposing Blount was former governor Fob James, motivated off the bench like a halfback who'd sat out a quarter after having his bell rung, but who could now spot the homecoming queen in the stands. James, who had finished third in the Democratic primaries in 1986 and 1990, was now a Republican, again. He had little trouble beating fancy-pants Winton III for the chance to take on Little Jim.

But where was Governor Folsom? Was he lying low or trying to rise above the circulating rumors of bribery and corruption, the news stories of aides under criminal investigation? "Folsom's responses," write Anne Permaloff and Carl Grafton, "were to deny everything except the [Cayman Islands] vacation, run professionally produced but vacuous television advertisements, refuse media requests for interviews, and decline his opponent's challenge to public debate."[43]

With Folsom refusing to engage, James — written off by pundits and pollsters only a month before the general election — sought advice, as he had in his successful 1978 campaign, from strategist Deloss Walker, the Arkansas native gifted for sniffing out voters like a truffle pig. Walker suggested that the onetime governor take to the radio airways with a live, daily call-in show broadcast throughout the state. Fob's friends-and-neighbors manner, effective radio voice, and ultraconservative answers to callers' questions turned a campaign that was "deader than dead air" into a ten-thousand-vote margin of victory over Little Jim. He also benefited from the national mood expressed in the midterm election in the presidential cycle, which gave control of Congress to the Republicans for the first time since the mid-1950s and, crucially, on election day, a light turnout of black voters. "If you've got a problem, let's talk," Fob said, slipping back into the governor's mansion in January 1995.[44]

Unique in Alabama politics for his election first as a Democrat and then as a Republican (and in claiming political-outsider status both times), Fob embodied the shift taking place throughout the South even if his own shifts in affiliation seemed especially opportunistic. Numerous aspirants and office-holders were jumping from the Democratic ship, the biggest Alabama splash belonging to U.S. Senator Richard Shelby, who already voted like a Republican. "He's looking at demographic changes that are like a big wall of water moving," said Jack Drake, general counsel for the state Democratic Party, "and they're not going to change." Also trying to get out in front of the water wall were nearly a dozen Birmingham judges, the secretary of state, state legislators, and members of the Public Service Commission, including George Wallace Jr.[45]

"During the first half of my life," commented J. L. Chestnut as he assessed the decades-long shift, "white Southerners literally hated the Republican Party for historic reasons mostly connected to slavery, reconstruction, integration and black people. Today, they support the Republican Party for reasons that have much to do with black people and racial matters. Nevertheless, only a few Southern whites will admit that obvious truth, even to themselves. It is interesting, that they admit almost nothing about racism."[46]

In pointing out that Alabama's recent population growth lagged far behind that of Florida, Georgia, Tennessee, and North Carolina, the *Huntsville Times* considered some of state's "basic needs still unmet," especially education, pegging failures on the "distorted and inadequate tax system." The paper also complained that "part of the state's problem is its poor national image. Although that image is changing, it changes slowly. Attracting the Mercedes-Benz plant helped, but other developments hurt — the racial troubles in Randolph County and another disputed election."[47] Bob Ingram, weathered politico, was cautiously hopeful: "After years of being the butt of jokes from without, after years of being viewed as a state which most of the other states would like to do without, we have appeared to turn the corner in recent years."[48] Around that corner the Alabama imaginary crashed head on into Fob James.

Governor James led his own parade as Alabama reinstituted the chain gang for prisoners, cut higher education spending, mocked the teaching of evolution, vowed interposition to protect school prayer, and gave the green light for teachers to paddle students. "Like it or not, James has Alabama in spotlight" announced an Atlanta headline.[49] Called "Alabama's current genius of bump-kin publicity" by Howell Raines, James seemed to glory "in the throes of an irresistible urge to attract attention in the worst possible way."[50]

Fob James's reinstatement in May 1995 of the whipping post and chain gang for prisoners evoked imagery of slavery times, of post-Reconstruction's bru-tally exploitative convict-lease system, of Alabama's historical penal practices of beatings and corporal punishment, of Hollywood's projections of southern sadism, and of George Wallace's law 'n' order ideology. Polls showed that a majority of black Alabamians opposed the use of chain gangs, but more than three-fourths of whites were in favor.[51] "People stop me all the time," remarked George Wallace Jr. approvingly, "and say, 'This sounds like what your father was saying.' The return of the chain gangs is a prime example. People want common sense. People are tired of crime."[52]

Television crews from Europe and Japan flew in to document the mostly African American convicts, shackled, busting rock, clearing drainage ditches, cutting weeds, and picking up trash along Alabama highways as guards with loaded shotguns stood watch.[53] "One shakes his chains at me like Marley's ghost as he goes past," wrote a reporter for London's *Guardian*. "'I know what my ancestors felt, man,' he says." Newspaper readers around the world opened to stories and photos of this latest Alabama outrage.[54]

If chain gangs didn't do enough to sustain the Heart of Dixie's most ret-rograde imaginary, listeners to National Public Radio's *All Things Considered* one morning in May 1996 would have heard host Bob Edwards report that "an Alabama lawmaker running for the U.S. Congress has defended the practice of slavery. In a speech, State Senator Charles Davidson of Jasper, Alabama, said slaves were treated well, and he quoted Bible verses to justify the practice of slavery."

NPR correspondent Debbie Elliott noted that "many state leaders are con-cerned that Davidson's speech will only confirm a negative image many out-siders have of Alabama," and offered up the comments of state representative Laura Hall: "I had a call from a reporter from Japan," said Hall. "So it doesn't just go through this United States, but across the world. That is not good for the state of Alabama. We don't need that type of image being projected about the state of Alabama." Chastised but unreconstructed, Republican Davidson withdrew from the congressional race to sulk with the constituents who'd sent him to the state senate.[55]

"Ala. questions evolution theory" headlined the *Boston Globe* after the six-to-one state school board vote in November 1995 that inserted a 250-word disclaimer in ninth-grade biology textbooks. Governor James, ex-officio president of the board, said he believed the Bible's version of creation and supported the insert, part of which read, "No one was present when life first appeared on earth. Therefore, any statement about life's origins should be considered as theory, not fact."[56]

"Because we keep electing those who refuse to acknowledge the reality we face, we never change that reality" editorialized the *Talladega Daily Home* as the second year of Fob Redux ended.[57] But whose reality? At the time Fob foraged across the state, over 60 percent of Alabamians believed that God created humans in their present form all at once no more than ten thousand years ago.[58]

FOB'S CIVIL WAR

When he returned to the governorship in 1994, after more than a decade of working with his sons in various coastal Alabama businesses, Forrest Hood James Jr. resumed his civil war. Abetting the governor, and destined for wider notoriety, was Roy Moore, an Etowah County circuit judge. On the wall near the bench of the Gadsden courtroom where he opened sessions with prayer, Moore hung what appeared to be a wood-burning-kit version of the Decalogue. Challenged in state court by the Alabama Civil Liberties Union on First Amendment establishment-clause grounds that the government could not favor one religion over another, or religion over nonreligion, Moore's plaque lost.

Sez-you. "The only way that the Ten Commandments and prayer will be stripped from Alabama's courts will be a force of arms," swore Governor James in February 1997, threatening to call out the National Guard. "This is just one more demonstration of hostility toward God by the U.S. government," insisted Thumper, although the ruling came from a Montgomery circuit court judge whose decision the state supreme court would overturn on technical grounds.[59] A poll of Alabamians revealed that nearly nine out of ten favored the Commandments remaining on Moore's courtroom wall, and more than half were proud their governor had declared he'd call out the Guard.[60]

"Evidence of moral and spiritual decay encroaches from every side," warned the Rev. Richard Land, an official with the Southern Baptist Convention and a featured speaker at the 1997 annual legislative prayer luncheon of Alabama religious and political leaders during which Governor James blasted the court ruling against Judge Moore. "We have got to fight for the recovery of religious faith," exhorted Land. "The continued existence of our civilization depends on it."[61]

Sanctimony peaked with an April prayer rally on behalf of prayer and plaque. Attended by thousands, the Montgomery event drew national attention and starred Governor James, Attorney General Bill Pryor, Christian Coalition leader Ralph Reed, and 1996 right-wing Republican presidential candidate and talk-show host Alan Keyes. "I became a lawyer," conservative Catholic Pryor told the crowd, "because I wanted to fight the ACLU."[62] *Times* columnist William Safire indulged those who flocked to Montgomery: "The parading religionists can't lose, except in court, where they win by losing. Most Americans believe our civilization is based on a Judeo-Christian heritage, and see no wrong — indeed, much good — in letting a few religious roses climb up the Founders' wall of separation between church and state."[63] As usual, the prayer hubbub provided politicians an Alabama getaway from the real problems of education, poverty, and health care.

In June 1997 Governor James sent federal district judge Ira DeMent a thirty-four-page letter arguing that the federal courts lacked the authority to adjudicate freedom of religion issues in the states and asking the judge to toss out a pending challenge, filed by an assistant principal in DeKalb County, of a 1993 Alabama law that allowed voluntary, nonsectarian, non-proselytizing prayer in public schools. DeMent, a conservative Bush appointee, consistently turned back both the governor and the Alabama school prayer statute, citing the nearly two-hundred-year history of the high court's ultimate authority as interpreter of the Constitution, and writing that James's position "threatens to erode this principle and, consequently, poses a serious threat to our system of democratic self-government." Vowing to "resist Judge DeMent's order by every legal and political means and with every ounce of strength I possess," Thumper fired off a fruitless appeal to the U.S. Supreme Court.[64]

"First came the chain gangs," complained the *Mobile Register*. "Then Alabama became synonymous with the rock pile, the hitching post and the National Guard protecting the Ten Commandments. Now here comes Gov. Fob James again, giving the rest of the nation more ammunition for jokes by saying he might pull out of the National Governors' Association, a Washington-based lobby group that represents all the governors. In fact, he would be the first member to officially resign."[65] And pull out he did, saying it was a waste of taxpayers' money.

James's appointment of women and African American Alabamians in key jobs ranked at the bottom of the fifty states. Unlike his earlier Democratic incarnation, Republican Fob failed to appoint any blacks to policy-making positions.[66] He signed an executive order banning same-sex marriages. His hiring freeze on state employees left too few revenue workers, leading to "a meltdown in collections of delinquent taxes" to the tune of $90 million, an amount that more than doubled between 1994 and the end of 1998.[67] Both of James's administrations were "characterized by assaults on higher education," observed the former president of the University of Montevallo, featuring "debilitating and dispiriting attacks on the state's colleges and universities," budget cutbacks, and demoralizing threats.[68]

During the summer of 1997 the Economic Development Association of Alabama voted their governor the state's number-one obstacle to business growth. Furious at Fob's unrelenting excursions into school prayer and states' rights and the accompanying negative national publicity, the EDA wanted their governor's time and energy focused on recruiting. "The best opportunity Alabama has had was Mercedes," complained the RSA's David Bronner, "and there has been pitiful follow-up."[69] Instead, Alabama's political imaginary, which regularly showcased racism, ignorance, and intolerance, now foregrounded theocracy and lost opportunities.

Due to the public fights over business recruitment strategies, Thumper's grandstanding, and his inability to push tort reform through the legislature, leaders of his own party, as well as key economic actors, increased their criticism. "It's an image problem for the state when the governor is quoted nationwide on highly emotional issues instead of on practical business issues," said Neal Wade, president of the Economic Development Partnership of Alabama, a consortium of the state's major companies prompted into being by the Alabama Power Company in 1991 after the recruiting ineptitudes of the Alabama Development Office. "He has the right to say the things he says, but they confirm the stereotypical image of Alabama as an intolerant climate."[70] The backward-facing Fob James remained trapped by the sez-you expectations for an Alabama governor.[71]

As election year 1998 took shape, business-first Republicans once again put forward Winton Blount III, now age fifty-four, to battle the hunkered-and-bunkered James, sixty-three. Called a "big fat sissy" by Governor James's wife, Bobbie (a strategy that always worked for George Wallace), challenger Blount, who far outspent his competitor thanks to family loans, was endorsed in the primary by the four largest city newspapers. After finishing second in a field of five and qualifying for a runoff with James, Blount hammered away at Fob's pledge to forcibly resist federal court rulings by recalling the futility of Wallace's schoolhouse-door stand. "He's hurt our image," Blount blazed over and over again. "No one is above the law, and I would never encourage anyone to violate the law." The challenger groaned over the national embarrassment caused by James's anti-evolution rants and his "dancing around like a monkey" at a 1995 appearance before the state board of education. "Well, I'm a monkey that's in good shape," the governor fired back. "I'm not a fat monkey, and I'm not a monkey whose daddy has put $2.5 million in my campaign, either."[72]

Thumper, who began campaign events praying "in Jesus' name," was promised "tremendous support" from the Alabama Christian Coalition, in addition to out-of-state backing from the evangelical right's Pat Robertson, James Dobson of Focus on the Family, and antifeminists such as Phyllis Schlafly. "Virtually alone among the nation's governors," wrote Rev. Jerry Falwell, Fob James "has stood up and vowed that he will no longer allow liberal judges to deny schoolchildren the right to pray." Ralph Reed, former Christian Coalition executive director and a James campaign consultant, claimed that a Fob loss would be a "major setback to the pro-family movement across America."[73]

"The rich get rich, the poor get fobbed," jabbed Thumper's opposition.

"More Fob!" roadside signs chanted back.

"More Fob?" asked incredulous Jim Vickery, former president of the University of Montevallo. "More admittedly visionless, unfocused leadership . . . More monkeyshines in public forums as he pursues his quixotic agenda to debunk scientific theories he dislikes and to put Christian prayer and sectarian religious artifacts back into public schools by advancing, unsuccessfully, legal theories rejected by the courts decades ago? More years of Alabama's lingering at or near the bottom of rankings of states in nearly every quality of life measure — from the status of children to per capita income?"[74]

"More Fob!" blared the bumper stickers.

Pulling from the bottomless Wallace croker sack of dirty tricks, the James reelection campaign ran television ads and distributed flyers connecting Blount by name and photograph with Richard Arrington, Birmingham's first African American mayor and a power broker in the state's Democratic Party. This racist scare tactic contended that the liberal mayor would be Alabama's real governor, having made a deal in exchange for mobilizing black Democrats to skip their own primary and cross over to vote for Blount in the Republican one, a practice that remained legal in Alabama. That Arrington had publicly announced his support of Blount during the last week of the primary campaign seemed a questionable strategy for the politically savvy mayor in what, up to that time, appeared to be a neck-and-neck campaign. The mayor's move resulted in a backlash of white-thinking voters. Governor James won the runoff and his party's renomination by more than a 10 percent margin, due in large measure to the successful mobilization of rural and suburban hard-line evangelicals and riled-up whites. And for the first time, more Alabamians voted in the Republican primary than in the Democratic. The national religious right was quick to claim credit and play up the significance of James's win, and anticipated an even greater victory in November against the Democratic nominee, Lieutenant Governor Don Siegelman, chief proponent of a state lottery for education.[75]

For all the high expectations for the fall election, the state's Republicans had fatally wounded themselves and spent their treasure in the bitter primary and runoff. Against Siegelman, Fob started late, thrashed about, and failed to inspire potential voters. For nearly a decade, when they'd been asked, the state's citizens had identified education, not states' rights, not prayer, not any social controversy, as their primary concern.

Building on an urban, labor, teacher, and African American coalition, challenger Siegelman rallied supporters to his lottery-for-education proposal while appealing to Alabamians, including Republicans, embarrassed and weary of James's public shenanigans and religious wars.[76] "The most important thing a Southern governor does," Georgia gubernatorial candidate Roy Barnes told a forum of high-tech business leaders in the fall of 1998, "is to keep his state off the front page of the *New York Times*. Nothing good is ever said about a Southern governor or Southern state on the front of the *New York Times*." Barnes's successful campaign made much of the claim that his Republican opponent would embarrass Georgia just as Fob James had done in Alabama.[77]

The November 1998 gubernatorial results weren't close. While Republicans won half of the fourteen statewide offices, Siegelman received 760,000 more votes than any candidate for governor in Alabama history, beating James by nearly 16 percent. Fervent anti-Fob feeling in both parties combined with the excitement stirred by Siegelman's anticipated lottery proposal to turn out 57 percent of registered voters, reversing a downward trend since the early 1980s. The governor-elect's total included as many as 200,000 African American ballots (same as the margin of victory). He won in both Etowah County (home of Ten Commandments judge Roy Moore) and DeKalb (battleground of school prayer).

The religious right could not deliver Fob from himself.[78] Historians' verdicts began to arrive amid the settling dust. "James," concluded Wayne Flynt, "was one of the most inept governors in memory."[79] Thumper reminded many, in and outside of Alabama, of the nastier side of The Guvner. Not since Wallace had a chief executive done so much damage to the state's image over an extended period of time as had James in his split terms as unrepentant parochialist. A pundit recalled the words of Dewayne Key, former school superintendent for Lawrence County, when he had once followed James as speaker at a meeting of the state board of education: "I guess the circus is over since the clown is gone."[80]

CHAPTER FIVE

The One-trick Pony and the Man on the Horse

My mom and dad gave me Alabama values, and that's all I need to be your governor. Alabama values run through my blood and have helped shape my life. Each and every one of you knows exactly what I mean by Alabama values . . . a heritage, a culture, a quality of life, tempered by self-reliance, rebellion and chivalry — it's all part of being an Alabamian. And I will build Alabama's future on Alabama values, the values we learned from our parents . . . the values we pass on to our children.
    — DON SIEGELMAN, Inaugural Speech, 1999

Even an intelligent governor would be a refreshing change.
    — BOB INGRAM, "Bronner Won't Seek Office"

The University of Alabama's fraternity and sorority mansions are planted along Old Row and Magnolia Drive in Tuscaloosa, on a campus that "looks like a museum of plantation houses," wrote faculty member Diane Roberts following the election of Don Siegelman in 1998. "Most of the buildings boast white columns, tall windows and satiny lawns." They boast white residents as well. Delta Kappa Epsilon is the oldest of these Greek letter organizations, established by a couple of visiting Yalies in 1847.[1] With great expectations, the golden-haired Don Siegelman landed on the Dekes' baronial doorstep in 1964. "Son of a piano salesman and beautician" was a favorite way for Siegelman to describe his origins, twining his roots around those of everyday Alabamians. A resolution adopted by the state legislature at his father's death in 2000 celebrated Leslie Bouchet Siegelman not only as a "successful piano salesman" but also as "general manager for the Jesse French Company, a Mobile music company."[2]

As the old-line white fraternities and sororities of the University of Alabama have maintained racial segregation into the twenty-first century, the political organization of the Greeks, known as the Machine, has continued to hold sway over student government. Don Siegelman, a political science major, won the Machine's nomination and became president of the Student Government Association in 1968. Previous SGA presidents went on to become U.S. senators and representatives, state political officeholders, and major players in the state's most powerful law firms and businesses. "I don't think there has ever been a president of the student body who didn't walk off the campus thinking he or she would be governor," former Alabama Democratic Party chairman (and onetime SGA president) Bill Blount told the *Birmingham News*. But the Dekes' Siegelman became the first to actually do so.[3] Frat brother became father to the Fratman.

At age fifty-two, Don Siegelman, who had been secretary of state, attorney general, and lieutenant governor, won the office he'd coveted "from his days in diapers."[4] The first Democrat to be elected governor since Wallace's last hurrah in 1982, Siegelman had run with one main proposal: an education lottery to be modeled along the lines of the Hope Scholarship program championed by Georgia governor Zell Miller. Miller himself was present at the inaugural, holding a Siegelman family Bible as well as the state's official Good Book (the Jeff Davis Bible) for swearing-in. "The next four years will be a defining moment for our children, our families, and for this state's future," Siegelman pledged to the capitol steps crowd along Dexter Avenue in his "New Day for Alabama" speech. Although he had made himself an ultimate insider during his series of moves from the Deke mansion on the hill in Tuscaloosa to the Neoclassical Revival governor's residence in Montgomery, Siegelman insisted, "I am part of Alabama, and you are part of me. I walk in your shoes."[5] When he finished, Parrothead-in-Chief Jimmy Buffett sang "Stars Fell on Alabama."[6]

Don Siegelman's 1999 inaugural speech is worth lingering over for the new governor's forced attempt to balance old incommensurables:

> It was here . . . that the Confederate States of America was born. On these steps President Jefferson Davis looked down the same street and saw civil war and sacrifice.

In that time he turned to General Robert E. Lee and said: "Lead us." And we honor General Lee today for his courage, his sense of duty and his sacrifice.

Ninety years later . . . a single, solitary African-American woman refused to give up her rightful place on a city bus. On that day Montgomery labor leader E. D. Nixon called the pastor of that church and said: "Lead us."

That pastor — Dr. Martin Luther King Jr. — stood on these same steps, looked down the same street as Jefferson Davis, and saw not civil war, but civil rights and sacrifice.

He changed this nation. And today we honor Dr. King for his courage, his sense of duty and his sacrifice.[7]

Standing on the "same steps" where Davis and King had stood, Siegelman tried to talk his way past the opposed historical meanings of Alabama's grayest days and its greatest ones. Talk past the oppositional significance of the events that these two men helped birth (with Rosa Parks, Claudette Colvin, and Johnnie Carr unmentioned) by appealing to shared, timeless virtues of "courage, sense of duty, and sacrifice" and by declaring, "That is our history. Those are our roots."[8] So long as this evasive balancing act remains necessary in gubernatorial inaugurals or official public speech, white Alabamians haven't understood their history. In attempting to balance the slaveholders' rebellion with the African American freedom struggle, Siegelman's narrative of public memory dodged the scales of social justice for the simplistic slogans of tourism brochures.

Siegelman, who spent decades measuring his way up the state's spiral staircase, touted a brighter day: "We will not live in the gray twilight. It is time for Alabama to believe in itself again. It is time to dare mighty things."[9] His speech and performance of public rituals on that third Monday in January put a happy face on an Alabama divided against and deceiving itself, a state still at odds with the nation. Instead of invoking the Lost Cause and omitting the slavery that shadowed the state's official Robert E. Lee holiday, the governor might have acknowledged that the coinciding MLK holiday already commemorated Alabamians who had set a high standard for believing in themselves and daring mighty things. Siegelman's day had begun by eating breakfast with Marty King at Dexter Avenue King Memorial Baptist Church. It ended with his laying a wreath at the Confederate monument on the capitol grounds. Between prayer breakfast and wreath laying, his first official act was to order that bond money already approved for school construction be used to replace three thousand portable classrooms strewn across Alabama. The portables, he would later say, were monuments "to the state's indifference to education."[10]

As lieutenant governor presiding over a Democratic-majority senate, Siegelman had appointed key committee chairs and shaped the legislative flow. He bottled up bills that would have put limits on jury monetary awards in damage suits against companies, and he smoothed passage of stronger drunk driver laws. The incoming lieutenant governor, party-switcher Steve Windom, became the first Republican to hold that office since Reconstruction. Siegelman and his senate allies moved to strip Windom of power, and the ensuing battle revealed Siegelman's ruthless side while taking up a third of the legislative session. It became a chuckleheaded blunder when Windom, as presiding senate officer, refused to leave the floor — for fear the governor's forces would win the day — and relieved his pent-up frustrations by peeing in a jug behind the podium.[11] Although he would go on to run for his party's nomination for governor, Windom's political reputation had sprung an irreparable leak. "It's embarrassing," said Jim Bates, a part-time security guard at the capitol. "When people ask me where I'm from, I tell them Kentucky."[12]

With the legislature rumbling into gear, among the first items to clear was authorization for a statewide lottery vote in the fall. Candidate Siegelman had campaigned hard for the lottery, claiming it would raise as much as $150 million to fund college scholarships, school technology, and pre-kindergarten programs. The moment appeared ripe. "For years, gambling's once-improbable march through the Bible Belt had seemed inexorable," wrote the *New York Times*. "There were casinos in Louisiana and Mississippi, lotteries in Georgia and Florida, and video poker machines in almost every gas station in South Carolina." Birmingham and a couple of Black Belt counties trotted out greyhound racing and bingo. Polls taken around the time of the 1998 election showed a majority of Alabama voters favored the lottery. Church-based opposition, however, vowed a pew-by-pew fight in October's special election.[13]

A beneficiary of hundreds of thousands of dollars in trial lawyer campaign contributions during his career, Siegelman as lieutenant governor had stymied efforts to put caps on jury monetary awards against companies found responsible for harm due to defective products or negligent service. The tort reform battle had intensified in the 1990s, attracting mind-boggling donations to legislative and state court candidates in opposing camps. Democratic plaintiffs' lawyers waving a banner of consumer protection fought Republican lobbyists who warned of damaging the state's business climate.[14]

As the 1999 legislature took up the contentious issue, Alabama's reputation as "tort hell" chalked up its latest outrage. "Why would you folks in Georgia be shocked over a little thing like the woman in Birmingham winning a $581 million judgment for her faulty $1,200 satellite dish?" wondered the *Atlanta Journal-Constitution*. "That was for her pain and suffering; she didn't get the 300 channels the company promised."[15] It was another Alabama moment, seized for national laughs, but not without consequences. Realizing that litigious flames were singeing his industry-recruiting hopes, now-Governor Siegelman became more obliging to business lobby legislation. Historians Sam Webb and Margaret Armbrester note that tort reform was one of several incentives sought by Honda in deciding to build a $400 million auto plant in Talladega County. Siegelman assented to tort-capping legislation, crowing, "We've proven Alabama was open for business."

In the war between trial and corporate lawyers, Siegelman's concession pragmatically acknowledged the Republicans' takeover, during succeeding elections, of a state supreme court that had, under Democratic justices, often upheld huge monetary jury judgments of company negligence. In helping to engineer the high court's shift, Republican operative Karl Rove, who had successfully advised supreme court candidates in Texas, urged Alabama corporate leaders to launch an offensive. Rovian-inspired campaign ads produced by the D.C.-based Republican media strategists at Stevens & Schriefer deployed hot-button accusations, such as demonizing a Democratic judge as being soft on criminals. When combined with the escalating flight of white voters into the Republican Party, the results were devastating. In 1994 no Republicans sat on the Alabama Supreme Court; by 2001 there were no Democrats and the state's two black justices had also been turned out. In the decade following 1993, election campaigns for supreme court seats, pitting big business against big plaintiff lawyers, raised some $41 million, the largest total for judicial candidates anywhere in the U.S.[16]

"A STATE OF FOOLS"

Honda announced for Alabama in May 1999. In June, Siegelman made a recruiting trip to Germany and France. "I think it's been fantastic," said David

Bronner, the usually caustic-tongued head of the RSA who invested billions of state employee pension dollars, when asked about the new governor's fast start. "I don't think anyone could have done any better."[17] Bronner, the innovative financial outsider who had watched many governors come and go, had been thoroughly disgusted by Fob James's misplaced zealotry.

In Alabama, footholds of protective social policy advance slowly. What would have been scandalous by its absence elsewhere — mandatory automobile liability insurance, for instance — offered grounds for progressive boasting when the legislature passed it in Siegelman's first year.[18]

As the summer of 1999 turned to fall, the antilottery movement gained momentum through grassroots opposition led by religious denominations and conservative groups such as the Alabama Baptists, the American Family Association of Alabama, and the state's Christian Coalition. Major opponents also included ALFA (the Alabama Farmers Federation), ambitious Republican attorney general William Pryor, and Americans for Tax Reform, the right-wing lobby headed by Massachusetts native Grover Norquist.

A strain of sez-you resistance to the lottery took the familiar form of "I don't care what they do in Atlanta." More thoughtful were Alabamians who learned that in Georgia, Siegelman's model state, poor and minority households purchased more lottery tickets than middle-class households, while white, middle-class students were disproportionate beneficiaries of HOPE college scholarships. The main purchasers of chance, the poor and blue collar, were helping to educate the children of the better off. Still, many African American voters backed the proposal as a pragmatic option for bringing in badly needed public school money.[19] Siegelman, rather than tackle entrenched resistance to fundamental tax reform, placed all his chips on the lottery.

He had won election in November 1998 by a 200,000-vote margin; less than a year later, thanks to the churches' mobilization, the lottery referendum lost by 100,000 (54 to 46 percent). "The religious groups are outraged by private sins," fumed Wayne Flynt, "but they don't seem as concerned about social sins, like a third of the kids in Alabama's public schools being poor. I haven't seen them mobilize to this extent in favor of anything that might actually improve education." As Dewayne Key recalls, Flynt's home church, Auburn First Baptist, "took a leading part in advocating tax reform and the church's role in reforming the state one town at a time. In 2000, Flynt and political scientist Gerald Johnson persuaded their congregation to approve a donation to the Auburn city schools of an amount equal to the property taxes the church would have paid the city if it were not exempt."[20] Unsuccessfully, Flynt introduced similar resolutions before the Alabama Baptist Convention. Might the day come when church property will be taxed and the revenue equitably distributed to support public education? Imagining such a prospect scandalizes mainline Bible Belters as surely as advocating the legalization and taxation of marijuana or gambling.

Stunned by the lottery's defeat, the governor said he "had no Plan B" for the state with the nation's lowest per capita spending on education. But not to worry. "I didn't get my black belt in karate some years ago . . . by being a wuss."[21] Siegelman didn't realize it at the time, but his administration and political career had reached their pinnacle. His descent would be precipitous.

In a serious hit to Alabama's jerry-rigged revenue machinery, the U.S. Supreme Court ruled the state's "franchise tax" illegal for placing heavier levies on out-of-state corporations' cost of doing business than on that of in-state companies. The franchise tax was a variation on the pleasures of sticking it to the outsiders. Having postponed this $120 million emergency until after the lottery vote, Siegelman now called the legislature into special session while he negotiated with business leaders for a thin spread of new taxes that would avoid cuts to prisons, mental hospitals, children's health insurance, and other social services dependent upon federal matching monies. Some of these state institutions and programs, facing court-ordered supervision or consent decrees, would be "underfunded even with the $120 million," said legislator Thad McClammy. "Without it, we're starting to look like a third-world state." With the cobbling together of a financial rescue scheme, Siegelman was quick to assure that "Alabama businesses will still be paying the lowest taxes in the nation."[22]

Early in 2000 newspapers praised the governor's "agility," and a poll of likely voters found two-thirds of them satisfied with Siegelman. Almost the same number, however, were dissatisfied with the state's public education system.[23] The post-Fob afterglow was fading. The state had desperate needs, but given its habits of judgment, few options. The governor persuaded the legislature to apply a portion of Alabama's accumulating natural gas royalties to a variety of infrastructural improvements.

With Alabamians' personal income growing at a slower rate than that of the citizens of any other state, with tax revenues down and the national economy

souring, the man aspiring to be the education governor found himself oversee-
ing cuts in the state's public schools, colleges, and universities. It was the return
of the accursed proration, a consequence of tying the misnamed Education
Trust Fund to volatile sales and income taxes while having no rainy-day stash;
nearly $270 million would have to be cut from the $4.3 billion education budget. Battle lines formed between K–12 supporters and partisans of higher ed
until the state supreme court ruled the cuts must be made equally across the
board. A hurriedly passed $110 million bond issue evaded the fundamental
problem. Even had Siegelman gotten his lottery, school funding would have
faced proration. Such is the recurring dilemma of public education in Alabama
since before the passage of the proration act in the Depression year of 1932.
Thrown by the failure of his lottery proposal, Siegelman was at a loss for what
to do next.[24] "We will become a persistent cautionary tale," warned a newspaper letter writer. "Politicians everywhere will say that if you neglect education,
you might become like Alabama: a relic retreating into the nineteenth century,
a state of fools."[25]

That it didn't have to be this way, even down South, was the message delivered at an Alabama education conference by John Dornan, of the Public School
Forum of North Carolina. Dornan detailed how his state had raised the sales
tax one-half cent and income tax by 1 percent for people making over $130,000
to offset an $800 million shortfall in its current education budget. Alabama
state superintendent of education Ed Richardson followed Dornan's report by
recounting his failed efforts to remove sales tax exemptions and corporate tax
loopholes. "Every time I talk to people about that," he said, "they just look
at me like I'm an idiot."[26] When polled, a vast majority of adult Alabamians
believed the state spent too little on public education, yet antitax fundamentalism stymied streams of new revenue.[27]

In Siegelman's 2001 State of the State address, the governor avoided any
mention of proration, tax reform, or constitutional reform. "He talked about
wonderful initiatives," commented Sophia Bracy Harris, director of the
Federation of Child Care Centers of Alabama, "but we've got to pay for them. I
would have liked for him to be as tough on making Alabama strong financially
as he was on crime."[28]

"The nature of politics in Alabama," concluded Auburn president William
Muse in 2001 as he was being chased from the Loveliest Village on the Plains
by the AU board of trustees for attempting to practice higher education, "has

. . . prevented the development of a long-range plan for the development of the state and inhibited the emergence of leadership that is so necessary to accomplish that objective." He was not optimistic that change would come anytime soon. "Alabama has been hampered by a tax structure that is both inequitable and inadequate. It places a disproportionate burden on the poor through an over-reliance on sales taxes and does not produce sufficient revenues to fund education, both elementary and secondary and higher education, on levels comparable to that of other Southern states. . . . The state's property taxes would have to be tripled to reach the national average and nearly doubled just to equal Mississippi's."[29]

As the insistent Muse fired a parting shot, the state's Republican Party went about its own version of changing the nature of politics in Alabama. Business-first Republicans looked and sounded different from Guy Hunt and Fob James. But racism remained an unacknowledged, encoded force, visible in the segregation of suburban residential space and the persistence of educational inequity and economic disparity.

More troubles were brewing for Siegelman. Reporters, particularly from the *Mobile Register* and *Birmingham News*, sniffed out trails leading to a fraternity of the governor's aides, insiders, supporters, and cronies profiting from bribes, no-bid contracts, and self-serving use of confidential information. By May 2001 the news stories prompted a state and federal investigation. The guilty pleas began accumulating in June. Prosecutions followed.[30] Between smiling announcements of the arrival of a Hyundai plant near Montgomery, a Navistar engine factory in Huntsville, and the expansion of Mercedes, Siegelman radiated irritability. "His demeanor has changed," observed a Republican state senator. "He doesn't appear as confident."[31] The *Register*'s pesky Eddie Curran got so far under the governor's skin that Siegelman ordered his staff and state agency employees not to speak to the investigative reporter or respond to his requests for information. This escalated into a general policy of requiring that all media queries about official records be made to the governor's legal office, hardly the way to win over the press or dampen public suspicions.[32]

As another campaign season loomed, Bob Ingram diagnosed the governor with a bad case of "re-electionitis," displaying the disease's "most telling symptom," the embracing by an incumbent of "all of the popular issues of the day even if it means reversing previously taken positions." So Siegelman "almost overnight became a champion of constitutional reform, an effort he had avoided like the plague throughout his administration." He also "imposed tough new disclosure rules on folks doing business with the state," although this seemed like "closing the barn door after the horse got out." In quasi-populist rhetoric late in his term, Siegelman began championing the closing of corporate loopholes. He spoke approvingly of Chief Justice Roy Moore's depositing his 5,300-pound granite Ten Commandments monument in the rotunda of the state judicial building (favored by 60 percent of registered voters) and called for placing copies of the Commandments in public schools. The governor went out of his way to take advantage of a third-grade boy's suspension from a Hoover school for wearing an ear stud to declare that men with earrings were "fools." "I don't think guys ought to be wearing earrings. . . . If God had wanted you to wear earrings, he'd have made you a girl."[33]

"Don't cry for Alabama, better times may be ahead," reassured the venerable Brandt Ayers, owner-publisher of the *Anniston Star*. Such longings in the Heart of Dixie periodically turn delirious, the waiting so fraught, the progress so maddeningly incremental, the brain-addling, ninety-degree shade and 100 percent humidity always on the horizon. "Public and private agreements unite business, government, higher education, the media and candidates of both political parties," read Alabama's fortune cookie, according to Ayers. This time stars were aligning, not falling. Publisher Ayers placed his bets again on Siegelman, hoping the Fratman would turn tentativeness into leadership. "Without violating any confidence or fear of contradiction, I can say this much: the best brains and some of the best hearts in the state will be assembled and focused — not on their special interests — but on the agenda of Alabama." Yet, Ayers hedged, "Something is stirring, fanned by media attention and civic activism, a force is building which Gov. Don Siegelman waited to feel before trying anything significant, momentum sensed by one of the governor's GOP challengers, U.S. Rep. Bob Riley."[34] Siegelman had to have been more shaken than stirred when, come November, over half of Alabamians surveyed rated his performance as governor as fair or poor.[35]

By spring 2002, the advantages of incumbency still foretold the first gubernatorial succession since Brother Guy Hunt's. "I think he's in reasonably good shape," assured a veteran political analyst. "He's a money-raising fool," chimed the AEA's Paul Hubbert, recognizing one on sight. After all, Siegelman could boast (and regularly did) of bringing new manufacturers into the state. Yet with federal agents subpoenaing records and a lengthening parade of Siegelman appointees and associates coming under legal scrutiny for activities ranging from fixing traffic tickets to conflicts of interest to extorting bribes, Alabamians started paying attention. By summer, a media poll showed that gubernatorial challenger Riley, a third-term GOP congressman from east Alabama (and publisher Ayers's district), had taken the lead.[36]

COWBOY OF CLAY

Clay County is best known to historians — but to few others — as the home of Hugo Black (1886–1971), whom locals remain slow to forgive for his U.S. Supreme Court voting record. "When he lived in Alabama," goes the down-home simplification of Senator Black's renunciation of Klan membership for a seat on FDR's court, "he wore a white robe and scared the blacks to death. When he got to Washington, he wore a black robe and scared the whites to death."[37] Present-day Clay County remains a ragged piece of east Alabama holding red earth together with vast tracts of pine trees, small pastures, and chicken houses. Its sparse population is over 80 percent white, and its poverty rate approaches 20 percent.[38]

Born in 1944, Bob Riley grew up in Clay and graduated from the University of Alabama some four years ahead of Siegelman. He went back home to poultry and eggs but also dealt in cars, cattle, and real estate. He had a knack for business. Riley first went to Congress in 1997, winning a formerly Democratic seat as the white tide of Republicanism continued to rise across Alabama and the South. He made the acquaintance of Karl Rove, Michael Scanlon, and George W. Bush. Riley boasted a 100 percent Christian Coalition voting record and won its "Friends of the Family" award. Well liked back home, Riley could have stayed in Washington for an extended run, except for a three-term-limit pledge he had made as a freshman. "If you know being in Congress is not going to be a career," he liked to say, "you can vote your conscience." Riding into new pastures, he fixed upon the figure of Ronald Reagan.[39]

As a member of Congress sending off the *Riley Report* newsletter to constituents, he worried publicly that "according to the Ronald Reagan Legacy Project, 38 states still haven't named a school, road, post office or other structure after the former president. Alabama is one, and I believe we should rectify that deficiency as soon as possible."[40] The fortieth president had visited the

Ronald Reagan Spirit of America Field (home to ball games and festivals) in Decatur in 1984, but Riley strategically perceived that by proposing to attach Reagan's name to Alabama bridges, roads, and post offices, Alabamians would attach his name to Reagan's.

You had to go back to the nineteenth century to find a successful member of Congress who'd made the move into the Alabama's governor's office. Riley anticipated his ascendance, laying groundwork and declaring his candidacy sixteen months before election day. Although little known outside of the fourteen-county district that boasted Anniston as its largest city, Riley had bought media advertising for his congressional campaigns in Montgomery, Birmingham, and Columbus, Georgia, markets with footprints that fell into his bailiwick. "Riley has a lot going for him," wrote Bob Ingram, assessor of scads of politicians over the decades. "He is a small town boy made good and he will come across on television as well as any candidate."[41]

Riley turned his distance from Montgomery into an advantage, pitching himself as unbought and detached from Goat Hill politics-as-usual. Testing the waters, he wrote newspaper op-eds and accepted speaking engagements around the state. Although he would call raising political money "the most demeaning thing I have ever done in my life," Riley excelled at it.[42] He took aggressive advantage of his situation as a member of Congress to build a war chest months before other candidates could legally solicit money for state campaigns. This earned him the title of Congressman Loophole from the *Anniston Star* as it totaled up tens of thousands of dollars in Riley contributions from Solutia (the industrial chemical giant and toxic polluter formerly named Monsanto), the tobacco industry, banking, and the National Chicken Council.[43]

Congressman Riley was one of several Republican candidates who basked in the media glow of President Bush's Alabama fundraising visit for right-wing U.S. senator Jeff Sessions in June 2001, which raised $1.7 million. Bush had won the state in 2000, and as GOP strategists sensed the prospect for snatching an incumbent Democratic governorship, the president promised to return soon and raise money for Riley.[44] Alabama had become the state with the greatest high-income voter gap — where the wealthy were most likely to vote Republican.[45]

With a Fourth of July rally in the Clay County seat of Ashland, a hamlet of some two thousand where he and his brother once sold nickel bags of peanuts in the shadow of the courthouse in which Hugo Black had practiced law, Riley officially began his campaign for governor, launching a bus tour of south Alabama, including Mobile, home of Republican rival Steve Windom. Ultimately, Riley had nothing to fear from the lieutenant governor whose most memorable public act remained pissing in a jug and whom Riley successfully lumped with the Goat Hill crowd of inept self-servers. "Few campaigns for governor in Alabama have so utterly collapsed as Steve Windom's," noted the *Huntsville Times*.[46] Well in advance of the Republican primary, Riley had undercut potential opposition by lining up influential endorsements such as that of Spencer Bachus, fellow Alabama member of Congress. Alabama's ten thousand realtors proclaimed that Riley "offer[ed] an opportunity to make the most positive changes ever in Alabama history."[47]

Bob Riley's July 15, 2002, Birmingham fundraiser headlining President Bush broke the national record for single-day, single-candidate fundraising, pulling in over $4 million.[48] While in the state, the president also filmed a Riley commercial. Alabama law allowed unlimited individual contributions to candidates, and some 2,800 people paid anywhere from $1,000 for entry to $50,000 to have their photo taken with W. Money in the Alabama governor's race had changed, big time. Back in 1954 Jim Folsom reported spending a total of $400,000 in his successful race. In 2002 a single lobbyist gave Don Siegelman $200,000. Riley and the incumbent governor each spent more than $10 million.[49]

Few among all those donors knew what Riley planned to do if elected. It was easy to oppose government waste and to speechify for education. The ninety-page booklet of policy proposals his campaign released in August 2002 called for more than a dozen study groups, from constitutional reform to highway building. Given his sustained attack on the ethics of the Siegelman administration, Riley advocated subjecting lobbyists to scrutiny and requiring them to account for the money they spent wooing state legislators and officials. But mainly, Riley presented himself as the un-Siegelman.[50] In white dress shirts and Lucchese boots, red ties, dark suits, and access to deep pockets, the man of Clay projected Christian straight-shooting, fiscal austerity, jingoism, and rock-ribbed Reaganism. Leaflets and TV ads showed the agribusinessman from hill-infested eastern Alabama on horseback, resembling Reagan in his California governor days, but looking even more a coonskin-capless Fess Parker from the 1960s *Daniel Boone* television series. Riley was the newspaper cowboy for all small-town car dealers, real estate agents, broiler-and-egg kingpins, and fast-food franchisees who mapped their trajectories onto his.

Siegelman, who had been stunned by the lottery's defeat in 1999, punched the ticket again in what seemed his best campaign call and his only idea for generating new money for education. "Siegelman is a one-trick pony," insisted Riley campaign spokesman David Azbell. "Siegelman tried a lottery, and the people said no. He tries again."[51]

Riley hammered away at corruption and cronyism in the Siegelman administration as well as the state's inability to support basic government functions. "Have you had enough of no-bid contracts?" he asked voters. "Have you had enough of proration? Then you want a different Alabama."[52] Neither Reaganite Riley nor the incumbent addressed property tax reform. Just how Governor Riley would make things different was not clear, but he came across as more poised, clear spoken, and confident, possessing an energy that was surprisingly missing from the Fratman.[53] With the smallest margin in the state's history, Riley won the governor's office by some 3,000 out of 1.3 million votes.[54]

Bob Riley and the Republicans had pulled big numbers in the rapidly growing whitelands — the suburbs in counties such as Baldwin, Shelby, Autauga, and Bibb. "Those outlying counties with freeway access to major areas of employment tend to be fairly well off," reported UA geographer Gerald Webster; "they are in many cases substantially whiter than the state as a whole, and they are increasingly Republican."[55] Siegelman's loss raised a Democratic fear that the day would soon come when the party would be unable to capture any statewide office.

Having battled to win the right to vote, black Alabamians found themselves electorally corralled within particular areas and neighborhoods of the state. Riley's election owed nothing to the voting bloc he called "Afro-Americans."[56] He projected racial fairness but seemed unmoved by evidence of endemic structural racism and what the pursuit of social equality would actually require.

And what of the Fratman? "Siegelman, too caught up in politics himself," wrote News columnist Joey Kennedy, "never would risk doing what's truly right and best for Alabama when he could get away with doing what's right and best for a favorite special interest. . . . The potential was amazing; the results, underwhelming."[57]

Don Siegelman had nourished an indulgent circle of sufferance and privilege. Tacit understandings covered scheming among the favor-doers, greedheads, easy-riders, and advisers working the angles. To his credit as governor, Siegelman didn't pitch racist politics, nor did he run for the cover of states' rights, or sez-you posturing, nor perform Thumper's embarrassing theatrics of anti-evolution. During the years of the Fratman's calculated rise, he had built friendships and alliances with key African American leaders and groups and had included women and blacks in his cabinet. In 1998 he'd won 94 percent of the black vote against Fob James.[58]

These African American ties endured even as Siegelman and HealthSouth founder Richard Scrushy were tried and convicted for corruption in 2006. When the Alabama New South Coalition (one of two major statewide African American political organizations) endorsed the gubernatorial candidacy of Lucy Baxley, Hank Sanders did so reluctantly, ruefully. "While far from perfect," wrote the state senator from Selma in his weekly column, "Siegelman had been more responsive to New South people than any other statewide elected official through twenty years as Secretary of State, Attorney General, Lieutenant Governor and Governor. To many of us, he is the best governor Alabama has ever had."[59] To others, Siegelman's best moments came with his first statewide-elected job, as secretary of state from 1979 to 1987, when he modernized and made more transparent Alabama's voting system, while making registration easier for the historically disenfranchised.[60]

Steeped from his Deke days in the inside game of Alabama politics, Siegelman had grown accustomed to settings and dealings inaccessible to ordinary Alabamians: major players' shifting large sums of money between untraceable pots for undisclosed intentions, the mutually understood understandings, the quid pro quos for retiring campaign debt. Who knows how many schemes ran in and out of the governor's roundhouse, how many he did or did not help get on track? Alabama's flimsy campaign-finance regulations and minimal ethics laws make it as difficult to clear names as it is easy to muddy them or to claim a ten-foot pole.

Historian Harvey Jackson captured the disillusion: "Don Siegelman understood the political culture of Alabama because he was part of it and his problems came when he could not rise above it. Siegelman knew, for example, that most of the services citizens expected the state to provide were underfunded — education being principal among them. He also knew that there were well-entrenched interests that would block any attempt to raise the money to pay for what the people wanted and needed." The lottery was Siegelman's attempt to avoid a fight with the interests. "Truth is," concluded Jackson, "Alabama today is not all that much different from Alabama four years ago. Auto plants are replacing paper mills, but fundamental economic problems remain."[61]

If once he seemed attuned to everyday Alabamians, Don Siegelman slipped with every passing year in Montgomery into chasing, acquiring, and deploying the sort of money that most Alabamians never touch in a lifetime. A half-million dollars in the governor's "contingency fund" disappeared without documenting what state business it accomplished; each year as governor, Siegelman made at least $250,000 in legal fees without practicing law.[62] Maybe it was all on the up-and-up or maybe it was all made up. Given Alabama's lack of disclosure laws, there was no way to know.

Engaged, the legal wheels ground inexorably, with official investigations leading to guilty pleas and convictions on crimes of bribery, tax fraud, and ethics violations for numerous Siegelman appointees, supporters, and consultants. Key to the prosecution of the governor himself was one-time aide Nick Bailey, who had worked his way up from personal driver and assistant to a seat in the cabinet as head of the Alabama Department of Economic and Community Affairs (ADECA) ("a cesspool if ever there was one," noted the *News'* Robin DeMonia). In June 2003 Bailey and two confederates pled guilty to bribery, but it was not until the summer of 2006 that a federal jury convicted Siegelman and Scrushy in an extortion and bribery scheme. Scrushy had arranged payments of $500,000 toward retiring a bank loan to the foundation Siegelman had created for the lottery campaign. In exchange for these "donations" to pay off Siegelman's personally guaranteed loan, the governor appointed Scrushy to the state board in charge of authorizing hospitals to expand or add services.[63]

Siegelman was "stymied," concluded Wayne Flynt, "by a rotten economy and, perhaps, the political ambition that kept him from taking on the toughest issues. I think he never realized anything like his possibilities or his potential. The tragedy, if you could call it that, of Siegelman is that he knew what ought to be done. He wanted to be a New South governor, but he could never pull it off."[64]

It was the *Register*'s investigative reporter Eddie Curran who recalled words of the young Siegelman when, as secretary of state in the 1980s, he had worked for the passage of what would become the Alabama Fair Campaign Practices Act. "Not only have we priced the average person out of politics," said Siegelman, but "people perceive politics as a dirty game."[65] As the indictments, convictions, and appeals played out, Siegelman fought against the gray twilight he had once decried, the fair-haired, Pat Boone sheen worn away.

"Alabama will have a lottery within the next four years," insisted the defeated incumbent. Was there a hint of bitterness? "The people are going to demand it. Bob Riley won't veto it. He's going to need the money for education." Certainly the state's education system was starved for money, but Siegelman's assertion that Riley would eventually support a lottery was one of several off-the-mark predictions—another being that a jury would find him innocent of bribery.[66]

The Fratman would protest his conviction for years, from the inside and outside of federal prison. He argued, supported by several national Democrats, that he'd been a target of Karl Rove's dirty tricks. Siegelman was allowed out on bond while his appeal and Rove's involvement in the firing of several federal district attorneys worked their ways through courts and rounds of congressional inquiry. While Rove instigated untold nasty acts against political enemies, not all the wrongdoing during the Bush years was Rovian. Siegelman had imploded through acquired habits and ineffectuality, amid a state political ethos unwilling to distinguish legal machinations from corrupt maneuverings. He grasped at the notion of a conspiracy like a frat brother for a fake ID. In a 2008 interview with Tavis Smiley, the fallen governor offered a grandiose and ultimately misleading set of reasons why the national GOP might target him:

> I think I represented a threat to the Republicans here in Alabama and to some extent, nationally. I was getting ready to start chewing on George Bush. I was opposed to his policies in Iraq, his economic policies and education policies, and had given a speech to the National Democratic Governors Association in December of 2002, and I was about to launch a campaign to help Democrats win across the country as they were running for Governor.[67]

One searches in vain for evidence that the Siegelman of 2002 or 2003 represented a serious threat to Republicans anywhere, or that he "was getting ready to start chewing on George Bush." After a federal court upheld his bribery conviction in 2009, Siegelman sought new grounds for appeal.[68]

ANOTHER "NEW DAY"

The day before his January 2003 inauguration, Bob Riley couldn't resist offering his own set of predictions: "I'll reform the tax structure. I'll reform the Department of Transportation, and I'll make our education system one of the best of the nation." Was there giddiness? "I'll build what I consider the most ethical government, at least in my adult lifetime. I will surround myself with the most talented people I can find and collectively begin a new day in Alabama."[69] Siegelman had tossed around the "new day" phrase four years earlier.

Very quickly, Governor Riley would discover how immediate and desperate was Alabama's need for revenue, and how limited were his options. The sun had risen on so many daybreaks in Alabama, only to have the storms roll in before evening.

"Have you ever seen the movie *Groundhog Day*?" Riley asked a Public Affairs Research Council of Alabama (PARCA) gathering in Birmingham one January morning in 2003. Outside of an all-but-extinct cadre of high school Latin teachers, Sisyphus labors unknown in the Heart of Dixie. Editorial writers' allusions to the man of La Mancha risk going where readers dare not go. *Groundhog Day*, however, provided Riley with a pop culture image that encapsulated the state's chronic dysfunction. The 1993 Hollywood film featured actor Bill Murray's vain, sarcastic, time-trapped character awakening over and over to the same Groundhog Day until, remaking himself into a well-rounded, empathetic fellow, he breaks the spell and wins the heart of Andie MacDowell's Rita. Riley, having spent a restless night in bed with the "State of the State" speeches of three preceding governors, awoke to his rendezvous with Alabama's time-space conundrum.

For generations, an assortment of journalists, activists, politicians, lawyers and judges, professors, policy wonks, and business boosters have called for rewriting the state's 1901 constitution, overhauling its grossly inequitable tax structure, and expanding home rule for counties and municipalities. The millennium arrived with reformers stymied and Alabama still mired among the bottommost states in indices of income inequality, education, social well-being, health care, female elected officials, prison incarceration, and environmental protection.

"Until we make . . . fundamental changes," Riley preached to the PARCA choir that day, "starting with the constitution, we're going to be having this debate ten, fifteen, twenty years from now." Alabama's revenue machinery, skewed worse than any other state's to the benefit of large property and timberland owners, began collecting income tax on families making less than $100 a week. "There's not a person in here who can defend that system," said the governor.[70] Riley pledged to work for a fairer system of taxation and a revamped constitution.

He promised improvement in the quality of life for the region of the state that the *Birmingham News* had begun calling "Alabama's Third World" — the crescent-shaped, multicounty Black Belt, with a majority African American population, extensive household poverty, and concentrated white land ownership. Despite the democratization of Black Belt politics since the late 1960s, the region continued to suffer great class disparity and unemployment, built on a legacy of racial exploitation.

"It will be an extremely hard sell," the *News* editorialized about Bob Riley's proclaimed intentions to make the tax system fairer. "Too many Alabamians and too many powerful special interests who are used to having their way in Montgomery want him to leave their windmills alone. Bringing them crashing to the ground will be a monumental task, yet it can't begin without a governor courageous enough to tilt at them."

Alluding to "windmills," the state's largest-circulation paper reminded readers that three years earlier a governor had startled this same public policy forum: "Then-Gov. Don Siegelman said he was no Don Quixote."

"I'm really not interested in tilting at windmills," he told a stunned audience at the annual meeting of the Public Affairs Research Council of Alabama. The windmills Siegelman had no interest in tilting at are Alabama's grievously flawed constitution and its immoral, unfair tax system. His astonishing indifference deflated a crowd that had just sat through sessions focused on fixing both.[71]

Given Riley's strong moral disapproval of a state lottery, he became convinced that only one option could make up the revenue shortfall of between $500 and $675 million forecast for the coming year — the largest looming deficit since the Depression.[72] He put the matter publicly in a comment so startling from the mouth of a southern Republican governor that it became a *New York Times'* "Quotation of the Day": "No one likes to raise taxes, least of all me. On the other hand, the inevitable is here."[73]

STATE BIRD: ALBATROSS

As history slept underfoot, Sunday, March 16, 2003, was Alabama Day at the National Cathedral in Washington, D.C. One of Alabama's most remarkable daughters, the socialist Helen Keller, rested in her crypt beneath the main floor as Rev. James Evans, pastor of Crosscreek Baptist Church in Pelham, stood in the pulpit where Martin Luther King Jr. had preached his final Sunday sermon. The National Cathedral designates a Sunday every four years in each state's honor, and among the eleven hundred or so people in attendance this day were perhaps as many as five hundred Alabamians. Rev. Evans took stock of the state's political imaginary by examining "values and traditions" (habits of judgment) and recounting lessons (good and bad) learned from his grandpa, who had died in 1985. Along with such values as hard work, "caring for your tools, and loving the earth that grows our food," Evans invoked his state's pervasive religious faith: "Something like 93 percent of the people of Alabama embrace some form of Christianity or Judaism." Yet, he wondered, would God guide Alabamians "to embrace all that is good from our forebears, and reject those things that work against justice and community"?[74]

Evans's intention was far from celebratory. "The legacy we have received from our forebears is a mixed bag," he conceded, offering again the example of his grandfather who had taught him how to smoke (and roll his own), a deadly habit that took Evans years to break. Having established his down-home credentials, the legacy this preacher wanted to address on Alabama Day was the curse of the 1901 state constitution, "apparent to anyone who reads history," which had disenfranchised blacks and poor whites and "concentrated inordinate power in the state legislature while allowing almost no local control to cities and counties. The constitution also created significant hedges to protect wealthy landowners from taxation." Evans connected the sins of the grandfathers to the ongoing fiscal crisis of Alabama:

> Today our state is suffering precisely because of the legacy of that constitution. Our schools are woefully underfunded. We also struggle to provide other basic services for the citizens of our state. As we search for revenue to improve this situation, we find that our hands are often tied by the tangled cords of our outdated state constitution.

Preacher Evans urged new Alabama governor Bob Riley to "get this albatross off the necks of the people of our state." Otherwise, "there is a real danger that we will lose what we really care about: a solid future for our children, adequate care for our elderly, and an economic environment that will allow the poor in our state the chance to work their way out of poverty."[75]

In town for their annual conference, and seated among the congregants at the National Cathedral, was a contingent from the Alabama Farmers Federation (ALFA), the major lobbying arm of the state's agribusiness and big landowning interests—and a persistent foe of tax equity, constitutional reform, and insurance regulation. ALFA sits atop a state insurance empire that generates untaxed millions of dollars in membership dues each year. ALFA money channeled through the organization's political action committee enables a statewide network to advance the group's causes and candidates. Not satisfied with the nation's lowest property tax rates, ALFA had mobilized in 1978 to further cap taxes and to base land assessments (such as vast timber holdings) on "current use" rather than market value. "The result," observed Wayne Flynt, "was incredible abuse of the system and chronic underfunding of schools."[76]

On Alabama Day 2003, the Alfans heard Rev. Evans preach that "in order to achieve the sort of environment we want in our state, we must . . . let go of our vested interests. The more we try to save ourselves, our standing, our economic advantage, our place of privilege, the more of our soul we will lose." Tempted by *Birmingham News* Washington correspondent Mary Orndorff to comment on Evans's sermon, Mike Kilgore, ALFA's executive director, said only, "I'm glad to be here to worship our Lord and savior. That's what I came for." Was that cathedral laughter welling from somewhere beneath Kilgore's feet?

The Alabama Day sermon echoed in the public voice of the state's largest religious denomination. Bob Terry, editor of the *Alabama Baptist*, reminded readers that two years earlier the state's Baptists had resolved that "the governor and the state legislature . . . develop and implement appropriate tax reform." Writing that "the welfare of Alabama citizens is at stake" and invoking the storm-tossed albatross image, the religious weekly listed the familiar categories in which the state sat at or very near the national bottom: social well-being, education, environmental protection, treatment of prisoners, and so on.[77] This litany had appeared in newspaper editorials and op-ed columns regularly for years. What was new was the wave of hope that accompanied Riley's early months in office and the run-up to the September 9, 2003, statewide vote on his modest package of revenue-raising proposals bundled together as Amendment One.

"Unlike the federal government, our state constitution requires us to have a balanced budget by October 1," Riley told the special legislative session convened on May 19 to produce his tax package. "We cannot balance our budget with cuts alone, not unless we are willing to lay off thousands of teachers and cancel all extra-curricular activities, open prison doors and put convicted felons back on the streets, and force thousands of seniors out of nursing homes and take away their prescription drugs. These are not scare tactics — this is reality — and I cannot, in good conscience, order such cuts." To square his action, Riley invoked the Gipper: "When Ronald Reagan was first elected Governor of California, he faced a similar crisis. When asked why he was raising taxes, he replied, 'Because I have no other choice.' Neither do we."[78]

Repeating often that while in Congress he never voted for a tax increase, Riley, through singleness of purpose and horse trades with strategic interest groups, shepherded a tepidly progressive, overly complicated package of income and property tax hikes through the legislature that, if approved by a majority of statewide voters, would raise some $1.2 billion. The money would address the looming deficit as well as support public education. Riley conceded that Alabama had been too often and too long on the wrong side of history. "We can for the first time in our 184-year history create a state worthy of the decent and moral people of Alabama."[79] It was a remarkable admission for an Alabama governor.

"RAT HEAD IN THE COKE BOTTLE"

At the time of Amendment One's legislative passage in early June, a poll found the public solidly in opposition.[80] Riley, however, felt he could win over enough Alabamians by September's statewide vote, just as he had sensed — although with much more time and money to work with, and less history to overcome — that as a little-known member of Congress, he could take the governorship. Through the spring and summer, he spent much of his freshly minted political capital campaigning for Amendment One. He shocked and divided his own party of whiteness into business-first, new economy conservatives versus old-economy, social and cultural conservatives. He startled, confused, and inspired numerous Democrats.

Riley's initiative attracted a different sort of international attention to Alabama for his statements that Christian responsibility to the poor fell heaviest upon those elected to public office. "The Governor of Alabama has said that the Bible inspired him to propose the largest tax increase in the state's history," wrote the *Times* of London. "Bob Riley, a Republican, has called for a $1.2 billion tax rise to bridge inequalities between rich and poor. 'Jesus said one of our missions is to take care of the least among us,' he said. 'We've got to take care of the poor.'"[81] Down home, the Alabama Christian Coalition, a significant political force in a state where over 90 percent of its citizens claimed to be Christian, fiercely disagreed: the poor had themselves to blame for their poverty; charity and minimal welfare assistance could take up the slack for the handful of deserving poor. The church should attend to saving souls and not be distracted by wondering if the state's tax structure itself might be iniquitous.

"In the coming weeks and months," Governor Riley had announced at the May opening of the special legislative session, "Alabama will witness a spirited debate over its future unlike any held in generations."[82] That debate never developed. Opponents of the amendment shorthanded it to the "tax increase" and fomented a swell of distortion and distraction that the governor and his disorganized supporters couldn't turn back. With a well-financed publicity campaign, opposition forces singled out parts of the multifaceted tax proposal with which to scare ordinary Alabamians, while they raised the specter of legislative corruption, and that old bugaboo: deep distrust of Montgomery politicians.[83]

Major "Vote No" opponents included the state Republican party chair and most of the party's steering committee as well as many of the corporate, timber, big-farming, and landowning interests that helped put Riley in office, including the Alabama Farmers Federation (ALFA), Gulf States Paper, and SouthTrust, a regional holding company that at the time held the largest assets of any Alabama-based bank.[84] Wallace Malone, SouthTrust's CEO, pandered fear by claiming Riley's plan "very probably will result in the loss of 30,000 jobs or more."[85] Former U.S. House majority leader Dick Armey, co-chairman of the right-wing Citizens for a Sound Economy, arrived to agitate the ranks of the wealthy and raise the threat that tax increases would keep manufacturers from locating in Alabama.[86] Local talk-radio cousins of Limbaugh, Hannity, and Beck hammered away. Many more white Alabamians pleasured in Birmingham-based, syndicated radio good ol' boys Rick and Bubba than ever cracked a Rick Bragg book to read a wrenching, personal take on the Heart of Dixie's animus toward critical thinking.

In the weeks prior to September 9, Susan Parker was one of many volunteers who traveled across Alabama speaking to small audiences and civic groups, trying to rally support for the referendum. Parker, a popular Democrat, had won the state auditor's job in 1998, ran unsuccessfully as the first woman nominated for an Alabama U.S. Senate seat against incumbent conservative Republican Jeff Sessions in 2002, and would, in 2006, be elected to the state public service commission.

As she campaigned for Amendment One, Parker pondered one of the most intractable Alabama problems. Why would low- and middle-income voters be against a plan to decrease their tax burden and provide their children with better educations? Polling done shortly before the vote suggested 52 percent of Alabamians in opposition. But in the least supportive group, only 22 percent of households with incomes between $20,000 and $40,000 favored the Amendment. Among black voters, only 32 percent said they would vote for the plan.[87] Parker found this "astonishing," concluding from conversations with people who attended her talks that the problem lay in the deep historical distrust by Alabamians "in our government and in our elected officials." Feeding this distrust in the current campaign was the bombardment of negative media ads against the tax package "paid for by groups like ALFA and the timber corporations, who have a vested interest in the failure of the plan."

"As a little girl," Parker wrote in an op-ed essay, "I remember George Wallace saying that we should give those government bureaucrats a good barbed-wire enema. It's no wonder then we have difficulty understanding that government is 'we the people' not 'they the enemy.'"[88] Distrust of another sort stirred among black Alabamians who doubted anything progressive could come from a governor of what had become the white people's party.

On board with Riley were the state teachers' union (AEA), the major newspapers, new technology businesses, and manufacturers with desires for a more educated workforce, Alabama Power, and the antipoverty coalition Alabama Arise.

According to UA law professor Susan Pace Hamill, whose close analysis and moral indictment of the tax structure put the biblical phrase "the least of these" into the political conversation, Riley's plan, modest as it was, represented a "monumental first step" toward the "genuine reform needed to bring Alabama into the twenty-first century."[89] In her widely quoted 2002 article in the *Alabama Law Review*, "An Argument for Tax Reform Based on Judeo-

Christian Ethics," Hamill and a team of law student researchers detailed how Alabama's constitution, with its constrictive revenue raising rules, imposes "the greatest burdens on the poorest Alabamians while allowing the wealthiest Alabamians to avoid paying their fair share."[90] Hamill, a United Methodist who devoted a sabbatical from teaching law to directing the tax study, came down hard on religious leaders' responsibility to protect the poor.

Challenging the piety of politicians and the politics of the pious, Hamill charged that "individuals claiming to be part of the People of God can no longer complacently tolerate Alabama's tax structure," which she assessed as "the worst in the whole country."[91] Dedicated to "Alabama's children . . . the most vulnerable and powerless segment" of the state's population, Hamill's study, one of the most remarkable research projects in recent Alabama history, exposed how a combination of income, sales, and property taxes "not only economically oppresses the poorest and most vulnerable Alabamians, but also denies the children of these families a minimum opportunity to seek a better life."[92]

Hamill's *Argument for Tax Reform*, which soon appeared as a paperback in Alabama bookstores and steadily attracted international attention, directed its strongest condemnation at the state's property tax structure (the nation's lowest rates) and its major beneficiaries, the large owners of forestland. Alabama, with more than 22 million acres of forest, was a leading wood-products producer, yet all other southeastern states collected property tax at a rate two to four times higher. With trees occupying over 70 percent of Alabama's land area, taxes on timberland comprised less than 2 percent of all property tax income. Hamill's research established that large landowners, pine plantations, and paper companies had so rigged the game that Alabama's tax structure "fails to meet any reasonable definition of fairness and violates the moral principles of Judeo-Christian ethics."[93] In urging that the elimination of a tax system oppressive to "the least of these" must be the true measure of Christian polity, Hamill's footnote-filled jeremiad challenged a religious right accustomed to claiming the moral high ground. Yet, as she pointed out, even if voters approved Riley's Amendment One, tax rates for large landowners and well-off households wouldn't change dramatically, and property tax assessments would remain among the nation's lowest.

"It's because we've never had the level of excellence in education and state government that we should," Governor Riley told a rally of five hundred

Amendment One volunteers in June 2003; "convincing ourselves we can do it, that might be the hardest part."[94] With the September 9 vote identified as a "defining moment" for the state and Governor Riley, the summer should have brought the spirit of camp meeting revivalism channeled into tax reform evangelism. But the pro-amendment leadership did a poor job in reaching or persuading the Alabamians who stood to be the real winners of the referendum. Critical to the outcome were church members, the voters who had doomed Don Siegelman's lottery. Mainline Baptists, Episcopalians, Presbyterians, and United Methodists had backed tax reform in general terms a few years earlier, but they were slow to mobilize for Amendment One.[95] All the while the Christian Coalition was ramping up holy opposition.

In response to an ALFA-backed campaign suggesting Riley's tax plan would doom the family farm, the *Anniston Star* editorialized: "Of all the 'special interests' that have thrown around their political muscle and PAC money in an effort to shape the state in their own image, few have been more callous in their disregard for fair play and corporate citizenship than the Alabama Farmers Federation and its equally greedy cohort the Alfa Insurance Co." The *Star* estimated that there were fewer than five hundred farms in Alabama exceeding two thousand acres — "the point at which the current use assessment will be replaced by an assessment based on fair market value. Shame on you Alfa."[96]

African American voters, nearly a quarter of the state's electorate, played a major role in absence as much as in support. Solidly Democratic, they had voted against Riley in the previous year's general election, but like everyone else, now did a double-take over his reformer's tone and referendum. In a scene that performed another reversal of what George Wallace had represented, Governor Riley, speaking in Selma in August, asked a gathering of black religious leaders to think of the tax reform amendment as comparable to voting rights marchers' crossing of the Edmund Pettus Bridge in 1965. "Just as that group came together and would not take no for an answer and moved across that bridge and literally changed this state, changed this country and to a large extent changed this world," said Riley, "there's another bridge to cross, and that bridge is going to be staring you straight in the face September 9."[97]

Why should black Alabamians trust a Republican governor? Riley's veto of a bill speeding the return of voting rights to ex-felons angered many of the state's black leaders and advocacy groups and revealed a historical blind spot the governor claimed he wanted to overcome. Rev. Manuell Smith III, pastor of Rising Star Baptist Church in Sylacauga, told a reporter he would vote no because "If it [the tax package] passes, he'll disrespect the black caucus as long as he's governor."[98] Going into the final week, the "Vote Yes" campaign grasped for *American Idol* winner, Ruben Studdard, whose sweet style of soul singing poured southern comfort on black and white alike as he headlined "Believe in Alabama" concerts in Mobile and his hometown of Birmingham.

A vicious *Wall Street Journal* editorial in late August accused the governor of "aping the worst kind of liberal demagoguery" and of going back on his March state-of-the-state pledge: "I will not entertain the idea of additional taxes until we reform the policies and practices that have created the problems we face today." Oblivious or callous to the state's historical underfunding of basic services and the perennial fiscal crisis, the *Journal* preached from its pulpit of privilege: "We're not sure where the Bible comes down on tax-and-spend politicians, but we have a pretty good idea of what it says about people who break their word."[99]

Riley's Amendment One failed badly. The summer campaign suffered from lack of mobilization by congregations, by grassroots organizations, by popular personalities who might have rallied working-class white support. Where were the nearly 100,000 AEA members? Susan Hamill spoke tirelessly at many "faith-based" events around the state, but a campaign song in a familiar drawl by the country band Alabama would have done more to mobilize the natives. And the churchy crowd? "Riley got precious little help from the ranks of the faithful," Robin DeMonia wrote in a *Newsday* retrospective. "While almost all major denominations support tax reform in principle, few pastors were willing to get out front on Riley's package as they had [in opposition] on the lottery."[100] Ultimately, a ninety-day sprint didn't pose a threat to entrenched antigovernment, antitax habits of judgment appealed to by anti-Amendment forces.

"If Bob Riley loses his attempt to raise taxes," blustered Grover Norquist a few days before the vote, "he will be humiliated and it will teach Republicans at the state level they can't get away with it."[101] The referendum defeat became monitory fodder for starve-government forces in many locations. "Across the nation," claimed Jack Kemp, co-director of the right-wing think tank Empower America, "voters are refusing to play enabler to their political leaders' spending addiction, and they are rejecting efforts to raise taxes . . . . California voters threw Gov. Gray Davis out of office in part because he couldn't resist raising the car tax. . . . Alabama voters rejected Republican Gov. Bob Riley's tax-hike referendum by more than a 2-to-1 margin. Seattle voters repudiated a tax on cups of coffee by a similar margin."[102] Antitax extremists tossed the Amendment One loss into an eclectic fear-bag of incomparable items (autos to lattes) with which to threaten any candidates or elected officials advocating any revenue increases or efforts at tax equity. And Riley? A danger to the Republican brand, he took vicious hits from the right wing. "Coca-Cola spends a lot of its time making sure there are no rat heads in Coke," said Norquist in one of his nastier rants. "The problem with the governor of Alabama is, he was a rat head in the Coke bottle."[103]

Faster than an Alabama snowflake, Riley's transformational moment melted by late summer 2003, about the time that NASCAR fans, sunburnt and beer-soused, filled the Talladega Superspeedway grandstands. Ultimately, it was their loss, the blue-collar Dixiehearts whom the Amendment One forces failed to reach.

GO DAY, COME NIGHT, GOD SEND HYUNDAI

A chastened Bob Riley set about salvaging his governorship by shifting attention away from the disregarded, by dangling huge tax breaks and incentives to incoming companies (German steelmaker ThyssenKrupp received $811 million), and by retreating into hackneyed, turnip-blood pledges to cut government waste and improve efficiency and accountability.[104]

As Alabama remained at or near the bottom in so many indices of social well-being, Governor Riley led the competition against other southern states to lure foreign manufacturers' auto assembly plants with hundreds of millions of dollars of long-term tax breaks, land giveaways, and non-union labor.[105] Resources used to entice automakers might have gone toward creating the "superior public education system" that Riley in his inaugural speech had pledged would be his "top priority."[106] Instead, inflated hopes rested on an imported, motorized salvation and the vagaries of auto sales. What if the state were to make the sort of all-out commitment to public education, from pre-K through college, that it musters for migrating manufacturers? Or to recruit and adequately pay talented teachers? What if the next generation of Alabamians were to gain analytical skills and technical competencies that taught them how to succeed in the global economy, rather than how to assemble this year's model?

Governor Riley pitched the value of education more than any Alabama governor since Jim Folsom. He was proud of the Alabama Reading Initiative (ARI), which he trumpeted as "a transforming moment in the state of Alabama." ARI trained teachers to improve student reading levels, drawing national attention and emulation in other states — an unprecedented Alabama feat.[107] Fully implemented in only one hundred of Alabama's approximately eight hundred K–3 schools in 2003, by 2009 the program had reached every school.[108] Yet without the political will or budgetary commitment to sustain and extend the initiative into upper grades, and to expand a nascent initiative in math, science, and technology, what would keep this "transforming moment" from becoming a lost moment as children became teens?[109] Even as the ARI took hold, Alabama fourth-graders remained among the nation's lowest scorers in national reading achievement.[110] Nor did the governor propose ways to enable the poorest Alabamians to attend college.

Bob Riley's version of operating Alabama like a business didn't repeat the blunders of prickly, Bible-thumping, belligerent Fob James. His two terms would be characterized by administrative efficiency and the absence of serious charges of corruption. That counts as a remarkable achievement in Alabama. Advised by Birmingham businessman Bill Cabaniss, a former legislator and ambassador to the Czech Republic, Riley deployed a cabinet of retired corporate execs. Touting "a wealth of experience," he tapped the experience of the wealthy. Drayton Nabers, a Princeton- and Yale-educated ex-insurance company CEO, began as Riley's finance director and would serve for a time as the state supreme court's chief justice. Nabers, who had clerked for U.S. Supreme Court justice Hugo Black, "appears to be committed to a lot of the things that the good government crowd is for," observed Birmingham-Southern College political science professor Natalie Davis, "such as tax reform, education reform and constitutional reform." For transportation secretary, Riley called upon a former executive with Alabama-based construction company Blount International. He persuaded a retired athletic equipment executive to serve as revenue commissioner. His chief of staff (and former campaign manager) came from the conservative Business Council of Alabama.[111]

As Riley put a corporate face on chief advisers and agency heads, he took steps toward recasting a few of the most egregious features of the Alabama imaginary. Some acts were symbolic — attending a commemoration of black students' efforts to desegregate the University at Tuscaloosa. It would take time to discover whether others were substantive — the creation of a Black Belt Action Commission for the region of the state with the lowest median income. Through appointments, grants, and promises, Riley's Republicans also hoped to chip away at the Democratic solidity of the black vote but met with little or no success.

Along with the state's Republican congressional delegation, including U.S. senators Shelby and Sessions, Governor Riley's gravest mistake in judgment was his gung-ho endorsement of the invasion of Iraq in March 2003. "It's certainly justified," he asserted at the war's inception. "What Americans have to remember is that after 9/11, today we have a moral right to remove a threat to this country wherever it exists." Riley's knee-jerk patriotism fed into the Bush administration's offensive of falsehoods and distortions. "If we have an opportunity to preemptively remove a threat," argued the governor (although there was no threat to the U.S. from Iraq), "it is much better than reacting afterward. I think that is what the president is doing tonight. . . . This is about protecting America."[112] Except among the state's black population and a minority of whites, Riley's unquestioning support of the disastrous Iraq war bolstered his popularity.

By the time another gubernatorial campaign season loomed, opposing forces seemed entrenched and determined, given Riley's thin 2002 victory margin and his failed effort at tax reform. "Governor's Race Shaping Up as Must-see Politics," headlined veteran AP correspondent Phillip Rawls, who anticipated the primary contests being "every bit as memorable" as any in modern Alabama history. He set the cast of characters:

> A Republican incumbent who alienated his base with a tax hike plan. A chief justice who lost his job over his Ten Commandments stand. A former governor under a racketeering indictment. A lieutenant governor who helped her ex-husband run for governor twice.[113]

More prescient was Samford University political scientist Randolph Horn, who predicted that Riley would use his incumbency to roll over a faltering Moore in the primary and move on with little trouble in the November election: "He's done a competent job. He hasn't embarrassed the state."[114] How long since even this faint praise could apply to an Alabama governor?

Moore's collapse as a viable political candidate suggests that a grandstanding theocrat can burn a bridge too far. A court composed of retired state judges had removed Moore from office in November 2003 for resisting a federal order to dislodge his Commandments monument from its place of prominence in the state judicial building. When Moore entered the governor's race in 2005, he pitched his rhetoric in distinctive Wallaceite tones, attacking familiar targets and vowing to "stand up" for Alabama:

> As our taxes continue to rise, the education of our children seems to decline. And at a time when morality seems to be disappearing, our courts are preoccupied with telling children they can't pray and telling public officials that they can't acknowledge the God that is the source of our morality. . . . The time has come for us as a people to stand up and to return the government of Alabama back to the people.[115]

As Moore's confrontational tactics drew upon the cultural model of the Little Fightin' Judge, perhaps his loss to Riley helped disperse the raging, shadowboxing specter of Wallaceism as an effective political style. Wallace had launched his Dixie diatribes with the rhetoric of states' rights and threats of "barbed-wire enemas" for federal judges, but whenever one of these jurists, famously native son Frank Johnson, ruled against him, The Guvner bitterly ceded the point of law to the execrable feds while playing to the home crowd. True-believer Moore pushed beyond states' rights to claim divine right. After some reflection, this didn't sit well with everyday Alabamians.

"I have never and will never use faith or my belief in our almighty God for political motives," asserted Bob Riley as he opened his reelection campaign amid friends, contributors, and rare, vintage motorcycles at the Barber Motorsports Museum east of Birmingham.[116] It was common knowledge that Riley held weekly Bible study sessions in the governor's office and talked to groups of preachers about witnessing for Christ, but the sanctimonious Moore so out-holied Riley as to be mistaken for Hazel Motes, Flannery O'Connor's street-corner shouter in tongues, pastor of the Holy Church of Christ Without Christ. Neither the coattails of Wallace nor Moses could deliver Roy Moore.

As for the Democrats and their approaching 2006 primary, ex-governor Siegelman remained hobbled by his and Richard Scrushy's corruption indictments and looming federal trial. It was a rainy day that had settled in for a season. Lucy Baxley dispatched Siegelman. Heading into the November general election, "I Love Lucy" signs went up along the roadsides, but Baxley, age sixty-eight, and the former wife of erstwhile liberal hope Bill Baxley, although likeable in the manner of a touring country music queen, was known mainly for her indistinctiveness. She called for an increase in the minimum wage and climbed aboard the Democrats' disingenuous attack on Riley's early months of courage when he pressed his revenue amendment.[117]

ALABAMA GHOSTS AND RILEY

In the 1960s and 1970s, the practice of Alabama officials' shirking their responsibilities of governance by kicking controversy into the federal courts became known by the name given to it by one of those judges, Ira DeMent: "the Alabama Punting Syndrome."[118] A primary receiver of Alabama's punts was federal judge Frank M. Johnson Jr., a champion of fundamental fairness for marginalized and historically oppressed groups who blasted the political leadership in Montgomery. "A state is not at liberty to provide its citizens only those constitutional rights it feels it can comfortably afford," wrote Johnson in 1979. "State government must begin to accept responsibility for its constitutional obligations. When a state fails to accept these obligations . . . people are deprived of their rights; the judiciary is overburdened; and even those in state government necessarily lose some of the flexibility and some of the authority of the office that is entrusted to them by the people they represent."[119]

During the second half of the twentieth century, so many of Alabama's responsibilities to its citizens, especially to its children and its institutionalized populations, were punted into federal court as a result of lawsuits filed by courageous Alabamians, white and black, representing various classes of the maltreated, that the state ran largely by court order and Judge Johnson was known as the real governor.[120] A partial list of lawsuits included *Gomillion v. Lightfoot*, ending racial gerrymandering; *Newman v. Alabama*, mandating medical care for state prisoners; *Wyatt v. Stickney*, ordering minimal standards of care for mental health patients; *Lee v. Macon County Board of Education*, ending segregated school systems; *R. C. v. Hornsby*, forcing Alabama to take better care of abused and neglected children; and *Knight v. Alabama*, attempting to remedy segregation in higher education.[121] As they punted, Alabama officials demonized the federal judges they were forcing to take over the tasks of state government.

In 2000 *Governing Magazine* designated Alabama the "make me" state, "the federal court order capital of the country." "Federal judges," observed Jonathan

Waters, "are making the state do so many different things that the federal courts might as well be recognized as a de facto branch of Alabama government."[122] The state so adamant in its boasting of states' rights has for extended periods turned its primary responsibilities over to the feds. During his two terms as governor, Bob Riley took steps to detach Alabama from its sez-you relationship with federal courts, courts now populated by more amenable, Bush-era judges. Riley realized that decades-long legal resistance and the paying-out of penalties and lawyers' fees were expensive hobbies for a state unable to fund its own minimal functioning. And for the culture of business-first to take lasting hold, sez-you needed hushing.

"Alabama truly is on the cusp of magnificence," Governor Riley rhapsodized to a late summer convention of Alabama bankers in 2006, confident in his reelection momentum. It was a phrase he repeated often in the fall campaign. Riley spoke of how his appointment of business executives to positions of public authority was transforming the political good-buddy culture of Montgomery, but he warned that this was a "tipping point" moment that mustn't be lost.[123] In a couple of years, some of these execs, along with major Alabama banks, would fall past their own tipping points as the worst recession since the Depression took hold. The business model of life and government soon came into question, but not by Alabama's economic and political leaders.

Riley easily won reelection. Jim Folsom, hardly a chip off the paternal populist block but supported by black voters, white Democratic loyalists, and ticket splitters, prevailed in the lieutenant governor's race by a small margin over corporate lawyer and political newcomer Luther Strange.

Riley's second term continued his pursuit of manufacturers, although the state fell back from the "cusp of magnificence." The governor persisted in his attempts to change the state's imaginary. "Our mission here," he told hundreds of cocktail-partiers at an event sponsored by the city of Huntsville at the 2007 Paris Air Show, "is to talk about a new Alabama, a reformed Alabama. We still have a negative image to some people in the world. All we have to do is get them to Huntsville one time." The high-tech north Alabama city, site of Redstone Arsenal and the Marshall Space Flight Center, benefited from the aerospace and weapons procurement business to the annual tune of tens of billions of dollars of Pentagon money.[124]

The Riley administration tidied up costly, long-lingering federal lawsuits and consent decrees while avoiding corruption scandals and indictments.[125] But the big problems remained: tax inequity and revenue inadequacy; the urgent need for constitutional revision; underfunded public education and great disparities between the richest and poorest school districts; crammed prisons and unemployable inmates; and the resegregation of urban space.[126] These were not problems to be remedied by Riley's refrain of tax cuts and a strong work ethic.[127]

How far had Bob Riley strayed from his early intentions? Called to conscience by Susan Hamill's tax iniquity study, his comments from the spring of 2003 were quoted from New York to London: "Jesus says one of our missions is to take care of the least among us. We've got to take care of the poor."[128] Governor Riley had pledged to raise the nation's lowest property tax rate in support of basic social services, primarily education. Battered by the antitax, antigovernment onslaught from ALFA and the state chapter of the Christian Coalition, Riley stumbled away from the defeat of Amendment One and back into the fold of conventional, trickle-down Republicans.

"Until we make . . . fundamental changes, starting with the constitution," Riley had told the Samford University–based public policy research organization PARCA, in his 2003 Groundhog Day comments, "we're going to be having this debate ten, fifteen, twenty years from now."[129] Speaking to PARCA three years later, Riley said he favored giving "limited home rule" to county governments by changing the constitution, but offered few specifics. As for a constitutional convention of Alabama citizens, well, hemmed the governor, that "brings on a whole other set of problems."[130] Riley had advocated an item-by-item approach to constitutional change in 2003. "Constitutional reform," he had said then, strangely, "is like eating an elephant. You have to do it a little at a time."[131] Given time, the GOP elephant turned on and chomped away Riley's best motives.

Bob Riley left office as the most competent and diligent among southern Republican governors. But consider the field: the shrewdly sinister Mississippian Haley Barbour, self-aggrandizing Bobby Jindal of Louisiana, right-wing Christian grandstander Jeb Bush, Sonny "Pray for Rain" Perdue of Georgia. Even with his antibingo crusade, Riley served up no public humiliations like those of South Carolina's Mark Sanford, who made a righteous rejection of hundreds of millions of dollars of Obama administration stimulus money (overridden by the state's legislature and supreme court), then topped that by a sensationalized disappearance that led to the disclosure of an extra-marital affair with an Argentine television producer.[132]

Riley kept the interests of business first. When he argued against taking federal money for those hardest hit by the Great Recession, the governor said that it would require changes in unemployment insurance laws to include benefits for part-timers and for those who left jobs due to family emergencies, and that when the stimulus funds ran out in four or five years, employers would have to pay more into the state's unemployment fund. "It would be a tax on businesses in this state, and that I can't support," declared the man who had once promised to ride to the rescue of "the least of these."[133]

"Christianity," writes Slavoj Žižek, "calls upon us to thoroughly reinvent ourselves."[134] For a few months in 2003, good Baptist Bob Riley seemed a man on the road to Damascus and out of the Heart of Dixie. After political and economic sandstorms blew in, Riley found himself a few miles further down the road, but still Alabama bound.

Toward the end of Riley's final term, as he was chosen to chair the Southern Governors' Association, the state and national economy entered the Great Recession. Perennial underfunding problems roared back, abetted by the consequences of Alabama's low median income and its large share of workers in cyclical manufacturing, including the auto industry.[135] The state had the fourth highest per capita rate of bankruptcy filings in the U.S. in 2008. Its unemployment rate was the highest in twenty-five years.[136] The Birmingham metro region lost some 64,000 jobs in the two years following December 2007, and figured its real unemployment rate above 14 percent, including those who had given up looking for work.[137] Wilcox and Dallas counties, in the Black Belt, suffered rates of unemployment over 20 percent.[138] Even the state's infant mortality rate ticked up, after years of incremental decline.[139] The legislature cut education spending and drained the rainy day fund. A billion dollars from the Obama administration's economic stimulus package saved 3,800 teachers' jobs, yet Alabama's Republican congressmen and senators were among those who most vehemently opposed federal support.[140]

As it had when Bob Riley was elected in 2002, the 40 percent high school dropout rate remained the state's number one economic dilemma, insisted Steve Suitts of the Atlanta-based Southern Education Foundation (SEF). "Alabama will suffer consequences worse than other states when the recession ends," Suitts, a native Alabamian, predicted, "if it doesn't figure out a way to deal with the dropout problem."[141] Although high paying by historical Alabama standards, the manufacturing jobs created during the Riley years benefited comparatively few workers as the state's median family income and per capita income nudged upward but remained among the bottom dwellers.[142] Was automobile-chasing the best way to make headway? "Alabama can attract and grow new industries with good paying jobs in the decades ahead," concluded an SEF study, "only if it systematically keeps more students in school, provides them with affordable higher education, and helps them graduate from high school and college on time."[143]

With the state's reserve funds emptied, federal stimulus money dwindling, and proration calling, whoever followed Riley as governor, warned David Bronner, chief of the Retirement Systems of Alabama, would inherit a "financial problem that's of biblical proportions."[144] Where was the revenue to avert a billion-dollar shortfall for the state's Education Trust Fund and General Fund?[145] How long would Alabama continue to boast of the lowest personal and business taxes in the country, as if privation and punitiveness counted for more than the health, education, and welfare of residents? How long? So long as Alabamians kept whistling "Dixie" past the graveyard.

The decades-long migration of the white majority toward Republican dominance of Alabama reached historic dimensions with the 2010 midterm elections, when Democrats failed to win any statewide offices while losing both houses of the legislature for the first time since Reconstruction. Unreconstructed voters flocked to retired Tuscaloosa dermatologist Robert Bentley, a hidebound conservative perceived by many as a nonestablishment candidate in a season of political reaction, economic retrenchment, and more than customary levels of corruption. Given the recession's devastating effects and Bentley's pledge not to raise taxes, what was the most that Alabamians might hope for? Campaign ethics legislation? Piecemeal constitutional revision? A clutch of assembly-line jobs in a degraded labor market? The election of Bentley, with his laissez-faire, limited government, "right-to-work," antiabortion, and antigay habits of judgment, as well as his white mandate, portended yet another long season of whistling "Dixie" past the graveyard.

PART THREE

Stakes in the Heart of Dixie

A people cannot be surprised into a more
rapid progress than it wills.
        —VICTOR HUGO, *Les Misérables*

CHAPTER SIX

Black Alabamas

Black Alabama is not a third-rate reproduction of white Alabama. It's
a different culture. It almost has a different language. It has a different
appetite, a different menu.

    — J. L. CHESTNUT, quoted in "J. L. Chestnut, Lawyer and Author"

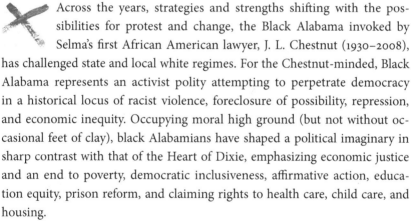 Across the years, strategies and strengths shifting with the pos-
sibilities for protest and change, the Black Alabama invoked by
Selma's first African American lawyer, J. L. Chestnut (1930–2008),
has challenged state and local white regimes. For the Chestnut-minded, Black
Alabama represents an activist polity attempting to perpetuate democracy
in a historical locus of racist violence, foreclosure of possibility, repression,
and economic inequity. Occupying moral high ground (but not without occasional feet of clay), black Alabamians have shaped a political imaginary in
sharp contrast with that of the Heart of Dixie, emphasizing economic justice
and an end to poverty, democratic inclusiveness, affirmative action, education equity, prison reform, and claiming rights to health care, child care, and
housing.

In his weekly newspaper column, "The Hard, Cold Truth," Chestnut called
to account white as well as African American political figures when he judged
their actions at odds with the best interests of Black Alabama. An incisive
commentator, Chestnut extrapolated the range of racial feeling in Selma to
make widely applicable judgments. At one end of a continuum of white attitudes, he pointed to the writers of unsigned letters to the editor who "hold
such extreme, foolish and racist views they are even careful about stating those
views in intelligent white company much less to blacks." He went on,

In the opposite direction, whites have sometimes privately expressed to me very positive views about racial integration that they could never afford to utter publicly. Then, there are some whites who put up false fronts to hustle potential black customers or black voters. Such fronts are relatively safe even in the South: however, any white person who steps beyond that front and establishes a genuine interracial relationship runs some risk of community censure, of being branded "nigger-lover" or a leftwing radical.[1]

Sought after as a public speaker for his candor and humor, especially after the publication of his co-authored autobiography, *Black in Selma*, Chestnut traveled widely, soaked up opinions and conversations, and never withheld his opinion. He expressed revulsion for Republicans such as Georgia native Clarence Thomas and Birmingham-born Condoleezza Rice, both of whom he felt had betrayed African Americans. Thomas, nominated to the high court by George H. W. Bush in 1991, had not paid his "civil rights dues," had opposed affirmative action when he directed the Equal Employment Opportunity Commission during the Reagan administration, and reminded Chestnut of those among "our slave ancestors who achieved emancipation, but not liberation." Thomas's appointment was also opposed by other voices of Black Alabama, including Chestnut's longtime law partner, state senator Hank Sanders, and state representative Alvin Holmes. "Unless Clarence Thomas has made a great change, as Saul did on the road to Damascus," insisted Holmes, "he is not the person to be on the Supreme Court. If he's against affirmative action — that's the reason he's where he is today, he's against everything to benefit blacks."[2]

APPROACHING THE BLACK BELT

The heartland of Black Alabama remains the Black Belt, a largely rural region of African American insurgence that has effectively taken over the meaning of the term from older senses and other geographies. For disenfranchised and oppressed black citizens of this multicounty swath of west central Alabama, Supreme Court decisions and congressional actions during the 1950s and 1960s accompanied a regionally based movement for political and civil rights. Places such as Tuskegee, Marion, Selma, Montgomery, Hayneville, and Eutaw became pivotal sites in the U.S. freedom struggle. At lunch counters, in city parks and courthouse squares, in registrars' and sheriffs' offices, and on the highways and streets, Black Belt Alabamians challenged the spaces and climate of segregation.

In the 1820s and '30s, the Black Belt identified a strip of rich, dark, cotton-growing dirt that drew immigrants from Georgia and the Carolinas in an epidemic of "Alabama Fever." Following the forced removal of Native Americans, the Black Belt emerged as the core of a rapidly expanding plantation area. Geologically, the region lies within the Gulf South's Coastal Plain in a crescent some twenty to twenty-five miles wide stretching from eastern, south-central Alabama into northwestern Mississippi. An unusually fertile Black Belt (or Black Prairie) soil, extensively eroded by historical agricultural practices, is produced by the weathering of an exposed limestone base known as the Selma Chalk, the remnant of an ancient ocean floor. Half of Alabama's enslaved population was concentrated within ten Black Belt counties where the exploitation of their labor made this one of the richest regions in the antebellum United States. During these "flush times," Black Belt river commerce centered around the cotton-transformed towns such as Montgomery, Selma, Demopolis, and Tuscaloosa and boosted the port of Mobile.

Proslavery, secessionist sentiment in the Black Belt led Alabama into the Confederacy in 1861. Following emancipation and the South's military defeat, African American men first went to the state's polls in 1867 and briefly held a variety of local, state, and national political offices. With the mid-1870s, however, came the restoration of white rule. Then, "for a hundred years," wrote J. L. Chestnut, "the Black Belt dominated state politics and the big landowners dominated the Black Belt."[3] Through violence and terror, appeals to white supremacy across class lines, and massive voter fraud, the Black Belt's oligarchs led the 1890s defeat of the Populists and inscribed their power in the racist and penurious cage of the state constitution.

The large presence of African Americans in the Black Belt during the antebellum era and the expansion of the Cotton Kingdom throughout the southern states produced a second meaning of the term as a broad area with majority-black population. In the first half of the twentieth century, years of soil erosion, the boll weevil invasion, the collapse of cotton tenancy, the failure to diversify economically, the urban exodus, and the repressive era of Jim Crow all combined to mire the Black

Belt in a disastrous decline. What had been one of America's richest and most politically powerful regions became one of its most distressed and ineffectual.

Black farmers had limited prospects in the modern Alabama Black Belt as, over successive decades, cotton fields ceded ground to vast pine tree plantations. Politically, the region's elites kept their hands on the levers of state politics through an inequitable structuring of legislative power based not on the population of electoral districts — the rural Black Belt steadily lost population to the state's cities — but on an inherited control over the apportionment and geographical distribution of representatives. This arrangement was not cracked until *Reynolds v. Sims* (1964), the one-person, one-vote decision argued before the U.S. Supreme Court by Birmingham attorney Charles Morgan Jr. As Brian Landsberg has detailed at length, Department of Justice litigation undertaken on behalf of disenfranchised Alabama blacks "provided the foundation" on which the 1965 Voting Rights Act was built.[4] The promise of fair reapportionment combined with the Civil Rights and Voting Rights acts to sustain the struggle for freedom and political justice in the Black Belt. Federal legislation, enforcement, and litigation eliminated a variety of strategies — poll taxes, literacy tests, registrar intimidation — used to disenfranchise black voters. Grassroots activists mobilized registration and election campaigns that drew national attention, put scores of African American candidates into office, and raised the expectations of social equality.

In 1967 Macon County, with an 80 percent black population, elected the South's first black sheriff since Reconstruction, Lucius Amerson, a Korean War veteran. Amerson's victory built upon years of groundwork by the Tuskegee Civic Association.[5] On July 29, 1969, in a special election ordered by the U.S. Supreme Court, four African American candidates of the National Democratic Party of Alabama (whose names had been intentionally left off the regular election ballot by a white circuit judge) won places on the five-member Greene County Commission. Also in Greene, in November 1970, Tom Gilmore was elected sheriff and William McKinley Branch became the South's first black to be elected probate judge.[6]

In nearby Lowndes County during the pivotal 1970 elections, John Hulett, a co-founder of the Black Panther Party, took the sheriff's office, a seat of historical racist terror.[7] "'Bloody Lowndes,'" writes Hasan Jeffries, "had always been a dangerous place for African Americans, but during Hulett's first term in office

. . . he not only ended police brutality, but also stopped random acts of racial violence perpetrated by ordinary white citizens."[8] The unflinching Hulett dared to arrest white lawbreakers.

During the 1980s Alabama's population grew only about 4 percent, insufficient to add a new member of Congress to the state's seven, but with the African American population above 25 percent, a minority representative or a lawsuit loomed, perhaps both. "There is nothing wrong — and a lot right — with having a black-majority congressional district," begrudged the *Montgomery Advertiser.* "But lawmakers should not twist and gerrymander such a district into creation simply to accomplish that end."[9] In 1992 a panel of federal judges in Mobile drew a new district, 67 percent black, that joined much of the Black Belt with a portion of metro Birmingham.[10] Voters elected Earl Hilliard, Alabama's first African American member of Congress since Reconstruction. Also in 1992, in the Black Belt, Barron Lankster became the state's first black district attorney.[11]

In the decades following the 1960s, African Americans in the Black Belt took charge of county commissions, sheriffs' offices, municipal governments, and school boards. They elected black mayors, state representatives and senators, and majority-black city councils. Black tax assessors discovered how pale predecessors frequently assessed African American property higher than comparable white property.[12] Lawyers at the Chestnut and Sanders firm in Selma successfully defended black activists in federal voting rights cases, dismantled at-large election districts, and won a class action suit against the U.S. Department of Agriculture that resulted in more than a billion dollars in payouts to tens of thousands of black farmers for years of discrimination in federal loan and support programs.[13]

Out of the Black Belt freedom movement also emerged youth organizations, a historic farmers cooperative, a regional festival of music, food, and the arts, as well as black-owned businesses and media.[14] Yet except for a few municipalities, segregated education continues as the norm, fed by white abandonment of public schools for private academies. Despite the efforts of the black legislative caucus and scores of local officials, economic democracy in the Black Belt remains thwarted in tapping the resources of a region that generates and concentrates wealth for a landowning white elite of individuals and corporations. Fast-growth pine tree plantations, cattle pastures, leased deer camps, and hunting preserves cover the Black Belt like the dew, their owners benefiting from the nation's most regressive property tax structure.

"The problem with the property tax, of course, like everything, goes back to race in Alabama," Republican state chairman John Grenier candidly told Howell Raines in 1990. "I think probably whites feel like they own the property, and the property tax goes up, and the proceeds will go to blacks."[15] Into the twenty-first century, Grenier's comments sting. So much in the Heart of Dixie turns upon deep structural inequalities, historical racism, and antidemocratic presumptions.

That the transformation of dominant social structures and institutions of economic power hasn't followed upon winning elective offices in the Black Belt calls democracy itself into question. Did a movement run out of collective steam? Do the persistent arrangements loom too large? "Democratization," insists Iris Marion Young, "requires the development of grass-roots institutions of local discussion and decision making. Such democratization is meaningless unless the decisions include participation in economic power."[16]

Writing about the difficulties of sustaining the grass-roots movement of social change in Lowndes County, Jeffries has lamented the "failure on the part of the advocates of freedom politics to execute the viable political program that they had devised."[17] Yet he also realizes that even if a once-emblematic figure of freedom politics such as Sheriff John Hulett ultimately turned to corruption and bossism, it was not an inevitable trajectory. While some black politicians took advantage of their new positions for personal gain, others pressed the public interest along new, widening paths. Although the long movement toward justice has not yet translated electoral victories into equivalent economic power, the clout of the Black Belt's legislative delegation, and that of the Alabama Black Legislative Caucus, has kept education, health care, and quality of life concerns in front of a generally retrograde body of state lawmakers. Gaining a foothold in the economic institutions that concentrate the Black Belt's wealth — whether local electrical cooperatives or transnational paper companies — remains a daunting prospect, as does gaining the authority to sufficiently tax large landholdings. "Investment and land use," adds Young, "will often cause or reinforce oppression when they are dominated by private corporate interests."[18]

As the Black Belt took on its new political incarnation, drawing national attention, African American breakthroughs bumped up against the barriers of undemocratic institutions, both private and public. In 1965 James Smith and Willlie L. Strain became the first African Americans employed by the Alabama Cooperative Extension Service (ACES), an education and outreach organization created around the time of World War I as a way to bring applied university research, mainly in agricultural and food practices, to rural, then eventually urban areas. The two men had been posted at Tuskegee in a "Negro unit," as it was called, prior to the 1964 Civil Rights Act. So that the previously all-white Extension Service program wouldn't lose federal funding, Smith and Strain were transferred in. Soon they became plaintiffs in a class-action suit that resulted in a 1971 ruling from federal judge Frank Johnson finding Alabama's Extension Service guilty of racially discriminatory practices and ordering employment in ACES to approximate the percentage of the state's African American population. The next hurdle was promotion discrimination, and Smith and Strain returned to U.S. district court in 1991 to show how they had been passed over for higher management and supervisory positions in favor of less qualified and experienced whites. Of the ACES's 147 specialists at the time the new suit was filed, only 3 were black.

"I can't believe that we are still facing this in 1991, but we are," said Dr. Smith, extending his criticism beyond Auburn's good-ol'-boy ACES network to the university's governing board. "The problem here is at the top," he insisted. "The people at the top have not made the effort to bring in more blacks. The Board of Trustees has never clearly articulated a very forceful commitment to affirmative action at the university."[19] Auburn's head trustee and effective boss during these years was Bobby Lowder, whose father, Ed, had worked with the extension service before starting the Alabama Farm Bureau Insurance Company (which grew into the right-wing lobbying bully ALFA). The younger Lowder's autocratic rule at Auburn did enormous damage to the university's academic reputation. "Whether because of his obsession with football," commented Wayne Flynt, "or his determination to recast the school according to his own inaccurate and myopic understanding of a what a land-grant university ought to be, Lowder has used his political influence to pack the board with trustees beholden to him."[20] When the Southern Association of Colleges and Schools put Auburn on probation in 2004, it cited Bobby Lowder's meddling across a range of university activities. Lowder wove a web of financial and ethical conflicts between Auburn trustees and his Colonial Bank operations before he was ultimately forced out during the bank's Great Recession collapse. Such are the encumbered, ol' boy relationships that resist democratization and inclusion. Yet sometimes, the Lowder they are, the harder they fall.

In 1997 David Wilson, then associate provost at Auburn, sounded a persistent theme in an op-ed essay: "If our state does not tackle its intractable problems, its social, cultural and educational future will mirror the present. Alabama today is still dealing with many of the same problems that confronted it at the turn of the century. I call these the Big Five — taxes, education, racism, poverty and leadership." Wilson, African American and a child of a Black Belt sharecropper's family, wrote about attending a one-room schoolhouse with a potbelly stove for heat. This was in the 1970s, not the 1930s. "I do not wish the experience I had growing up in Marengo County on anyone. It should be illegal to put children in this state through the trauma and cruelty I had to endure growing up here. . . . It is an act of pure luck that I was able to escape those conditions." Luck and considerable talent.

As for contemporary Alabama, Wilson wrote of white children enrolled in segregated academies while African American children continued to attend "county schools where little or no education is taking place." "Is anyone listening to the cries of children in this state?" he demanded. "Is anyone concerned about the uncommonly high rate of illiteracy in Alabama? Is anyone concerned about quality education, or the lack thereof, statewide?"

Wilson listed the familiar statistics: high levels of child poverty and school dropout rates, low per capita income. Who was addressing Wilson's Big Five? Not the governor at the time. "I wondered if Gov. Fob James lived in the same Alabama as I did when he said last year that there was no race problem in the state."

He called for Alabama leaders "who are culturally and socially diverse and not chosen because of the color of their skin, club membership or because he, and more often than not it is a he, is a 'good ol' boy.'"[21]

Wilson's coming-of-age trajectory led out of rural Marengo County to Tuskegee Institute and then to Harvard for a master's and doctorate in educational planning. With a sense of mission he returned to his home state to work at Auburn, committed to improving the educational prospects of all Alabamians. In 1999 he supported Governor Siegelman's proposed lottery, seeing it "as a ray of hope for poor students," and was critical of religious denominations that, concerned about the sin of gambling, had organized in opposition. "The way we treat our poor," he wrote in an op-ed essay, "is a greater sin than gambling could ever be."[22] Only Alaska had a lower percentage of children from low-income families graduating from high school and going on to college.[23]

Over the course of ten years as an Auburn vice president, Wilson increased the university's outreach budget from $5 million in 1995 to $25 million. Before making his Alabama getaway. In 2005 Wilson announced his move to the University of Wisconsin to become chancellor of its two-year colleges and head of the UW extension system. His farewell statement expressed disappointment in Auburn and state officials: "My heart and work and commitment kept me here in Alabama, but I have been ready for a long period of time to give to Auburn and the state of Alabama greater leadership. I thought that opportunity would present itself here." The *Birmingham News* reported that Wilson "had been mentioned as a candidate in several presidential searches but had stayed in Alabama, hoping to move up in the ranks in his home state." The Auburn higher administration and board of trustees failed David Wilson. Undoubtedly, attempting to work with the commodity groups in agriculture that form the core of the right-wing Alabama Farmers Federation was also a frustrating assignment for an African American who grew up poor in the Black Belt and sought to change that experience for a younger generation.[24]

THE LONG SEZ-YOU

In 1985, during the last George Wallace term as governor, Johnny Reynolds, an African American employee of the Alabama Highway Department, became the courageous first plaintiff in a federal lawsuit challenging racially discriminatory practices in hiring and promotion. The state fought the suit, not agreeing to settle until 1994, and then failing to meet the terms of a consent decree worked out under the authority of Judge Myron Thompson. One of two African American federal judges appointed in Alabama by Jimmy Carter, Thompson was taking his turn receiving Alabama punts. White employees added to the litigation's contentiousness and complexity, complaining that their own promotions were being stymied by the unresolved complaint.

By 2003 attorneys' fees, court fines, consultant costs, and outside contractors' fees in *Reynolds v. Alabama* approached $200 million. "I think every day of my life that this thing is going to be over today. But it never is," lamented Johnny Reynolds, who had become a Department of Transportation district engineer.[25] "This thing is completely out of hand," said newly elected Bob Riley.[26] The governor brought in Joe McInnes, a retired executive vice president of construction giant Blount International with a quarter-century of corporate experience, to head the Department of Transportation. Four years and tens of millions of additional dollars later, near the beginning of Riley's second term, Alabama finally satisfied the hiring practices and promotion goals of Thompson's consent decree. A department of some four thousand employees, once rife with cronyism, whiteness, and nepotism, was now 35 percent black, including 31 percent of the DOT's professionals.[27] Johnny Reynolds didn't make it to his fiftieth birthday, dying before settlements began to be paid to the plaintiffs. To the end he believed the heart attacks he suffered stemmed from the stress of the overhanging lawsuit and the hostility he had fielded for years at the DOT.

As grievous as Reynolds's passing was the murder of African American DOT accountant Freddie Golthy of Grove Hill in July 2001. In a case exposing persistent, racially based workplace resentments, Golthy, age fifty-three and one of the *Reynolds v. Alabama* plaintiffs, was killed by sixty-year-old Marvin Graves, a retired DOT employee who had engaged in a bitter, ongoing argument with Golthy about the *Reynolds's* discriminatory practices legal settlement. Marvin Graves's son Daniel, a DOT civil engineer, had transferred to Birmingham after black workers at Grove Hill complained about his habit of carrying to the office a cell phone with a Confederate flag cover on it.[28]

Suggestive of the deep habits of judgment entwined around this murderous incident, Daniel Graves had hired attorney Kirk Lyons, known for his ties to white-supremacist groups, in a fruitless attempt to challenge the DOT ban on Confederate items in state offices. In an EEOC complaint, the younger Graves claimed that since his national origin was southern American, he was being discriminated against. His confusion was understandable. The Confederate battle flag remains iconic for many white Alabamians and is embossed on dozens of items in the gift shop in the state capitol in Montgomery.

At the Golthy murder trial, prosecution documents and testimony revealed an underlying history of racial slurs, physical attacks, and near-lynching that Freddie Golthy had experienced seventeen years earlier when he had first worked at the Grove Hill DOT office. He had returned there reluctantly, for a promotion and pay increase. Golthy's wife, Mary, was a member of the Grove Hill City Council and an equal employment opportunity officer at the DOT office. "He didn't want to go back," Johnny Reynolds told the *Birmingham News*. Golthy and Reynolds had become friends shortly after the 1985 suit was filed. "He cried about going back. He said, 'Johnny, I really don't want to go back. But that's where they want me — I guess that's where I have to go.'"

In April 2002 a jury of four blacks and eight whites found Marvin Graves, deacon and former Sunday school teacher at Thomasville's Pineview Baptist Church, guilty of Freddy Golthy's murder. He was sentenced to twenty-five years in prison. How tragically and inextricably the worst habits of judgment still hold some number of white Alabamians in thrall.

PROM NIGHT

In 1994 the hamlet of Wedowee, in rural, predominantly white, east Alabama, drew the sort of national media attention that reinforced the "what do you expect?" reflex. In a student assembly at Randolph County High, Principal Hulond Humphries declared that rather than allow interracial couples to attend that year's school prom, he planned to call it off. Principal Humphries was reported to have told junior class president Revonda Bowen, a prom organizer, "Your mom and daddy made a mistake, having a mixed-race child."

Humphries, principal for twenty-five years, had been written up in a 1989 U.S. Department of Education civil rights report for maintaining racially segregated buses and for his "disparate treatment of black and white students" in disciplinary matters. The Randolph County school board suspended Humphries and the prom went on. Perhaps things *were* different now. "Slowly, quietly, relentlessly, often painfully," wrote *New York Times* columnist Bob Herbert, "integration continues its advance, its long and terribly difficult walk away from fear and backwardness."[29] Then backwardness danced back onto the floor.

With strong white parental support, and a four-two vote, the school board kept Humphries as principal. The board's only black member resigned in protest, and several black parents withdrew their children from Randolph High and sent them to classes held in local churches. "Reports are that federal mediators have now arrived in Wedowee," wrote syndicated columnist and Auburn graduate Rheta Johnson, "proving that not that much has changed since the 1960s when giant Mossbacks walked the Earth. It still takes 'federal meddlin', as George Wallace used to say, to see that blacks are taken seriously — as students, taxpayers, people."[30]

The months passed in Wedowee with Klan rallies and African American protest marches and national news media drifting in and out. In early August a suspicious fire destroyed Randolph County High, and Principal Humphries was dismissed after he tried to chase away a black Birmingham TV photographer. A jury of eight whites and four blacks found the only person tried for setting the fire, a young African American man, innocent. Former principal Humphries was tasked to oversee the rebuilding, and in November 1996 was elected school superintendent in this white majority county. "It's frustrating," said Wedowee mayor Tim Coe of his town's reputation. "I can go to Chicago, or wherever, and they will have heard of us, and it will be only because of that."[31]

The battle over prom night in rural east Alabama provided one of those I-told-you-so moments reconfirming for outsiders that the Heart of Dixie thumps beneath a thin skin of civility, where narrative motifs congeal in still-unbroken molds.

ALABAMA'S "THIRD WORLD"?

"I am hardly a Southerner in the classic sense," insisted the venerable J. L. Chestnut in his mid-sixties. "Indeed, I believe only white people qualify for the dubious title. Black people have been little more than a displaced people here, and we now reject so much of what the white South holds dear."[32] Chestnut's reservations about southernness remain common in Black Alabama. "I'm a Southerner, too, as Southern as funeral home fans, collard greens and Ray Charles," writes Cynthia Tucker. "But my love is neither irrational or uncritical."[33]

Tucker was born in 1955 in Monroeville, at the southern edge of the Black Belt. Her parents "grew up in land-owning families who worked small plots for subsistence in fertile territory east of the Alabama River." Her ancestors, "as far back as I can trace them, tilled the soil of the Deep South, first for white slave owners and later for themselves, eventually owning property that they left to their children and grandchildren."

After graduation from college (her father from Tuskegee, her mother from Central College in Pella, Iowa), Cynthia Tucker's parents did not become part of the southern out-migration, but returned to their home region. Her mother became a high school English teacher who hoped that the *Brown* decision would lead the children of her daughter's generation into desegregated public education where resources and opportunities would improve. It didn't work out that way. As Tucker later wrote, "using the court's language of 'all deliberate speed' as an excuse to do nothing, Alabama continued its system of second-class schools for black students until the early 1970s."[34] The creaky wheels of deliberate speed accounted for less than the determination and optimism of Tucker's parents combined with her own talents and ambition to land her at Auburn University. Having written for the campus *Plainsman* while she majored in journalism and English, she was ready for a reporter's job at the *Atlanta Journal* in 1976.

Tucker's career took her to the *Philadelphia Inquirer*, then back to the *Journal* as an editorial writer and columnist. She held a Nieman Fellowship at Harvard in 1988–89, became editorial page editor of the *Atlanta Constitution* in 1992, and a few years later was writing two columns a week for the combined *Atlanta Journal-Constitution* as well as making appearances as a commentator on national television news programs. In 2007 she won the Pulitzer Prize for editorial writing, and in 2009 moved to Washington as an AJC political columnist. Tucker's is the exceptional story, as she honed her critical talents to write for a large readership about major social and political issues of Atlanta, the South, and the U.S. Following regular trips back home, she continued to protest and lament the lost potential of black children caught in underfunded and resegregated Alabama public schools.

To take the measure of change in the rural Deep South, Tucker often compares memories of her childhood with fresh gleanings from trips to the Alabama town famous as the setting for *To Kill a Mockingbird* and to the counties surrounding Monroe. On a 1990 visit, she and her mother talked with a black couple who had retired to a 110-acre Butler County farm after years of working in Detroit. The return-migrants reported a white population accommodating to middle-class African Americans. White racial intimidation and violence seemed rare. Their daughter had married a "down-home white Georgian" at a Valentine's Day ceremony on the family farm. On the other hand, reported Tucker, "the white administrator of a nearby federally funded clinic treats the black physician with disdain and withholds from poor black patients federal funds they should be getting for prescriptions."[35]

That the rural Black Belt is a poor region consisting of poor counties full of poor black people has been fixed in the Alabama imaginary for generations.

"Once the heart and soul of Alabama when cotton was king and plantations dictated a different way of life, today the region is among the poorest in the nation," wrote the Black Belt's most indefatigable reporter of the late twentieth century.[36] True, the Black Belt holds a larger percentage of its citizens in poverty than any other swath of counties in Alabama. And it presents the greatest disparity between rich and poor. But it also has wealthy inhabitants, wealthier absentee (individual and corporate) landowners, and broad tracts of vastly underassessed and minimally taxed forests. The Black Belt, home to some of the poorest U.S. citizens and with counties having among the highest infant mortality rates in the country, is a region that generates wealth for the few. The poverty of a third of its population is sustained by unjust structures of land ownership and taxation embedded in the state's constitution. "If we ever expect to be in a position to take care of ourselves properly, we must raise property taxes," concluded newly elected African American officeholders such as Greene County Commission chairman Garria Spencer.[37] It's an authority that counties don't possess. Despite the political takeover of the Black Belt, economic leverage remains weak. "Democratization is meaningless," Iris Young writes, "unless the decisions include participation in economic power."[38]

As John Gaventa concluded years ago about Appalachia, anywhere that some are wealthy while many are poor, "we must assume the presence of injustice and identify the institutions, structures, and practices which sustain it."[39] Popularly, the Black Belt is depicted and imagined as home to the undeserving, unemployable poor, a place beyond the pale, dragging down the rest of the state. A longtime African American activist in Greene County called the region "a scar on the underbelly of the state." The perception, repeated, helps shape the Alabama imaginary. "The scar is familiar to the rest of the country," writes the *Birmingham News*, "for it is laid bare periodically in prominent national newspapers and magazines. The image is often seen in movies, read of in books. For many across the nation, life in Alabama is indistinguishable from life in the Black Belt."[40]

In the Alabama Black Belt, wrote the *Economist* in a 2003 essay, "more than half the people are black; and almost everyone is poorer, unhealthier, less well-educated and with worse jobs than those in the rest of the state. Almost half the counties have 12 percent unemployment or higher. Median household income in the Black Belt is more than $10,000 less than Alabama's average, and life expectancy nearly two years shorter." As it puzzled if, and how, the region might find its way to a better future, the *Economist* noted, as such journalistic forays typically do, that newly recruited industries, such as auto manufacturers, avoid the Black Belt, but that economic developers were "optimistic, advertising a loyal workforce largely untouched by unions — and plenty of tax breaks. The state has also promised worker training and other forms of aid." This, the *Economist* concluded, "could be the best way to break the Black Belt's cycle of poverty."[41] The *Economist* didn't acknowledge the deep, interconnected social structures sustaining injustice: the region's vast, untaxed land and timber wealth, the constitutional straightjacket on local revenue, and the state's inequitable funding of school districts.

For decades, manufacturers have been loath to locate here, offering reasons that boil down to some variation of racial logic. "We found that when you got over 30 percent black population," a regional director of the Alabama Department of Economic and Community Affairs (ADECA) told reporters, "you would tend to get a unionized plant. So most of the businesses just didn't look at an area that was over 30 percent black."[42] Potential manufacturers cited reasons ranging from the low educational levels and skills to inadequate infrastructure and fears of worker unionization. Or worse. In the mid-1980s an economic development worker in Wilcox County asked a state official why so few industrial prospects visited the Black Belt. He was told, "You've got too damn many niggers down there." The authors of a five-part *Atlanta Journal-Constitution* series on the southern Black Belt wrote that "the same axiom has applied for half a century: The blacker the county, the more likely business will bypass it."[43]

The AJC writers heard another familiar refrain from white state officials: that the Black Belt's majority African American population were apathetic about their situation and unlikely to change. "I don't know what to do for that area," said another ADECA official. "I don't think those areas care themselves sometimes."[44] "Those areas" sounds a lot like "those people."

Starved for jobs and lacking in clout, the Black Belt has found itself sited for speculative ventures. The region has hosted prisons, dog-racing tracks, and catfish farms. The Tennessee-Tombigbee Waterway, an Army Corps of Engineers boondoggle on a grand scale, took advantage of the geophysical location by digging and dredging major rivers, then building a series of locks allowing passage between the Gulf of Mexico and the Ohio River. All of the region's infrastructure (schools, hospitals, etc.) could have been newly built from the ground up for the cost of the Tenn-Tom. Through a land sale beyond the control of the people of Sumter County, Chemical Waste Management sited and built the nation's largest toxic waste dump in the Selma Chalk near the Mississippi state line in Emelle, Alabama.

Had the image of the Black Belt and its economic circumstances changed by the end of the twentieth century? In 2002, a team of *Birmingham News* reporters combined extensive statistical research with in-person reporting to produce an important series with a provocative title: "The Black Belt: Alabama's Third World."[45] In writing about the Black Belt at least as far back as the 1930s, journalists and travel writers have approached the region as anachronistic, a vestige of the Old South, detached from modernity. The circumstances that have led to the depiction of the Black Belt as a world apart from the rest of Alabama, its majority black residents as abject, are frequently mystified by omitting the connections between their ongoing plight and the deep historical structures that Black Belt landowners cemented into place back at the beginning of the twentieth century. The *News* series' strength lay in documenting the extent of concentrated land ownership and the effects of unjust property tax structures, in bringing to wider attention "an illegal dual school system in Greensboro," and in making vivid the impoverishment and desperation of most black Alabamians who live in the region. But the Third World analogy projected a place exotic, detached, and beyond comprehension, "a world so foreign to many Alabamians that it might be another country."[46] In describing its series, the *News* lapsed unreflectively into "our state's Heart of Darkness,"[47] as if the Black Belt were a strange hinterland and not inextricably entwined with Alabama's capital city, Montgomery — which straddles east and west along the historical Black Belt — and the political power vested there, from the planter-instigated constitution to the state's retrograde system of taxation. The inequities and widespread poverty that characterize the contemporary Black Belt are fundamental to the state's larger structuring of inequality, evident in both the depopulated countryside and the extremes of urban centers. While hunting camps and weekend farm retreats give testimony to how affluent city residents make use of Alabama's "Third World," many inner-city blocks of Birmingham have more in common with Black Belt locales than with the upscale neighborhoods closer by.

Because one of the secret strengths of concentrated economic power in Alabama is the obscurity of who owns what, some of the most important work by the *News* team involved the examination of nearly 150,000 property tax records for ten Black Belt counties to determine the specifics of absentee ownership. "Almost two-thirds of all land in the region is owned by people or companies located outside the county lines. And . . . more than two-thirds of the land qualifies for a tax break that lowers the taxable value of property by $1.1 billion. In Lowndes County, bordering on Montgomery County and the state capital, 78 percent of the land is owned by people and companies outside the county. . . . Perry and Macon counties are close behind. . . . More than a quarter of Bullock County's land is owned by people who don't even live in Alabama."[48] Who, then, is responsible for the desperate plight of public schools, for the poverty of the Black Belt?

The *News* determined that 1 percent of Black Belt landowners owned more than half of the region's land. The largest, a collection of timber and paper companies headed by Gulf States Paper, International Paper, Weyerhaeuser, Rayonier Woodlands LLC, and McMillan Blodel, claimed some 679 square miles, 10 percent of the region. Under Alabama's "current-use" tax structure, land is assessed on an estimate of the value of timber or crops produced, not on the land's market value or potential use. And the tax rate for Alabama timberland is the lowest in the U.S. The *News* reporters drew upon and confirmed the work of UA law professor Susan Hamill.

Not only does Black Belt timberland get an unjustifiable tax advantage, but the vast acreages leased to deer hunting clubs are also not taxed at a rate that represents the real worth of the land for hunters. Hunting doubles the value of timberland, but not the assessed value.

"The lure of the deer, the quiet nights and the taste of the rustic life," wrote the *News*, "have led wealthy residents from Birmingham, Mobile, Tuscaloosa and Montgomery to snap up property across the Black Belt, using the land for hunting lodges and weekend getaways." These country lodges of rusticated escape exist alongside the residences of some of the poorest citizens of the state. A Birmingham attorney who had bought three thousand acres of timbered Lowndes County and built a weekend cabin and lake told reporters, "It's a complex problem that there are no obvious answers to. It's really, really tough."[49]

In fact, it's a simple problem with an obvious but intractable solution, tangled for more than a century in the state's constitution and tax restrictions, and before that in the political economy of the Black Belt's plantation power.

AS POWERFUL AS ANYPLACE

For all the stars that fell on Alabama, the North Star pointed a getaway for many African Americans. What good could come from staying here? In a place where reporters and researchers find an ecology of despair and underdevelopment, those who have passed much of their lives in the Black Belt and whose political revolution has remapped the "terrortory" reflect upon the reasons why they stayed. In one of his weekly newspaper "Sketches," Hank Sanders recalled the compelling conviction that landed him and his wife, Rose, both fresh from Harvard Law School, in the Black Belt, where they would partner with J. L. Chestnut to create a powerhouse law firm and base for political activism.

> Back in 1971, Rose and I could not decide on a place to settle down and practice law. After we visited and or otherwise explored all obvious options, I suggested we visit Selma. Rose objected vehemently. Her father's brother, Jethro Gaines, had lived in Selma and every visit had left a bad taste. However, my feelings were strong enough for me to visit Selma by myself.
>
> I drove from Huntsville where we both worked at the Madison County Legal Aid Society helping poor people. I drove to Montgomery and then took U.S. 80 west to Selma. I did not have a specific destination in Selma because I had not made any arrangements. I crossed the Edmund Pettus Bridge, traveled one block to Alabama Avenue, turned right and traveled one block to Washington Street. At that moment the feeling became overwhelming. I knew this was the place I must cast down my life bucket and draw from the stream of struggle. I just knew it.
>
> I could not explain the feelings. I did not feel I could say to Rose, "I just have these feelings." I took other objective evidence and tried in vain to convince her. After Rose and I could not agree on coming to Selma, we made a deal: I would choose our living location for the first five years and Rose would go regardless of the place. Rose would choose our living location for the second five years and I would go regardless of the place.[50]

Long-settled in Selma, five years going on forty, Sanders wrote in 2005 of great expectations for the newly created Black Belt Action Commission, an initiative of Governor Bob Riley, prompted in part by the *News*' 2002 Black Belt series.[51] Sanders acknowledged ancestors who ran away from the plantation, evaded the slave catchers, crossed rivers and swamps. "They . . . could always get back on track by locating and following the North Star. Our North Star is our vision. For the Black Belt Action Commission (BBAC), that vision is a transformed Black Belt in key areas of life. If change is going to come, we must have a shared vision that keeps us moving toward a new modern-day freedom."[52] In his mid-sixties when he made these comments, Sanders, along with his wife, Rose, had committed their adult lives to pressing the aspirations of Black Alabama against racism and formidable economic realities. The BBAC, created by a Republican governor, had come as a surprise. Not that it would tempt many blacks to vote Republican. But it was one among several unexpected moves by an Alabama governor unthinkable in the administrations of Fob James and Guy Hunt. And although Don Siegelman had gestured in the Black Belt's direction, there was "little evidence he accomplished much," concluded the *Decatur Daily*.[53]

The moving democratic horizon requires tactics for all occasions and institutions for passing along political skills, historical consciousness, and purpose. Since the mid-1980s, the 21st Century Youth Leadership Movement (21C), an offspring of Alabama New South Coalition (ANSC), has developed county chapters to enlist African American youth in leadership training, to teach political solidarity, and to tend the historical memory. Encouraging young blacks to stay and work on Alabama problems, 21C conducts summer leadership camps and a yearly mock legislative session in the Alabama House chamber in Montgomery.[54]

A lightning rod for political controversy, Rose Sanders helped create 21C. Among many tasks, Sanders (who later changed her name to Faya Rose Touré) wrote and directed musical plays performed by high school students that addressed topics such as teenage pregnancy and racially biased student tracking. In a keynote address at the 2005 ANSC convention held at Alabama A&M in Huntsville, Malika Sanders, daughter of Rose and Hank, surveyed the mission of her generation "to make real the promise of democracy in Alabama and in America. . . . Young people are moving. We are working for environmental justice; extension of the Voting Rights Act; to end tracking in our schools and education systems; and to fight racism everywhere it manifests itself.

"We must fight for decent health care, affordable housing, good education, a fair justice system; we must fight across the board for justice. We must move from a movement for civil rights to human rights. We must work across cultures in a genuine way to build power. We must dismantle white racism."[55]

Rhoda Johnson, a former 21C board member, graduated from Tuskegee in 1968, went to graduate school at the University of Michigan and the University of Alabama, where she became a faculty member and chair of the Department of Women's Studies. Johnson, whose research includes the study of minority women in the rural South, has worked to improve Black Belt public schools. Johnson represents the ideal of a 21C volunteer, observed Hank Sanders, a person who "continues to reach back as she moves forward," supporting the upcoming generation by emphasizing "community focused rather than individual focused" leadership.[56] With the aging and passing of the 1960s civil rights generation, the 21st Century Youth Leadership Movement provides a way to sustain the memory of the long revolution while identifying the next generation's steps toward social equality and democratic inclusion.

"Some of the strongest views on race," concludes Hank Sanders, "are coming up in a new generation of young folks. You can go into a restaurant or a store and see kids working together, but when they leave Hardee's, or J. C. Penney's, or Kentucky Fried Chicken, the whites go back to their community and to their world. And the African Americans go back to their community. They go back to separate social, educational, political, and other kinds of institutions. And the question is how to be able to bridge it. We can't hardly afford one education system. How can we afford two? We certainly cannot afford two political systems. Racism is such a powerful force in this country, you have to always be jumping on it with both feet just to be able to hold it down, hold it in check. But it's been such a force in our history. How do you overcome it in an area like the Black Belt where it's as powerful as anyplace?"[57]

BLACK ALABAMAS

By 1992 Alabama counted 706 elected black officials, more than any other state.[58] In 2008 there were more than 800 from a variety of black-majority jurisdictions, beneficiaries of voter mobilizations and redistricting successes as the long movement for social justice moved from the streets to the ballot boxes and courtrooms. The black voter registration rate now equals or exceeds that of white Alabamians. And, in proportion to their percentage of the state's population, in 2010, blacks held 8 of 35 state senate seats, and 27 out of 105 house seats. The increasing number of black Alabamians in political life has created outspoken alternative and oppositional voices to whiteness-as-usual, affecting practical matters from road paving to police behavior, child care to elder care. County courthouses have transformed from places of fear to sites of public participation. Through their votes as members of municipal, county, and state political bodies, in speeches, writings, media interviews, in demonstrations and marches, litigation, official acts, and commentary, black Alabamians have undone political normalcy.

The reputation of the state morphs slowly and not without reason, its flagrant demeanor having been racist and reactionary for so long. In more than a century, only two African Americans have won statewide elective office, and only after each one was first appointed to that office by a governor.

The visible presence of black elected officials in local governments has meant more than a seat at the welcome table for divvying up public monies and services. It has served to redress large grievances and daily indignities. The white mayor of Huntsville can't say to a black councilman, "I'm not going to let you get uppity any more," without a lesson in racist etymology. "I have never heard that connotation associated with the word," apologized Mayor Loretta Spencer, "and certainly would not have said it, had I been aware of its background."[59] This counts as Alabama progress.

On the fourth Monday of each April, state offices close for Confederate Memorial Day. On the fourth Tuesday in April 2007, after weeks of effort, the Alabama House and Senate passed a resolution apologizing for slavery. During the debate, Republicans fretted and balked. "What I have a problem with is apologizing for something I didn't do," said Rep. Jay Love from Montgomery. "Opposition," noted AP writer Phillip Rawls, "came from white Republicans who expressed concern the resolution would be used to seek reparations." "Nobody in this state can call me a racist," said Charles Bishop, the major opponent in the senate.[60] Instead, he declared himself "somebody who hates to see lawyers take advantage of the General Fund of the state of Alabama and suck it like a leech."[61] Senator Hank Sanders reminded Bishop of a moment in the early 1980s, when both men were new to the legislature. Bishop had called Sanders "big boy," nearly provoking a fight before he apologized, saying he didn't realize calling a man in his forties "boy" was, as Sanders put it, "a legacy of slavery."[62]

To secure passage, the slavery apology's sponsors, Mary Moore in the house and Sanders in the senate, included language expressing "the intent of the Legislature that this resolution shall not be used in any form of litigation."[63]

Former Alabama state senator Charles Steele of Tuscaloosa, who now served as president of the Southern Christian Leadership Conference, suggested that southern state resolutions of apology might lead to such reparations as scholarships and job training.[64]

"It's been a long time coming," said house sponsor Mary Moore from Birmingham, evoking Sam Cooke's 1960s ballad of change. The resolution nudged against the perception of Alabama. "We have an opportunity for people to start looking at us differently because of this."[65]

The house approved the apology resolution by voice vote. In the senate, where names were taken, no Republican voted in favor, no Democrat voted against.[66] Governor Riley said he would sign the resolution "in a heartbeat," and did. Following the lead of Virginia, Maryland, and North Carolina, Alabama became the first Deep South state to authorize this official expression. "I believe that the resolution helps us to stand on our history of slavery," concluded Hank Sanders, "rather than having it stand on us."[67]

With increased black political participation came heightened personal ambitions, rivalries, jealousies, corruption, go-it-aloneness, betrayals, generational differences, and resolute contrary opinions that thwart any monolithic Black Alabama. Black legislators, councilmen, and commissioners began to share temptations once reserved for white public officials and found themselves caught in sleaze, kickback schemes, and malfeasance, sometimes removed from office and imprisoned.[68] The emergence of rival political organizations as well as intragroup conflicts and maneuverings also testified to the lessened threat to political survival for Black Alabama. Daily dramas from around the state involved factions, betrayed loyalties, deal making, and shifting alliances that await their historians.

In a statewide organizational meeting held in Birmingham in January 1986, revolting against the strongman style of Alabama Democratic Conference (ADC) chairman Joe Reed, a group of black leaders including Chestnut, Hank and Rose Sanders, Richard Arrington, and Michael Figures began the insurgent Alabama New South Coalition (ANSC).[69] The ADC, the state's most powerful African American political organization, had endorsed candidates and advanced the cause of black electoral participation since its 1960 founding. Over the decades, the ADC under Reed's leadership seized upon leverage provided by federal voting rights laws to effectively draw all manner of election lines — from local school boards to the state legislature — creating winnable, single-member districts for African American candidates.[70] That black representation in the Alabama legislature came to accurately reflect the state's African American population percentage owed much to Reed's shrewdness, courage, and tirelessness. Candidates, black and white, appeared before the ADC convention knowing that the organization's endorsement brought with it the machinery to mobilize large numbers of black voters.

A student leader at Alabama State in the 1960s, Joe Louis Reed became a teacher, then rose to be the head of the Alabama State Teachers Association. When the ASTA merged with the white teachers' organization in 1969, Reed became second in command in the fiefdom of Paul Hubbert's Alabama Education Association — one of the state's most formidable lobbying groups.

Although a critical breaking point between the two black political organizations was the ANSC's support of the presidential candidacy of Jesse Jackson in contrast with the ADC's endorsement of Walter Mondale, the split was also based upon the participatory democracy promised in the new organization and upon its broader vision of action. "We felt there was a need for another black organization — one that was interested in economic development, the youth, education," said Michael Figures, "not just politics." Figures, a Mobile Democrat, was the first black president pro tem of the Alabama Senate. "We had seen," he said, "during the Jackson campaign that while ADC was strong in Montgomery and the Wiregrass, it had little support in Mobile, Birmingham and the Black Belt. Instead there were local black organizations in those areas that operated on their own. Our intent was to form a coalition of these groups. That's what we have done and that's where our name came from."[71] There seemed neither intended irony nor awareness of the origins of the phrase "New South" among late-nineteenth-century white supremacists in places such as Atlanta, Richmond, Louisville, and Birmingham.

The Alabama New South Coalition grew out of the 1985 Campaign for a New South, a grassroots political organization credited with the successful election of African American candidates, including legislators Hank Sanders and Lucius Black. As described at the time in the *Greene County Democrat*, the Campaign for a New South was "an umbrella organization for many of the recently activated local county civic league organizations." The local groups grew quickly during the Jackson-for-President effort; then, according to acting chairperson Rose Sanders, the campaign turned into a "re-vitalization program that encompasses a continued struggle for basic rights, and to also move on the questions of economic development, preservation of our cultural heritage, education and motivation of our youth and equity in the distribution of jobs, benefits and services among all classes and races of people."[72] Among its first activities, the campaign came to the defense of Black Belt activists being prosecuted by the federal government for alleged vote fraud, raising money for legal defense, and successfully opposing the nomination of federal prosecutor (and Selma native) Jeff Sessions for a federal judgeship.

Drawing strength and membership from different geographies, the ANSC and ADC became quite different black organizations. With the death by stroke of Michael Figures in 1996, his wife, Vivian, assumed his place in the senate and consistently won reelection. New South relied on a number of stalwarts and leaders, and opened itself to a diversity of personalities, ages, styles, and missions. As for the ADC, Joe Reed held tight to power and seldom shied from picking fights. For Reed, old habits couldn't die. "What black folks have got to understand is," he told Gwen Ifill for *The Breakthrough*, her book on new-generation African American politics, "if you were a warrior by training and a warrior by philosophy, you can't all of a sudden not be a warrior."[73]

In 2006 Reed used his power over a subcommittee of the state Democratic Party to attempt to deny the nomination of Patricia Todd, a white, openly lesbian winner of a party run-off for the state legislature, because she was not black. Todd had won election by fifty-nine votes over a black candidate in this majority-black district of Birmingham. To disqualify Todd, Reed, insistent that the district must elect an African American nominee, dug up a long-ignored party rule dealing with campaign finance reporting.

For national commentators, the incident became one of those here-we-go-again moments typical of the Heart of Dixie: the state Democratic Party was acting prejudicially against a gay candidate or against a successful white candidate in a black district. Understood down home, this was one more instance of Joe Reed being Joe Reed. "We here in Alabama have to take enough crap as it is from Democrats and Republicans alike in the rest of the country about being backward and hate-filled," e-mailed a Birmingham Democratic "foot soldier" to the *Atlantic* online.[74] "This is about Joe Reed controlling the party," Todd told the *New York Times*, "and trying to get his way, and he's just a bully."[75]

Reed's decision was overturned by the state party's executive committee thanks to votes by African American state representative Alvin Holmes and Reed's boss at the AEA, Paul Hubbert.[76] In 2007 Patricia Todd, associate director of AIDS Alabama, became the first openly gay legislator in a state in which over 80 percent of voters had just approved a constitutional amendment banning homosexual marriage.[77]

Joe Reed, who had grown up as a leader in the 1960s civil rights movement and who risked and did much to advance black electoral participation, had become, with the passage of years, an obstacle to inclusive democracy. Uncompromising in his unwillingness to relinquish hard-won personal power, he lost his seat on the Montgomery City Council, lost again when his chosen candidate, incumbent member of congress Earl Hilliard, was defeated by relative newcomer Artur Davis.[78] And, because he so strongly believed a black candidate could not be elected president, Reed backed Hillary Clinton over Barack Obama. The Alabama New South Coalition endorsed Obama, the popular favorite of black Alabamians.

"Joe and I, we're old men," acknowledged Alvin Holmes, who in 2008 was the state's longest serving black legislator, no one's understudy, and a close friend of Reed's since they were student activists together at ASU. "The new generation? Hell, they only know that Martin Luther King made the 'I have a dream' speech and they get a day off for his birthday. They don't know who Ralph Abernathy was, who Fred Shuttlesworth is, who Thurgood Marshall was, let alone who Joe Reed is. . . . They go more their own way, and I think Joe is having a hard time dealing with it."[79]

In a crowning embarrassment, Reed, in his seventies, saw his name chiseled off the Joe L. Reed Acadome, a 7,400-seat arena and the signature building on the ASU campus, his alma mater and where he'd been chairman of the board of trustees. A complicated story simplified, the erasure came from an autocrat's unyielding habits of judgment.

BIRMINGHAM: BLACK, BROKE, AND BADLY BENT

"Well, today I can tell you with confidence that there really is a move under way to combine many of the cities and towns in our area into one big city," wrote the *News*' Joey Kennedy on April 1, 2009. "Secret negotiations have been under way for months."[80] A photograph showed a consolidated Birmingham stretched to the horizon. The prospect of one regional government extending from the city's heart in all directions to encompass the burbs, including affluent Mountain Brook and Hoover, turned out to be Kennedy's April Fool's joke.

What makes the most civic sense seems furthest from realization in this metro region of unequal municipalities and neighborhoods expressive of extreme localism, fragmentation, resegregation, and vast differentials in wealth.

"Divisions by race, politics and geography have long held back this region and threaten our future," wrote columnist Eddie Lard in support of Kennedy's notion. "Ironically, many of the people who despise the city work in Birmingham and depend on it for their livelihoods." Land continued,

> UAB, in Birmingham, is the state's biggest employer, with many of those workers, if not most, living outside the city. Downtown, despite the hit the banking industry has taken, is still the state's financial center. Large companies such as Alabama Power, Energen and AT&T have their main offices downtown. Many other professionals — lawyers, accountants, architects, doctors, etc. — also work downtown.[81]

At the time, Jefferson County was effectively bankrupt from a self-inflicted sewer-finance deal that left the county flooded with rising and unpayable levels of credit swaps and overleveraged debt, unwinding months before the onset of the Great Recession. John Archibald relentlessly pounded the city and county's "divided, self-absorbed politicians." "Look at the Jefferson County legislative delegation," he wrote bitterly. "It is so split by party and race and ideology it cannot act even when the communities it represents are in peril. This year the Legislature failed to address Jefferson County's debt and the dead-and-gone occupational tax. What was it last year, the budget? Transit? I lose track of all the things that don't get done. There is always something. There is always nothing — nothing for the Birmingham area."[82]

City government in Birmingham had grown increasingly chaotic since the 1999 retirement of the city's first black mayor, Richard Arrington. A place so significant in shaping the historical meaning of Alabama steadily lost population as it lurched toward ungovernability, its politicians ineffectual, self-centered, often corrupt, and at cross purposes, its businesses losing momentum. The year Arrington left office, Birmingham was home to six Fortune 500 corporations; ten years later there was only one, Regions Financial, clinging to the 280 rung on the ladder.[83] Under CEO Dowd Ritter, Regions' stock had gone from a high of thirty-eight dollars a share in 2006 to under three dollars in early 2009 as billions in loans in Florida and Georgia went bad.[84]

Arrington, who first won election as mayor in 1978, built and commanded a formidable political organization, the Jefferson County Citizens Coalition.[85] He was strongly identified with increasing minority hiring and redressing the city's long record of police brutality against blacks. Arrington, writes Wayne Flynt, "won the support of the business community, renovated downtown, helped diversify the economy, helped develop the University of Alabama at Birmingham as the economic engine driving the city forward."[86] Yet the ever-whitening landscape beyond downtown was suspicious, often hostile. "During my nearly twenty years as mayor," Arrington reflects in his memoir, "I had found no elected official in the county government or suburban government who felt politically comfortable being allied with me."[87]

Mayor Arrington also felt stymied by his lack of official authority when dealing with the inept leadership of a Birmingham school system in steady decline. He observed that the city's board of education operated in fear of the Alabama Education Association (AEA). The AEA "was very good at protecting its members," writes Arrington in his memoir, "but I never learned what it did to improve the school system overall. The union would probably argue that education begins with the teachers, and I agree. But it also includes ridding this system of underperforming teachers and administrators." Arrington concludes, in a critique that has become central to contemporary Alabama's public education debate, "I was soon convinced that it was the poor teachers, poor administrators, poor lunchroom managers, poor janitors, poor bus drivers, and so forth who needed and relied on the union for job security. But the powerful AEA has such undue influence with Alabama legislators that no one dares oppose it."[88] The teacher-centric organization constructed over decades by Paul Hubbert and Joe Reed was becoming as much of an obstacle to school reform as a leadership force for improving education.[89] As recently as 2008, the Southern Education Foundation reported that there were "virtually no standards or incentives by which schools in Alabama are held accountable for student dropouts."[90]

When Arrington left office, he left no perpetuating political machine, no protégé. In his wake, latent factionalism, corruption, cronyism, and less devoted leadership rushed in.

The economic hub of Birmingham is UAB, especially its medical center, generating national headlines for pathbreaking health research and state-of-the-art therapies and replacing the city's former paleotechnic face of coal and iron. While scientists and biomedical specialists know UAB from its steady stream of discoveries and spin-offs, among sports fans Dr. James Andrews's Sports Medicine and Orthopedic Center gained celebrity for career-saving, orthopedic surgeries on college and professional athletes. "Every athletic trainer, physical therapist, strength-and-conditioning coach in the land," reports ESPN, "seems to have Andrews' cell phone number."[91] That UAB achieved so much with comparatively little state support led the *Montgomery Advertiser* to complain "that the state's political leaders haven't quite figured out that a research university . . . can be as important as a Mercedes or Honda automobile plant."[92]

Birmingham's Civil Rights Institute (opened in 1992), Kelly Ingram Park, Sixteenth Street Baptist Church, the Museum of Art, and Eddie Kendricks Park anchor a downtown cultural district remarkable for memorializing the city's role in the freedom struggle.[93]

In the years after Arrington, the Birmingham City Council and Jefferson County Commission, fraught with turf wars and irreconcilable personalities, became increasingly dysfunctional. Mayors Bell and Kincaid gave way to the flimflam vanity of cheerleader Larry Langford. In 2010 Langford, having been removed from office for accepting $235,000 in cash, loans, and gifts (watches, expensive clothing, plasma TVs) in exchange for $7 million of Jefferson County's sewer bond business, was sentenced to fifteen years in prison. Bill Blount and Al LaPierre, the white men who bribed Langford, had served, respectively, as chairman and executive director of the Alabama Democratic Party. Both received fines and prison terms.[94] It was yet more proof, like the conviction of Democratic governor Don Siegelman, of the need for clear, tough state ethics laws. "I hope that every elected official learns that you can't accept these kinds of gifts without the person wanting something in return," said Birmingham state legislator Patricia Todd.[95] Amid recession and stuck with over $3 billion in jerry-rigged bond debt — some of it resulting from the Blount-LaPierre deals — Birmingham faced its most calamitous crisis since the mid-1960s.

"Jefferson County is so far gone, so short-sighted and so filled with mind-boggling ineptitude," agonized the *News'* Archibald, "that it needs a receiver to run all county operations."[96]

Diane McWhorter's compelling narrative of Birmingham's civil rights battles of the mid-1960s ends with the trial in 2002 of Bobby Frank Cherry, the last of the Klansmen convicted for the Sixteenth Street Baptist Church bombing. In one sense, the trials of Cherry and, in 2001, of Thomas Blanton were public theater, closing acts for the long arm of justice and the city's reputation, but less relevant to Birmingham since the 1960s as whites steadily vanished from the Magic City into over-the-mountain suburbs. Birmingham's black population increased from 55.6 percent to 63.3 percent in the 1980s, to 75 percent by 2010, while its total population dropped from over 340,000 in 1960 to around 200,000 during the next half-century. More than a quarter of the city's people lived below the federal poverty line. Blocks of downtown seemed lost to drug-driven crime.[97]

Contradictions abounded. John Archibald pointed out that the Birmingham school system, once the state's largest, was soon to fall to sixth in size even as its bloated administrative costs — protected by cronyism, inertia, and the AEA — remained, by far, the highest in the state.[98]

While Birmingham and Jefferson County were losing residents across the decades, southward, over Red Mountain, white suburbanites were achieving spatial segregation and pledging allegiances to booming municipalities. Shelby, the state's fastest-growing county during these years (and 87 percent white in 2008), became the homeland of Republican upsurge.[99] Its population grew from 38,000 in 1970 to nearly 200,000 in 2010.[100] The squires of Shelby boasted million-dollar homes, gated "communities," and hunting preserves, and felt little or no allegiance to Birmingham.[101]

"Racially stratified metropolitan space remains a basic foundation for racial distinctions and for social inequality in the suburban south," observes Andrew Wiese. "In an era of increasingly subtle, covert, and, perhaps, fading discrimination against individuals, racial discrimination applied to the places where most African Americans live remains the most significant basis for racial inequality in the early twenty-first century."[102] Wiese's comments clearly apply to the Birmingham metro area and to other Alabama cities, whether Dothan, Montgomery, or Mobile. As for Birmingham, the outlying white municipalities share common interests with the heavily black city, including interdependencies of work, transportation, environmental quality, and health care. Lacking and needed is an effective regional government that can draw upon the wider tax base. One of Richard Arrington's major disappointments as mayor — and a foreshadowing of the city's still-unarrested crisis — was the failed, racially split 1998 vote on a package of metro-wide economic projects.[103]

"Issues of proper scope of the polity arise in just such situations," writes Iris Young, "when the scope of social and economic interactions does not match the scope of political jurisdiction." Young concludes: "The scope of a polity ought to correspond to the scope of relations across which obligations of justice extend. In many parts of the world with dense metropolitan regions this principle implies that the scope of politics should be regional." Rephrase Young's legal-critical language, and you'd have Joey Kennedy's April Fool's Birmingham. Then add layers of participatory democracy. "Regional governance is deeply democratic," insists Young, "only if combined with neighbourhood and community-based participatory institutions, many of which are differentiated by group affinities on a model I call *differentiated solidarity*."[104]

Young's proposals for broadening the democratic horizon through the participatory, differentiated solidarity of coalition building across various social groups complements the idea of proportional representation offered by attorney and legal theorist Lani Guinier. Guinier experienced firsthand white Alabama's entrenched resistance while successfully helping to defend Black Belt voting rights activists from partisan federal prosecution as pursued by U.S. attorney Jeff Sessions in the mid-1980s. In subsequent law review articles collected as a book, Guinier proposed a variety of remedies that would promote proportional representation of a polity's social groups as an alternative to the tyranny of the majority. "Democracy in a heterogeneous society," writes Guinier, using the example of race, "is incompatible with rule by a racial monopoly of any color."[105] Her proposals grew from frustration over the alienating effects of winner-take-all politics, the limitations that single-member election districts imposed upon the expression of contending group interests, and the inability of diverse minorities to participate in the governing institutions that affect their lives. Moving beyond the hard-won principle of "one person, one vote," both Young and Guinier call for more inclusive elective bodies to ensure the participation and representation of all of a polity's significant social groups in the major decisions that affect them. For contemporary urban areas that extend from the core of an older central city, regional governance would bring all interested parties to the table.

If the residents of metro Birmingham were to shape a polity to chase apartheid's specters and an economic restructuring based upon tax equity, Joey Kennedy's April Fool's proposal of regional consolidation would be a place to start, as well as a place to come home to. As of today, that prospect is about as likely as the citizens of Hoover renaming their city Shuttlesworth.

CHAPTER SEVEN

Baghdad as Birmingham

Nobody can go back and reinvent the past.

— CONDOLEEZZA RICE, on *CBS 60 Minutes*

What I would expect from Rice, however, is a better understanding
of the history of the civil rights movement and the lessons it taught,
or should have taught, the nation and the world.

— EUGENE ROBINSON, "Baghdad Isn't Birmingham"

Not even Bear Bryant, perhaps because he walked on water, could
boast of a million-barrel crude tanker with his name on it. But from
the mid-1990s until early 2001, the double-hulled *Condoleezza Rice*
floated on a rising tide that lifted some boats far more than others. Its youthful namesake, fresh from service on George H. W. Bush's National Security
Council, joined the Chevron board of directors in 1991, armed with her
knowledge of the former Soviet republics and the oil-rich Caspian region.
Republican, African American, female, and native of civil rights crucible
Birmingham, Rice was the public face of Chevron's public policy committee.
As for the *Condoleezza Rice*, she was a frequent visitor to West Africa, hauling
crude out of this region of multi-billion-dollar Chevron investment and making stops, according to reporting by Ken Silverstein, in "Nigeria's Niger Delta,
where continual oil spills have left the groundwater poisoned (and where a
Chevron-hired 'kill-and-go' security squad gunned down two protesters in
1998); in Angola, where Western oil money, often in the form of signing bonuses to the government, continues to finance a 25-year-long civil war; and in
the Democratic Republic of Congo . . . embroiled in its own brutal war."[1]

Highly paid for her corporate service, Condoleezza Rice unambiguously tied the global interests of U.S.-based oil companies with the national interest: "I'm very proud of my association with Chevron," she told Fox TV in 2000, "and I think we should be very proud of the job that American oil companies are doing in exploration abroad, in exploration at home, and in making certain that we have a safe energy supply."[2] Rice's ascendance from Titusville, Alabama, to University of Denver grad, to Stanford faculty member, to government service in D.C., to Stanford provost had been rapid, and she was not widely known. When Rice's ship sailed big-time as George W. Bush's national security advisor in January 2001, Chevron, seeking to downplay its connection to an administration known for its inseparability from Big Oil, renamed the *Condoleezza Rice* the *Altair Voyager*. "In the old sailing ship days," warns Pat Moloney, maritime historian, "they'd say it was bad luck to change the name of a ship."[3] If she ever heard this superstition, Condoleezza would have poohpoohed it. She made her own luck.

In 2004 and 2005 *Forbes* magazine ranked Rice as the most powerful woman in the world. The first African American woman secretary of state followed Colin Powell, the first African American. Both had ties to Birmingham's black middle class. Condoleezza, born in 1954, was the only child of a Presbyterian minister and a teacher; Colin Powell's wife, Alma Johnson, not quite a generation older than Rice, was the daughter and niece of principals of all-black Birmingham high schools.[4] For Republicans in the new century, Condoleezza and Colin became highly visible figures in an effort to erode a solid Democratic bloc. How advantageous for the lapsed party of Lincoln was a black woman whose childhood had crossed paths with the most horrific event of the 1960s civil rights movement — even though her family rejected the street protest tactics that directly challenged desegregation in her home city.

As the Bush presidency entered its lame duck phase, few African Americans had switched allegiance, and there were no black Republican members of Congress.[5] Republicans might quote Lincoln more often in speeches, but the Democratic Party remained the home of African American voters. Long committed to progressive politics, they were outraged over Bush domestic policy and embarrassed and angry that Rice and Powell had pitched so hard and deceptively for Bush's Iraq invasion. "If it's nice to see a black face in high places," wrote Patricia Williams, "that pleasure is more than outweighed by Rice's deployment as spokeswoman for an unprecedented policy of preemptive war."[6] Far from the high places, the percentage of black army recruits dropped steadily during the Iraq War, approaching the lowest point since the beginning of the all-volunteer military in 1973.[7] "With blacks," said Birmingham recruiting Sgt. First Class Abdul-Malik Muhammad in August 2007, "there is not really a great support for the war." Sgt. Muhammad told the *New York Times* that the parents of one potential African American recruit warned their son that that if he enlisted, they would cut all ties with him. That summer's polling showed 83 percent of blacks thought the U.S. should not have invaded Iraq (as compared with 46 percent of whites).[8] Characteristically, Condoleezza Rice was at odds with black consensus on this issue, as on most others.

COSSETED IN TITUSVILLE

In a skillful profile for the *Washington Post Magazine* published two days before the September 11, 2001, terrorist attacks, journalist Dale Russakoff, herself a Birmingham native two years older than Rice, drew on telephone and in-person interviews to uncover the braided narratives of family history, racial striving, upward mobility, and self-composition through which Rice's parents prepared her for success in white society while maintaining a wary distance from the concerns of everyday African Americans. Russakoff gathered a core of revelatory family stories that would appear again and again in articles about Rice, varying little in subsequent tellings. The effect for readers and historians is that of encountering a scripted identity, of someone less concerned with introspection than with strategies of personal ambition. For a few childhood years Russakoff and Rice had the battle of Birmingham in common, although Russakoff's elite, white Mountain Brook society was far from the black neighborhood of Titusville in the valley below. Russakoff's parents, like a significant minority of white Alabamians, despised George Wallace, and she interpreted the events of 1960s Birmingham as a "mass movement of the powerless, coupled with the force of federal law, triumphing over oppression." In contrast, Rice's narratives told of "generations of ancestors navigating oppression with individual will, wits and, eventually, wallets." The mass-movement narrative was not their style. "My parents were very strategic," Rice said. "I was going to be so well prepared, and I was going to do all of these things that were revered in white society so well, that I would be armored somehow from racism. I would be able to confront white society on its own terms."[9] In attempting to insulate their only child from the daily weather of Jim Crow Birmingham,

Rice's parents also separated her from much of the lived experience, the emotional resources, and the political savvy of rural and urban Alabama's black working-class culture. The Rices' was a more selective, individualistic Alabama imaginary.

The Rice family portrait foregrounds a mixed-race lineage from antebellum plantation masters and house servants in contrast to black Alabamians whose enslaved ancestors worked fields of cotton and corn. This toehold of advantage and separation is illustrated in the story of Condoleezza's "Granddaddy Rice," a staple of commencement addresses and a widely quoted moment at the 2000 Republican National Convention.[10] Coming of age in rural Greene County, Alabama, following emancipation, Granddaddy Rice parlayed his rudimentary literacy and striving for education into a getaway from the widening trap of sharecropping:

> Granddaddy Rice . . . decided to get book-learning. And so he asked, in the language of the day, where a colored man could go to school. They said that a little Presbyterian school, Stillman College, was only about 50 miles away. So he saved up his cotton to pay for the first year's tuition. After the first year, he ran out of cotton and he needed a way to pay. Granddaddy asked the school administrators how those other boys were staying in school, and he was told that they had what was called a scholarship. And, they said, "if you wanted to be a Presbyterian minister, you could have a scholarship too." My grandfather said, "That's just what I had in mind."[11]

Rice fed upon narrative kernels of indomitable individual effort, rarely taking race, much less black nationalism, into account. Her later equivocation about affirmative action was colored, Russakoff discovered, by "her lifelong view that her grandparents liberated themselves well before the federal government stepped in." Rice's academic and public-policy careers depended on and yet denied generations of African American political struggles.[12] The Alabama oral tradition on both the Rice and Lee sides of her family touted exceptionalism, religiously disciplined and unceasing work, and the forging of what Russakoff calls an "impregnable sense of self." Family stories distanced and distinguished their tellers from identification with the black majority, as some plantation house servants might disdain field hands, black or white.

To the inherited narratives Rice added new ones, such as two scenes in Birmingham department stores during the early 1960s in which her mother courageously backed down white saleswomen who had refused to let the child Condi try on a dress or handle a hat. "Condoleezza," instructed her mother, "go touch every hat in this store." To avoid the indignities of downtown clerks, Angelena Rice occasionally took her daughter shopping in white, affluent Mountain Brook, where money bought citizenship in the consumer's republic.[13] Here on some serendipitous day, Dale Russakoff and Condi Rice might have shared floor space for a passing moment, exchanged glances. From childhood, pricey clothes and practiced manners (*con dolcezza*) armored Rice against the everyday, convincing her of elite status. No Bama she.

Inside the city of Birmingham, Rice's childhood neighborhood of Titusville was a black, middle-class enclave, her family's house a two-bedroom bungalow. Under the scrutiny of Angelena, her self-possessed, schoolteacher mother, and the Reverend Rice, high school guidance counselor and popular youth activities organizer, Condoleezza's out-of-school regimen resembled her in-school one, with homework, constant reading, and classical piano practice. "I don't play gospel very well," she would tell a Sunday school class years later, excusing her unease at free-forming the piano around congregational call and response. "I play Brahms."[14] Onetime coach John Rice inspired Condo, as he called her, to be a lifelong football fan, but forbade her dressing up as one of the Supremes in a variety show. *That* would be "undignified."

"When the civil rights movement came to Birmingham," writes Russakoff, "the Rice family — like middle-class blacks in general — kept its distance." Rice's father, a registered Republican since 1952, practiced personal uplift but disdained the bold desegregation tactics of fearless working-class Baptist minister Fred Shuttlesworth and his Alabama Christian Movement for Human Rights (so named after the state attorney general, John Patterson, outlawed the Alabama NAACP). "If we'd waited for the middle class to lead us, we'd still be waiting," Shuttlesworth would say.[15] He had survived the bombing of his family's home in 1956 and a Klan beating a year later as he and his wife (who was stabbed) tried to enroll their children in an all-white school.

Shuttlesworth persuaded Martin Luther King Jr. to make Birmingham a major civil rights theater in what became known as Project C (for Confrontation). The breakthrough in Birmingham came during the Easter season of 1963, when hundreds of black children and students, ages six to twenty, roused by the charismatic James Bevel, marched to a victory of conscience and shaming over Bull.[16] For decades to come, indelible images fixed Birmingham and the Heart of Dixie in the world's imagination as the heartland of vicious racism.

Condoleezza Rice has said that she believes federal law pulled down a structure of segregation that was already falling under its own weight.[17] Veterans of the Birmingham campaign strongly disagree. Rice slights the power of grassroots participation at the core of the freedom struggle and the courage, ingenuity, and endurance of working-class, black Alabamians across generations. Her lack of understanding of the motive forces, long-term collective commitment, and strategic timing needed for oppressed people to effect social change complements an abstract, universalizing notion of "freedom" that she would overlay on Lebanon, Brazil, and Baghdad. Rice's theory does not emerge from the location of the Birmingham movement, but from her paradoxical distance from it.

That Sunday morning in September 1963, eight-year-old Condoleezza heard the blast and felt the tremor from Sixteenth Street Baptist, two miles away from her father's Westminster Presbyterian church where she and Denise McNair, one of the four girls blown up in the basement, had shared the same kindergarten.[18] The city's oldest black church, Sixteenth Street was a rallying place for the Birmingham campaign, but the bombing rained fear on every African American doorstep, including those in Titusville. When other nonfatal blasts and attempts at bombings drew closer, John Rice joined his neighborhood's nighttime shotgun patrols and lookouts. The momentum in the downtown desegregation battle shifted with the jailing of King and Ralph Abernathy, the marches and arrests of hundreds of youths, federal-court-ordered school openings, and the outrage over the Sixteenth Street bombing. It would be fourteen years before the first of the Klansmen who had bombed the church would be convicted by a jury, but congressional passage of the Civil Rights Act of 1964 owed much to the Birmingham mobilization and its nonviolent incitement of white outrages.

Rice was eleven when the family left Titusville, her father taking a job as a college administrator, first at Stillman (his alma mater and the historically black Tuscaloosa school where Granddaddy Rice had strategically assumed Presbyterianism), and then in 1967 at the University of Denver. Not until Catholic private school in Colorado did Rice sit in an integrated classroom.

At age sixteen, she enrolled in her father's university. A year or so later, after a summer-school session at the Aspen Music Festival, she realized that her years of disciplined piano practice were not going to lead to a career as a performer. She lacked range and depth of musical feeling. It was a critical moment for Rice, who would cast about for a new major before finding, in her words, "love at first sight" in Czech refugee Josef Korbel's courses on international relations. Korbel, former diplomat and father of future secretary of state Madeline Albright, inspired Rice to take up Soviet Studies and set her on a path that would lead to academic and administrative achievements — as well as criticism from women and minority faculty — at Stanford, and soon into the highest levels of U.S. policymaking.[19] Rejecting the Democratic Party's pluralistic courtship of diverse social groups, and convinced that Jimmy Carter's foreign policy wasn't tough enough in dealing with the Soviets, Rice became a Republican in the excitement of Ronald Reagan's jingoistic militarism and Cold War escalation.

Star ascending, Rice's conservative positions on issues from gun control to disarmament attracted the attention of several patrons. Kissinger associate and national security professional Brent Scowcroft was so impressed in a Stanford question-and-answer session in 1984 that, writes Nicholas Lemann, he "began grooming Rice for a position in government, by arranging for her to be invited to seminars and conferences and to meet people." A Council on Foreign Relations fellowship in 1986 took Rice to the Pentagon, as an assistant to the director of the Joint Chiefs of Staff.[20] By all accounts she enjoyed the Pentagon camaraderie, with its glimpses into deadly hardware, throw-weights, and strategy, and she tossed around her football analogies like one of the boys. When Scowcroft became George H. W. Bush's national security advisor in 1989, he named Rice to the National Security Council. Present at the dissolution of the Soviet state, Rice deployed her East European expertise and diplomatic aplomb when dealing with Gorbachev, Yeltsin, and upper-level diplomats.

At the end of Bush's term, Rice returned to the Stanford faculty, becoming in 1993 the university's youngest, first female, first black provost. President Gerhard Casper made the appointment. "It would be disingenuous," Casper told Nicholas Lehman, "for me to say that the fact that she was a woman, the fact that she was black, and the fact that she was young weren't in my mind."[21] Rice was a quick study and a lively presence, possessing a "distinctly Southern charm," which she had practiced for as many years as she had the piano.[22] But beneath what Stanford historian David Kennedy calls her "veneer of utter graciousness," Rice possessed the steely habits of an autocrat, bristling at criticism, vindictive against critics.

"I am myself a beneficiary of a Stanford strategy that took affirmative action seriously," Rice acknowledges, "that took a risk in taking a young PhD from the University of Denver."[23] She benefited at Stanford from funds set aside for minority hiring, and her original appointment, a window of opportunity, meant the usual open search was not required.[24] Unlike her hiring, Rice's tenuring in 1987, she has always argued, had everything to do with her scholarship and nothing to do with her race or gender.[25]

As provost, Rice carried out severe budget cuts in a ruthless style, angered minority students through an unsuccessful attempt to house a variety of campus ethnic centers in one building, took a hard line against faculty who advocated affirmative action in tenure decisions, and was accused in a U.S. Labor Department complaint of unfair treatment of women and minorities. "It was a very difficult time at Stanford for those of us concerned about equity in faculty appointments and promotions," history professor Estelle Friedman told the *L.A. Times'* Mark Barabak. "You can't pin that entirely on the provost. But the provost does set a mood and an agenda, and in my opinion the atmosphere has improved enormously since then."[26]

Among Rice's mentors, George Shultz, former secretary of state and a Distinguished Fellow at Stanford's Hoover Institution, helped her become an adviser to George W. Bush as he planned his presidential run.[27] Shultz, credited as the intellectual source of Bush's doctrine of preemptive war, was also godfather to the policy specialists known as the Vulcans.[28] This Roman deity, armament maker to gods and heroes, ceaseless toiler at anvil and forge, was the name chosen by Rice and her working group of military-minded, foreign-policy advisers in Bush's 1999–2000 campaign. Ultimately rewarded with administration posts, the Vulcan short list included Rice, Dick Cheney, Richard Perle, Colin Powell, Donald Rumsfeld, Robert Zoellick, and Paul Wolfowitz.[29]

Vulcan, the world's tallest cast-iron statue, was a vivid personal landmark to anyone growing up in modern Birmingham. Posted high atop Red Mountain, Vulcan held up a fateful torch during the evenings of Rice's Titusville childhood. The light of the torch, red or green, depended on whether or not the day's highway traffic had offered up a fatality.

"Vulcans," writes James Mann, "captured perfectly the image the Bush foreign-policy team sought to convey, a sense of power, toughness, resilience and durability."[30] Together, they melded an uncritical faith in U.S. military strength, "free" markets, godliness, and imperial intentions. Yet the powerful Vulcan of myth was also vulnerable. As the Greek Hephaestus, he was scarred from working too close to molten fire and caustic metals, and lame either from birth or from having been bounced out of Olympus. Bush's Vulcans admitted little caution and vulnerability and certainly no error. Rice would soon forget her own prescription, expressed in a *Foreign Affairs* campaign essay in early 2000: "America can exercise power without arrogance and pursue its interests without hectoring and bluster."[31]

U.S. popular culture provides another instructive set of Vulcans, the seemingly logic-driven, self-controlled, rational-choice strategists of *Star Trek*. These Vulcans, the Wikipedians remind us, while claiming to be free of emotions, actually practice a strategic denial of emotion and are capable of vast irrational damage.[32] September 11 was the terror that unhinged White House Vulcans. Desirous of taking quick advantage of broad international support for the pursuit of Al Qaeda in Afghanistan, they added the Iraq invasion as a two-for-one special, a way, as Norman Mailer wrote in July 2003, for the U.S. to satisfy its "need to get a choke-hold on the Middle East" and at the same time get a quick-win war that would be good for national psychic rejuvenation.[33] Condoleezza Rice turned out to be the ideal apologist for putting a rational cover on the Vulcans' mad purpose.

GRAND DELUSIONS

"One of Rice's defining ideas—now Bush's idea," writes Russakoff in her 2001, pre-9/11 profile, "is that the U.S. military should refrain from what she and Bush disparage as 'nation-building,' or what supporters of that idea call helping nations develop democracy and rule of law. In Rice's view, the world's greatest democracy cannot, and should not, do for strife-riven peoples what they can't do for themselves. . . . The responsibility rests with the people who live there." Catalyzed by the September 11 attacks, and challenged by the most hawkish among Bush's foreign-policy consultants, Rice turned her prior resistance to preemptive intervention upside down during the fall and winter of 2001. Oversimplified historical comparisons combined with an irreproachable belief in U.S. exceptionalism to fuel the Bush foreign policymakers' shift from resisting nation-building to attempting its far-flung military imposition.[34] Throughout the following years of squander — of lives, material resources, money, international reputation and goodwill — Rice maintained her stubborn certitude, imperiously defending Bush administration actions by claiming privileged insight. Smarter-than-thou Rice, wrote Fred Kaplan, "invokes her academic credentials to evade responsibility for decisions that she's made or for policies that she's helped devise."[35] "I'm a student of history," she would predictably announce, waving away scrutiny, dismissing the mounting waste as the necessary cost of freedom, as if she already knew what history would teach.

Was it Rice's conviction of historical vindication that led her and other high Bush officials in the summer of 2002 to approve and justify, as later reported by the *Washington Post*, "the CIA's use at secret prisons of harsh interrogation methods, including waterboarding," a technique of torture that simulates drowning? Throughout the Bush years, Rice had maintained, in her words, that the "United States government does not authorize or condone torture of detainees. Torture, and conspiracy to commit torture, are crimes under U.S. law, wherever they may occur in the world."[36] A Senate Intelligence Committee timeline released in April 2009 showed that Rice gave a verbal okay to waterboard an alleged Al Qaeda terrorist and passed along the Bush administration's approval to CIA director George Tenet. Further, reported the Associated Press, "dissenting legal views about the severe interrogation methods were brushed aside repeatedly." Vice President Cheney, White House counsel Alberto Gonzales, and Rice participated in a spring 2003 meeting that reaffirmed the legality of these methods of interrogation.[37] In the spring of 2009 Rice defended the Bush torture policy, saying, "By definition, if it was authorized by the president, it did not violate our obligations under the Conventions Against Torture." For many commentators, and historians, her words recalled the royal defense offered by Richard Nixon: "When the president does it, that means that it is not illegal."[38]

THE DOCTRINE OF PREEMPTION

Rice's reading of the new century's moment of historical opportunity measured the usefulness of situations and societies for the purposes of the U.S. corporate state, couched in an uncritical, universalist language of "freedom." "She flashes the same pride and determination describing her grandparents' lonely odyssey out of the plantation South," wrote Russakoff, "as she does in defending the separate course Bush is charting for the United States in the world." Rice used the narrative of her Alabama family's climb and the inevitability she voiced about her rightful ascendance — "My family is third-generation college-educated. I should've gotten to where I am" — to create a hermetic time-space escape from history and geography.[39]

Exactly how did U.S. foreign policy move so quickly to the disastrous go-it-alone, preemptive Bush Doctrine? In the crush of blame-shifting, self-justifying Washington memoirs, we may never know. But the post-9/11 panic and nationalistic rallying-round presented opportunists and true believers in expansive U.S. power the means to act on the notion that the world had changed forever, that the U.S. had suffered an attack equivalent to Pearl Harbor, and that it faced an enemy comparable to the empire of Japan or Hitler's Germany.[40] For months, international sympathy for 9/11 victims and outrage over the terrorist attacks washed across the U.S. All too soon the president and his advisers began to erode this goodwill as the U.S. military response shifted from attacking Al Qaeda in the mountains of Afghanistan to justifying and preparing to launch preemptive war in Iraq. Religious epiphany, conversion narratives, and a defiant sense of mission substituted for realistic analysis, thoughtful policy, and the building of international consensus. Bush and Secretary of Defense Donald Rumsfeld, Vice President Cheney, and National Security Advisor Rice underwent what David Kennedy called "the policy equivalent of a born-again religious conversion." Where formerly they were "openly contemptuous of the role of idealism in foreign policy, they have embraced an agenda so utopian as to make Woodrow Wilson look like a hard-bitten cynic. They seek nothing less than remaking Iraq in the Western image, thereby changing the political equation of the entire Middle East and beyond."[41] As she hopped aboard the transformational train of American messianism, perhaps Condoleezza heard the voice of Granddaddy Rice, "That's just what I had in mind."

The new imperative was set out in a document that Rice as national security advisor had primary responsibility for, "The National Security Strategy of the United States of America," released in 2002 around the first anniversary of 9/11.[42] This overview of U.S. international strategy trumpeted the preeminence of the United States' "single sustainable model for national success: freedom, democracy, and free enterprise" and set out the intention to extend this trinity globally. "We will actively work to bring the hope of democracy, development, free markets, and free trade to every corner of the world." To protect itself from "today's adversaries" while carrying out its world mission, "the United States will, if necessary, act preemptively."[43] While the Bush Doctrine of preemption, coming largely from the Defense Department, became the justification for the Iraq invasion and received the most international criticism, the National Security Strategy's rhetoric promoted nation-building as a melding of "democracy" with the march of "free" markets and "free" trade. From her cosseted childhood in Titusville through her ascendancy in academia, her highly paid service on corporate boards, and her national-security appointments, Condoleezza Rice never had the opportunity to appreciate the implications of broad inclusiveness borne by the word *democracy*, nor had she expressed the least skepticism in the myth of free markets.

"What seems to be happening now is that we're endowing a new establishment," declared Robert Bartley, editorial page editor of the *Wall Street Journal* in 2003. "We had an establishment in this country, the generation that came out of World War II. Dean Acheson was the epitome — he called his memoirs *Present at the Creation*. They were the experts, the smart guys, and everyone deferred to them. What the liberals have to worry about now is that it's all happening again — this time to the benefit of the conservatives. Dick Cheney and Condoleezza Rice and Rumsfeld and Wolfowitz will be figures in our history like Acheson and [George] Marshall were."[44] For his contributions to journalism, Bartley won the Presidential Medal of Freedom in 2003.

Condoleezza Rice told and retold the family narrative — at her Senate confirmation hearing when she became secretary of state, at international conferences, and at commencements: Vanderbilt, Michigan State, Stanford, Boston College. Boilerplate in place, Rice could hear explosions from the other side of the world and mistake them for the growing pains of democracy. She "milked her upbringing in the South," observes Glenn Kessler, "using it as an example of how even democracy in the United States is not perfect."[45] But what had she learned from her hometown's freedom struggle except how to appropriate her proximity to this legitimizing tragedy?

"How can someone with this past in their bones," wonders British cultural theorist Stuart Hall, "refashion themselves into the spokesperson and instrument of Bush's domestic attack on the poor — the majority of whom are black — and his international assault on other peoples and civilizations around the world?" While Rice might be smart, Hall concludes, she is "not, in a deeper sense, a person of tough intelligence or moral conviction."[46] What if, across the blundering years, U.S. policymakers had asked African American veterans of civil rights battles, men and women of proven "moral conviction," for their judgment and "tough intelligence" about whether or not to start the next war? What if, for instance, another native Alabamian, John Lewis, had exercised an influence equivalent to that of Condoleezza Rice? As a member of Congress from Atlanta, Lewis spoke early and often against George Bush's "beating the drums of war" and voted against the Iraq invasion's authorization. In his campus speeches, Lewis also deployed family narratives, but his were more contingent than Rice's, more questioning of inherited habits of judgment, more vulnerable in amazement, more struck by the wonder of his journey, by what he called his "walking in the wind."

"I was born the son of sharecroppers on a small farm outside of a little town called Troy, in the heart of rural Alabama," Lewis recounted to a Howard University audience in September 2002. "And if you had told me when I was growing up on that farm — or sitting in for civil rights — or going on the Freedom Rides — or marching from Selma to Montgomery for the right to vote — if you had told me then that I would be here, as a Member of Congress, I would have told you 'you're crazy, you're out of your mind, you don't know what you're talking about.'"

John Lewis came to understand his Alabama disobedience as an attempt to build the "beloved community" evoked by Martin Luther King Jr.[47] "During the 1960s," he said to the Howard students, "I saw many young people — many students — grow up by sitting down. By sitting down and sitting in, they were standing up and speaking out for what is best in America: Justice. Equality. Freedom. . . . We literally put our bodies on the line. We used extra-legal means and methods to remove many of the scars, stains, and symbols of racism."

Angry that "too many of us — black, white, Hispanic, Asian, and Native American — are being left out and left behind," Lewis urged the new generation to "find a way to get in the way" and not accept injustice, inequality, and intolerance.

"When I was growing up in Alabama," he continued, "my mother and father would tell me not to get in trouble. But I got in the way; I got in trouble. And it was good trouble — it was necessary trouble. You must be maladjusted to the problems and conditions of today." Using a phrase adapted from King, John Lewis sounds the importance of refusing to adjust to unjust and discriminatory conditions. His actions raise Judith Butler's question — "who will be a subject here and what will count as a life?" — about the formation of self in maladjustment to socializing structures and dominant habits of judgment.[48] At risky moments of social disobedience — stepping off the Freedom Rider bus into an Alabama mob intent on mayhem, marching across the Edmund Pettus Bridge into the skull-cracking billyclubs of state troopers — Lewis and his comrades in the movement walked into new selves. Confrontations in Alabama and throughout the South taught Lewis to weigh and assess the moment-to-moment dangers and costs of the freedom struggle, its strategic possibilities, and its requirements for sacrifice and solidarity. Condoleezza Rice's well-fashioned trajectory, insistent will to power, and posture of surety landed her in situations where her lack of understanding contributed to enormous human tragedy.

"We must not allow our success and our strength," Lewis counseled the Howard audience, "to make us complacent or arrogant. . . . Being arrogant will lead us — unilaterally to war. . . . Still, our President proposes war. He proposes that we, the strongest nation on earth, invade a sovereign nation. He asks that we go to war unattacked — unprovoked — unilaterally. This I cannot and will not support."[49] By September 2002, native Alabamians John Lewis and Condoleezza Rice had arrived at diametrically opposed positions.

As national security advisor, Condoleezza Rice, concluded the *Economist* in 2007, "bears almost as much responsibility for the mess in Iraq as Mr. Bush, Dick Cheney and Donald Rumsfeld. Her fingerprints are on some of the worst mistakes of the first Bush term."[50] With Secretary of State Powell, Rice helped sell the clear threat and the preemptive strike. She also helped convince policymakers, legislators, pundits, and the public that Saddam Hussein had tried to buy concentrated uranium for nuclear bomb-making from the African country of Niger. Most unfounded and provocative was Rice's warning, heard round the world, against discovering too late that Saddam had gone nuclear: "We don't want the smoking gun to be a mushroom cloud."[51] The Vulcan Rice, whose parents' battle cry had been "twice as good as," out-hawked even the bullying Cheney and his cluster of hard-liners — Wolfowitz, Richard Perle, Elliott Abrams — as she provided the most memorable phrase misleading the nation into war.

HER EYES WERE WATCHING CONDOLEEZZA

Condoleezza Rice's "self-presentation," wrote Patricia Williams in the winter of 2004, "belies the degree to which she is ideological — rather, she comes across as obedient, dutiful, understated, an anchor in the storm. I can't help thinking that to be her, one would have to live in fear of what would happen if you veered from the path of conformity."[52] Rice trod the ideologue's path in countless pairs of expensive new shoes that only seemed to keep her feet dry. Come Katrina, she was in over her head.

In the late summer of 2005, nothing so starkly revealed the great divide between the precarious lives of many African Americans and the lifestyles of the distant and mighty than the role Rice played as a public face for the Bush administration after its derelict response to tens of thousands of people flooded, stranded, exhausted, and displaced in New Orleans and along the Gulf Coast in the aftermath of Hurricane Katrina. "If you go through each one of them," points out Tulane historian Douglass Brinkley in Spike Lee's *When the Levees Broke*, and say, 'where were you when the golden hour came?' Dick Cheney? Fly fishing. Karl Rove? Nowhere around. [Secretary of Homeland Security] Chertoff going to Atlanta on a disease prevention kick. You see Condoleezza Rice shopping."

The preemptive dressing-up that had protected Rice — from Sunday school as a child to congressional hearing rooms — ran aground in the public storm accompanying Katrina. "What was Dr. Condoleezza Rice doing that looked very poorly?" asked Michael Eric Dyson. "She was at Ferragamo's buying shoes. . . . Then she goes to *Spamalot* that night and when the cameras frame her familiar figure, once the lights come on and they see it's Dr. Condoleezza Rice — 'Boo!' They began to boo her. And then the next day she's hitting tennis balls with Monica Seles at a club. So Blahniks, Broadway, and balls are more important than black people who look like her, for this woman from Birmingham."[53] Dyson had drawn his summary from various news and website accounts. The widely circulating stories conveyed public outrage at Rice's seeming indifference. Her claim to be surprised by the flood of criticism confirmed her detachment from the lives of everyday Americans, even if she had been brought up not to think of herself as black. "I thought of myself as secretary of state," she told biographer Marcus Mabry. "I didn't think about my role as a visible African American national figure. I just didn't think about it."[54]

Amid the delayed, chaotic response to Katrina by the Federal Emergency Management Administration and the nonchalance of President Bush, came the NBC television benefit "A Concert for Hurricane Relief" and the ad-lib criticism by rapper Kanye West that concluded with "George Bush doesn't care about black people."[55] Although Katrina had hit Florida on August 25, it was not until September 2 that Bush made landfall in the hurricane's wake. Secretary Rice arrived a couple of days later, proffering authenticity.

"I am an African American," she insisted in Bayou La Batre, south of Mobile, on September 4. "I'm from Alabama," she added. "I can tell you that this response is not a response about color. This is a response about Americans helping Americans. No American wants to see another American suffer."[56] While cameras rolled and clicked, Rice toured a relief center and helped load a box of supplies. Then, as quickly as she had dropped in, she made her Alabama getaway, leaving the wreckage of the Republican Party's strategy for wooing black voters amid Katrina's debris. "Our history, I believe, will return to haunt her," wrote the Chicago-born, African American playwright and critic Bonnie Greer, months before the hurricane blew in. To Greer, Condoleezza Rice, "the most powerful black woman since the Queen of Sheba," was a study in the pursuit and machinations of power.[57]

PIMPING THE MOVEMENT?

Condoleezza Rice returned to Alabama again in the fall of 2005, this time with British foreign secretary Jack Straw. They made official appearances in Birmingham and lectured at the University of Alabama in Tuscaloosa, where Rice tossed the coin before the Tennessee-Bama football game. But this visit was also a test of Rice's appeal as a possible political candidate.[58] This was Bush country and she was W's most loyal operative. White Alabamians overwhelmingly supported the Iraq War, as they had from its inception, and the state's Gulf Coast had come though Katrina relatively unscathed when compared with Mississippi and Louisiana.[59]

Invited to travel with Rice was *Washington Post* editorial writer Eugene Robinson, who wondered from the start how Rice could be such a Bush loyalist when the president's policies were overwhelmingly disliked by African Americans. "How did she come to a worldview so radically different from that of most black Americans? Is she blind, is she in denial, is she confused — or what?"

Upon hearing her childhood narrative, Robinson decided that "if there's a 'Rosebud' to decode the enigma that is Condoleezza Rice, it's . . . her beloved Titusville, the neighborhood of black strivers where she was raised." Shielded in this protective bubble, Rice was "able to see the very different reality that other African Americans experience but not to reach out of the bubble — not able to touch that other reality, and thus not able to really understand it."

"I've always said about Birmingham," Rice told a startled Robinson, "that because race was everything, race was nothing." She talked "without visible emotion" of the Sixteenth Street bombing and reminisced about "piano lessons and her brief attempt at ballet — not of Connor setting his dogs loose on brave men, women and children marching for freedom, which is the Birmingham that other residents I met still remember." Rice presented African American history from the perspective of a privileged Washington insider, not from the situation in which most black Americans perceived themselves. And she seemed to have missed a "guiding principle" of black ascension, "that as you climbed, you were obliged to reach back and bring others along." Robinson doubted the "lame excuse" that the absence of qualified minority candidates was the reason Rice could name only one black professional she had brought into the State Department.[60]

Among the toughest critics of Condoleezza Rice were veteran Alabama civil rights activists. In his weekly newspaper column, J. L. Chestnut took up where Gene Robinson left off: "I know more about the Rices' family relation to the civil rights movement and the black struggle than Mr. Robinson because I was in Birmingham during the tumultuous civil rights years." Chestnut argued that Condoleezza's parents "did a helluva lot more than shelter Ms. Rice. They mis-led her about the justice of the civil rights movement, misled her about the courage of Fred Shuttlesworth, misled her about the greatness of Rev. Martin King, and misled her about all the dedicated people risking their lives in the streets and jails in Birmingham."

"Ms. Rice's father," adds Chestnut, "a prominent pastor in Birmingham, looked down on Shuttlesworth and his small working class congregation and publicly called them 'uneducated, misguided Negroes.'" As for Rice's "race was nothing" statement, Chestnut counters, "So, forty years after her father de-nounced us, Ms. Rice reduces segregation, the movement, all the deaths and sacrifices to one word, 'nothing.' In a sense, she is in 2005 where her father was forty years ago. I have a feeling she would spit on the grave of King and on all those brave souls whose life and death sacrifices put her where she is now. . . . Let there be no doubt that while white Alabama celebrates Ms. Rice, there is much reserve and distrust in black Alabama about the second black Secretary of State. Also, let there be no doubt why."[61]

For journalist George E. Curry, an African American native of Tuscaloosa, Rice's selective and strategic use of civil rights–era memories to justify her father's disdain for the 1963 Birmingham desegregation campaign helps explain how she "feels so comfortable defending George W. Bush, arguably the worst president on civil rights in more than 50 years." Curry, a syndicated columnist and editor-in-chief of the National Newspaper Publishers Association, wrote about Rice's appearance on CBS television's *60 Minutes* in September 2006: "I expected the same old run-of the-mill defense of the Bush administration and, in that respect, she was predictably predictable. But when the discussion turned to her upbringing in my native state of Alabama, it was clear that this smart, able and doctrinaire bureaucrat was basically pimping the Civil Rights Movement."

Most offensive to Curry was how Rice's retelling of her Birmingham childhood, including her invocation of the four girls killed in the Sixteenth Street Church bombing, appropriated the historical high moral ground of that horrendous event to legitimize U.S. foreign policy, while failing to appreciate the organization and critical timing of the groundswell movement with its mass boycotts, marches, and confrontations in Kelly Ingram Park. "Rice," writes Curry, "was eight years old when that bomb exploded in Birmingham. I was 16 years old at the time. Perhaps because of our age difference, I knew then and I know now, that there was no way any parent could shield their children from the indignities of *de jure* segregation." Curry, whose mother was a domestic worker, participated in demonstrations as a teen by cutting school and traveling to Birmingham with a tenth grade classmate "to protest the deaths of those four girls. . . . Our parents didn't want us harmed. They didn't want us beaten. They didn't want us tear-gassed. They loved us as much as Condoleezza Rice's parents loved her. But our parents also knew that the system was wrong. And while they worried about our safety, they allowed us to fight for our rights." Although many of Birmingham's black youth participated in the marches, Curry doesn't fault Rice's parents for not sending her into the streets, but he and Chestnut suggest they neglected essential lessons. "Unlike her parents, she is not on the sidelines — she's on the wrong team."[62]

As national security advisor, one of the venues where Rice told her Birmingham story as a freedom allegory justifying the Iraq invasion was to a national convention of black journalists in Dallas. "But let our voice not waver in speaking out on the side of people seeking freedom. And let us never indulge the condescending voices who allege that some people are not interested in freedom or aren't ready for freedom's responsibilities. That view was wrong in 1963 in Birmingham and it is wrong in 2003 in Baghdad."[63]

As secretary of state, Rice transposed her version of Birmingham upon a variety of global situations, appealing to an essential, universal "human spirit" while downplaying cultural differences, U.S. strategic interests, and unilateral actions. Her approach elided the differential social histories of power, resistance, and insurgence in particular places.

Heeding the call to assume their predestined roles, Rice and the Vulcans had transformed the post-9/11 situation into a "moral mission" under U.S. command. "In many ways, the opportunity before us today is similar to that we faced in the wake of World War II," trumpeted Rice as ebulliently and condescendingly as the *Wall Street Journal*'s Bartley. "Like the transformation of Europe, the transformation of the Middle East will require a commitment of many years."[64]

But what of her central conceit: Baghdad as Birmingham? That would suggest that the tinhorn, one-eyed, former baseball broadcaster and professional racist Bull Connor, or even the banty segregationist George Wallace, might be likened to Saddam Hussein. And what in the blasting away at heavily militarized Iraq was comparable to the movement for desegregating lunch counters and fitting rooms, the hiring of black department store clerks, the claiming of voting rights? What comparable to the "shock and awe" bombing campaign? The U.S.-led invasion and occupation? With its beginnings in late-nineteenth-century wars between labor and capital in mine and mill, the long battle for Birmingham proceeded in fits and starts through the opposition to convict-lease, the working-class movements of the 1930s, the post–World War II homecoming of black vets demanding full citizenship, the building of political organizations. It was an intergenerational history threaded through neighborhood institutions and informal networks. The Birmingham movement forced white business owners, the courts, elected officials, the federal executive, national civil rights organizations, and broad public opinion to engage the Heart of Dixie. Baghdad and Birmingham were incommensurable.[65]

Ultimate loyalist and burner of after-midnight oil for her president, Condoleezza Rice kept any second thoughts, regrets, or apologies out of sight.[66] As a black girl in Titusville, she was taught the appearance of being in control as a tactic, a habit to mask vulnerability and victimization. "Childhood matters," she told Russakoff, adding, from a second-person point of view: "Your outward image is critical to reminding people that you still have control. They're not diminishing your humanity."[67]

Even aided by the archival film footage of the 1960s on display at today's Birmingham Civil Rights Institute and the chilling delineations of sociopathic Klansmen as rendered by Diane McWhorter in *Carry Me Home*, it's impossible to emotionally reinhabit the foundry of daily pressures and humiliations, abuse, brutality, foreclosure, and terror with which Jim Crow Birmingham oppressed its black population. John and Angelena Rice sought to advance themselves and their only child through a strategy that combined the acquisition of white cultural capital with emotional distancing and torturous self-control. The Rice family left Titusville and the Heart of Dixie not long after the Sixteenth Street bombing. How to trace the effects of such a childhood? Condoleezza Rice embodies "a more contradictory legacy of Birmingham than any of us would like to admit," writes Patricia Williams. "She is a tightly fitted mask of compulsive politeness pulled over both great grief and corrosive, unhealed cruelties."[68] Intent on putting as much distance as she could between herself and Birmingham's streets, Rice never publicly questioned the formative habits and family ideology that armored her life and secured her Alabama getaway.

CHAPTER EIGHT

Invasions of Normalcy

No, we will not allow Alabama to return to normalcy.
— MARTIN LUTHER KING JR., "Our God Is Marching On!"

Across recent decades, growing numbers of Alabamians have ratcheted up their critiques of the Heart of Dixie. Their raids on normalcy have taken many forms, from gender and disability-discrimination litigation, to challenging inequities in the state's tax structure and the funding of education, to creating a National Voting Rights Trail and confronting the tenacious ghost of George Wallace. Citizen groups bang against the constitutional gearbox where the state's governmental machinery remains jammed. Black Alabamians continue to press for economic justice and statewide democratic inclusion. Activists of many stripes, as well as critical journalists, artists, and musicians, sustain the march toward a widening horizon. As this chapter suggests, the transformation of Alabama and its political imaginary proceeds along many fronts, lurching ahead here, stuck in habitual mud there, throwing off sparks one night, passing generational torches the next.

SPECTERS OF WALLACE

"Perhaps the best way of encapsulating the gist of an epoch," suggests Slavoj Žižek, "is to focus not on the explicit features that define its social and ideological edifices but on the disavowed ghosts that haunt it, dwelling in a mysterious region of nonexistent entities which nonetheless *persist*, continuing to exert their efficacy."[1] A frozen image in high school textbooks, a flutter of film footage sampled in TV documentaries and Hollywood flashbacks, George Wallace floats in history's peripheral vision. Glimpsed at the corner of an Alabama eye, the disavowed Guvner prowls long after leaving office in 1987 and the hustings of the living in 1998, his shadowy persistence troubling the state's political imaginary.

An indelible afterimage, Wallace stands, as Chet Fuller writes, "the sinister figure . . . in the doorway," modeling defiance in a failed attempt to stop the desegregation of the University of Alabama in June 1963.[2] Along with the interposition at Foster Auditorium, a second Wallace scene remains vivid for The Guvner's ritual performance of official bigotry. In January 1963 Wallace stood atop the capitol steps in Montgomery at his first inaugural (where Jefferson Davis had taken the Confederacy's presidential oath) and vowed "segregation today . . . segregation tomorrow . . . segregation forever."[3] Wallace's reinvigoration of the theatrics of obstruction in the name of states' rights lingers in circulating images and echoing words that continue "to exert their efficacy."

Churning memories, semblances of Wallace materialize anew. Alabama's most notorious politician has become its chief haint, diminished yet indelible, a blurring tattoo, "encapsulating the gist of an epoch," and a reminder, whenever familiar code words are uttered, of the persistence of the dilemmas he exploited. "Hauntology," writes Christopher Peterson, elaborating a term of Jacques Derrida's, "means to displace the binary opposition between presence and absence, being and nonbeing, life and death. Hauntology is thus another name for the spectrality that conditions all life."[4] In considering the dogged presence of The Guvner, hauntology puts a fresh face on death warmed over and breathes meaning into specters. Hauntology, in this sense, invokes not a dead Wallace but the intertwined social obsessions, inertias, and compulsions signaled by his presence—the Heart of Dixie habits still extant. Consider, for instance, Pat Buchanan, adviser to Nixon, Ford, and Reagan, and a candidate for president himself in 1996, lapsing into theatrics modeled after The Guvner's as he stood "before dozens of television cameras . . . at the great gates of Charleston's Citadel military academy and vowed that under his presidency no more women would enter that all-male institution."[5]

Just as black Tallapoosa County farmer Ned Cobb taught that "all God's dangers ain't a white man," George Wallace can't take the rap for all of Alabama's racist mayhem in the 1960s, nor all of the doorway stands today.[6] He has, however, become a semantic touchstone that urges an investigation of the meanings and tenacity of Wallaceism, an Alabama export even in afterlife.

Specters of Wallace are not Alabama bound, but await their casting calls into present dramas, sometimes speaking through unexpected voices. Backs to the wall, political candidates who know better can find themselves channeling The Guvner. Hillary Clinton, desperate for voters in rural West Virginia and Kentucky to fend off a surging Barack Obama in the 2008 Democratic primary season, boasted of her appeal to "hard-working Americans, white Americans." In quickly chiding Clinton, *New York Times* columnist Bob Herbert maintained that although some whites still "will not vote for a black candidate under any circumstance," things had changed enough that "the United States is a much better place now than it was when people like Richard Nixon, George Wallace and many others could make political hay by appealing to the very worst in people, using the kind of poisonous rhetoric that Senator Clinton is using now."[7] Herbert's calling out of the spirit of Wallace loosed among the Democrats brought to mind the catalog of sorrows provoked by The Guvner. What could have been, or could be otherwise, suggests Avery Gordon, depends upon the "willingness to follow ghosts, neither to memorialize nor to slay, but to follow where they lead, in the present, head turned backwards and forwards at the same time."[8]

Wallace's ghost stirred more than once in the 2008 presidential campaign. Sensing a potential for racial violence in the atmosphere created during John McCain–Sarah Palin rallies when, at the mention of Obama's name, voices in the nearly all-white crowds called out "traitor" or "terrorist" or "off with his head," civil rights veteran and Alabama native John Lewis felt a familiar chill.[9]

"During another period, in the not-too-distant past," warned the Georgia congressman in comments that circulated beyond the U.S., "there was a governor of the state of Alabama named George Wallace who also became a presidential candidate. George Wallace never threw a bomb, he never fired a gun, but he created the climate and the conditions that encouraged vicious attacks against innocent Americans who were simply trying to exercise their constitutional rights. Because of this atmosphere of hate, four little girls were killed on Sunday morning when a church was bombed in Birmingham, Alabama.

"As public figures with the power to influence and persuade," Lewis continued, "Sen. McCain and Gov. Palin are playing with fire, and if they are not careful, that fire will consume us all. They are playing a very dangerous game that disregards the value of the political process and cheapens our entire democracy."[10]

At Hofstra University, during the third presidential debate of that political season, Lewis's comments prompted this rejoinder from Republican nominee John McCain:

> Well, this has been a tough campaign. It's been a very tough campaign. . . . And I regret some of the negative aspects of both campaigns. But the fact is that it has taken many turns which I think are unacceptable.
>
> One of them happened just the other day, when a man I admire and respect — I've written about him — Congressman John Lewis, an American hero, made allegations that Sarah Palin and I were somehow associated with the worst chapter in American history, segregation, deaths of children in church bombings, George Wallace. That, to me, was so hurtful.[11]

For Lewis's warning, drawn from firsthand experience of tactics deployed by The Guvner, the *Wall Street Journal* charged the former chairman of SNCC with fanning racial tensions: "Mr. Lewis's over-the-top analogy is nastier by far than anything the GOP nominees have said during this campaign."[12] Lewis's sense that the white-heat "atmosphere" of McCain-Palin crowds had turned dangerously alarming was lost on the *Journal*.

Wallace sometimes appears as a rallying figure of speech, useful for galvanizing opposition to subsequent banty pharaohs and repressive social policies, as in the movement for sexual rights. "Rock star Melissa Etheridge chuckled years ago," journalist Eric Deggans wrote in 2005, "when I told her folks who criticize her openly lesbian life now will feel years later like former Alabama Gov. George Wallace, who eventually recanted his decision to stand in the doorway at the University of Alabama to keep black students out."[13]

"At some point in our lifetime," suggested actor George Clooney when California voters overturned the state's same-sex marriage law in 2008, "gay marriage won't be an issue, and everyone who stood against this civil right will look as outdated as George Wallace standing on the school steps keeping James Hood from entering the U. of Alabama because he was black."[14]

The Guvner's stand has become a motif for obdurate bigotry. "Much has been written about a president's interest in his legacy," observed a letter writer to *USA Today* in 2004. "As President Bush gave his radio address July 10 demanding a constitutional amendment to ban same-sex marriage, the unforgettable image of another politician popped into my mind. I saw George Wallace in the doorway of the University of Alabama. . . . This is the image with which he will always be associated."[15]

For a 1998 series on the Wallace legacy, *Atlanta Journal-Constitution* reporter Mike Williams interviewed several African Americans formerly of Alabama, such as Charles Howard, who grew up in 1940s Birmingham, but "knew he had to leave" for a place with better prospects. He studied electrical engineering at Tennessee State University and made a career as an Air Force meteorologist, stationed mainly outside the South. In the mid-1950s, Howard was stationed at Maxwell Air Force Base in Montgomery, where he served as a driver for blacks participating in the bus boycott. "George Wallace," Howard reflected, "is the worst thing that ever happened to the state of Alabama, period. He went deeper than anybody in a long time into playing the race card, and the stigma is still there. It's really put this state behind."[16]

Older whites with ties to the state will sometimes admit the damage done during the Wallace heyday. Mary Williams Wood was born and raised in Vance, Alabama, before marrying and moving to Baltimore, then returning later in life to her hometown, where she was interviewed in 1998 at the age of sixty-seven. "When George Wallace stood in the schoolhouse door," Wood recalled, "he was doing what the people wanted. But it hurt us. It gave Alabama a bad name. I could hear it in what people outside the state were saying about us." Living for years in the upper South gave Wood "a new perspective on her Alabama roots" and on black migration. "The blacks who grew up here didn't feel welcome here, and they moved away. They went to Detroit and Chicago and the cities up North. Now that they are retiring, they are coming home to Alabama. We've had a bad name, but we're slowly living it down."[17]

The specter lurks when politicians turn to interposition. "Not since George Wallace stood in that schoolhouse door at the University of Alabama had a pandering politician done something so bold in support of something so wrong," wrote *Newsday*'s Ellis Henican when in 2003 Florida governor Jeb Bush, along with Republican members of Congress, including House leader Tom Delay, rushed to defy federal court rulings that would have allowed Terri Schiavo, for years in a persistent vegetative state, to die.[18]

But sometimes Wallace offers a measuring stick of progress: "In the nearly half-century in which we have gone from George Wallace to Barack Obama . . ."[19]

Yet one wonders whether we have come so far after all. In November 2004 "the descendants of Bull Connor and George Wallace and Lester Maddox and Leander Perez were still out there yesterday, doing the familiar, dirty work, trying to keep decent people away from the polls."[20]

Or that we may have come further, if measured by breakthrough moments: "When the Massachusetts governor went to Boston Common . . . to endorse Obama," observed Gwen Ifill, "ten thousand gathered to cheer the two black men, who stood, hands clasped, on the same bandstand used by segregationist George Wallace as he campaigned for president in 1968."[21]

References to Wallace resurfaced as the Great Recession touched off boiling rage against Wall Street bailouts, executive bonuses, and government complicity. Legitimate complaints were quickly exploited by media demagogues such as talk show host Glenn Beck, whose "ideology," wrote Frank Rich, "if it can be called that, mixes idolatrous Ayn Rand libertarianism with bumper-sticker slogans about 'freedom,' self-help homilies and lunatic conspiracy theories." Beck's ranting traced its lineage through a history of right-wing paranoia that Rich referenced from Father Charles Coughlin in the 1930s to The Guvner: "Wallace is most remembered for his racism, but he, like Beck, also played on the class and cultural resentment of those sharing his view that there wasn't 'a dime's worth of difference' between the two parties."[22]

Reenactments of Wallace's moments of high trauma — but this time performed with deliberate reversals — attempt to send The Guvner's specters back into the crypt. On June 11, 2003, recently elected governor Bob Riley participated in a three-day "Opening Doors" commemoration of the University of Alabama's desegregation. "Once again," reported the *Tuscaloosa News*, "the state governor stood before the schoolhouse doors. Onlookers gathered, and police paced in the distance. News cameras again rolled . . . and James Hood and Vivian Malone Jones again found themselves outside Foster Auditorium, 40 years after Gov. George Wallace tried to block their entrance."[23]

Governor Riley listened to and spoke with Hood and Jones — and with Autherine Lucy Foster, who had desegregated the university for three days in 1956 until school trustees and administrators, claiming they could not protect her, suspended her. Riley kissed Jones's cheek and told an audience of several hundred that in Alabama's past "there are certain parts we celebrate, certain parts we regret. . . . Now we have to show the rest of the world what it's like to bring the races together."[24] How many counter-commemorative moments will it take to erase Wallace's belligerent snarl and call to account "the different modes of today's racism" that sustain unquiet spirits of prejudice and resentment?[25]

In Seattle, Washington, in 2004, King County executive Ron Sims, an African American, performed a "planned exercise in political theater," reenacting the schoolhouse door stand by barring "six carefully selected couples" who were seeking same-sex marriage licenses. Later, Sims joined with gay rights activists at a news conference, where he welcomed a legal challenge to the state law. "When I was a kid," Sims told the *Boston Globe*, "I remember Governor Wallace standing at the door with his arms folded. It was important to me to open the door to these couples seeking to be married. We felt our strategy in the long run was the most sensible strategy. We were able to say, 'Let the courts interpret the constitution in the state of Washington.'"[26] By repeating ritual in order to break it, a symbolic intervention can change the sense of the real and break with habits of judgment.[27]

"GEORGE WALLACE IN HELL"

"And you know race was only an issue on TV in the house that I grew up in," says Patterson Hood of the Drive-By Truckers on the band's 2001 album, *Southern Rock Opera*. "Wallace was viewed as a man from another time and place, but when I first ventured out of the South I was shocked at how strongly Wallace was associated with Alabama and its people. Racism is a worldwide problem, and it's been like that since the beginning of recorded history and it ain't just white and black, but thanks to George Wallace, it's always a little more convenient to play it with a southern accent."[28]

When Patterson Hood was growing up in north Alabama, his father David was a legendary session musician on 1960s and '70s hit tracks with black and white, northern and southern artists in the creation of the soul-based Muscle Shoals Sound.[29] "I left the South," adds Patterson Hood, "and learned how different people's perceptions of the Southern Thing was from what I had seen in my life, which leads us to George Wallace."

Several members of the Truckers, sprung from the same cultural geography, have variously celebrated and raged about the "duality of the southern thing" — great-great-grandfathers who didn't believe in slavery yet put on a rebel uniform and got shot at Shiloh, the sectional loyalty of Robert E. Lee versus the liberatory courage of Martin Luther King Jr., the cotton fields and the "cotton picking lies" that kept white and black apart. "To the fucking rich man all poor people look the same," they sing.[30] "The Southern Thing" — both song and obsessive dilemma — is a knotty net of potent, devastating, simultaneous contradictions.

"In 'The Southern Thing,'" says Patterson Hood, "every line contradicts another line in the song. That was to me the point of it. You can't just say this or that is the Southern Thing, because it encompasses all of it. Regardless of your stance or feelings about somebody politically, or sociologically, there's no denying the fact that Martin Luther King was absolutely a southerner, as was Robert E. Lee. And, regardless of your feelings about what one or the other was supposed to have stood for, it's all connected."[31]

In *Southern Rock Opera*, the Truckers' song "Wallace" wrestles with the conciliatory image cultivated by The Guvner late in life as contrasted with the thuggish racist in fighting trim. Told "from the Devil's point of view," the song begins in September 1998, the month of Wallace's death. Eager for his new resident, the devil (whose car bears a Wallace sticker) orders his lackeys to toss "another log on the fire. . . . George Wallace is coming to stay." Even if The Guvner "wasn't a racist" and was just pandering for votes, the devil concludes that African Americans would "still vote him this way."

"Wallace" is a remarkable moment in southern musical history, as the Drive-By Truckers, an all-white band with biracial Alabama roots and a soulful, twanging ensemble of ear-bursting instruments and accents, push back against the Heart of Dixie and Wallaceism: "And Hell's just a little bit hotter cuz he played his hand so well."[32]

"To remain haunted," writes Avery Gordon, "is to remain partial to the dead or the deadly and not to the living."[33] Certainly, specters of Wallace still float in the political imaginary. "We are the nation that produced George Washington and Abraham Lincoln, Kennedy and the Rev. Martin Luther King Jr.," editorialized the *Los Angeles Times* as it considered the challenges facing the U.S. at the end of George W. Bush's presidency. "But we also inhabit the land of George Wallace, Joe McCarthy, the robber barons, the John Birch Society and the Ku Klux Klan."[34] The *Times'* formulation seems too easy, not acknowledging the ways in which Wallace racialized such words as *crime* and *welfare* for succeeding politicians to exploit.

Some future treatment of Wallace might include a one-man drama of the addled Guvner making solitary, late-night phone calls, voicing noisome spirits,

in the way that Robert Altman's 1984 film, *Secret Honor*, imagined a possessed, interior Richard Nixon. But how much time must pass before apparitions of Wallace dissolve? Similar malignant specters of southern history have
passed into near invisibility. Who today has heard of the Great White Chief,
Mississippi's vicious Vardaman, charismatic champion of lynching, shiny
locks streaming atop his ox-drawn wagon? Or the loony Theodore G. Bilbo?
Pitchfork Ben Tillman? Talmadge? Maddox? Faubus? High-profile politicians
in their day, and white supremacists all. Wallace may possess more staying
power because of those indelible, auratic film clips and photos — the 1963 inaugural speech, the schoolhouse door, the faces of four black girls — and his
effects on national political rhetoric and strategy. Resident docent in the Heart
of Dixie, The Guvner will haunt Alabama so long as the state fails to reconcile
the quandaries he only stoked.[35] Politics for George Wallace was like whiskey
poured into a drunkard's dream. Like whiskey, politics doesn't make you do a
thing, it just lets you.

LEDBETTER THAN NEVER

"The Supreme Court struck a blow for discrimination this week," wrote the
Times in the summer of 2007, "by stripping a key civil rights law of much of its
potency."[36] This was the equal-pay case of Lilly Ledbetter, a former Goodyear
supervisor at a Gadsden, Alabama, tire plant who, after nineteen years with the
company, discovered that her $45,000 annual salary was $6,500 less than the
lowest-paid male supervisor.[37] Ledbetter filed a complaint and won a federal
jury verdict under Title VII of the 1964 Civil Rights Act. Goodyear appealed
and the Eleventh Circuit Court in Atlanta overturned the verdict, ruling that
Ledbetter had not shown intentional discrimination in the 180-day time period
allowed for filing a complaint. Two of the three members of the panel of judges
ruling on the appeal were Bush father-and-son appointees, including former
Alabama attorney general Bill Pryor.[38] In a five-to-four decision, with the Bush
administration siding with Goodyear and against its own EEOC's position in
the lower court, the U.S. Supreme Court ruled against Ledbetter, ignoring the
Catch-22 through which the company's policy of salary secrecy had prevented
her from discovering the pay differential until well past the complaint dead-
line. "In our view," dissented Justice Ruth Bader Ginsburg, "this court does
not comprehend, or is indifferent to, the insidious way in which women can

be victims of pay discrimination."[39] Left unredressed by legislation, the court's unreasonableness in appreciating the long-term and continuing effects of pay discrimination would have made Title VII suits extremely difficult to sustain while shoring up employers' ability to discriminate with impunity. "I'm disappointed for all the females who are out there working today," said Ledbetter. "The practical effect of the court's ruling," commented Karen Mathis, president of the American Bar Association, "is to make Title VII . . . almost useless in combating pay discrimination in the workplace."[40]

Following the 2008 election, a new Congress rewrote the law to ease the statute of limitations so that women in Ledbetter's situation could pursue pay discrimination complaints. The Lilly Ledbetter Fair Pay Act was the first piece of legislation signed by President Obama. Among Alabama congressmen, only African American representative Artur Davis voted in favor of the act. Ledbetter, who had made campaign appearances for Obama, was present in the White House for the signing. "Goodyear will never have to pay me what it cheated me out of," she said. "In fact, I will never see a cent. But with the president's signature today I have an even richer reward."[41]

KNIGHT V. WHITENESS

Seeking to eliminate "vestiges of historical, state enforced, racial segregation and other forms of official racial discrimination against African Americans in Alabama's system of public universities," a group of plaintiffs led by Alabama State University administrator (later state representative) John Knight initiated *Knight and Sims v. Alabama* in 1981 in Montgomery.[42] It entered the federal court system for the Northern District of Alabama in 1983 and over twenty-some years wound its way to the bench of federal judge Harold Murphy, based in Rome, Georgia. *Knight* became another of those long-running, litigative attempts to create a more inclusive and equitable state in the face of constitutional barriers. The lawsuit sought to preserve the identity of historically black Alabama State and Alabama A&M while supporting new programs of study and enhancing existing ones that would attract students of all races. *Knight* also aimed at increasing black enrollment, as well as black faculty and administrative hirings, at the state's historically white universities.

In a break with Alabama gubernatorial habits vis-à-vis federal courts, the Riley administration (cushioned by a momentary bulge in the state's education purse) settled *Knight*. On December 12, 2006, Judge Murphy declared the end of "the vestiges of de jure segregation" in the state's university system and signed off on a set of agreements that would, by 2014, cost some $500 million.[43] "There's no question that more has been spent in Alabama than in any other state on [higher ed] desegregation remedies to this point," said lead plaintiff attorney Jim Blacksher.[44] Among the results was the combining of what had been two separate (black and white) agricultural extension services; new degree programs, diversity scholarships, classrooms, and building repairs at A&M and ASU; and money for the recruiting of black faculty and administrators at the state's historically white universities.[45] "I don't know many things that have happened in Alabama where courts have not played a role," Knight said plaintively. "Without federal courts intervening, nothing seems to happen."[46]

Although "nobody really contends that we have reached the end of the road when it comes to ending vestiges of segregation," acknowledged Blacksher, agreements between the parties in *Knight* sought to shift the next steps of the process away from the courts and into the colleges and universities.[47]

But what of racially discriminatory structures and practices — the effects of property tax limits and disparities of resources — upon K–12 public school districts? This question, which emerged in *Knight*, continued as a separate proceeding. "We are breaking new ground here," commented Blacksher. "But it is a very logical extension of the case law."[48] Blacksher's legal team and expert witnesses detailed the state's intentional history of white racist education and asked the court to find the offending portions of Alabama's tax system unconstitutional.

Knight's sequel, *Lynch v. Alabama*, was filed in 2008 on behalf of children in Lawrence (north Alabama) and Sumter (Black Belt) counties. *Lynch* plaintiffs asked the federal court to dismantle the racially discriminatory features of the state's property tax provisions dating back to the 1875 and 1901 constitutions (and including subsequent tax-capping amendments, or "lid bills," in the 1970s) so that adequate revenues could be raised to support public schools. As egregiously unjust as the state's tax structure is, it seemed very unlikely that a federal judge — not even Frank Johnson in his heyday — would intervene to alter such a constitutionally embedded arrangement. Nor would such a ruling likely be upheld. Given federal appellate courts' shift to the right with the appointment of Bush-era judges, even egregious patterns of state-inflicted racial discrimination such as Alabama's have been judged out of bounds for challenge under a narrow interpretation of the legal doctrine of "standing." Conservative jurists at all jurisdictional levels have resisted opening up the historical actions of Alabama's state and local governments to citizens' scrutiny and redress. "We end up having this wrong without a remedy," concluded attorney Ed Gentle in 2010, after the state supreme court tossed out a challenge by black citizens that proved the 1901 constitution was ratified with thousands of fraudulent votes cast by the Black Belt's planter elite. "The plaintiffs cannot claim that they personally were deprived of their voting rights in 1901 because they were not voters at that time," ruled the court. Never mind the resulting century of inequity.[49] Until reformers win the legislative chambers (or somehow achieve a constitutional revision) and write equity into the people's document, Alabama will remain captive to its white-supremacist, antidemocratic past.

NORMALCY RETURNS KICK FOR TD

In 2007, as Alabama ranked forty-seventh in the U.S. in high school graduation rates, the University of Alabama signed football coach Nick Saban to an eight-year contract valued at $4 million annually.[50] "I feel like he is the right man for the job," said Bama center Antoine Caldwell, "and he will be good in getting Alabama back on track."[51] Caldwell meant the football team, but for many Alabamians the state's image is bound up in the fortunes of football, as it has been since the godlike Bear Bryant won six national championships before retiring (then immediately dying) after the 1982 season. "I do not believe that sport is the very essence of Southern life," writes Rick Bragg, who grew up deep within east Alabama's working-class culture and whose two wrecked knees testify to his headlong, oblivious passion for high school football. "I know God and work and family precede football, except perhaps on Alabama-Auburn game day — but what it really is, is the grandest of all escapes from that life."[52] When sport went sour, as Bama endured losing seasons and turned over coach after coach in search of the next Bear, life threatened to crowd out escape.

"Mission Accomplished," trumpeted the *Mobile Press-Register* when the Crimson Tide landed Saban.[53] The new coach, welcomed at the Tuscaloosa airport by hundreds of exuberant fans in red sweatshirts and A-caps chanting "Roll Tide," signified "a new era of Crimson Tide football," said UA athletic director Mal Moore. Saban's arrival affirmed Alabama's "commitment to provide our student-athletes and fans with a leader who will continue our commitment to excellence across the board."[54] In smaller fonts and in fewer newspapers, other headlines that day told of a perennially unaccomplished mission: "Study says education struggling," and "Alabama kids face long odds."[55] Accompanying stories reported that *Education Week's* ranking of state policies for improving K–12 education placed Alabama among the bottom five in offering children a "chance for success." Evaluating educational readiness across a lifetime — "whether young children get off to a good start, succeed in elementary and secondary school, and hit key educational and economic benchmarks as adults" — Alabama fell significantly behind the national average and far below leading states Virginia, Connecticut, Minnesota, New Jersey, Maryland, Massachusetts, and New Hampshire. "It's clear that it matters where children live," wrote the editors.[56]

It also matters where coaches (and boosters) live. Contributors to the UA athletic department receive 80 percent tax deductions and choice stadium seats.[57] Coach Saban's yearly salary easily doubled the amount of annual financial aid that Alabama designated for over 100,000 low-income college students. The Southern Education Foundation reported that "Alabama helped less than 4 percent of students with a demonstrated financial need to attend college."[58]

The chair of the Education Finance and Appropriations Committee in the Alabama House questioned the "strong statement" Saban's hiring made "in a state that funds education at one of the lowest per-pupil rates . . . in the country. I think we've let it get out of hand."[59] Saban's celebrity salary was "sending the wrong signals about what's important in a poor state beset with tons of problems," editorialized the *Birmingham News*. "You couldn't have a more stark picture of education priorities," said Jim Carnes of the grassroots coalition Alabama Arise. "How do you explain to the people of Alabama the needs of the university when you have these kinds of resources available to pay the coach?" asked Cleo Thomas, former UA trustee.[60] Although Alabama exhibited the tendency in its extreme, the *Chronicle of Higher Education* reported on the doubling and tripling of tax-exempt donations to major university athletic programs throughout the U.S., while gifts to academic programs showed no advance.[61]

Alabama trustees, including Paul Bryant Jr., lined up on defense. "The president and athletic director have recommended this salary," said Finis St. John IV, "because of the impact athletics has on student recruiting, donor giving and the overall mission of the university." Fellow trustee John McMahon agreed: "Our fan base expects the university to compete at the highest levels. We have not done that, and if you ever lose your fan base, it is very difficult to get it back."[62] Sure enough, as summarized by *Rammer Jammer Yellow Hammer* author Warren St. John, "Saban quickly turned the ship — and the ego of an entire state — around."[63] In January 2010 the Tide won its first national title since the 1992 season. Unlike the spectacle, obsession, vindication, and escape of football, education in Alabama, having scant history of excellence and few expectations, has no large fan base to lose.

SIMPLE PERVERSITY

In 1990 journalists Ron Casey, Joey Kennedy, and Harold Jackson wrote a Pulitzer Prize–winning series of editorials for the *Birmingham News*, "What They Won't Tell You About Your Taxes," which brought the state's tax inequities and their consequences to public attention. In 2003 Kennedy quoted from the series to show that nothing much had changed: "Alabama nickels and dimes its people to death . . . its sales tax hits the poor and middle class hardest. . . . While some states exempt food and over-the-counter drugs from their sales taxes to give poorer families a break, Alabama doesn't. Alabama handcuffs more of its tax money than any other state. . . . Alabama earmarks nearly 90 percent of its revenue. The national average is only about 28 percent. Our tax system endures . . . because of the political muscle flexed by those who set it up."[64]

Coincident with the *News* publishing "What They Won't Tell You," Howell Raines at the *New York Times* pointed to the difference in property taxes paid on a large chunk of land that straddled the Alabama-Georgia line: "Kimberly-Clark pays 93 cents an acre on the Alabama side and $4.36 an acre in Georgia." Raines offered a succinct economic history of his home state: "From 1901 until the decline of the iron furnaces in the mid-1970's, Alabama property taxes were tailored for United States Steel. Now they are tailored for companies that own pine trees. It comes to the same thing. Property taxes are so low that it is more economical for the big firms to sit on their land than to develop it or sell it to someone who will." He noted that "thirteen out-of-state corporations — including International Paper, Kimberly-Clark, Scott Paper, Union Camp, Tenneco and USX, the successor to United States Steel — hold more than 11 percent of the state's land."[65]

Large owners of Alabama property wrap themselves in antitax and antigovernment rhetoric. Social-issue politics — school prayer, Ten Commandment displays, the teaching of creationism, English-only initiatives, Sunday liquor laws, bingo parlors — have sucked energy and diverted attention from cutting the atavistic knot that stifles the state's revenue structure, perpetuating widespread civic cynicism. "The only thing that runs deeper than faith in God here," observes Robin DeMonia, "is a lack of faith in government."[66]

The 1990 *News* series put tax reform into serious public discussion, where it has stayed, as public pressure for change builds. "We have one of the most regressive tax systems of any state in the country," complained Alabama Supreme Court justice Janie Shores in 1992. "Our taxes fall heaviest on the people who are least able to pay them, and that's always been true."[67] Grassroots political organizations, nonprofits, and citizen-interest groups such as the Alabama New South Coalition, Alabama Arise, A+, and the Alabama Citizens for Constitutional Reform (championed by too-soon-deceased Bailey Thompson and Thomas Corts), along with the Public Affairs Research Council, hammered away at the state's perversely interconnected constitutional and tax machinery.

In 2003, a dozen years after the *News* team won their Pulitzer, Don Logan, Alabama native and media executive (*Southern Living*, Time Warner), recalled "the wave of enthusiasm that followed the publication of those editorials. There seemed to be so much momentum that parents with children in kindergarten in 1991 had every right to expect Alabama would get its house in order and fix our schools. . . . Those children will be graduating from high school this spring. The problems were never fixed. We let those parents down. We let those children down. And we let ourselves down."[68]

News columnist Eddie Lard summed up decades of futility: "A failed education reform plan under Gov. Guy Hunt, the gutted equity court ruling, another failed education reform initiative under Gov. Jim Folsom, Gov. Fob James' piddling funding plan that passed the Legislature but did little to fix inequities, a failed education lottery vote under Gov. Don Siegelman and Riley's failed tax plan. . . . The way we fund education in Alabama is simply perverse."[69]

Perversity in Alabama education draws from shallow wells and teaches its own lessons. Although most Americans can't name one of the Gospels, while 70 percent of Alabamians can name all four, too much Good-Book learning can get you killed for spite:

A Dadeville, Ala., man who lost out in an early-morning Bible-quoting contest last week is accused of killing the man who bested him. Police Chief Terry Wright said 38-year-old Gabel Taylor was shot once in the face. The suspect, whose identity was not released, was being sought. According to witnesses, Taylor and the suspect were discussing their Bible knowledge when Taylor, whose brother is a preacher, began quoting Scripture. The suspect then retrieved his Bible and realized his recollections were wrong.

"He said Taylor did know more and that made him mad," Wright quoted witnesses as saying.[70]

A little learning eked out over a long time is a deadly thing. In its 1993 "Kids Count" survey, the Annie E. Casey Foundation ranked Alabama forty-eighth among U.S. states across a range of factors affecting children's health, education, poverty, and life chances.[71] The 2009 edition of "Kids Count" found that Alabama had not budged from its near-bottom rung, still stuck at forty-eighth.[72]

THE DAY AFTER YESTERDAY

What is owed to the Confederate dead? And their long-waving acolytes? And what is the meaning of all this looking away, looking away? "We're losing the things that make the South the South," lamented the leader of a group seeking to return the Confederate flag to the capitol dome, at least for annual Confederate holidays. "When tourists come to Montgomery, and they go to the visitors' center, the first thing they ask is where they can buy Confederate stuff. Take away all those symbols, and we'll lose our tourism."[73] In truth, although key chains, miniature flags, and other Confederate trinkets are still sold in the state capitol gift shop, today's Montgomery tourists are more likely to inquire about the location of Maya Lin's Civil Rights Memorial, or Martin Luther King's first church, or if someone thought to save the Rosa Parks bus.[74]

In the Heart of Dixie, it's always the day after yesterday and each April is Confederate History Month, although symptoms of Lost Cause melancholy diminish with passing generations. Soon all the schoolkids who dressed in gray during the Civil War Centennial and played Stonewall Jackson or Bedford Forrest will be old men whose grandkids will have never worn a Johnny Reb cap or a battle flag belt buckle, never swooped down from the high ground in a rock fight upon hapless playmates designated as Yankees-for-a-day.

Rick Bragg writes in *The Prince of Frogtown* of the Confederate monument on the courthouse square in his hometown of Jacksonville, Alabama, erected "forty-five years after the war ended, paid for by the General John H. Forney Chapter of the United Daughters of the Confederacy. The inscription reads: *Times change, men often change with them, principles, never. Let none of the Survivors of These men offer in their behalf the Penitential Plea, 'They believed they were right.' Be it ours to Transmit to Posterity our Unequivocal Confidence in the Righteousness of the Cause for which these men died.*"[75]

And what was that cause? "The Civil War was a states' rights issue and wasn't about slavery," said seventy-three-year-old Bob Radford, principles intact, at the 2002 Battle of Selma reenactment. Radford's great-grandfather fought at Chickamauga.[76]

The popularity of Ken Burns's *Civil War* documentary series, which first aired on television in 1990, fed into the reenactor phenomenon to boost attendance at events like the Battle of Selma. Begun on a small scale by local Kiwanis in 1986, the Selma reenactment counted some two thousand participants by 1992 before enthusiasm began to wane. Going through the military motions year after year proved as vacuous as the repetitious fiddle theme from Burns's series. Lacking attendance and support, Selma organizers waved the white flag and called off the 2009 reenactment. Were Dixie's gray ghosts fading? Not for some. At least one prime mover, businessman James Hammond, wasn't ready to surrender. "I'm calling this a rebuilding year. It'll be similar to Auburn's football team. They've got a new coach and a new spirit. I can see that happening here, too."[77]

The intensity of the still-tingling nub of spectral memory often substitutes for historical perspective among a minority of white Alabamians and other southerners. In a review of John M. Coski's *The Confederate Battle Flag*, Diane McWhorter notes the extent to which the debate over public displays of the Confederate flag is driven by "the raw emotion of soul injury." As for keepers of shrines to Confederate veterans, whether literal or spiritual descendants, McWhorter revisits the foundations of southern nationalism, writing that "the ideal that urged the secessionists on to their blood-drenched sacrifice was the freedom to subject a race of people to enslavement."[78]

This is the judgment of history rejected by the wearers of "Heritage Not Hate" T-shirts who place militarism and blood ties to a mythologized homeland above racial justice. "They were fighting to maintain their independence after having been invaded by a foreign country," said a member of the Sons of Confederate Veterans at a 2000 ceremony in Prattville. "It's important to remember and important to teach our children what Confederate Memorial Day is all about," echoed an employee of Alabama's Department of Archives and History. "It has nothing to do with race. It commemorates our ancestors' sacrifices."[79]

It still sticks in some craws to confess the tragic historical error of ancestors who fought beneath the rebel flag. Or, pushing the history further back, that the old family homeplace itself might sit atop a site of earlier horror when Native Alabamians were chased from their sacred geography.

But as sure as some McWhorter or Coski questions present-day rebel flag wavers, whether on Confederate Memorial Day or race day at Talladega Superspeedway, they can expect a "Letter to the Editor": "My more than two dozen maternal ancestors who fought for the South made it clear, in their letters, memoirs and books, what that Lost Cause was: they were fighting for their homeland — not for slavery, but for their families, homes and country."[80] But without slavery, there would have been no "homeland" to fight for, no paradoxical southern "freedom" to declare; nor have historians uncovered more than a handful of antislavery secessionists or free black Confederates. Old times here, selectively forgotten.

UNTIL PANHELLENIC FREEZES OVER

In March 1991 the 76th Old South Parade held by Auburn University's Kappa Alpha fraternity drew both African American protesters and Civil War–costumed white students waving Confederate flags. Ninety-five percent of Auburn's 22,000 students were white. "It's not that they don't want us," an officer of the Black Student Union told an AP reporter. "It's like they just have this picture in their minds of the Auburn family — of what Auburn should be."

"Yeah, and it's this white guy with a sweater and blonde hair," added another BSU officer. "It's not me."

"My mother grew up in Auburn," said an African American student whose home was in New York. "And she told me how she'd walk by the school and students would spit on her. She said she felt proud that now I could actually go there.

"But it seems like nothing has changed. No, it's changed, but it's all on the outside. You don't feel like you belong."[81] Certainly the faces of Auburn athletes in the money sports of football and basketball had changed. If not the faces in the crowds, the national image of Auburn was much blacker than the enrollment figures.

Atlanta reporter Jim Yardley wrote that both blacks and homosexuals at Auburn shared a "harsh climate" made tangible in controversies over free speech and assembly. The state house of representatives had commended Auburn's student senate in 1991 for voting twenty-three to seven not to charter a campus gay and lesbian group, a decision overruled by the school's president. Gay students received threatening phone calls and feared making their names public. "We have no idea in Alabama of what a university is," commented Auburn history professor Wayne Flynt. "It's a place where various viewpoints are debated. It needs to be a place where people can discuss ideas."[82]

In 1992 the Old South celebration was repeated amid a country music soundtrack with KAs (Kappa Alphas) in rebel uniforms sporting two-week beards, coeds in colorful hoop dresses, and white students and Auburn residents lining the parade route. Blair Robertson described the scene:

> Moments before the parade began, Darrel Crawford, a senior and former linebacker with the Auburn football team, set fire to a Confederate flag and raised his muscular arm in the air to show the flame to white parade supporters across the street.
>
> "Everything the Old South stands for is injustice for the black man," [said Crawford], "and I don't see why they have something like this knowing that it offends us. What is the need for this parade? It's just a blatant display of hatred. This is the way things are. This is the way things always will be."

The unreconstructed included a senior from Montgomery waving a battle flag: "Blacks preserve their heritage with Martin Luther King and everything," he said, "but when we try to preserve our heritage, they put us down and call us racist. If they have everything their way, pretty soon we'll end up with nothing."[83]

"They are propping up a way of life that saw a lot of our great-grandmothers raped and black men lynched just for looking at a white woman," said a black student about the KAS. "We're protesting a way of life that saw us oppressed and they're celebrating a way of life that saw us oppressed. I don't think there's going to be any compromise."[84]

The 1992 Old South parade was the last at Auburn, the last time the KAS covered their house with the giant battle flag and paraded in rebel uniforms, though they carry on the tradition in Old South lawn socials, balls, and band parties.[85]

Meanwhile, over at Tuscaloosa, "If University President Andrew Sorensen and the university administration have their way," wrote UA faculty member and journalist Diane Roberts in 1998, "the white fraternities and sororities and their African-American counterparts will be nudged toward democratizing their membership with integration the goal — someday."[86] Not one of the three dozen white fraternities or sororities had ever admitted a black brother or sister.

"I shudder to think that there would be a mandate to integrate," Joycelyn Carr, a UA graduate student in English and member of Delta Sigma Theta, told Roberts. "I totally disagree with pushing for integration. One principle of all Greek organizations is that you are free to choose the people you admit as members. Not every woman — regardless of race — is Delta material."

Hundreds of white UA students protested President Sorensen's change in the 2000 rush schedule, one of his strategies to encourage voluntary desegregation. "What Happened to Freedom?" and "What Happened to Student Voice?" read their signs.[87]

In the fall of 2001, the first University of Alabama "white" fraternity desegregated. It was hardly one of the old-line Machine frats, but newly arrived and Christian Lambda Sigma Phi. For its "signal that minorities are welcomed, included, appreciated, and treated fairly," the fraternity won a commendation from the faculty senate.[88] That same year, Melody Twilley, a black student who sang first soprano in the campus choir and had a nearly perfect grade point average, was rejected, for the second time, by all of the university's fifteen all-white sororities. "It's not a racial thing," insisted the Panhellenic vice president.[89] In 2003 a white sorority, Gamma Phi Beta, begun at Tuscaloosa in 1988, admitted its first black member.[90] "Baby steps to a distant, distant destination," editorialized the *Birmingham News*.[91]

Sorensen came and went. His successor, Robert Witt, said on his first day as UA president that he would like the white fraternities and sororities to begin accepting black members, but "I do not think it would be appropriate to force the issue."[92] "Witt tackles diversity" read the local headline.

Given persistence and time, normalcy gives way, but often too late for another generation. "We're torn between welcoming the progress and not forgetting the pain of our past," says George Curry, syndicated journalist and son of Alabama. "To this day, I never pull for a University of Alabama team. In fact, I pull for them to lose. The pain is too much to ignore or to forget."

Born and raised in Tuscaloosa, Curry attended college in Tennessee but has lived outside the South ever since. "I still consider myself a Southerner," he writes. "I say that with a mixture of pride and discomfort." While Curry acknowledges that many younger Alabamians lead less segregated lives than his coming of age in the 1950s and 1960s, "those of us that witnessed Alabama Gov. George C. Wallace standing in the schoolhouse door at the University of Alabama in a futile effort to maintain segregation, those of us who remember Bear Bryant's all-white football teams at 'Bama and those of us that marched in order to ride in the front of the bus or to get rid of humiliating 'Colored' water fountains have a difficult time cheering for Alabama — even when some of their athletic teams could pass for being on a Historically Black College."

But Curry, who was a high school sophomore when President Kennedy sent in the National Guard to order Wallace out of the doorway, writes that "the progress at 'Bama is undeniable and they are to be applauded for it."[93] With the state's black population at 26 percent, black students made up 12 percent of UA's total enrollment of over 28,000 in 2010. Progress.

In 2009 a Bama freshman confirmed once more that the secretive Machine, "a coalition of white fraternities and sororities," still controlled "nearly all aspects of student life. . . . My school has made a lot of progress since George Wallace stood in the doorway. . . . We are in no way, however, healed. I don't know if we ever will be, so long as the status quo that actively permits racial discrimination continues."[94]

The decades and the Tide roll on, university presidents and faculty come and go. White fraternities and sororities persist, along with the Greek system itself, living artifacts, hard kernels of socialization, passing habits of judgment and feeling to another generation of privilege, practicing for social life after college in the all-white country clubs of Alabama towns and cities.[95]

Come "Old South Days" 2009, and there were the KAS, celebrating in Confederate uniforms and waving rebel flags on the street in front of the black

Alpha Kappa Alpha sorority house. Following a letter of protest, university officials were reviewing the situation.[96] A year later national KA officials ruled that fraternity members could no longer wear their Confederate garb to campus events.[97] Hereafter perhaps they would heed Stonewall Jackson's dying words and "cross over the river and rest under the shade of the trees."

STREET FIGHTS

The state published its first brochure on black tourism in 1983. "It's good for Alabama's image to promote its black history," Lisa Shivers, director of tourism and travel told the *Times'* Peter Applebome in 1990. It was also good for the economy, as visitors toured Black Belt plantations, battlefields, quilting cooperatives, and sites of civil rights protest. African Americans who had long ago left Alabama and the South began to return to visit and to assess the extent of social change, bringing their children and grandchildren.[98] In steadily increasing numbers, cultural tourists and human rights pilgrims, as well as teachers and students from around the planet, travel the historic landscape and consider the hard and far-from-finished lessons of Black Alabama.

Of late, the naming and renaming of streets, along with the commissioning and siting of monuments, has provided contested turf for the Alabama imaginary. In the early 1990s Camden, Alabama, home to some 2,400 people, was a fairly typical Black Belt town. Whites controlled the downtown business district and had a tenuous majority on the city council. Surrounding Wilcox County was predominantly black. Black city council members sought to rename Broad Street in honor of Martin Luther King Jr., and Whiskey Run Road in memory of local black activist Rev. Thomas L. Threadgill, whose church sat along the street. The effort failed, split along racial lines. But the controversy didn't go away.

"They can name all the streets downtown for whites, but when it comes to naming one or two for blacks, it doesn't seem like they want to do that," said a Wilcox resident who lived near Whiskey Run Road. "We have the power with our shopping dollars to bring it about, but I don't know if that will ever happen."[99]

In Perry County, childhood home to Coretta Scott, a civil rights leader proposed state legislation to create a thirty-four-mile parkway named for Martin Luther King Jr. The parkway would require renaming sections of Jefferson and

Washington streets. "They will stay the way they are if we have anything to do about it," responded the white Marion city attorney.[100] And they did. After the Marion city council refused to change the street names, Hank Sanders persuaded the state legislature to name a one-hundred-mile section of Alabama Highway 14 for King.[101] The route was dedicated in 1992; the stealing and defacing of the new King Highway markers began immediately.[102]

No piece of Alabama geography provides a more compelling heritage than the fifty-four miles of U.S. Highway 80 that runs through the heart of the Black Belt, from Selma to Montgomery, marked at one end by the Edmund Pettus Bridge and at the other by Maya Lin's Civil Rights Memorial.[103] In 1996 Congress designated this stretch of road as the National Voting Rights Trail.[104] Along the route is the Lowndes County site where Viola Liuzzo, driving marchers home on March 25, 1965, was shot from a car carrying three Ku Klux Klansmen and an FBI informant.[105] A group of SCLC women erected a tall stone monument at the Liuzzo site in 1991. It quickly became a place of pilgrimage as well as a target for the spray painting of Confederate flags.[106]

As the twenty-first century arrived in Selma, the forces of Confederate general Nathan Bedford Forrest fought with local activists led by attorney Rose Sanders. First, in 1996, a community effort succeeded in changing the name of Nathan Bedford Forrest Homes (a public housing project) to that of a revered black nurse, Minnie B. Anderson.[107] The next skirmish became a teaching moment in public memory and memorialization.

In October 2001, outside Selma's Smitherman Historical Museum, the Friends of Forrest Monument Committee unveiled a bronze bust of the general atop a granite base — five tons, costing $25,000. It stood as a private monument on a public space in an African American neighborhood, bearing names of Forrest's battles and an engraved rebel flag.

Among African Americans, the historical Bedford Forrest remains anathema: a wealthy antebellum slave trader and planter; a Confederate military commander who condoned a massacre of black federal troops at Ft. Pillow, Tennessee; defender of the munitions stronghold of Selma before it was burned to the ground by Union forces during the first week of April 1865; bitter opponent of federal Reconstruction; and a paternal spirit and Grand Wizard of the Ku Klux Klan.[108]

As over a hundred monument supporters attended the statue's unveiling, a dozen protestors heckled, some chanting "Nathan's got to go" and others

"Nathan slaughtered hundreds of African Americans." They held up a dummy in a Klan costume. "Toward the end of the program," reported Alvin Benn, "the blacks began to sing 'We Shall Overcome,' but were quickly drowned out by a rendition of 'Dixie' by the much larger group."[109]

"The children who look out their doors and windows each morning see Nathan Bedford Forrest," wrote Hank Sanders at the time, "who wrecked such havoc on our forbears. . . . Each time they walk or ride down Alabama Avenue in their neighborhood, or play on the basketball court just across the street, they are faced with Nathan Bedford Forrest held up as a symbol of honor to be emulated."[110] It was a moment that called for disruption. "Disorderly, disruptive, annoying, or distracting means of communication," insists Iris Young, "are often necessary or effective elements in . . . efforts to engage others in debate over issues and outcomes."[111] During a six-month campaign, protestors challenged the Forrest monument, dumping garbage around it, chipping it with a thrown cinderblock. The president of the local SCLC chapter led a group of residents in trying to pull the statue over with a rope.[112]

"It is difficult to believe," the *Montgomery Advertiser* editorialized, "that Martin Luther King Jr., renowned as a proponent of nonviolence, would have approved of the ridiculous attempt to pull down the Nathan Bedford Forrest monument in Selma on Monday — the national holiday honoring King."[113] Perhaps. Or maybe King would have lent a hand.

It was March 2001 when one of the three white members of the Selma City Council voted to make it five to four in favor of moving the Forrest monument to Old Live Oak Cemetery near the remains of some 150 Confederate soldiers and several generals. Former mayor Joe Smitherman, a tactician of white racism for almost four decades, had approved the original siting of the monument. Selma's first African American mayor, James Perkins, supported the relocation.[114] Unlike a tree standing by the water, General Forrest was moved.

SELMA BRIDGE: ALWAYS UNDER CONSTRUCTION

In one of the stranger scenes of the 2008 presidential campaign marathon, a dozen Gee's Bend quilters joined hands with candidate John McCain, singing "Old Ship of Zion" as they ferried across the Alabama River in the rural Black Belt.[115] The Wilcox County quilters, known for their spectacular, handmade textile art exhibited in museums from New York to Houston to Atlanta and issued as first-class stamps by the U.S. Postal Service, lent a gracious moment of local color to the candidate's "Forgotten Places" tour.[116] Quilter Mary Lee Bendolph, aged seventy-two, told a reporter that McCain had "touched her heart" by visiting this region that includes counties with some of the highest rates of poverty and highest percentages of Democratic voters in the U.S. "I truly thank him for coming. It was wonderful to meet him, but no, I think another has my vote."[117]

Earlier that day, upriver in Selma, with the Edmund Pettus Bridge as skeletal backdrop, McCain had spoken to a small, heavily white gathering, announcing that he would be "the president of all the people." But most of the people in this 70 percent African American city demonstrated their solidarity by staying away. "McCain's policies unify us," said lawyer and longtime civil rights activist Faya Rose Touré. "That's why you don't see black people here."[118]

Selma and the Pettus Bridge signify victories by a people in a place forgotten since the mid-1960s by the GOP, except when prosecuting voting rights activists. With McCain's dismal civil rights record throughout years in Congress, including his (later retracted) opposition to the Martin Luther King Jr. holiday, a lot of water has passed under his bridge, and a lot of other stuff, too. Still, there stood the senator on the Selma riverbank, "framed in camera shots by the bridge where white police officers beat black demonstrators trying to march to Montgomery in 1965," wrote Elisabeth Bumiller of the *New York Times*, "and where Senators Hillary Rodham Clinton and Barack Obama converged last year in a political spectacle to commemorate the footsteps of the marchers."[119] The Bloody Sunday beatings by Dallas County deputies and Alabama state troopers provoked international outrage, led to the Selma-to-Montgomery March, and gave rise to the national clamor that pushed the Voting Rights Act into law.

Since 1965, the Edmund Pettus Bridge has taken on the meanings and features of a venerated public place.[120] Anniversaries of the march drew widely scattered veterans of the original events back to Selma. Historians gathered oral histories and wrote books. Local activists began museums and commemorative parks where the bridge touched either side of the Alabama River. And since the early 1990s, the "spectacle" of an annual Bridge Crossing Commemoration has become a tourist destination and an authenticating ritual for politicians of various stripes seeking to reaffirm or newly signal their ties to the meanings evoked by what is now one of the world's most well-known structures.[121]

Binding memories to landscape, the bridge at Selma locates transitions from one time and space to another. Named for Edmund Pettus, Confederate brigadier general and post-Reconstruction white-supremacist U.S. senator from Alabama, the landmark bridge was finished in 1940, the heyday of Jim Crow. In March 1965 it became not just a means of getting from one side of the river to the other but also a site where a people crossed out of repressive racial territory and into a social geography that they were remaking to suit themselves. In annual Bridge Crossing speeches, the Alabama River often becomes the Jordan or the Red Sea, passageways to freedom.

As the Bridge Crossing has grown in attendance and visibility, a diverse cast of civil rights, religious, and political figures, musicians, and media celebrities have walked the walk. In 2000 President Bill Clinton and Coretta Scott King led a thirty-fifth anniversary crowd of twenty thousand. Urging celebrants to "look at the South on the other side of the bridge," Jesse Jackson in 2003 warned against nostalgia, against resting on laurels and letting the memorial rituals displace present-day activism: "Beyond the bridge is crippling poverty, people working without fair wages."[122] In 2005 the Bridge Crossing celebrated "Invisible Giants," unsung worthies who tilled the grassroots and filled the ranks of marchers but went largely unmentioned in popular accounts. This year, Rep. John Lewis (who always brings along a congressional delegation) and the Reverends Jackson and Al Sharpton were the headliners. "I don't think it really matters who shows up to speak," said Sam Walker, a Bridge Crossing organizer, "because this thing is bigger than any of us. It just keeps getting bigger each year."[123]

The presidential campaign implications of the 2007 Bridge Crossing set the bar high with empathetic allusions and aspirational bonds. Addressing a mostly black audience at First Baptist Church before setting foot on Pettus Bridge, Hillary Clinton shifted into the kind of exaggerated drawl that falls painfully on the ears before leaping to YouTube. Reciting gospel lyrics familiar to fans of James Cleveland, she spoke in what trollish critics pounced upon as her "black-cent": "I want to begin by giving praise to the almighty. I don't feel no ways tired. I come too far from where I started from. Nobody told me that the road would be easy."[124] Straining to speak in the voice of the bridge, Senator Clinton's affirmation of endurance and persistence — "the march is not over" — became a moment of unintended caricature.[125]

Also on hand that day in 2007 was Bill Clinton, deciding at the last moment to show up for induction into Selma's Voting Rights Hall of Fame, but who seems largely to have made the trip as a mission of campaign bridge building. The Clinton whom Toni Morrison had called the nation's "first black president" sought to parlay his popularity among African Americans into momentum for Hillary.[126] Yet before another year had passed, John Lewis, the standard for courage and constancy, would first support Hillary, then switch to Barack Obama. For Hillary, observed an NPR commentator about this latest "battle of Selma," it's "almost like she's running against a younger, blacker version of her own husband."[127] The spirit of the bridge was shifting away from past alliances and toward a possibility unimagined at the last Bloody Sunday anniversary.

"If it hadn't been for Selma, I wouldn't be here," Barack Obama said to attendees (some wearing "Alobama" T-shirts) at a prayer breakfast that same March morning in 2007. "This is the site of my conception. I am the fruits of your labor. I am the offspring of the movement. When people ask me if I've been to Selma before, I tell them I'm coming home."[128]

Later that day, before joining Bill and Hillary and thousands of others for the crossing, Obama spoke at Brown Chapel AME Church, one of the most important civil rights rallying spots of the 1960s and the starting point for the original Selma March. The senator from Illinois recounted how, during the Kennedy administration, his Kenyan father benefited from an education program in Hawaii where he met Obama's mother, a white student from Kansas. "There was something stirring across the country because of what happened in Selma, Alabama," he said, "because some folks are willing to march across a bridge. So they got together and Barack Obama, Jr., was born." Lest reporters and bloggers think that here was a gotcha moment, a campaign spokesman quickly pointed out that Barack Junior, born in 1961, more than three years before the March, was "speaking metaphorically about the civil rights movement as a whole." A fact-obsessed family history misses the meaning in Obama's appropriation of the Pettus Bridge for the work of what he calls the "Joshua generation" — as contrasted with the civil rights veterans' "Moses generation." "We've got to remember now that Joshua still has a job to do," he said. "There are still battles that need to be fought; some rivers that need to be crossed."[129]

More than a year after the Selma prayer breakfast and his Brown Chapel speech, as Obama claimed the requisite delegates to become the Democratic nominee, he offered a cheering St. Paul, Minnesota, crowd a list of actors and moments through which, "every so often," compassionate people in particular places call upon their "fundamental goodness to make this country great again": "that band of patriots in Philadelphia hall" who opted for a more perfect union; "all those who gave on the fields of Gettysburg and Antietam their last full measure of devotion" to save the union; the "greatest generation" of World War II; "the workers who stood out on the picket lines; the women who shattered glass ceilings"; and "the children who braved a Selma bridge for freedom's cause."[130]

Children amid Bloody Sunday? Children (more accurately teens and youth) are usually linked in the freedom struggle imaginary not to Selma but to Birmingham's Children's Crusade in 1963, where they strategically provoked Bull Connor's overreaction, where they were hosed and chased by police dogs, watched by the world.[131] Taking their inspiration from Birmingham, hundreds of African American high school students demonstrating in support of voting rights were arrested and incarcerated in Selma in the months before March 1965. But a state trooper's killing of twenty-six-year-old Jimmie Lee Jackson on February 18 produced such an "extraordinary tension" that the marchers who crossed the Selma Bridge on March 6 were preponderantly adults led by protest veterans such as John Lewis, Amelia Boynton, Hosea Williams, and Albert Turner.[132]

Obama's joining of the Children's Crusade with the troopers' assault upon the six hundred at the Selma Bridge was much like the factually incorrect but figuratively crucial story of his conception — "because some folks are willing to march across a bridge." It revealed the hoped-for trajectory of a new generation coming to political age after the long season of reaction that followed the gains of, and shaped the resistance to, the Civil Rights Act of 1964 and the Voting Rights Act of 1965. Obama's inclusive narratives of himself as a child of the Selma Bridge, and of "the children who braved a Selma bridge for freedom's cause" re-placed a venerable — if increasingly distant — public memory of heroism with a generative purpose for the present. Monuments, memorials, and the rituals of commemoration remain vital only if the living can shift their meaning and emotional power into possibilities for an impending or imagined future. From Selma to Selma to Selma, the Edmund Pettus Bridge is built and rebuilt by those who march across it.

ECHOES FROM THE TERRORTORY

When contemporary Alabama lapses into throwback scenes from the Heart of Dixie, a few backsliding moments can evoke historical memory and raise the question: Will it be different this time? A pattern of incidents in late-twentieth-century Montgomery that likely would have gone unnoticed or unchallenged in earlier years caught the attention of two black Montgomery council members. Several white police officers in the Cradle of the Confederacy were found to have brutalized black suspects and planted evidence. "What I see happening here," said first-term councilman James Nuckles, "is a motivation to do what has been done in the past, and that is to instill fear into the black population. It's systemic."

Nuckles, wrote reporter Todd Kleffman, "suggests that there is a ghost that still haunts the police department from the civil rights days and beyond."[133] What, if anything, had changed? "Could it be that the reason we have these high-profile incidents is that we're looking for them," wondered Montgomery police chief John Wilson, "and when we find them we're not going to put a lid on them?"

Chief Wilson was operating under new mayor Bobby Bright, a white lawyer and criminal-justice professional whose 1999 election over law 'n' order hard-line incumbent Emory Folmar had depended on black voters. Speaking of two police brutality incidents that occurred shortly after Bright took office, attorney Roy Anne Conner told Kleffman, "If those incidents had occurred under the previous administration, the public would have never known about them."[134] She should know. Conner worked as a police officer from 1971 to 1981. Her father and grandfather were also Montgomery policemen.

Montgomery's black citizenry kept the pressure on, calling for the resignation of Chief Wilson, initiating protests. The SCLC brought in Montgomery-born Martin Luther King III to speak against racism and police brutality. The FBI and U.S. attorney's office investigated for civil rights law violations. In February 2002 eight third-shift white officers resigned and three others faced dismissal. "What these officers did," said Chief Wilson on the *CBS Evening News*, "tarnished not only my badge, but every badge of every law enforcement officer in this country, just like the impact that the Rodney King case had on us."[135]

It was, concluded the *Advertiser*'s Kleffman, "another case that puts Montgomery on the national radar with a negative blip." But it also signified an important blip of another color on the Alabama imaginary. What had once enjoyed impunity, the daily intimidation and brutalization of black citizens, life in the terrortory, was now likely to see the light of day — and in doing so, shifting the meaning of Alabama.

For those too young to remember past projections, the Alabama imaginary can form fresh with one click of a mouse. Consider the YouTube video "Birmingham Police Beat Unconscious Suspect."[136] In January 2008 five Birmingham police officers kicked and battered an already unconscious black man who had been thrown from his wrecked vehicle onto the roadside following a high-speed chase that ended in the over-the-mountain city of Hoover. Captured on a patrol car camera, the incident and the existence of the video were covered up for fourteen months within the police department. The evidence came to light when a Jefferson County assistant district attorney preparing a case against the black driver, who had struck an officer with his vehicle during the chase, noticed a gap in the police video and requested the full recording, which showed the beating. Calling the incident "shameful" and saying he knew nothing of it until the DA called, Birmingham police chief A. C. Roper fired the five officers (black, white, and Hispanic) who participated in the beating.[137] "This was a diverse, equal opportunity beat-down," wrote *News* columnist John Archibald (actually, all the officers were male).[138] State investigators and the FBI launched inquiries while the national media reached for a predictable storyline.

This time, it was different.

"The culture of the past was that police brutality was acceptable," said the city's black mayor on NBC's *Today*. "In Birmingham, Alabama, in the present day it is not acceptable."[139]

The *News* alluded to the "terrible, well-documented history of brutality" that was part of the history of Birmingham PD and editorialized about "the renewed shame this brings to all police officers, to city officials and, yes, to each of us."[140]

Governor Riley weighed in: "You have to give police officers some latitude, to go through what they go through every day, and the adrenaline's pumping and everything is moving very quickly, but you should never tolerate that type of reaction from any segment of law enforcement."[141]

Archibald, a University of Alabama grad and twenty-year veteran at the *News*, listed several episodes in the city's history of uniformed brutality and the turn that Birmingham's first black mayor, Richard Arrington, made to move away from the "bullying reputation" of the police department. "And it all came apart last week, when the world watched five cops beat an unconscious man. . . . That's Birmingham, those people thought, because they don't know Birmingham and they don't know better." Archibald acknowledged the city's tenacious notoriety but vouched, "We will not go back."[142]

"F" FOR OPENNESS

"If I do nothing else during the next four years," pledged Bob Riley on the day of his inauguration as governor in 2003, "Alabama will lead this nation in uniting our races once and for all." Full of the hyperbole of daybreaks and new beginnings, Riley made his promise during a birthday commemoration for Martin Luther King Jr. at the Dexter Avenue Baptist Church in Montgomery where King, at age twenty-five, had held his first pastorate. As if one outrageous vow wasn't enough, Riley went on to "declare once and for all that racial problems in this state are going to cease, beginning now."[143]

Governor Riley gestured magically toward the rehabilitation of Alabama's political imaginary at its most calamitous fault line. The 2008 presidential election tally unwrapped his delusion. The Republicans took Alabama, as they had done since 1980. John McCain amassed 60 percent of the total vote, the largest percentage of victory in any Deep South state. Exit polling by the *New York Times* showed that only 10 percent of white voters voted for Obama, the smallest percentage of any state. Obama received 98 percent of the black vote. Alabama was one of the few states in which a greater percentage of white voters had cast ballots for John Kerry in 2004 than they did for Obama.[144] To judge by voter behavior, the races in Alabama were united largely unto themselves.

There were other signs that suggested more continuity than departure from Alabama traditions. Surveying the race and gender composition of appointments to over three hundred of the state's boards and commissions during the Riley years, the Examiners of Public Accounts revealed that the numbers hadn't changed. In a state that was 26 percent black and 52 percent female, white men held two-thirds of the appointed seats and women filled about one-quarter — essentially the same as when Riley took office.[145]

"Have you had enough of proration?" Riley asked during his 2002 campaign, promising a "different Alabama."[146] Come spring of 2010, his governorship winding down and tax collections still falling, Riley ordered a second year of proration. A third followed in 2011. Alabama, rainy day fund depleted, wore its ranking as forty-ninth for local and state tax collections as a badge of honor.

Electoral tea leaves foreshadowed continued racial bifurcation, as some 84 percent of white Alabama voters under age thirty told CNN pollsters they voted for John McCain in the 2008 presidential election.[147] As Alabama's GOP had become the white people's party, the dominant politics of the Deep South continued to recoil against national Democrats.[148] This did not bode well for the quixotic 2010 gubernatorial candidacy of African American Artur Davis, who gave up a safe congressional seat for a history-making run at a breakthrough. "Pipe dreams, building air castles," snapped veteran Alabama voting rights activist Jerome Gray about Davis's chances.[149] In a state where white voters composed 75 percent of the total, a successful black candidate would have to turn out a solid African American vote and win nearly 40 percent of the white electorate.[150] Having served as Alabama chairman for the Obama campaign, Davis — whose upward trajectory from a working-class, female-headed household to an Ivy League education shared features of biography with the president — was easily tied to the national Democratic Party by his political opponents. "Of all states," D.C. representative and veteran political commentator Eleanor Holmes Norton told journalist Gwen Ifill, "that's the worst state I could think of now to run in. A terrible state. . . . The country's so polarized; I do not see a southern governor as our next step, frankly."[151]

Trimming his sails throughout the gubernatorial primary season, Rep. Davis was the only member of the Congressional Black Caucus to vote against national health care legislation (which passed by a 219 to 212 vote), despite his district being the fifth poorest in the U.S.[152] "Artur Davis gained nothing in his race for Governor by his vote," noted one comment on the *Birmingham News* blog. "If he thinks conservative reactionary white voters in Alabama will support him because he voted NO . . . then he doesn't understand Alabama Politics. Conservative voters will thank him for his no vote and then vote for Byrne or whoever wins the GOP primary."[153] Candidate Davis so angered the state's traditional black leadership that he neither asked for nor received the endorsement of influential African American political organizations.[154] "It's one thing to position ourselves to secure votes that we do not usually get in a statewide political race," complained Hank Sanders. "It's another to stomp on our own people in the process. And Artur Davis has stomped on us time after time."[155] Davis lost the primary to Agricultural Commissioner Ron Sparks, who in turn was thrashed by Republican Robert Bentley in November.

Among the numerous low points of the 2010 governor's campaign was the discovery that the Alabama Education Association had shuttled nearly $600,000 into the True Republican PAC for attack ads against GOP candidate Bradley Byrne, scolding him for favoring the teaching of evolution in schools. In rebuttal, Byrne, who as chancellor worked to clean up the state's corrupt two-year college system, rushed to assure voters, "I believe the Bible is the Word of God and that every single word of it is true. . . . As a member of the Alabama Board of Education, the record clearly shows that I fought to ensure the teaching of creationism in our school textbooks." That Byrne would scurry into know-nothing land, and that the AEA, angry over Byrne's efforts to keep community-college teachers from also holding jobs as legislators, would appeal to anti-evolutionist voters, seemed especially perverse and drew the inevitable wrath of national observers such as HBO's Bill Maher and *New York Times* columnist Gail Collins.[156]

As the Great Recession rolled in like a Gulf hurricane or a BP oil plume, the predicaments of other states and the foibles and outrages of somebody else's governors — New York, Alaska, Illinois, South Carolina, Arizona — distributed a measure of the embarrassment and dysfunction usually reserved for Alabama. "California, it has long been claimed, is where the future happens first," wrote Paul Krugman as the Golden State crashed into mountainous indebtedness and constitutional "ungovernability." "If it is, God help America." But Krugman might have been writing about Alabama as he described the "straitjacket" of California's Proposition 13, capping property tax rates and requiring a two-thirds legislative majority to increase any state tax. California's is a "tax system that is both inequitable and unstable."[157] As a "partisan power struggle in the State Senate brought New York's government to new heights of chaos," calls began for "a more radical approach: a constitutional convention to rewrite the state's very political DNA."[158] Rewriting Alabama's political DNA first requires being able to read the writing on the wall.

Would New Yorkers and Californians take the lead on constitutional conventions and rewrites? If they did, would it be contagious? "California's current constitution rivals India's and Alabama's for being the longest and most convoluted in the world," observed the *Economist*, "and is several times longer than America's. It has been amended or revised more than 500 times and now, with the cumulative dross of past voter initiatives incorporated, is a document that assures chaos."[159] On the map of constitutional chaos, California bordered Alabama, New York, and India.

Republican contenders in the 2010 Alabama governor's campaign raced each other to denounce Obama policy proposals. When the president addressed Congress on health-care reform, pointedly noting that in Alabama almost 90 percent of the insurance market was controlled by just one company (Blue Cross and Blue Shield), candidate Tim James turned that into a sez-you moment, claiming the feds "have one goal and that is to control our lives." Obama's "intent" was to "socialize our medical care," insisted Roy "Ten Commandments" Moore. Ultimate winner, retired dermatologist Robert Bentley, declared federal health-care legislation as "the worst thing that has ever happened in this country." Invoking the specter of George Wallace, Bentley vowed, "As governor I will stand up and fight it."[160]

Meanwhile, contestants across the U.S. lined up for the worst state legislature award. Federal stimulus money might bail out the miserly Alabama budget for a couple of years, but then what? "Year in and year out," wrote the *Huntsville Times*,

> the Legislature refuses to address the core problems of this state, some of them structural in nature, others of them political. . . .
>
> Asking the voters if they want to create a constitutional convention would seem innocuous enough. Not so. Entrenched (and hysterical) opponents imply that the citizens can't be trusted to make such a decision and that if a convention were called, special interests would control it.
>
> Well, the legislators ought to know. Special interests — everything from business groups to the powerful Alabama Education Association — run joyously unchecked in Montgomery's halls of power. They employ highly paid lobbyists to promote their own agendas and to block anything deemed to be even remotely counter to their own welfare.[161]

Nor was there yet any way to trace political campaign money as it laundered from PAC to PAC to candidate.[162] The Campaign Disclosure Project funded by the Pew Trust gave Alabama an "F" for openness.[163]

And what of that sacrosanct, apolitical branch of government, the courts? In the spring of 2009 the U.S. Supreme Court ruled that judges ought to disqualify themselves in cases in which they have been the recipients of large campaign contributions from one of the litigating parties. Who would be left to hear Alabama cases? "The massive amount of money flowing into judicial races certainly impacts the perception of whether courts can be fair," Sue Bell Cobb, chief justice of the Alabama Supreme Court, told the *Wall Street Journal*. "Judge Cobb," wrote Nathan Koppel, "was elected to her current post in a 2006 race in which she and her opponent raised more than $7.5 million — one of the highest campaign totals in any state supreme court race. . . . Campaign contributions have not skewed results in Alabama, she said, but it has eroded trust in the court."[164] Where did erosion lap onto skewing, skewing onto corruption?

But didn't existing Alabama law limit campaign contributions to judges to a few thousand dollars (the amount depending upon judicial level), before they have to recuse themselves from cases involving donors? Surely judges couldn't disregard the law? "It's a pretty good statute," said H. Thomas Wells of Birmingham, president of the American Bar Association. "The problem is Alabama has no transparent way to track campaign contributions to judges, so that statute can't be used."[165]

"DO I MAKE YOU PROUD?"

A state anxious for a makeover searches the starting lineups and sidelines, the writing on the walls and faces among the wallflowers, the studios of New York, Nashville, and Hollywood for ways to count among the winners in the world.[166] What was the sound of America singing as the new century opened? In *American Idol*'s first five seasons, all the winners were from the South, two from Alabama. Singers with strong ties to Birmingham were runners-up in 2004 and 2005, and won again in 2006 when Taylor Hicks, a crowd-pleasing embodiment of black and white southern streams visible in his gray hair, came across to thirty million viewers as if Elvis had been rehabbing at Weight Watchers for the last quarter-century.

And what to make of Ruben Studdard, 2003's idol from Birmingham, jersey size XXL, area code 205? "Roo-ben, Roo-ben," fans would chant for the big man, smooth and soulful in song, voice of sectional sensitivity and the southernization of America, southern comfort to the Fox-TV nation.

Appearing on the nation's highest-rated TV show for weeks and charming its diverse audience, Studdard's genial presence polished the state's image. "To have an African-American from this community touting Birmingham on national TV the way Ruben did," exulted Chamber of Commerce president David Adkisson, "it blows away a lot of negative stereotypes about this city."[167] Unfortunate phrase, "blows away," coming from Bombingham, but Adkisson meant well. Celebrity judge Paula Abdul said Ruben could be elected governor. Governor Riley proclaimed "Ruben Studdard Day."

"Ruben Studdard . . . is practically unhateable," praised the New York Times. "He is a big guy with a shy smile and a smooth voice, and he manages to play up his teddy-bear image while still feigning mild embarrassment." Music critic Kelefa Sanneh seemed as sold as the Fox fans. She polled the political imaginary for phone-in votes. If Ruben the Un-rapper could win the heart of Nielsen nation, what did that mean for the Heart of Dixie? "He united red-state and blue-state voters," rhapsodized Sanneh, "he consolidated his base while reaching out to undecided voters, he promised to be a breath of fresh air (he never let us forget he was from Alabama, proof of his outsider status) even as he made sure to stick close to the mainstream. In this way he won on 'American Idol,' the most hotly contested musical election of the year."[168] If rose-colored Ruben softened the appearance of Birmingham, only a curmudgeon would complain about unfinished agendas of race and class. Imagined as an ambassador from some reconstructed Alabama, soulful Studdard seemed a getaway from murderous, drug-ridden, rap-wracked, inner-city enclaves. Was he an extra-large mirage? "The White House announced that Ruben Studdard is going to perform at one of President Bush's inauguration celebrations," joked Conan O'Brien. "Republicans said they chose Studdard because he's one of the red states."[169]

QUAGMIRES

Semblances of the old Alabama normalcy remain, often in high places, throwing up barriers to invasion. As the first decade of the twenty-first century slipped into history, the state's most visible public figures were its two right-wing Republican U.S. senators, still pumping the Heart of Dixie.[170] Despite resistance from African Americans and a significant minority of white voters, Alabama's dominant politics remained in thrall to what Bob Herbert called "the party of just-say-no."[171] Shored up by core supporters among business and professional elites (economically powerful and self-interested) and by the majority of white voters (from socially conservative to reactionary), Senators Shelby and Sessions, like the GOP itself, were "bizarrely detached from the real world," at odds with the long-term needs of state and nation. They savored their votes against progressive legislation ranging from the micro (embryonic stem cell research) to the macro (economic stimulus during the Great Recession, national health care).[172]

"When it came to looking out for the interests of ordinary working Americans," wrote Herbert, "the party of just-say-no could hardly have cared less. Referring to the catastrophic ordeal of Detroit's automakers, Senator Richard Shelby of Alabama, the senior Republican on the banking committee, told us . . . 'The financial situation facing the Big Three is not a national problem but their problem.'" Shelby, made of money, could count $15 million in his coffers before his 2010 reelection campaign formally began.[173] Attacking the creation of an independent consumer protection agency, he readily acknowledged that he'd rather protect banks.[174] "On the side of the plutocrats," as Paul Krugman observed, Shelby opposed legislation that would increase federal scrutiny of large banks and financial companies in order to prevent their taking advantage of government backing with the sort of shadowy, deregulated practices that led to the Great Recession.[175] Perhaps most egregiously, Shelby pronounced the 2010 national health care legislation a "terrible mistake," despite the fact that over 640,000 Alabamians lacking health insurance could now receive coverage.[176]

And here was junior senator Sessions voting against legislation (which passed, seventy-eight to twenty) to provide child care support for low-income families and welfare recipients so that parents would have time to work. "You can't get from welfare to work without child care," explained Connecticut senator Christopher Dodd.[177]

As the ranking minority member on the judiciary committee, Sessions pledged "fair and honest" treatment of Obama's nominees. His high visibility gave the national media reason to revisit his rejection as a Reagan nominee for federal district judge. In 1986 the Senate Judiciary Committee had turned U.S. Attorney Sessions away for his overzealous, partisan handling of the failed prosecutions of Black Belt voting rights activists as well as for a series of disparaging comments about the civil rights movement and its sympathizers.[178]

A career Justice employee testified that Sessions had branded the NAACP and ACLU "un-American and communist-inspired." A former black assistant U.S. attorney in Alabama said that Sessions had called him "boy," warned him about the way he spoke to white people, and disparaged a white lawyer who took civil rights clients as a "disgrace to his race." The 1986 Sessions appointment was opposed by organizations such as the NAACP, the Leadership Conference on Civil Rights, and People for the American Way. "Mr. Sessions," said Senator Edward Kennedy at the confirmation hearings, "is a throwback to a shameful era which I know both white and black Americans thought was in our past. It's inconceivable to me that a person of this attitude is qualified to be a U.S. attorney, let alone a United States federal judge."[179] The deciding vote that denied Sessions's federal judgeship was cast by Alabama's Howell Heflin, who argued that his "duty to the justice system is greater than any duty to any one individual."[180]

Since there are few surer ways to win statewide office in Alabama than being on the receiving end of a blast from a Massachusetts Kennedy, sez-you voters punched Sessions's rejection ticket to the U.S. Senate in 1996, following Heflin's retirement. His voting record consistently landed him among hardcore, right-wing ranks in opposition to civil rights, affirmative action, child care, and environmental legislation. He defended Bush's judicial nominees, such as Mississippi's Charles Pickering, who had civil rights reputations as bad or worse than his own. He was one of only nine senators voting against a ban on torturing military detainees.[181] Sessions, reelected to his third Senate term in 2008, represented a national political party that had shrunk to fit the ideology of white, mainly southern and western conservatives.

Faced with Barack Obama's nomination of Judge Sonia Sotomayor to the Supreme Court in the summer of 2009, Sessions, who had voted against Sotomayor's appointment to federal appellate court in 1998, promised her a "fresh start . . . to convince us if we were wrong before."[182] He then took the Senate floor for a series of five "teaching moments" that ranged from setting out his belief in originalist judicial interpretation (what did the Constitution's framers intend?) to expressing his opposition to gun control, affirmative action, and voting rights for ex-felons.[183] Oblivious to persisting class, gender, and racial inequality in the U.S., while assertive in his states' rights overtones, Sessions's patronizing lectures tapped into the worst of Alabama's yesterdays.

Senator Sessions intended his sez-you loud and large. Knowing that the Sotomayor hearings would give him the most national visibility since his arrival in the Senate in 1997, he added to his media staff. The suspense of a "fresh start" quickly dissolved. During the televised hearings, Sessions appeared unchastened by his own history of racial and gender politics as he hammered against what Judge Sotomayor could bring from her working-class, Latina experience. Once again a south Alabama accent broadcast exclusion and parochialism.

Hearings over, Sessions announced his unsurprising conclusion in an op-ed essay for *USA Today*: "I don't believe that Judge Sotomayor has the deep-rooted convictions necessary to resist the siren call of judicial activism. She has evoked its mantra too often. As someone who cares deeply about our great heritage of law, I must withhold my consent."[184] And, as he had in 1998, Richard Shelby also opposed Sotomayor. "During her confirmation hearings and after meeting with her privately," announced Alabama's senior senator, "she was unable to allay my concerns regarding two major issues she has considered — Second Amendment rights and race-based preferences."[185] Oblivious that their words and votes conveyed long-persistent, historical postures of white supremacy, states' rights, and ol' boy privilege — Sessions and Shelby seemed like Dixie cave dwellers in a state famous for its troglodytes.

LONG JOURNEY HOME

Rodney Jones, native poet of cave-riddled Morgan County, having worked at many menial and meaningful jobs and traveled far before settling down to write and teach in Carbondale, Illinois, says that although north Alabama has focused his imaginative energy, he remains in a "permanent psychological exile from my homeland. . . . When I lived there as a kid I thought I had some kind of political obligation to change things in a way that as an adult I saw couldn't be accomplished in my lifetime."[186]

Many of Jones's contemporaries describe similar Alabama getaways. Thirty-six years after his 1961 graduation from Theodore High School in Mobile, Larry Lee reflected on what had become of a group of seven friends who had enrolled together at Auburn University. All graduated. Six left the state for a variety of jobs: engineer, mathematician, city employee, preacher, school administrator, and college professor. "During the most productive years of each of these lives," writes Lee, "Alabama has not benefited from their contributions. . . . And this is Alabama's great tragedy of too many decades."[187]

Rather than value homegrown talent and potential, Alabama is intent upon projecting a manufacturing metamorphosis — potlatch-style — shoving tax abatements, free land, state-backed development bonds, and non-union labor at migrating auto assembly outposts from Germany, Japan, South Korea: Mercedes, Honda, Hyundai. The fever for car chasing has overwhelmed second thoughts about the enormous costs of enticements. Yet even to suggest that boosting state support for education on a scale approaching the incentives lavished on auto manufacturers would offer a surer way of allocating resources for the long-term good of Alabama's citizens remains beyond the bounds of political discourse. Meanwhile, the Alabama Commission on Higher Education awarded an F to the state for the affordability of its colleges and universities.[188] The high school dropout rate ranks among the nation's highest, posing the greatest drag on Alabama's potential.[189] The obvious first steps — sufficiently funding early childhood learning, focusing on dropout prevention, and establishing adequacy and equity among school districts — require political will, leadership unfettered by lobbyists, and widespread mobilization that has yet to materialize.

As for reshaping the Alabama imaginary, invasions of normalcy have achieved mixed results. Time here, once stopped by exploding bombs, ticks off the passing heartbeats of civil rights veterans and would-be constitutional reformers, the pace of spatial resegregation, the roll call of black county commissioners and legislators, the minutes between the Interstate exits of transnational automakers, the days until Auburn-Alabama, the span of life without parole, the weeks of hunting and fishing seasons, the ever-springing hopes for the next election.

History's compulsions in Alabama stand revealed in the persistence of social inequality, vast disparities of well-being, and antidemocratic political and economic institutions. "Because disadvantaged and excluded sectors cannot wait for the process to become fair," writes Iris Marion Young, "because there are often so many contending interests and issues, oppressed and disadvantaged groups have no alternative but to struggle for greater justice under conditions of inequality."[190] Having come this far, how far has Alabama come? Not so far, Mobile's Satchel Paige might say, that it can look back and not find the past gaining on it. But far enough yet to look the day after yesterday in the eye?

Epilogue

Goodlier than the land that Moses
Climbed lone Nebo's Mount to see.
— JULIA TUTWILER, "Alabama"

Oh Moon of Alabama
We now must say goodbye.
— BERTOLT BRECHT, "Alabama Song"

RACE WEEKEND

The sound of Sez-you massed, revved, and capitalized? That would be more than 150,000 NASCAR fans and some four-dozen candy-colored stock cars inside the Talladega Superspeedway at summer's end. Is this, as a *New York Times* writer claimed, a space for "the opposite of politics"?[1] Or are race weekends the Heart of Dixie's last pit stop?

In 2003 NASCAR dads, a pollster's catchy term, were said to hold the keys to the November elections. The simplistic label attempted to capture a demographic of white men who worked with hands and machinery, cement and sheet metal, nail guns and electrical wire, with a military stint in the immediate family, accompanied to the track, in fewer numbers, by wives and girlfriends, by kids with multicolored backpacks, rolled-up posters, and visor caps. Come the morning of September 28, NASCAR dads mainly held the keys to RVs, SUVs, and pickups with pull-behinds, en route to 'Dega, or already encamped around the Alabama racetrack.

Between Atlanta and Birmingham, along the southernmost fingers of the Appalachians, the exit off I-20 leads to Speedway Boulevard and flatland acres of motor homes, trucks, pop-up campers, and tents. Temporary quarters are marked with flagpoles flying driver numbers, stars and stripes, Confederate fighting colors. Waved along by state troopers in smoky hats and black racing stripes up their blue pants legs, fans park in ranks of tight rows among license plates from Alabama and Georgia, but also from Missouri, Ohio, Wisconsin, then wander with thousands over to the shopping midway, dazzled by the metallic glimmer and luminous reflections of eighteen-wheeler trailers, sides flipped up into storefronts for moving all that colorful merchandise beneath the morning sun. From racetrack to racetrack the rolling souvenir caravan follows the NASCAR circuit.

Another sort of crowd gathers around the Dale Earnhardt truck for Sunday morning services. Someone is preaching. A black, red, and silver-trimmed silhouette of the Intimidator looms near the congregants, his arms outstretched. The Sacred Earnhardt of Dixie crashed the wall of death so fastidiously at Daytona in 2001 that no one who witnessed it believed it.

Across the Talladega grounds, a carny scene deploys, in all shapes, in jeans, shorts, driver T-shirts, baseball caps, sunglasses, carrying plastic bags full of trinkets and gewgaws, holding cups of beer or fluorescent-green plastic bottles of Mountain Dew. A sweaty throng with barrel-shaped men wearing shirts that read: "Addicted to beer and blow jobs." These must be the NASCAR dads.

The scene looms flat and treeless near the track, hotter by the minute. In the Corporate Display Area, a pumped-up Viagra exhibit stands close by the tallest structure in sight, the black and gold "An Army of One" tower where recruiters welcome blue-collar kids to refuel the war wagon. "Our fans and competitors will show the world that we stand united in support of our troops in the war against Iraq," said Grant Lynch, president of the Talladega Superspeedway and former PR manager for R. J. Reynolds Tobacco Company, soon after the U.S.-led invasion.[2]

From out of the Army recruitment tower emerge guys who'd jump for each other into a firefight or a house-to-house against slim odds on the other side of the world. Sloggers bonded by football, hunting, drinking, Holy Ghost, nation, mission, Toby Keith. Team players who'd have each other's back if it killed them. Guys who refused to believe, because the magnitude of duplicity, squander, and arrogance went beyond their wildest unwilling experience or worst boss, that a president and his cronies, including the Alabama native who was national security advisor, waving the flag while plying the rhetoric of fear, would send them into death's quagmire for no good cause.

Shortly before the 2003 invasion, soldier-turned-novelist Christian Bauman had complained bitterly about romanticized U.S. Army recruiting pitches, the sort of gung-ho, Be-All-You-Can-Be-Army-of-One imagery that pulled him to enlist, to spend four years in Somalia and Haiti, and then to write his realistic novel *The Ice Beneath You* (2002) about the lives of ordinary troops. "We do not acknowledge who is in the Army and why they are there. We watch shows on the Discovery Channel about Green Berets or Rangers or Navy Seals and think this is the military. . . . The real Army is made up of . . . people who had no choice, people trapped and suffocating without enough education and a real job. . . . When some poor private from Alabama, who never had a chance in life, gets killed in Iraq, he won't know why."[3]

The first Alabamian killed in Iraq, in March 2003, was a private named Howard Johnson II, age twenty-one, from Mobile. He had joined the Army of One two weeks out of 99 percent black LeFlore High School. His father, Howard Johnson Sr., a Missionary Baptist pastor, told a reporter that his son "didn't shy away from it. . . . He never expressed any displeasure in going." Johnson had watched a news story on Sunday TV about his son's company being ambushed near Nasiriyah. "It seemed like I heard him call my name, 'Daddy,' and I felt a pain for him."

At his office the next day, Pastor Johnson felt his son's presence. "I walked to the wall where I have several pictures of him, and I kissed one of the pictures, praying for the Lord to be with him." It was late afternoon on Tuesday when an Army officer arrived with the news.[4]

Back at the Talladega Superspeedway, the startlingly blue day glows hotter still, shirts come off, coolant goes down. The vast crowd streams the grandstands. It's easy to lose yourself in a picture this big.

Overlooking the start-finish line, the Moss Thornton Tower is the choice place to sit. A ticket there sets you back $120. The cheap seats, where fans barely see one section of the track, go for around fifty bucks.

Jets from the 203rd Marine Attack Training Squadron fly over the pre-race rituals, patriotic sky jumpers leap with a giant American flag and a Winston flag while Lee Greenwood sings "God Bless the USA." Many in the stands sing along. Down on the infield stage, Krista Allison, whose father, Davey (second-generation Alabama Gang), died when his helicopter crashed here in 1993, offers a prayer, asking for a blessing on our troops who are fighting for freedom. Two-thirds of Alabamians polled in July 2003 felt that the Iraq War was worthwhile and that President Bush was handling it well.[5]

Just after noon comes driver introduction time. Ericka Dunlap, Miss

America 2004, begins shaking hands with the lineup of NASCAR stars. A bronzed, shirtless drunk a few rows up in the grandstand yells, "Look at the nigger! Get the nigger off!"

Then for a while it's all about the consuming speed, the circling engine drones, the micro-nearness to mayhem at a track so fast the cars' power is limited by restrictor plates on the engine intakes. According to the "Official Souvenir Program," a Talladega racecar costs around $300,000. There are forty-three cars driven by forty-three white men in the starting line-up. Fans know the drivers as kin, heroes, and villains. Fuel, tires, and crew sweat into the sun as a toxic swirl of stars rises to the Alabama sky, round and round in the same place. Titanium nerves and microsecond reflexes. The thrill of banged-in, close-pursuit fender bumping at 190 mph. Team strategies radio from crew to drivers and back.

The race doesn't feel much like fun, more a speed parade, but not one you'd want to run in, with the rainbow, logo-plastered cars, four- or five-wide, bunched inches in front, behind. The drivers are rich celebrities — Michael Waltrip, Tony Stewart, Bill Elliott, in metallic suits plastered with corporate brand logos. Talladega fans are passionate in love and in enmity, as for Jeff Gordon, the anti-Earnhardt, who is booed and jeered and given the finger every time the 24 car comes round.

Dale Junior is the clear favorite, many of the white mass wearing red. Junior is chasing his fifth consecutive Winston Cup victory at Talladega. This is the last season a tobacco company sponsors the cup, NASCAR's top racing series; next year it will be Nextel, as the sport is reimagineered. But it seems unlikely that Talladega will cease anytime soon being a place to smoke like a fiend, grill slabs of meat, drink like a fish, get sick as a dog. What would the campground be without rebel yelling, grab-assing, and ogling short shorts? It's a free space for mouthing and antics not allowed on a paycheck job. Not the opposite of politics, but an escape hatch. A Heart of Dixie the size of a tri-oval, packed with fans of all sizes, plenty of widebodies, overhanging, restless hands digging at nachos and cheese, steak burgers, hot dogs, "American fries," cans of Bud, tits. When the stock car culture is imagined for pop culture laughs in the Hollywood movie *Talladega Nights*, the turf invader is an egotistical, gay, French Formula One driver.[6]

On a rented scanner with noise-reduction headphones, you hear the drivers shout orders, cuss their pit crews or egg them on, snap at some young gun's reckless maneuver, fume when hung out to dry by a drafting buddy. A few laps short of the 188 that make up today's five-hundred-mile race, focused frenzy binds the contenders. Squeezed in a turn, bumped, the M&M's car goes airborne with the crowd rising to watch the shell of what it wants, plain or peanut, end over end four or five times in a beach ball of colors. Out comes the red flag invoking a new rule that holds drivers to their places while the accident is cleared.

"I like that rule," veteran driver Rusty Wallace says after the race. "I have never liked everyone screaming around the racetrack, and a guy's sitting there on fire."[7]

This time the guy lucky not to be flambé is Elliott Sadler, who's been racing since elementary school when he was Virginia go-kart champ. Sadler is helped from the unmelted but broken shell of his car, helicoptered to UAB hospital to be examined, observed, and released.

The finish comes down to a four-lap scrum and a stretch flourish with Michael Waltrip blocking the slick Jeff Gordon high and his teammate Junior low to win by a car length.[8] Escape takes the checkered flag. Suddenly, the workweek looms as spent fans spill out of the grandstands to start their engines for the long drive home.

HOSPITALITY'S NUTSHELL

The pecan is the Alabama state nut.[9] In Montgomery, you'll find pecans for sale at every turn, down every street, year round. As you make an Alabama getaway, you'll need some of this year's crop to take along, to bring home and roast in the oven on a baking sheet with butter and salt. Take your pick of vendors: trinket carts, grocery stores, the refurbished Union Station and RiverWalk arcades, the souvenir shop of the Southern League's Montgomery Biscuits. Pecans in colorful tins and cello bags, raw or roasted, fancy mammoth halves or pieces, salted, unsalted, baked in granulated sugar and sprinkled with cayenne or cinnamon, tied in ribbons, dipped in milk or dark chocolate, flattened into pralines, poured into brittle, sprawled with caramel and chocolate into turtles. Pecans squared into fudge or whipped into the angelic, achy-sweet, barometrically correct, crispy-crusted, egg-white puffery of childhood memory: divinity.

I stop in front of a building where Alabama pecans are commercially processed, sold online, and shipped all over the world. There is a small, glassed-in shop at the front for walk-ins. A woman who could be one of my aunts, smiling, plump, attentive, and dressed for Sunday School or a pecan showroom, asks if she can help. As I collect bags of raw, shelled halves, we talk about cows grazing the pecan groves, the crack of branches in thunderstorms, a family's livelihood of trees snapped into hurricane tinder.

I tell her about fall visits as a child to my grandmother Hatcher's pecan grove outside the south Alabama town of Hartford, of climbing the limbs with cousins to shake and dance the dappled brown, black, silvery nuts onto white bedsheets spread over the cow-cropped grass.

"We did that too," the pecan lady tells of her Wiregrass kin.

I hand her money. She counts change.

She wonders what brings me to Montgomery. I say I'm writing about the state's image, its slow-to-change political climate, its largely fossilized legislature. Its unwillingness to educate many of its children.

"Alabama is doing all right," she says.

"Well, no, not really. Maybe one day Alabama will catch up, but not until we do a lot better with our schools."

"I don't owe anybody an education."

"Well, yes, we do."

She laughs the laugh of hospitality betrayed. "Let me tell you something about that."

Moving toward the door, I smile and raise a pecan salute. "We better not get started."

NOTES

ABBREVIATIONS FOR MEDIA

AC *Atlanta Constitution*

AJ *Alabama Journal*

AJC *Atlanta Journal-Constitution*

AP Associated Press

APT Alabama Public Television

AS *Anniston Star*

BN *Birmingham News*

CNN Cable News Network

FTR *For the Record*, Alabama Public Television

GCD *Greene County Democrat*

HT *Huntsville Times*

MA *Montgomery Advertiser*

MPR *Mobile Press Register*

MR *Mobile Register*

NPR National Public Radio

NYT *New York Times*

SC *Southern Changes*

TN *Tuscaloosa News*

WP *Washington Post*

WSJ *Wall Street Journal*

INTRODUCTION

1. Robin Toner, "Stakes High in Contest for Alabama Governor," NYT, Sept. 26, 1990.

2. In a pattern repeated throughout black majority jurisdictions in the rural South, the election of black sheriffs greatly dampened the long era of white terror. See, for instance, the discussion of Lowndes County, Alabama, and the importance of the election of Sheriff John Hulett in Hasan Kwame Jeffries, *Bloody Lowndes: Civil Rights and Black Power in Alabama's Black Belt.*

3. "Alabamastan" at http://boortz.com/more/boortztionary.html (accessed Mar. 15, 2009).

4. Lydia Saad, "Political Ideology: 'Conservative' Label Prevails in the South," at http://www.gallup.com/poll/122333/Political-Ideology-Conservative-Label-Prevails -South.aspx (accessed Aug. 21, 2009).

5. George Talbot, "Alabama a Global Player," MPR, Sept. 9, 2009; Dan Luzadder, "Financing Cultural Change," NYT, Oct. 28, 2009.

6. Brian Lyman, "Report Finds Household Incomes Lag," MPR, Sept. 5, 2007.

7. Wanda Rushing, *Memphis and the Paradox of Place*, 85.

8. Iris Marion Young, *Justice and the Politics of Difference*, 173.

9. Susan Pace Hamill, "Reform in Alabama," SC 24, nos. 3–4 (2002), 10; and see Hamill's full study, "An Argument for Tax Reform Based on Judeo-Christian Ethics."

10. Horace Mann Bond, *Negro Education in Alabama*, 247. Bond quotes from a Brookings Institution survey of 1932.

11. Eddie Lard, "We'd Rather Hunt and Fish Than Educate Our Children," BN, Dec. 12, 2004. Dewayne Key, "Scholar as Activist," 200–202.

12. Rahkia Nance, "Alabama's Rising Dropout Rate Could Slow State's Economic Recovery," BN, Feb. 11, 2009.

13. In 2007 Alabama collected $455 per capita, Georgia $1,010, Florida $1,482, New Jersey $2,485. See Tax Foundation, "State and Local Property Tax Collections Per Capita by State, Fiscal Year 2007," at http://www.taxfoundation.org/taxdata/show/251 .html (accessed Oct. 22, 2009); David Cay Johnston, "Professor Cites Bible in Faulting Tax Policies," NYT, Dec 25, 2007.

14. "Alabama Income Taxes the Highest for Families Living at Poverty Line," AP, Apr. 30, 2010.

15. Wayne Flynt, "A Tragic Century: The Aftermath of the 1901 Constitution," 37.

16. As the gap between rich and poor widened, median U.S. income between 1979 and 2005 went up only 12 percent. David Leonhardt, "In the Process, Pushing Back at Inequality," NYT, Mar. 24, 2010.

17. Jim Williams, "Economic Development and the Alabama Constitution," remarks to the Alabama State Bar Convention at Point Clear, Alabama, July 16, 2009.

18. Applied to a U.S. state, rather than a nation-state, my rendering of the political imaginary nonetheless draws upon the discussion in Susan Buck-Morss, *Dreamworld and Catastrophe*, 2–39.

19. Alabama Department of Archives and History, "Official Symbols and Emblems of Alabama," at http://www.archives.state.al.us/emblems/heart_of_Dixie.html (accessed Nov. 25, 2005). Implementation of the motto on auto tags began in 1955.

20. Jonathan Daniels, *A Southerner Discovers the South*, 262.

21. "Holmes Questions Critic's Interracial Marriage," MA, Jan 22, 2001.

22. Drew Jubera, "Debate over 'Dixie,'" AJC, May 6, 2002; Jannell McGrew, "Woman fights illegal-tag ticket," MA, Apr 18, 2002; Karen Taylor, an African American lawyer and criminal justice professor at Alabama State was ticketed by a state trooper for taping over "Dixie" in the "Heart of Dixie."

23. "'Choose Life' Tag Approved for State," AP, Oct 25, 2001. Public opinion polling places Alabama among the foremost states in opposition to abortion rights. "Pro-Life vs Pro-Choice," Survey USA, Sept. 12, 2005, at http://www.surveyusa.com/50State2005/50StateAbortion0805SortedbyProLife.htm (accessed Mar. 10, 2010); Thomas F. Schaller, *Whistling Past Dixie*, 100–102.

24. "Stars Fell on Alabama," at http://en.wikipedia.org/wiki/Stars_Fell_on_Alabama. The historical reference is to a meteor shower visible over the state in 1833.

25. "Alabama Official Emblems, Symbols, and Honors," http://www.archives.state.al.us/emblems/emblems.html (accessed Mar. 24, 2010).

26. John Lewis and Michael D'Orso, *Walking with the Wind*, 368.

27. Gary Younge, "Racism Rebooted."

28. "Alabama *Survivor*," eBaum's World at http://www.ebaumsworld.com/jokes/read/211683, posted in 2009 (accessed July 10, 2009).

29. Phillip Rawls, "California Wine Company Capitalizing on 'Banned in Bama' Label Controversy," AP, Jul. 31, 2009.

30. Kim Chandler and Eric Velasco, "Alabama Supreme Court Upholds Sex Toy Ban," BN, Sept. 12, 2009. Representative John Rogers quoted by John Archibald, "Rogers Out to Bust Sex Toy Ban," BN, Jan. 20, 2008.

31. Hank Sanders, "Senate Sketches," GCK, June 13, 2007.

32. Slavoj Žižek, The *Fragile Absolute*, 141.

33. "Got-rocks" is a term especially associated with Big Jim Folsom, who applied it to the banks and Birmingham corporations that used their wealth to oppose his reform agenda. Source: Oral-history interview with James Folsom, by Allen Tullos and Candace Waid, Dec. 28, 1974, Cullman, Alabama. Interview A-0319, Southern Oral History Program Collection (#4007), Southern Historical Collection, Wilson Library, University of North Carolina at Chapel Hill.

34. Victor Hugo, *Les Misérables*, 44.

35. "Guvner" is how it sounds in Lynyrd Skynyrd's "Sweet Home Alabama," *Second Helping* (MCA Records, 1974). Robert Christgau claims this to be "the first state song ever to make the top ten." See his *Consumer Guide Reviews* at http://www.robertchristgau.com/get_artist.php?name=Lynyrd+Skynyrd (accessed Dec. 20, 2008).

36. "Measuring Progress," Opinion, BN Aug. 24, 2003.

37. Rena Havner Philips, "Despite Budget Cuts . . .", MPR, Oct. 6, 2009; Marie Leech, "Alabama Students Show No Significant Progress in National Math Assessment," BN, Oct. 15, 2009.

38. Anna Velasco, "Alabama Children's Care Ranks 14 in U.S.," BN, June 4, 2008; Markeshia Ricks, "Eligibility for Alabama Program That Insures Kids to Expand," MA, July 13, 2009.

39. Hank Sanders's phrase in "Senate Sketches," GCD, Mar. 10, 2010.

40. Markeshia Ricks, "Ala. Lawmakers Predict Indictments Ahead in Bingo Investigation," MA, May 6, 2010; Campbell Robertson, "U.S., after Inquiry, Charges 11," NYT, Oct. 5, 2010.

41. Frances Coleman, "Tired of Being at the Bottom of the Ratings," MPR, Nov. 22, 2009.

42. "Gov. Bob Riley Meets with Irish Counsel General to Discuss Trade," AP, Sept. 18, 2009.

43. Roy L. Williams, "Activists Protest Drummond Co.'s Employment Practices," BN, Nov. 21, 2008; Bob Johnson, "Suit: Drummond Co. Funded Colombian Terror," May 29, 2009; Russell Hubbard, "Drummond Co. Fires Colombian Union Leaders," BN, Sept. 18, 2009.

44. Robert Trent Jones Golf Trail at http://www.rtjgolf.com/trail (accessed July 20, 2009).

45. Alabama Travel website at http://www.alabama.travel/media-room/lee_sentell (accessed Mar. 17, 2009).

46. "State's History Major Resource," Editorial, MA, Jan. 29, 2004.

47. Jay Reeves, "Hyundai Joins Alabama's Growing List of Car Companies, AP, Apr. 2, 2002.

48. David White, "Alabama Ranks Among 15 States with a Jobless Rate of More Than 10 Percent," BN, July 27, 2009. Jeff Amy, "Alabama Unemployment Tops 11 Percent," MPR, Mar. 10, 2010.

49. Louis Uchitelle, "When, Oh When, Will Help Be Wanted?" NYT, July 19, 2009; "Study Says Jobs Alabama Lost Could Be Gone Until 2013," AP, Nov. 16, 2009.

50. Rick Bragg, The Most They Ever Had, 24.

51. Iris Marion Young, Inclusion and Democracy, 50.

52. Joan Didion, Where I Was From, 18.

53. Diane McWhorter, Carry Me Home, 15.

54. McWhorter, Carry Me Home, 28.

55. Jake Adam York, "A Field Guide to Northeast Alabama," Southern Spaces, http://www.southernspaces.org/contents/2008/york/1a.htm (accessed Mar. 14, 2010).

56. Gregory Donovan, "An Interview with Jake Adam York."

57. "Leaving Alabama," in Don Noble, ed., Climbing Mt. Cheaha: Emerging Alabama Writers, 252.

CHAPTER ONE. *The Sez-you State*

1. Clayton Collins, "Southern Fried Kiddin'," *Christian Science Monitor*, June 16, 2006, at http://www.csmonitor.com/2006.0616/p11s01 (accessed May 1, 2007).

2. "The Vent," AJC, May 6, 2005.

3. Sandy Grady, "Pa.'s Male, Pale Past," *USA Today*, Apr. 22, 2008; Carrie Budoff Brown, "Extreme Makeover," *Politico*, Apr. 1, 2008, at http://www.politico.com/news/stories/0408/9323.html (accessed Apr. 30, 2008).

4. [n.a.], "Top of the World Alaska's Rugged Beauty, Friendly Folks, Getting Lost All Part of the Adventure in a Volvo xc70," *Winnipeg Free Press*, 28 Mar. 2003.

5. Peter Ruehl, "It Seems a Poor Way to Define Poverty," *Australian Financial Review*, 18 Mar. 2004.

6. Richard L. Eldredge, "Punch Lines Take a Bite Out of Alabama's Image," AJC, May 4, 1997.

7. *The Nation*, July 29–Aug. 5, 1996, back cover.

8. Adrienne Rich, introduction to *My Mama's Dead Squirrel*, by Mab Segrest, 13, 14.

9. "Alabama Isn't So Different," *Economist*, Oct. 18, 1997.

10. Eddy L. Harris, *South of Haunted Dreams*, 232.

11. *Urban Dictionary* at http://www.urbandictionary.com (accessed June 11, 2009).

12. "Bama Day Wasn't Compliment to State," MA, Nov 22, 2000.

13. Robin DeMonia, "There's Reason to Put Faith, Hope in Artur Davis," BN, June 12, 2005.

14. Bob Johnson, "Governors: Trained Workforce Key to Success in Poor Region," AP, May 14, 2007.

15. Sarah Woolfolk Wiggins, "John Gayle, 1831–1835," in Samuel L. Webb and Margaret E. Armbrester, *Alabama Governors*, 31–33.

16. See Alabama State Archives website at http://www.archives.state.al.us/emblems/st_motto.html (accessed Dec. 28, 2006).

17. Delbert Freeman, "Allow Us to Live with Results," Letters to Editor, MA, Jan. 7, 2004.

18. Albert Brewer, foreword to *Alabama Governors*, by Samuel L. Webb and Margaret E. Armbrester, ix.

19. Herman Melville, *The Confidence Man* (New York: Dix, Edwards & Co., 1857), 265–66. Electronic Text Center, University of Virginia Library, at http://etext.lib.virginia.edu/toc/modeng/public/MelConf.html (accessed Jan. 2, 2007). As invoked by AJC writer Tom Baxter: "The dark side of this modesty is a studied disregard for the opinions of outsiders, a nose-thumbing, show-the-world tendency so deep-rooted, Herman Melville gave it to an Alabama character in his 1857 novel *The Confidence Man*." "You Never Know What You're Going to Get," AJC, Dec. 11, 1994.

20. George Wallace, "No Easy Walk, 1961–1963," part 4 of *Eyes on the Prize* (1986).

21. Chet Fuller, *I Hear Them Calling My Name* (Boston: Houghton Mifflin, 1981), 159–60.

22. Andy Miller, "Around the South," AJC, Sept. 7, 1995.

23. David White, "Alabama Senator Richard Shelby Says States Shouldn't Depend on Federal Government," BN, Feb. 10, 2009.

24. Damian Paletta, "Consumer Agency Stalls Senate Talks on Financial Overhaul," WSJ, Oct. 31, 2009.

25. Mary Orndorff, "8 of 9 Alabama Congressmen Oppose President Barack Obama's $787 Billion Stimulus Plan," BN, Feb. 14, 2009.

26. David M. Herszenhorn and Carl Hulse, "Democrats in Congress Are Ready to Pare Budget," NYT, Mar. 25, 2009; Cosby Woodruff, "Shelby Helps Lead Opposition Against Stimulus Package," MA, Feb. 10, 2009; "How They Voted," BN, July 23, 2006.

27. Judith Butler, *Giving an Account of Oneself*, 20.

28. Harvey H. Jackson III, *Inside Alabama*, x, xi.

29. Harvey Jackson on FTR, original air date May 30, 2005, APT. *Inside Alabama*, 224.

30. Jackson, *Inside Alabama*, 225.

31. Kevin Phillips, "The GOP's Southern Exposure," AJC, Jan. 5, 2003.

32. John Archibald, "The South's Trying to Do It Again," BN, Feb. 15, 2009.

33. Brad Winters, "Coach Paul Bear Bryant Quotes," at http://www.coachlikeapro.com/coach-paul-bear-bryant.html (accessed Dec. 12, 2009).

34. Warren St. John, *Rammer Jammer Yellow Hammer*, 226, 124.

35. St. John, *Rammer Jammer*, 149.

36. St. John, *Rammer Jammer*, 207.

37. Joey Manley, *The Death of Donna-May Dean*, 42.

38. Virginia Foster Durr, *Outside the Magic Circle*, 51–58. See the discussion in Fred Hobson, *But Now I See*, 122–25.

39. Hobson, *But Now I See*, 132.

40. Anne Rivers Siddons, *Heartbreak Hotel*, 130–31. With the screenplay by Tom McCown, *Heartbreak Hotel* becomes the 1989 movie *Heart of Dixie*.

41. Siddons, *Heartbreak Hotel*, 210.

42. Mab Segrest, *My Mother's Dead Squirrel*, 20.

43. Vicki Covington, *Gathering Home*, 12.

44. Butler, *Reader*, 356.

45. "Decoration Day," lyrics and music by Jason Isbell, 2002 House of Fame Music on the album *Decoration Day* by the Drive-By Truckers (New West Records, 2003).

46. Butler, *Reader*, 333–34.

47. McWhorter, *Carry Me Home*, 584–85.

48. McWhorter, *Carry Me Home*, 585.

49. Judith Butler, *Reader*, 333.

50. "For the Record: Governor Candidate Nathan Mathis (D)," AP, air date: May 24, 2006.

51. John Davis and Alvin Benn, "Gay Marriage Ban Easily Approved," MA, June 7, 2006.

52. "Alabama's Southern Baptists Denounce Homosexual Lifestyle," AP, May 28, 1992.

53. Matt Smith, "Alabama Enters Fight over Gay Rights Referendum," MA, Feb. 2, 1995.

54. Hobson, *But Now I See*, 133.

55. Hobson, *But Now I See*, 133.

56. Mab Segrest, *Memoir of a Race Traitor*, 2.

57. Segrest, *Memoir*, 4.

58. Hobson, *But Now I See*, 133 n.12.

59. Minnie Bruce Pratt, "No Place," in *Crime Against Nature*, 18, 19, and at http://southernspaces.org/contents/2004/pratt/2a.htm (accessed July 8, 2008). For reflections on Bibb County and her family, see Pratt's "When I Say 'Steal,' Who Do You Think Of?" at http://southernspaces.org/contents/2004/pratt/1a.htm (accessed July 8, 2008).

60. Tara McPherson, *Reconstructing Dixie*, 228, 229; Minnie Bruce Pratt, *Rebellion: Essays, 1980–1991*. And see McPherson, "Re-imagining the Red States: New Directions for Southern Studies," *Southern Spaces*, Dec. 14, 2004 at http://southernspaces.org/contents/2004/mcpherson/1a.htm (accessed July 8, 2008).

61. McPherson, *Reconstructing Dixie*, 230.

62. Judith Butler, *Undoing Gender*, 1.

63. "APT Gets Few Protests over Nixing Gay Show," MA, June 26, 1992.

64. "Station Shelves Another 'Ellen' Episode," AP, May 9, 1997.

65. "How the House Voted on Gay Marriage Bill," NYT, July 13, 1996.

66. "Anti-gay Rally Held Outside Courtroom," AP, July 31, 1996.

67. Rick Bragg, "O.K., So How Many Alabamians Does It Take . . ." NYT, June 24, 2009.

68. Kevin Sack, "Judge's Ouster Sought After Antigay Remarks," NYT Feb. 20, 2002.

69. Claudia Pryor Malis and Forrest Sawyer, "Assault on Gay America," *Frontline*, Feb. 15, 2000. Transcript at http://www.pbs.org/wgbh/pages/frontline/shows/assault/etc/script.html (accessed May 15, 2005).

70. Michelangelo Signorile, "Our Media-Made Martyrs," *Advocate*, Oct. 12, 1999. Background stories include David Story, "The Sad Death of Billy Jack," *Advocate*, May

11, 1999; Val Walton, Rose Livingston, Frank Sikora, "Slaying of Quietly Gay Man Shocks Rural Alabama Area," Newhouse News Service, Mar. 7, 1999.

71. "Statement by the President," White House, Washington, D.C., Mar. 2, 1999.

72. John Quiñones, Diane Sawyer, Sam Donaldson, "Small Town Secrets," *20/20*, Mar. 10, 1999.

73. Interview with Steven Mullins excerpted from ABC's *20/20*, in "Assault on Gay America," transcript at http://www.pbs.org/wgbh/pages/frontline/shows/assault/etc/script.html (accessed July 14, 2009).

74. Statement of Steven Eric Mullins to Sylacauga Police, Mar. 3, 1999, at http://www.pbs.org/wgbh/pages/frontline/shows/assault/billyjack/statement.html (accessed July 14, 2009).

75. Mullins interview. Except where noted, this and other direct quotations in the following paragraph are excerpted from ABC's *20/20*, in "Assault on Gay America."

76. "Skinhead on Trail Describes the Beating Death of a Gay Man," AP, Aug. 5, 1999; "Suspect in Murder of Gay Man Known for Skinhead Beliefs," AP, Mar. 6, 1999.

77. Mubarak Dahir, "The Urge to Kill," *Advocate*, Sept. 12, 2000.

78. Dahir, "The Urge to Kill."

79. "Man Guilty of Slaying Homosexual," AP, Aug. 6, 1999; "Killer of Gay Man in Alabama Gets Life in Prison Without Parole," NYT, Aug. 7, 1999.

80. "Assault on Gay America."

81. Kevin Sack, "Judge Trades on Renown in Race," NYT, June 5, 2000.

82. Neil Boortz quoted Aug. 8, 2003, posted at "'Holy Rock' Judge Suspended," http://www.flutterby.com/archives/viewentry.cgi?id=6461 (accessed Jan. 6, 2008). See Boortz glossary at http://boortz.com/more/boortztionary.html.

83. Anthony McCartney, "New AG to Bring Personal Touch," HT, Mar. 14, 2004.

84. "Judicial Nominees and Gay Rights," Editorial, NYT, May 19, 2003.

85. Meredith May, "Gay Rights Affirmed in Historic Ruling," *San Francisco Chronicle*, June 27, 2003.

86. "Prosecutor: Gay Teen Pleaded for Life During Slaying," AP, May 8, 2007; David Ferrara, "Haunted by His Crime," MPR, June 3, 2007, Laura Douglas-Brown, "Ala. Killing May Be Anti-gay Hate Crime," *Southern Voice*, July 30, 2004, at http://www.southernvoice.com/2004/7-30/news/national/alakill.cfm (accessed May 11, 2007).

87. Crystal Bonvillian, "Crimes Against Gays Targeted," MA, Aug. 27, 2004.

88. Deitrich Curry, "Gay Rights Activists Hold Rally," MA, Feb. 20, 2006.

89. Jamie Kizzire, "Bill to Add Homosexuals to Hate Crime Law Falters," MA, May 11, 2007; David Crary, "Comfort Level Grows for Many Gays, Lesbians," AP, May 21, 2006; Bob Moser, "Unsweet Homo Alabama," *Out*, Jan. 2005 at http://www.out.com/print_article.asp?id=8607&catid=35 (accessed May 21, 2006).

90. Charles J. Dean, "Good Ol' Boys Still Rule Roost in State Positions," BN, Dec. 30, 2007; David White, "Baxley Takes Oath in Historic Role," BN, Jan. 21, 2003.

91. Charles J. Dean, "Good Ol' Boys." Kay Ivey became lieutenant governor in the GOP sweep of 2010.

92. "The Alabama River had the highest amount of toxic chemicals causing developmental disorders in the nation in 2007." "Over 230 Million Pounds of Toxics Discharged into American Waterways," press release to accompany report released by Environment America, *Wasting Our Waterways: Industrial Toxic Pollution and the Unfulfilled Promise of the Clean Water Act* (Boston, Oct. 21, 2009).

93. Bob Johnson, "Number of Women Legislators Low in Alabama, Southeast," AP, Apr. 8, 2006.

94. New Hampshire and Vermont rank highest at 37 percent. "Alabama Ranks 3rd Lowest in Women in Legislature," AP, July 24, 2009.

95. "Women in Elective Office," Center for American Women and Politics, 2004, at http://www.cawp.rutgers.edu/Facts/StbySt/AL.html, and "Women in State Legislatures," http://www.cawp.rutgers.edu/Facts.html#leg (accessed Nov. 25, 2007); "Alabama Near Bottom Nationally in Number of Female Lawmakers," AP, Jan. 5, 1991; Mary Orndorff, "Democratic Runoff for 7th Congressional District Seat Could Be Historic," BN, June 3, 2010; Mary Orndorff, "As Winners Craft Agendas," BN, Nov. 4, 2010.

96. "Alabama: Women in Elective Office — Historical Summary," Center for American Women and Politics, 2004, at http://www.cawp.rutgers.edu/Facts/StbySt/AL.html.

97. Center for Women in Government & Civil Society, *Appointed Policy Makers in State Government: Five-Year Trend Analysis, Gender, Race and Ethnicity*, State Univ. of New York at Albany, Winter 2004. See table, "State by State Listing of Appointed Policy Leaders."

98. Charles J. Dean, "State Lags in Cabinet-level Women," BN, Dec. 7, 2007.

99. Ben Raines, "State Environmental Council Head Sees No Conflict in Lobbying for Major Business Group," PR, Feb. 11, 2010; "Lobbying, Alabama Environmental Board Don't Mix," Editorial, MA, Feb. 12, 2010.

100. Charles Grayson Summersell, *Alabama History for Schools*, 444–46; Alabama Department of Archives and History, "Alabama Constitutional Officers" at http://www.archives.state.al.us/conoff.html (accessed Dec. 20, 2009).

101. Ann Crittenden, "The Muscle State," review of Marie Wilson's *Closing the Leadership Gap*, in *American Prospect*, April 2004, 59; Crittenden, *The Price of Motherhood*.

102. *Making the Grade on Women's Health: National Report Card on Women's Health*, National Women's Law Center and Oregon Health and Science University, 2007, at

http://hrc.nwlc.org/Reports/State-Report-Card.aspx?stateID=ALABAMA (accessed Jan. 9, 2008); "Women's Health," *Women's Health Weekly*, May 27, 2004.

103. Dean, "Good Ol' Boys," BN, Dec. 30, 2007.

104. Mike Sherman, "Women Take On Leadership Roles," MA, Feb. 4, 2003.

105. "State 4th Lowest in Number of Female Legislators," AP, Dec. 29, 2006.

106. Scott W. Wright, "Judge Says Alabama College System Discriminated Against Women," *Black Issues in Higher Education*, June 26, 1997.

107. Anna Velasco, "Nurses Running Three Major Birmingham Hospitals," AP, Jan. 26, 2004.

108. Gita M. Smith, "Watkins: See Poor, Ailing Firsthand," MA, Jan. 24, 1992.

109. Angela Kuper, "Harris Receives National Honor," MA, June 18, 1991.

110. Crystal Bonvillian, "Pair of Local Civil Rights 'Warriors' Mourned," MA, Dec. 17, 2005.

111. Gardiner Harris, "A Doctor from the Bayou," NYT, July 14, 2009.

112. "Healthy Choice," Editorial, LAT, July 14, 2009; see also "Regina Benjamin: Serving and Healing in the Bayou," MPR, July 14, 2009.

113. Bob Ingram, "Alabama Scene," GCD, Sept. 6, 2006; Dave Parks, "Alabama Gets Fatter," BN, Aug. 30, 2006; Elizabeth Becker and Marian Burros, "Eat Your Vegetables? Only at a Few Schools," NYT, Jan. 13, 2003; Penelope McClenny, "Alabama in Denial About Its Health?" MPR, Apr. 1, 2007.

114. Claire Suddath, "Why Are Southerners So Fat?" *Time*, July 9, 2009.

115. Kevin L. Bardon, "Alabama . . . by Its Sad Numbers," BN, Letters, Jan. 11, 2004; Janice Francis-Smith, "State Ranks 43rd in Think Tank Guide," *Oklahoma City Journal Record*, May 13, 2004.

116. Among Medicare patients, the state ranked forty-eighth in the use of flu shots and forty-ninth in using pneumonia vaccine. Dave Parks, "Study: State Ranks 42nd in Medicare Treatment Quality," BN, Jan. 17, 2003.

117. Rick Bragg, *All Over but the Shoutin'*, 150.

118. William Neuman, "Tempest in a Soda Bottle," NYT, Sept. 17, 2009; David Leonhardt, "The Battle over Taxing Soda," NYT, May 19, 2010.

119. Bob Hall and Mary Lee Kerr, *1991–1992 Green Index: A State-by-State Guide to the Nation's Environmental Health*.

120. Dennis O. Grady and Jonathan Kanipe, "Environmental Politics in the Tar Heel State," in Christopher A. Cooper and H. Gibbs Knotts, *The New Politics of North Carolina*, 257–61.

121. Only four states had a higher number of vehicle miles traveled per capita. Brian Wingfield and Miriam Marcus, "America's Greenest States," Forbes.com, Oct. 17, 2007; Ben Raines, "Alabama Rates Low in 'Green' Survey," MPR, Dec. 27, 2007. An excellent

study of one Alabama city's shameful environmental history, including years of dumping upon African American neighborhoods, is Ellen Griffith Spears, *Toxic Knowledge: A Social History of Environmental Health in the New South's Model City, Anniston, Alabama, 1872–Present*, PhD diss., Emory Univ., 2007. A mammoth, celebratory chronicle of Alabama Power, with scant, uncritical coverage of its environmental practices is Leah Rawls Atkins, *"Developed for the Service of Alabama."*

122. Ben Raines, "Environmental Groups Give State D+ Grade on Water Quality," MPR, Sept. 4, 2009.

123. "New Study Faults Alabama Power Plant for Air Pollution," AP, Apr. 5, 2002.

124. Thomas Spencer, "Coal-fired Plant in West Jefferson County Puts More Mercury in Air Than Any Other in Nation," BN, Nov. 21, 2008.

125. American Lung Association, Lung Action Reports, at http://lungaction.org/reports/sota07_cities.html

126. Sean Reilly, "State Stands to Feel Effects of Climate Bill," MPR, July 6, 2009.

127. Neela Banerjee, "Alabama's Power Struggle," NYT, June 23, 2002.

128. Bruce Barcott, "Changing All the Rules," *NYT Magazine*, Apr. 4, 2004.

129. Banerjee, "Alabama's Power Struggle."

130. Ari Berman, "The Dirt on Clean Coal," *Nation*, Mar. 26, 2009, at http://www.thenation.com/doc/20090413/berman (accessed July 30, 2009).

131. Leonard Doyle, "U.S. Power Company Linked to Bush Is Named in Database as a Top Polluter," *Independent* [London], Nov. 16, 2007.

132. On the Bush-Cheney anti-environmental offensive see Barcott, "Changing All the Rules."

133. Judicial candidate Hopkins received a partial "Not Qualified" rating from the American Bar Association. Her nomination was advanced by Senator Shelby. See "Statement of Senator Patrick Leahy" at http://leahy.senate.gov/issues/nominations/Hopkins.html (accessed July 27, 2009); Katherine Bouma, "U.S. Judge Rules Utility Complied with Clean Air Act," Aug. 16, 2006; Cathy Cash, "Federal Court Rules in Favor of Alabama Power," *Global Power Report*, July 31, 2008.

134. "Collapse of the Clean Coal Myth," Editorial, NYT, Jan. 23, 2009.

135. Correspondence from Wayne Flynt, July 27, 2009. Flynt also notes that the Alabama Conservancy has been battling Alabama Power for years over the destruction of shellfish species due to hydroelectric dams and coal-fired power plants.

136. See "Etymology of State Name" in *Wikipedia* at http://en.wikipedia.org/wiki/Alabama#Etymology_of_state_name

137. Summersell, *Alabama History for Schools*, 137, 139. And see Herbert J. "Jim" Lewis, "Canoe Fight," *Encyclopedia of Alabama*, at http://www.encyclopediaofalabama.org/face/Article.jsp?id=h-1815 (accessed July 23, 2009).

138. Leah Rawls Atkins, "Creeks and Americans at War," 53.

139. Ove Jensen, "Battle of Horseshoe Bend."

140. J. L. Chestnut Jr., "The Hard Cold Truth," GCD, Oct. 25, 2006.

141. Chestnut, "The Hard Cold Truth."

142. "HJ Res 114," Oct. 10, 2002, at http://clerk.house.gov/evs/2002/roll455.xml and "U.S. Senate Roll Call Votes 107th Congress–2nd Session," at http://www.senate.gov/legislative/LIS/roll_call_lists/roll_call_vote_cfm.cfm?congress=107&session=2&vote =00237 (accessed Jan. 2, 2008). For reasons largely unrelated to his opposition to the Iraq War, Rep. Hilliard lost his seat in 2002 to another African American, Artur Davis.

143. Salim Muwakkil, "The Blame Game," *In These Times*, Jan. 6, 2003.

144. Phillip Rawls, "Possible War Prompts Heated Debate in Senate," AP, Mar. 18, 2003.

145. Jeffrey McMurray, "Iraq Set to Strike, Shelby Warns," MA, Aug 3, 2002.

146. Garry Mitchell, "More State Soldiers Join War Effort," AP, Jan. 30, 2003.

147. Liz Marlantes, "A Battle Cry from the 'Volunteer County,'" *Christian Science Monitor*, Mar. 12, 2003; Carla Crowder, "Clay County Goes to War," BN, Mar. 20, 2003; "Background on Alabama National Guard," AP, Jan. 3, 2004.

148. "Ashland, Alabama Pro-war," *Dateline NBC*, Mar. 20, 2003.

149. Marlantes, "Battle Cry."

150. Crowder, "Clay County Goes to War"; "Clay County, Alabama," *Wikipedia*, http://en.wikipedia.org/wiki/Clay_County%2C_Alabama (accessed Dec. 30, 2003).

151. Marlantes, "Battle Cry."

152. John Fleming, "Lost in Noise of Cowboy Diplomacy," AS, Mar. 2, 2003; Brandt Ayers, "Empire — If Not Us, Who?" AS, Jan. 12, 2003.

153. Polling numbers as well as quotes from VFW commander, Sosebee, and Snow in Sam Hodges, "Poll Gives OK to War in Iraq," MR, Jan. 1, 2003. Snow thought the war would spell defeat for Bush in 2004.

154. John Lewis, "Drums of War," Howard University Convocation, Sept. 27, 2002.

155. Sean Reilly, "Poll: Alabamians Distrust Muslims," MR, July 7, 2002.

156. Vivi Abrams, Benjamin Niolet, and Mary Orndorff, "Alabamians Stand Behind Soldiers as Battle Unfolds," BN, Mar. 20, 2003. The Sessions family names point back to Jefferson Davis and Confederate general P. G. T. Beauregard.

157. Michael Lind, "Bush Whistles Dixie," *Newsweek International*, Dec. 23, 2002.

158. "The United States Army Aviation and Missile Command," at http://en.wikipedia.org/wiki/United_States_Army_Aviation_and_Missile_Command, (accessed Feb. 6, 2009). For a background summary of post–World War II southern military dependency, see "Missiles and Magnolias," chapter 6 of *From Cotton Belt to Sunbelt*, by Bruce J. Schulman, 135–73.

159. "Redstone Arsenal: Facts," at http://www.garrison.redstone.army.mil/sites/about/facts.asp (accessed Jan. 5, 2008); Dawn Kent, "Riley Hopes to See State Jet Industry Flying High," BN, June 17, 2007.

160. "Robert E. Cramer," *Wikipedia*, at http://en.wikipedia.org/wiki/Robert_E._Cramer (accessed Jan. 5, 2008); Abrams, Niolet, and Orndorff, "Alabamians Stand Behind Soldiers"; "Alabama," in "The 1994 Elections: State by State," NYT, Nov. 10, 1994; Sean Reilly and Joe Danborn, "Congressmen Silent About Tax Plan," MPR, Aug. 19, 2003.

161. Tom Gordon, "Iraq Invasion Popular with Many in State," BN, Sept. 11, 2006.

162. "Poll: State Skeptical on War in Iraq," AP, Jan. 13, 2007.

163. Sean Reilly, "Bush's Job Performance Rating Slumps in State Poll," PR, July 29, 2007.

164. Kelli Hewett Taylor, "Army Becomes Tough Sell," BN, Jan. 9, 2005.

165. "Dress Blues" recorded at Stubb's in Austin, Tex., Apr. 29, 2006, YouTube, at http://www.youtube.com/watch?v=aJb1_EGnapY (accessed Nov. 17, 2007).

166. Jason Isbell, "Dress Blues," *Sirens of the Ditch* (Los Angeles: New West Records, 2007).

167. Tom Smith, "Marine's Death in Iraq Generates Scholarship in Alabama Home," AP, Aug. 30, 2006.

168. Wendy Kaminer, "A Wing and a Prayer: Religion Goes Back to School, *The Nation*, Dec. 15, 1997.

169. Gita M. Smith, "Lawmakers to Join Alabama Rally for Public Prayer," AJC, Apr. 11, 1997.

170. "A Justice for All?" *Now with Bill Moyers*, PBS, July 11, 2003.

171. "Interview: Alabama Chief Justice Roy Moore," Aug. 22, 2003, *Today*, NBC News.

172. David White, "Alabama Republican Candidate for Governor Roy Moore Blasts President Obama's Economic Policies and His Comment That America Is Not a Christian Nation," BN, Sept. 6, 2009.

173. U.S. Census, "United States Foreign-born Population," American Community Survey, 2003; "Statistical Portrait of the Foreign-born Population in the United States, 2007," table 10, "Foreign Born, by State: 2007" (Washington, D.C.: Pew Hispanic Center, 2007).

174. "Census Proves Alabama Moving Forward," MA, Feb. 24, 2002.

175. D'vera Cohn, "Magnet or Sticky?" Pew Research Center, Social and Demographic Trends, at http://pewsocialtrends.org/pubs/728/magnet-sticky-states-typology (accessed Aug. 12, 2009).

176. Tom Gordon, "Population of State Gets Less Home-grown," BN, Nov. 22, 2007.

177. "German Students Get Taste of Alabama Hospitality," AP, MA, Apr. 19, 2002.

178. Sean Reilly, "Sessions Hard-liner on Immigration Bill," MR, Mar. 31, 2006.

179. Kyle Wingfield, "Alabama Purposely Slow in Providing IDs to Noncitizens," AP, Nov. 24, 2003.

180. Kyle Wingfield, "Immigrants Sue State over Driver's License Rules," AP, Apr. 26, 2004.

181. "The Candidate from Xenophobia," Editorial, NYT, Apr. 29, 2010; Mary Orndorff, "Adwatch: Analysis of a TV Ad from Tim James," BN, Apr. 29, 2010.

182. Thomas Spencer, "Foreign Students at Alabama Colleges Face Greater Scrutiny," BN, Jan. 9, 2003.

183. Judith Butler, *Reader*, 356.

CHAPTER TWO. *The Punitive Habit*

1. Avery F. Gordon, *Ghostly Matters*, 197, 63.

2. *Lockup: Holman Extended Stay*, five-part documentary series first aired by MSNBC in Dec. 2007, at http://www.msnbc.msn.com/id/22083055 (accessed Apr. 17, 2009).

3. Incarceration rates are for 2005. Marc Mauer and Ryan S. King, *Uneven Justice*, 15.

4. Robin DeMonia, "Eye-for-eye Justice Is Blinding," BN, Feb. 28, 2003.

5. David Cole, "Can Our Shameful Prisons Be Reformed?" *New York Review of Books*, 56: 18 (Nov. 19, 2009).

6. Marie Gottschalk, *The Prison and the Gallows*, frontispiece and 1, 4.

7. Adam Liptak, "1 in 100 U.S. Adults Behind Bars," NYT, Feb. 28, 2008; "Statistics for the State of Alabama," National Institute of Corrections, http://www.nicic.org/Features/StateStats/?State=AL#3 (accessed Apr. 25, 2009).

8. http://en.wikipedia.org/wiki/Capital_punishment_in_the_United_States (accessed Apr. 25, 2009).

9. Edward L. Ayers, *Vengeance and Justice*, 34, 35; Gottschalk, *The Prison and the Gallows*, 47–49.

10. C. Vann Woodward, *Origins of the New South*, 212.

11. Woodward, *Origins*, 213.

12. Steve Suitts, *Hugo Black of Alabama*, 384, 582 n.6.

13. Mary Ellen Curtin, *Black Prisoners and Their World, Alabama, 1865–1900*, 10, 11. Drawing upon a "deluge of evidence," Curtin examines the situations of black men and women prisoners during the convict lease era.

14. U.S. Bureau of Labor Statistics, cited in Walter Wilson, *Forced Labor in the United States*, 34.

15. A horrific chronicle centering upon Alabama's practices of forced labor ("neo-slavery") in the New South era is Douglas A. Blackmon, *Slavery by Another Name.*

16. Alex Lichtenstein, *Twice the Work of Free Labor*, 13.

17. Allen Tullos, "The Alabama Prison System: Recent History, Conditions, and Recommendations," undergraduate honors thesis (University of Alabama at Tuscaloosa, 1972), 20, 21, 43. Published as a monograph by the American Civil Liberties Union of Alabama, Tuscaloosa, 1973.

18. Larry W. Yackle, *Reform and Regret*, v, vi, 30.

19. Yackle, *Reform and Regret*, 10–13, 45–47, 55–61.

20. Gottschalk, *The Prison and the Gallows*, 176–77.

21. Ray Jenkins, "Alabama Prisons Ruled Unconstitutionally Cruel," NYT, Jan. 4, 1976.

22. Wendall Rawls, "Alabama Prison Changes Called Remarkable Gains," NYT, May 4, 1981.

23. See the discussion of Weaver in Glenn C. Loury, *Race, Incarceration, and American Values*, 12–14.

24. Yackle, *Reform and Regret*, 119, 120.

25. Yackle, *Reform and Regret*, 126–29.

26. Yackle, *Reform and Regret*, 166, 167.

27. Ralph Knowles, "Monitoring Committee on Prisons in Alabama Folds," *Journal of the National Prison Project* 20 (Summer 1989), 2; *Newman v. Alabama*, 349 F. Supp. 278 (M.D. Ala. 1972).

28. Information on the state's prisons drawn from "Alabama Department of Corrections History," at http://www.doc.state.al.us/history.asp (accessed May 18, 2008); Curtin, *Black Prisoners and Their World.*

29. "Jailhouse Blues," *Economist*, Mar. 25, 1978.

30. Yackle, *Reform and Regret*, 137, 171.

31. Yackle, *Reform and Regret*, 176, 190; Matthew 25:44–45.

32. Knowles, "Monitoring Committee on Prisons in Alabama Folds," 6. For details of Graddick's antics, see Yackle, *Reform and Regret*, 194–221.

33. Alabama's prisoner growth rate topped that of fifteen southern and border states between 1981 and 1991. Dan Morse, "Alabama Prison Terms Top in South," MA, Aug. 21, 1992.

34. "Jailhouse Blues," *Economist.*

35. Morse, "Alabama Prison Terms."

36. Gregg Barak, "Behind the Numbers on Black Crime," SC, 8: 6 (1986), 8–9.

37. Ralph Knowles, "Monitoring Committee on Prisons in Alabama Folds," 7.

38. Knowles, "Monitoring Committee," 1.

39. Yackle, *Reform and Regret*, 256–60.

40. Rick Bragg, "Chain Gangs to Return to Roads of Alabama," NYT, Mar. 26, 1995.

41. Bragg, "Chain Gangs."

42. Fob James Jr., "Prison Is for Punishment," *USA Today*, Aug. 28, 1995.

43. "Sessions Says He Would Win Race," MA, Aug. 26, 1995.

44. "Chain Gang Members Do Rock-breaking Work," AP, MA, Aug. 22, 1995.

45. Bragg, "Chain Gangs."

46. Jessica Saunders, "Prisons Chief Out," MA, Apr. 27, 1996; "Jones' Ouster Leaves Agency at Crossroads," MA, Apr. 29, 1996; "After Jones," Editorial, MA, Apr. 30, 1996.

47. Stephen Bates, "Ghosts of Old South Rattle Chains," *Guardian* (London), May 20, 1995.

48. "Productive Work," Editorial, MA, July 9, 1996.

49. "Between 1970 and 2003, state and federal prisons grew sevenfold. . . . The entire correctional population of the United States [jails and prisons] totaled nearly seven million in 2003, around 6 percent of the adult male population." Bruce Western, *Punishment and Inequality*, 3, 78, 105.

50. Mike Sherman, "Swollen Prisons Create Crisis," MA, Mar. 3, 2003.

51. Western, *Punishment and Inequality*, 189–90

52. Quotations in this paragraph taken from Gottschalk, *Prison and Gallows*, 12.

53. "Prison Summit," Editorial, BN, Sept. 3, 2002; "Prison Numbers Compelling," Editorial, MA, Sept. 6, 2002.

54. D. Miller, "Building Prisons Not Answer," Letters to Editor, MA, Sept. 8, 2002.

55. Gene Owens, "Change Could Benefit Prisoner, Taxpayers," MR, July 13, 2003.

56. "Smarter Sentencing," Editorial, BN, Apr. 29, 2003.

57. Chris Suellentrop, "The Right Has a Jailhouse Conversion," NYT, Dec. 24, 2006.

58. Gottschalk, *Prison and Gallows*, 11.

59. Carla Crowder, "'Dehumanizing, Overcrowded': Who Would Want a Prison Job?" BN, Nov. 17, 2003; "The Ultimate Optimist," Editorial, BN, Sept. 3, 2002.

60. "Alabama Department of Corrections History"; Sherman, "Swollen Prisons"; Bob Johnson, "Judge Rejects Tutwiler Plan," AP, Feb. 4, 2003; "Tutwiler Freeze," Editorial, BN, Jan. 3, 2003.

61. Mike Cason, "Suit Blasts Prison Conditions," MA, Aug. 20, 2002.

62. Melanie Peeples, "Overcrowding at Alabama's Only Women's Prison," *All Things Considered*, NPR, Dec. 27, 2002.

63. Cason, "Suit Blasts Prison Conditions"; Carla Crowder, "Tutwiler Warden Copes with 'Ticking Time Bomb,'" BN, Apr. 8, 2003; Crowder, "Prisoners' Families Seek Political Voice," BN, Apr. 20, 2003; Stan Bailey, "Number of Inmates at Tutwiler Down to 750," BN, June 26, 2003.

64. Nick Lackeos, "Inmates Ask for 58 Guards," MA, Jan. 22, 2003; Stan Bailey, "Judge Presses Riley for Relief at Prison," BN, Jan. 22, 2003; David White, "Riley May Export Inmates," BN, Feb. 20, 2003; Stan Bailey, "Riley Gives Court Plan to Defuse Tutwiler," BN, Feb. 22, 2003; Kim Chandler, "State to Move 600 Male Inmates," BN, Apr. 15, 2003.

65. Kim Chandler, "70 Inmates Shifted to Louisiana," BN, Apr. 15, 2003.

66. "Private Prisons Less Accountable," Editorial, MA, Apr. 10, 2004.

67. Carla Crowder, "Sick Prisoners Prove Costly in Louisiana," BN, June 21, 2003; Crowder, "Private Firm Has Seen Riot, Escapes, Drugs at Prisons It Operates," BN, Apr. 15, 2003.

68. "Breakdown of Inmates Sent out of State Because of Crowding Problems," AP, Jan. 16, 2004.

69. "A Stigma That Never Fades," *Economist*, Aug. 10, 2002.

70. Solomon Moore, "Justice Dept. Data Show Prison Increases," NYT, Dec. 6, 2007.

71. "U.S.: Record Numbers for World's Leading Jailer," *Human Rights News*, Dec. 5, 2007, at http://hrw.org/english/docs/2007/12/05/usdom17491.htm (accessed May 21, 2008); Adam Liptak, "Inmate Count in U.S. Dwarfs Other Nations," NYT, Apr. 23, 2008; Mike Sherman, "Swollen Prisons Create Crisis," MA, Mar. 3, 2003. Alabama's cost per prisoner in 2004 was $9,000. "Alabama Is No. 5 in Percent of Population in Prison," AP, May 28, 2004.

72. Western, *Punishment and Inequality*, 57.

73. Gottschalk, *The Prison and the Gallows*, 2, 3.

74. Stephen L. Carter, "Affirmative Distraction," Op-ed, NYT, July 6, 2008.

75. Western, *Punishment and Inequality*, 105.

76. Gottschalk, *The Prison and the Gallows*, 15.

77. Carla Crowder, "Advocates Seek Youth Justice Reform," BN, Aug. 05, 2005.

78. Sam Dillon, "Study Finds That About 10 Percent of Young Male Dropouts Are in Jail or Detention," NYT, Oct. 9, 2009.

79. Western, *Punishment and Inequality*, 24–28; Stephen J. Carroll and Emre Erkut, *The Benefits to Taxpayers from Increases in Students' Educational Attainment*, 74–75.

80. Larry Yackle notes the efforts of several journalists in the 1970s to bring the conditions of Alabama prisons to public attention: *Birmingham News* editorial writer Walter Massey and reporter Stan Bailey, Ed Watkins's series based on visits to Alabama's prisons for the *Tuscaloosa News*, articles by the *Montgomery Advertiser*'s Harold Martin following the 1974 prison violence, and reporting by the *Birmingham Post-Herald*'s Ted Bryant. Yackle also shows how prison commissioner L. B. Sullivan sought to use the press to undercut reform litigation. See *Reform and Regret*, 45, 46, 66–69.

81. Stan Bailey, "Judge Fines State for Jails' Backlog," BN, June 15, 2002; "Frustrated Judge Seeks Solutions," Editorial, MA, Dec. 13, 2002.

82. Stan Bailey, "State May House Inmates in Tents," BN, July 14, 2002.

83. Representative Allen Treadaway, who sponsored the failed legislation in 2009, commented: "This has been a practice in Alabama for many years and is the only place in America that allows elected officials to legally pocket excess tax dollars." E-mail to author, June 5, 2009.

84. FTR, May 13, 2002.

85. Jay Reeves, AP, May 17, 2008. "By comparison, the government pays schools $2.47 for serving a single free meal under the National School Lunch Program for low-income students."

86. Adam Nossiter, "As His Inmates Grew Thinner, a Sheriff's Wallet Grew Fatter," NYT, Jan. 9, 2009.

87. Stan Bailey, "Audit: Prison Health Care Poor," BN, Feb. 13, 2003; Adam Liptak, "Alabama Prison at Center of Suit Over AIDS Policy," NYT, Oct. 26, 2003.

88. Carla Crowder, "'Medical Failure' Blamed in HIV Inmate Deaths," BN, Aug. 28, 2003.

89. "State Prison Deaths Comparatively High," AP, May 12, 2003.

90. Debbie Elliott, "Alabama State Prison System Being Sued by Inmates," *All Things Considered*, National Public Radio, Sept. 30, 2003.

91. Elliott, "Alabama State Prison System."

92. "Inmate Dies Two Days After Filing Lawsuit," MA, May 17, 2003.

93. "*Bradley v. Haley*," Southern Poverty Law Center, at http://www.splcenter .org/legal/docket/files.jsp?cdrID=13, and the following court documents posted by Human Rights Watch: Kathryn Burns and Jane Haddad, "Expert Report: Mental Health Care in the Alabama Department of Corrections," 2001, http://hrw.org/ reports/2003/usa1003/Alabama_Expert_Report_Hightower.pdf; Jane Haddad, "Alabama Department of Corrections Improvements in Mental Health Services for Inmates," 2003, http://hrw.org/english/docs/2003/10/22/usdom7148_txt.htm (accessed June 25, 2008).

94. "Imprisoned and Ill," Editorial, BN, Oct. 27, 2003.

95. Yackle, *Reform and Regret*, vi.

96. The 0.8 percent growth in the prison population in 2008 was the smallest annual increase that decade and significantly less than the 6.5 percent average annual growth of the 1990s. Jeff Carlton, "U.S. Prison Population Drops for First Time Since 1972," *Huffington Post*, Dec. 20, 2009 (accessed Dec. 22, 2009); William J. Sabol and Heather C. West, *Prisoners in 2008* (Washington, D.C.: Bureau of Justice Statistics), Appendix, Table 2.

97. Todd Kleffman, "Officials Discuss Prisons," MA, Sept. 5, 2002; "The 'T-word,'" Editorial, BN, Sept. 11, 2002.

98. Stan Bailey, "No Fines Over Crowded Jails," BN, Jan. 31, 2004.

99. Phillip Rawls, "Riley Sees Prison Problems Firsthand," AP, Mar. 7, 2003.

100. "Warning Shot," Editorial, BN, Aug. 18, 2002; "State Must Have Different Options," MA, Mar. 17, 2003; Rawls, "Riley Sees Prison Problems Firsthand."

101. Kyle Wingfield, "AL Prison Overcrowding," AP, Mar. 5, 2004.

102. "1,400 Inmates to Be Sent to Mississippi," MA, June 27, 2003; Ellen Barry, "Dispatch from Tutwiler, Miss.," *LA Times*, June 5, 2004.

103. "Montgomery Businesses Worry Prison Changes Will Hurt Work-release Programs," AP, Jan. 21, 2004; "Private Prison Costly to State," AP, Feb. 6, 2004.

104. Lichtenstein, *Twice the Work of Free Labor*, 193.

105. Gottschalk, *The Prison and the Gallows*, 16.

106. "Settling Cases," Editorial, BN, July 1, 2004.

107. Crowder, "Marijuana Conviction Seals Life Behind Bars for Vietnam Veteran," BN, Mar. 28, 2004.

108. John Davis, "Riley's Office Quiet on Prison Chief's Departure," MA, Feb. 11, 2006; "Pitiful Prisons," Editorial, BN, Feb. 14, 2006.

109. Carla Crowder, "State Offers Few Extras for Prisons," BN, Dec. 25, 2003.

110. John D. Milazzo, "Senate Committee Authorizes Bond Issue to Build New Prison," MA, Feb. 7, 1992.

111. Desiree Hunter, "Riley: Moving Inmates from County Jails Faster Isn't Possible," June 5, 2007.

112. For a glimpse of one Alabama prisoner's release, see Ben Harmon and Catalina McCormick, "Ten Dollars and a Bus Ticket," *Southern Spaces*, Dec. 16, 2009, at http://southernspaces.org/contents/2009/tendollars/1a.htm (accessed Dec. 22, 2009).

113. See the monthly "Statistical Reports" for 2007 and 2008 at the Alabama Department of Corrections website, http://www.doc.state.al.us/reports.asp; "A Stigma That Never Fades," *Economist*, Aug. 10, 2002; Glenn C. Loury, *Race, Incarceration, and American Values*, 21, 32.

114. Marc Mauer and Tushar Kansal, *Barred for Life*, Washington, D.C.: Sentencing Project, 2005; Shaila Dewan, "Fighting to Regain Right Some Felons Never Lost," NYT, Mar. 2, 2008.

115. "Felony Disfranchisement Laws in the United States," The Sentencing Project, Washington, D.C., Nov. 2005; Dewan, "Fighting to Regain Right"; Kim Chandler, "Felon Voting Bill Ensnares Riley," BN, June 22, 2003; Val Walton, "Bill Proposes Automatically Restoring Voting Rights," BN, Jan. 19, 2006.

116. And see Kara Gotsch and Kenneth Glasgow, "At 'Bloody Sunday' Commemoration Leaders Urged to Join New Movement for Voting Rights," Press Release, Alabama Restore the Vote, Feb. 28, 2007.

117. Dewan, "Fighting to Regain Right." Glasgow was also state coordinator for Alabama Restore the Vote.

118. Bruce Western, *Punishment and Inequality*, 189–90.

119. Gottschalk, *The Prison and the Gallows*, 195.

120. "Conditions in Prisons Must Not Be Ignored," Editorial, MA, May 9, 2003.

121. "About the Center," Southern Center for Human Rights at http://www.schr.org/aboutthecenter/index.html (accessed Sept. 6, 2008).

122. Eighty-seven percent of all U.S. state court judges are elected. A study of Pennsylvania state judges found that "all judges, even the most punitive, increase their sentences as re-election nears." Adam Liptak, "Rendering Justice, with One Eye on Re-election," NYT, May 25, 2008; Anthony Lewis, "Is It a Zeal to Kill?" NYT, Dec. 8, 1995.

123. J. L. Chestnut, "The Hard Cold Truth," GCD, Jan. 11, 2006.

124. Samira Jafari, "Alabama's Habitual Offender Laws Filling State Prisons," AP, Feb. 20, 2006.

125. Bob Ingram, "Alabama Scene," GCD, July 9, 1997.

126. Crowder, "Marijuana Conviction."

127. Gene Owens, "Change Could Benefit Prisoner, Taxpayers," MR, July 13, 2003; "Inmate's Case Highlights Habitual Offender Dilemma," AP, Apr. 22, 1991.

128. Brett J. Blackledge, "Low-Level Crooks Top Parole Plan," BN, Sept. 29, 2003.

129. Chris Suellentrop, "The Right Has a Jailhouse Conversion," NYT, Dec. 24, 2006.

130. Mile Wilkerson, "Alternatives Must Be Used to Address Prisons," MA, Apr. 6, 2003.

131. Website for the Alabama Sentencing Commission, at http://sentencingcommission.alacourt.gov/about.html (accessed June 9, 2008).

132. William L. Gillespie, "State Sentencing Policy," 205–10.

133. Blackledge, "Low-Level Crooks."

134. Mike Cason, "Prison Panel's Advice May Die," MA, June 15, 2003; Phillip Rawls, "Legislature Approves Sentencing Commission Plans," AP, June 16, 2003.

135. Mike Cason, "State Says Shoplifters Are Robbing Prisons of Space," MA, Apr. 20, 2003; Fox Butterfield, "With Cash Tight, States Reassess Long Jail Terms," NYT, Nov. 10, 2003.

136. Carla Crowder, "Drug Laws Face Scales of Justice," BN, Mar. 1, 2004; "Drug Law Review an Important Step," Editorial, MA, Mar. 3, 2004; "Comparison of Alabama's Minor Marijuana Sentencing Laws," AP, Apr. 3, 2005.

137. Samira Jafari, "Legislature OK's New Sentencing Guides," AP, Mar. 31, 2006.

138. *Decatur Daily* quoted in "More Recent Editorials from Alabama Newspapers," AP, Dec. 31, 2003.

139. Carla Crowder, "Tighter Sentencing Gets OK," BN, Apr. 10, 2004; "Commission

OKS New Sentencing Structure," AP, Apr. 10, 2004; "Keeping Drug Court a National Model," Editorial, BN, Dec. 30, 2006; "A Wise Choice: More Circuit Drug Courts," Editorial, MR, Sept. 4, 2007.

140. Gottschalk discusses this seeming contradiction in *The Prison and the Gallows*, 9.

141. "Good News That's Not So Good," Editorial, BN, Apr. 29, 2005; Phillip Rawls, "Riley Gets Third Try at Filling Parole Board Seat," AP, Jan. 27, 2004.

142. "Campaign for Reform Goes On," Editorial, BN, Aug. 7, 2005; Marty Roney, "District Attorney Against Releases," MA, Feb. 16, 2004.

143. Troy King interviewed on *For the Record*, APTV, Oct. 19, 2007.

144. Paterson quoted in Gottschalk, *The Prison and the Gallows*, 239.

145. "State and Federal Prison Counts," *Prison Count 2010*, Pew Center on the States, March 2010, at http://www.pewcenteronthestates.org/report_detail.aspx?id=57653 (accessed Mar. 15, 2010); Prison Commissioner Michael Haley speaking on FTR, APTV, May 13, 2002; "Governor Riley Wants State and Faith Groups to Help Ex-Prisoners Avoid Return to Crime," Press Release, Office of the Governor, Mar. 17, 2008, at http://www.governorpress.alabama.gov/pr/pr-2008–03–17–01-faith-crime.asp.

146. Klass, "Support for Ex-prisoners Key to Lower Recidivism," MA, Mar. 30, 2008; see "Improving Prisoner Reentry Services Through Faith and Community-Based Partnership" at http://www.whitehouse.gov/government/fbci/pdf/improving_prisoner _reentry.pdf (accessed May 15, 2008); CIA Roundtable Report, "Improving Prisoner Re-entry Services Through Faith and Community-Based Partnerships," Mar. 22, 2007, at http://www.whitehouse.gov/government/fbci/pdf/march_cia_roundtable_ report.pdf.

147. "Governor Riley Wants State and Faith Groups to Help Ex-Prisoners Avoid Return to Crime."

148. Anthony C. Thompson, *Releasing Prisoners, Redeeming Communities: Reentry, Race, and Politics*, 180.

149. George Bush mentioned a version of Second Chance in his 2004 State of the Union address. Dan Eggen, "Bush Signs into Law a Program That Gives Grants to Former Convicts," WP, Apr. 10, 2008.

150. Val Walton, "State's First Black Federal Judge," BN, Oct. 19, 2008.

151. "Anti-death Penalty Bills Keep Death Row Debate Alive," AP, May 2004.

152. See the discussion of inadequate counsel at the website of the Equal Justice Initiative, http://eji.org/eji/deathpenalty/inadequatecounsel (accessed Apr. 16, 2009).

153. DeMonia, "Eye-for-eye Justice Is Blinding," BN, Feb. 28, 2003. For a political history of the death penalty, see chapters 8 and 9 of Gottschalk, *The Prison and the Gallows*.

154. Quotations from Goldberg in Gottschalk, *The Prison and the Gallows*, 210ff. These paragraphs draw extensively on Gottschalk.

155. Gottschalk, *The Prison and the Gallows*, 206.

156. Gottschalk, *The Prison and the Gallows*, 211–12.

157. Gottschalk, *The Prison and the Gallows*, 225.

158. Robin DeMonia, "Four Deaths on the Way to Inglorious Milestone," BN, Dec. 4, 2005.

159. Quotations from Pryor and Doyle come from Sara Rimer, "Questions of Death Row Justice for Poor People in Alabama," NYT, Mar. 1, 2000.

160. Carla Crowder, "Death Row Most Crowded by State's Size," BN, Jan. 19, 2003.

161. Nat Hentoff, "A Jail like a Slave Ship," *Village Voice*, Oct. 2, 2001.

162. Philip Alston, "Press Statement," United Nations Human Rights Council, New York, June 30, 2008.

163. Howell Raines, "Alabama Bound," NYT, June 3, 1990; "UN report critical of Alabama death penalty," AP, July 2, 2008.

164. Mike Sherman, "Lethal Injection Bill Alive," MA, Feb. 17, 2002; Alabama Crime Victims Compensation Commission, at http://www.acvcc.state.al.us/commissioners .htm (accessed Apr. 30, 2008); Anthony McCartney, "A Question of Numbers," HT, Dec. 21, 2003.

165. Robin DeMonia, "Eye-for-eye Justice Is Blinding," BN, Feb. 28, 2003.

166. Rick Bragg, *The Prince of Frogtown*, 13.

167. "Alabama AG Files Brief Supporting Death Penalty for Teens," AP, Apr. 20, 2004.

168. Patricia J. Williams, "Absolutely No Excuse," *Nation*, Dec. 7, 2009.

169. Eric Velasco, "Alabama Leads Nation in Life Sentences for Felons, Black Youths," BN, Jul. 23, 2009.

170. "Court Ruling on Lethal Injection Puts Stay on Execution," *Irish Times*, Sept. 29, 2007.

171. Matthew Bigg, "U.S. Court Upholds Lethal Injection," Reuters, Apr. 17, 2008.

172. DeMonia, "Race Issues Troubling on Death Penalty Cases," BN, Dec. 10, 2006.

173. Recent research indicates the extent to which the makeup of the jury affects sentencing: when five or more white males sit on a capital trial jury, there is a 70 percent chance of a death penalty outcome. If there are four or fewer white males, the chance of a death sentence is only 30 percent. Rachel Lyon and Jim Lopes, "Race to Execution," *Independent Lens*, PBS, at http://www.pbs.org/independentlens/racetoexecution/film .html, Feb. 20, 2007 (accessed May 9, 2008).

174. DeMonia, "Race Issues Troubling on Death Penalty Cases," BN, Dec. 10, 2006.

175. Shaila Dewan, "Study Finds Blacks Blocked from Southern Juries," NYT, June 1, 2010. See *Illegal Racial Discrimination in Jury Selection: A Continuing Legacy* (Montgomery: Equal Justice Initiative, 2010).

176. Western, *Punishment and Inequality*, 191.

177. Western, *Punishment and Inequality*, 86, 194.

178. Glenn C. Loury, *Race, Incarceration, and American Values*, 28.

179. Western, *Punishment and Inequality*, 196.

180. Comments of Loïc Wacquant, "Forum," in Loury, *Race, Incarceration, and American Values*, 59.

181. "Probation, Parole Officers Swamped," BN, Sept. 14, 2003.

182. "Time to Spend More Wisely on Our Corrections System," MR, Dec. 31, 2003.

183. Two thousand convicts were in the Community Corrections programs, while 25,000 to 28,000 were inside state prisons. Robert McClendon, "Alabama Rates High in Locking People Up, Lower in Probations," MPR, Mar 3, 2009; and see "State and National Correctional Spending," Table A-2, in Pew Center on the States, *One in Thirty-one: The Long Reach of American Corrections* (Washington, D.C.: Pew Charitable Trusts, March 2009); Phillip Rawls, "Alabama Prisons Eye Releases as Worst Case Option," AP, Dec. 15, 2009.

184. Sebastian Kitchen, "Prisons Are 'Time Bomb,' Officers Say," MA, Feb. 3, 2009; Jay Reeves, "Guards Side with Inmates in Lawsuit," AP, May 7, 2009.

185. Southern Center for Human Rights, "Alabama Department of Corrections Significantly Underreports Assaults on Incarcerated Men," Dec. 9, 2009, at http://www.schr.org/action/resources/alabama_department_of_corrections_significantly_under reports_assaults_on_incarcerat (accessed Dec. 22, 2009); "SCHR Responds to ADOC. Data Reveals Assaults on Corrections Officers at Donaldson Also Underreported," at http://www.schr.org/action/resources/schr_responds_to_al_department_of _corrections_data_reveals_adoc_also_underreports_a (accessed Dec. 22, 2009).

186. With a resulting loss of nearly $3 million to the prison operating budget. Tom Gordon, "Recession Has Affected Work-release Jobs for Prisoners," BN, Apr. 19, 2009.

187. Bob Johnson, "Prisons Need More Funding, Chief Says," AP, May 9, 2009.

188. "Lockup: Inside Holman Correctional Facility," MSNBC, at http://www.msnbc.msn.com/id/15952548.

189. Djilas, *Of Prisons and Ideas* (1986), quoted in Alex Lichtenstein, *Twice the Work of Free Labor*, xi, 195; Gottschalk, *Prison and Gallows*, 236.

190. Robert Hunter, lyrics, the Grateful Dead, "Alabama Getaway," *Go to Heaven*, Arista Records, 1980.

CHAPTER THREE. *In the Ditch with Wallace*

1. Gary Younge, "Alabama Diary," *Guardian*, Dec. 29, 1997.

2. Former governor Albert Brewer, foreword to *Alabama Governors*, ix.

3. Rick Bragg, *The Prince of Frogtown*, 8.

4. Permaloff and Grafton, *Political Power in Alabama*, 304.

5. Robert Drew, exec. producer, *Crisis: Behind a Presidential Commitment*.

6. Sebastian Kitchen, "Senate Gets Early Start on Drama," MA, Feb. 15, 2009.

7. George R. Altman, "Survey Rates Alabama Ethics Commission Among Weakest in the Nation," MPR, Nov. 8, 2009.

8. Jim Williams, "Economic Development and the Alabama Constitution."

9. "A Price Tag on Sewer Mess," Editorial, BN, July 5, 2007; Shaila Dewan, "Alabama Area Reeling in Face of Fiscal Crisis," NYT, Aug. 1, 2009. Matt Taibbi unwinds the sordid complexities of Jefferson County's sewer scam in "Looting Main Street," Rollingstone .com, Mar. 31, 2010, at http://www.rollingstone.com/politics/story/32906678/looting _main_street (accessed Apr. 2, 2010).

10. Dan T. Carter, *The Politics of Rage*, 389–91, 400ff; Stan Bailey, "Gerald Wallace Dead at 72," BN, Aug. 4, 1993.

11. Howell Raines, "Alabama Bound," *New York Times Magazine*, June 3, 1990.

12. Howell Raines, "The Politics of Embarrassment in Alabama," NYT, June 7, 1998. See the discussion of Wallace's two-year college patronage network in Anne Permaloff and Carl Grafton, *Political Power in Alabama*, 177–85.

13. Carter, *Politics of Rage*, 424. The following paragraphs also draw upon 455–59.

14. Dale Russakoff, "The Wallace Phenomenon," reprinted in SC 1, no. 5 (1979): 7–9.

15. Bob Ingram, "Alabama Scene," GCD, Jan. 4, 2006.

16. Carter, *Politics of Rage*, 386–95; Howell Raines, "Alabama Bound."

17. Wayne Flynt, "The Wallace Legacy," BN, Sept. 20, 1998.

18. Howell Raines, "The Birmingham Bombing," NYT, July 24, 1983.

19. David Frum, "Send Them a Message," *Forbes*, Dec. 5, 1993.

20. Bill Peterson, "Alabama's Born-Again Democrats," WP, Sept. 25, 1978.

21. Raines, "Alabama Bound."

22. Marjorie Hyer, "Evangelical Christians Meet to Develop Strategy for 1980s," WP, Jan. 30, 1981.

23. William H. Stewart, "Forrest ('Fob') James Jr.," 243–46; Kevin Sack, "Alabama G.O.P. Governor Sees a Different New South," NYT, Sept. 29, 1997; "Sweeps: Democratic Party Celebrates," MA, Nov. 4, 1998.

24. Frank E. Moorer, "Wallace Wasn't State's Greatest Son," MA, Oct. 16, 1998.

25. Art Harris, "George Wallace's Visions and Revisions," WP, Sept. 1, 1982.

26. A rare instance of a nearly all-white county electing a black Democrat to the legislature in the new millennium is instructively explored in Nicholas Dawidoff, "The Visible Man," *New York Times Magazine*, Feb. 28, 2010, 30–44.

27. Art Harris, "George Wallace Is Back," WP, May 22, 1982; Ronald Smothers, "Alabama at a Crossroads," NYT, June 14, 1983.

28. Office of the Alabama Secretary of State, Election Results Archive — Governor (1946–2002), at http://www.sos.state.al.us/downloads/dl2.cfm?div1=Elections%20 Division&types=Data (accessed Apr. 30, 2006).

29. Roy Reed, "Wallace Redux," NYT, Nov. 6, 1982.

30. Randall Williams vividly captures Folmar's rule as mayor in "Witness in Montgomery," SC 5, no. 4 (1983): 1–6.

31. Office of the Alabama Secretary of State, "Historical Election Results, Governor — 1982 Election," at http://www.sos.state.al.us/cf/election/her/her-sw2.cfm (accessed Apr. 30, 2006); Carter, *Politics of Rage*, 464.

32. Rick Bragg, *All Over but the Shoutin'*, 140.

33. Bill Peterson, "Wallace Set to Announce Intentions on Fifth Term," WP, Apr. 2, 1986. For gubernatorial polls in October 1985 and January 1986, see Patrick R. Cotter and James Glen Stovall, *After Wallace*, 23. A survey of Alabamians taken in June 1986 bathed the weary and debilitated Wallace with farewell sympathy as some 63 percent of whites and 80 percent of blacks agreed that he "has gained respect for Alabama in the nation as a whole." 35–36, 207 n.14.

34. Carter, *Politics of Rage*, 465.

35. Raines, "Alabama Bound."

36. Raines, "Alabama Bound."

37. Jeff Frederick, "Interest Groups and Political Culture in Alabama," 190.

38. "Babies Get Chance," Editorial, MA, Aug. 21, 1992.

39. Jeff Frederick, *Stand Up for Alabama*, 406.

40. Bill Peterson, "Alabama's Born-Again Democrats," WP, Sept. 25, 1978.

41. Randall Williams, "In Wallace's Wake," SC 8, no. 3 (1989), 10–12.

42. William E. Schmidt, "Alabama Contest a Reminder of the Old Days," NYT, June 23, 1986.

43. Letter by Don Black published by the GCD, June 18, 1986; Bill Peterson, "Graddick Edges Baxley," WP, June 25, 1986.

44. Bill Peterson, "Stooping on the Campaign Trail," WP, June 22, 1986.

45. Kendal Weaver, "Democratic Runoff to Succeed Wallace Is Name-Calling Brawl," AP, June 20, 1986. Baxley divorced his wife, Lucy, and married the reporter, Marie Prat.

46. Bill Peterson, "Democrats Keep Slugging After the Bell," WP, July 4, 1986.

47. William E. Schmidt, "Alabama Democrat Sees No New Runoff," NYT, Aug. 6, 1986. The federal panel consisted of Frank Johnson, Truman Hobbs, and Myron Thompson.

48. Cotter and Stovall, *After Wallace*, 129–31.

49. William E. Schmidt, "Reagan's Visit Lifts Alabama G.O.P.," NYT, Sept. 19, 1986. See the discussion in Cotter and Stovall, *After Wallace*, 91–100.

50. Schmidt, "Alabama Contest."

51. Cotter and Stovall, *After Wallace*, 97.

CHAPTER FOUR. *Oafs of Office*

1. Dudley Clendinen, "Wallace's Successor Ushers in Conservative Era," NYT, Jan. 20, 1987.

2. Robin Toner, "Black Democrats Map March on Alabama Capitol," NYT, Feb. 13, 1987.

3. Raad Cawthon, "Protesters Say Blacks 'On Back of the Bus' in Alabama Politics," AJ, Feb. 5, 1987.

4. William H. Stewart, "Guy Hunt," 250–251.

5. Sallie Owen, "Rallying Around the Flag," MA, Mar. 3, 2000. The *Economist* wrote it was to "show his contempt for federal plans to desegregate the University of Alabama" ("The Accidental Governor," *Economist*, May 1, 1993, 28–29). The battle banner had served as the Dixiecrat flag in 1948. McWhorter, *Carry Me Home*, 69.

6. Dudley Clendinen, "Wallace's Successor Ushers in Conservative Era," NYT, Jan. 20, 1987.

7. Booth Gunter and Mike Williams, "Toxic Waste Cadillac," SC 6, no. 3 (1984).

8. Howell Raines, "Alabama Bound," *New York Times Magazine*, June 3, 1990.

9. Hoyt Harwell, "Environmental Group Endorses Hubbert, Seeks ADEM Changes," MA, Oct. 10, 1990.

10. Raines, "Alabama Bound."

11. Raines, "Alabama Bound."

12. "Teacher Union Head Wins Alabama Primary," NYT, June 28, 1990.

13. "The Record," Editorial, MA, Oct. 3, 1990.

14. Peter Applebome, "New South Has New Face for Black Tourists," NYT, Sept. 10, 1990.

15. Quotes from Barnard and Hubbert in this and the following paragraph come from Robin Toner, "Stakes High in Contest for Alabama Governor," NYT, Sept. 26, 1990.

16. Peter Applebome, "Alabama Governor on Spot over Flying to His Sermons," NYT, Oct. 6, 1991.

17. Peggy Roberts, "Hubbert Says He'll Stay in State Politics"; Ragan Ingram, "Hunt Ads Racist, Reed Says," MA, Nov. 8, 1990.

18. Wayne Flynt, *Alabama in the Twentieth Century*, 80; Bill Poovey, "Folsom Takes Early Lead," MA, June 8, 1994; Applebome, "Alabama Governor."

19. "Black Vote May Have Helped Hunt," MA, Nov. 10, 1990.

20. Gwendolyn M. Patton, "Why Would Blacks Vote for Hunt?" MA, Dec. 12, 1990.

21. Applebome, "Alabama Governor."

22. "'More the Merrier' for Tax Overhaul," AP, Nov. 18, 1991; "Keep Them Open," Editorial, MA, Oct. 13, 1991; Ronald Smothers, "Alabama Fails to Act on Tax and School Plan," NYT, May 20, 1992.

23. Phillip E. Austin, "Alabama Running out of Time to Reform Taxes," Op-Ed, MA, June 28, 1992; Phillip Rawls, "Tax Reform Beneficial for Hubbert," AP, May 24, 1992.

24. Dan Morse, "Governor Plans to Present New Tax Reform Plan," MA, June 19, 1992.

25. "Bush State Chairman Says Clinton a 'Bad Dream,'" AP, May 8, 1992.

26. Bill Poovey, "Democratic Chief Criticizes Folmar for Cadillac Joke," MA, May 9, 1992.

27. Dan Morse, "Bush Spokesman Defends Folmar's Comment," MA, May 21, 1992.

28. "Alabama's Hunt Should Step Down," Editorial, AJC, Dec. 31, 1992. Five years later, when the former governor had fulfilled his service and paid restitution with money gleaned from friends and supporters, Alabama's Board of Pardons and Paroles declared him innocent of his 1993 ethics conviction and granted him a pardon. Such a declaration of innocence was so rare that it had been issued only once before, in 1976, to one of the "Scottsboro Boys." Hunt immediately entered the governor's race, where he was beaten badly in the Republican primary. Kevin Sack, "Pardoned Ex-Governor Enters Alabama Election," NYT, Apr. 4, 1998.

29. Tom Baxter, "Hunt's Fall No Milestone for Alabama," AJC, Apr. 26, 1993.

30. David Usborne, "Alabama Spoils Image of the New South," *Independent* (London), Feb. 9, 1993.

31. Two decades after the *Economist* article, the number of amendments to Alabama's miserable constitution approached a thousand.

32. "The Accidental Governor," *Economist*, May 1, 1993, 28–29.

33. Mike Williams, "For Good and for Ill, Wallace Legacy," AJC, Sept. 20, 1998.

34. Bob Ingram, "'Little Jim' Sees Stature Increase," MA, Oct. 3, 1993.

35. James Bennet, "Mercedes Selects Alabama Site," NYT, Sept. 30, 1993.

36. E. S. Browning and Helene Cooper, "Ante Up: States' Bidding War over Mercedes Plant Made for Costly Chase," WSJ, Nov. 24, 1993.

37. "'Free' Enterprise," Editorial, MA, Nov. 29, 1993.

38. Bob Ingram, "'Little Jim' Sees Stature Increase."

39. Bob Ingram, "GOP Will Raise Race Issue in '94," MA, Oct. 10, 1993.

40. "Under the Dome," MA, Apr. 2, 2001.

41. "Who's In Charge?" Editorial, MA, Dec. 22, 1993; Bill Poovey, "State Paid Special Counsel to Folsom $228,000 in 1993," AP, Dec. 6, 1993; Sallie Owen, "Rallying Around the Flag," MA, Mar. 3, 2000; "Unfulfilled Promise," Editorial, MA, Apr. 17, 1994; Tanner Freed from Prison," AP, Sept. 13, 1997.

42. Alvin Benn, "Candidate Expects More GOP Voters," MA, Aug. 4, 1993.

43. Anne Permaloff and Carl Grafton, *Political Power in Alabama*, 312.

44. Gerrie Ferris, "Talk-show-hosting Governor Meets Friends, Foes on Radio," AJC, Sept. 16, 1995; Bob Ingram, "It Could Have Been Worse for GOP," MA, Nov. 8, 1998; Marlon Manuel, "Alabama Ex-Democrat Takes Statehouse for GOP," AC, Nov. 10, 1994; Joe Strauss, "GOP Governors in the South Ride Airwaves to Power," AJC, Feb. 5, 1995.

45. "The 1994 Elections: State by State," NYT, Nov. 10, 1994; David M. Shribman, "GOP's Dixie Rise," *Boston Globe*, Jan. 20, 1995; Flynt, *Alabama in the Twentieth Century*, 103.

46. "The Hard Cold Truth," GCD, Dec. 14, 2005.

47. "What Others Write," MA, Jan. 7, 1995.

48. Bob Ingram, "Chain Gang Idea Bad for Alabama," MA, Mar. 26, 1995.

49. Andy Miller, "Like It or Not, James Has Alabama in Spotlight: Chain Gangs Are Back, College Funding Down," AJC, Sept. 7, 1995.

50. Howell Raines, "Editorial Notebook: A Genius of Bad P.R.," NYT, Sept. 3, 1995.

51. "Most Alabamians Support Chain Gangs, Poll Shows," AP, Apr. 17, 1995.

52. "James Reminiscent of Wallace, Some Say," AP, June 6, 1995.

53. Flynt, *Alabama in the Twentieth Century*, 202; Katherine M. Skiba, "Bustin' Rock," *Milwaukee Journal Sentinel*, Nov. 12, 1995.

54. Stephen Bates, "Ghosts of Old South Rattle Chains," *Guardian*, May 20, 1995; "Alabama Chain Gang," Reuters Pictures, May 3, 1995; "Jones Ends State Career," AP, Jan. 13, 2000.

55. "Alabama State Senator Writes Speech Justifying Slavery," *All Things Considered*, NPR, May 10, 1996; n.a., "Alabama State Senator Forced to Quit U.S. House Race after Defending Slavery," *Jet*, May 27, 1996.

56. Diego Ribadeneira, "Ala. Questions Evolution Theory," *Boston Globe*, Nov. 18, 1995. When, in 2001, the state board of education approved a new science curriculum, it included a preface calling evolution "a controversial theory." Bob Johnson, "New Science Curriculum Stirs Debate," AP, Feb. 9, 2001.

57. *Talladega Daily Home* editorial in "What Others Write," MA, Dec. 14, 1996.

58. "State Puts Faith in Creationism, Survey Shows," MA, Mar. 22, 1995.

59. Sandee Richardson, "James Denounces Courtroom Prayer Ruling," MA, Feb. 6,

1997; Kevin Sack, "Alabama Governor's Race Tests Strength of Christian Conservatives," NYT, May 19, 1998.

60. "Poll: 88 Percent Believe Commandments Should Stay," AP, Mar. 3, 1997.

61. Richardson, "Governor Denounces Prayer Ruling."

62. Kelly Greene, "Bill Pryor Hopes to Ride Court Crusade to the Top," WSJ, May 21, 1997.

63. William Safire, "The Commandment Solution," NYT, Apr. 16, 1997.

64. Kevin Sack, "Alabama G.O.P. Governor Sees a Different New South, NYT, Aug. 29, 1997; Sandee Richardson, "James Loses Bid to Dismiss Prayer Suit," MA, Aug. 1, 1997; Sack, "Alabama Governor's Race"; Terry M. Neal, "Alabama GOP's Bitter Runoff Mirrors Party's Divisive Issues," WP, June 16, 1998.

State attorney general William Pryor, a conservative Catholic Republican from Mobile who had his eye on larger prizes and would later play his cards into a fiercely contested appointment to a federal judgeship in the George W. Bush administration, did not support Governor James's legal theatrics. Acknowledging that the Bill of Rights did apply to the states, Pryor filed a separate motion couched in terms of free speech with the U.S. Court of Appeals, Eleventh Circuit, in Atlanta, where he would one day sit. Pryor's argument prevailed and Judge DeMent was reversed. David Firestone, "School Prayer Is Revived as an Issue in Alabama," NYT, July 15, 1999.

65. "Fob vs. Alabama's Image," Editorial, MR, May 22, 1997. Governor Siegelman rejoined the group. Bob Johnson, "State to Rejoin Governors Group," MA, Nov. 15, 1998.

66. "Empty Words," Editorial, BN, July 21 1997. James appointed an African American as director of the Bureau of Tourism and Travel. See William Stewart, "Forrest ('Fob') James," 246.

67. Bill Poovey, "Delinquent Taxes Double," MA, Feb. 23, 1999.

68. James Vickery, "Leaders Must Give Hope, Vision," Opinion, MA, Mar. 15, 1997; "James' Cease-Fire," Editorial, MA, Oct. 17, 1997.

69. Mike Sherman, "James' Recruiting Reviewed," MA, Aug. 4, 1997; Phillip Rawls, "Business Recruiters Upset with James' Development Efforts," AP, July 27, 1997.

70. Sack, "Alabama G.O.P. Governor"; Gita M. Smith, "Alabama Governor Seeks Public Support," AJC, July 28, 1997; Flynt, *Alabama in the Twentieth Century*, 153.

71. David Firestone, "Bastion of Confederacy Finds Its Future May Hinge on Rejecting the Past," NYT, Dec. 5, 1999.

72. "Winton Blount," Editorial, MA, May 17, 1998; "Out There Again," Editorial, MA, May 9, 1998; Kevin Sack, "Gov. James, in Runoff, Tries Body Blows," NYT, June 4, 1998; Mike Cason, "James Responds to Blount," MA, June 4, 1998; Jill Lawrence, "Fob James Wins Alabama Runoff," *USA Today*, July 1, 1998.

73. Sack, "Alabama Governor's Race"; Terry M. Neal, "Alabama GOP's Bitter Runoff Mirrors Party's Divisive Issues," WP, June 16, 1998.

74. Jim Vickery, "'More Fob' Means More Problems," Letters to the Editor, MA, June 7, 1998.

75. Bob Ingram, "Logic Favors James Today," MA, June 30, 1998. See articles by Kevin Sack of the NYT: "Democratic Mayor's Support of Governor's Rival Muddles Alabama Race," June 26, 1998; "Alabama Governor Wins Runoff in Triumph for the Right," July 1, 1998; and "G.O.P. Right Stakes a Claim in Decisive Alabama Victory," July 2, 1998; Marty Connors, "The Sea Change of Alabama Primary Politics," website of the Alabama Republican Party, at http://www.algop.org/chair2.htm (accessed Nov. 10, 2001).

76. Patrick R. Cotter and James G. Stovall, "Siegelman Brilliantly Blended Lottery and Education," MA, Nov. 8, 1998; Bob Ingram, "Actually, Republicans Fired Fob," MA, Nov. 10, 1998.

77. Kathey Pruitt, "Barnes: Millner Would Turn State into a Laughingstock," AJC, Oct. 20, 1998.

78. "Primary / Primary Run-off / General Election Statistics, State of Alabama," Elections Division, Office of the Secretary of State, Montgomery, Revised July 5, 2006; Bob Johnson, "Turnout Tops Expectations," MA, Nov. 5, 1998; Mike Cason, "Lawmakers Say Voters Want Lottery," MA, Nov. 5, 1998; Kim Chandler, "Siegelman Urged to Use His Mandate," MA, Nov. 8, 1998; Bob Ingram, "It Could Have Been Worse for GOP," MA, Nov. 8, 1998; "Religion Issue Wasn't as Billed," Editorial, MA, Nov. 10, 1998.

79. Flynt, *Alabama in the Twentieth Century*, 100.

80. Bob Ingram, "Alabama Scene," GCD, Sept. 4, 1996.

CHAPTER FIVE. *The One-trick Pony and the Man on the Horse*

1. Diane Roberts, "Black, White and Greek," AJC, Nov. 29, 1998; "Historical Markers," Alabama Department of Archives and History, at http://www.archives.state.al.us/ markers/ituscaloosa.html (accessed July 3, 2006); Nick Beadles, "Built on a Hill," *Crimson White*, Apr. 28, 2006.

2. Siegelman, "Inaugural Speech," Alabama Senate Joint Resolution SJR71 22063-32, Feb. 1, 2000.

3. Tom Gordon, "Siegelman Scores Several Firsts," BN, Dec. 3, 1998; Jason Zengerle, "Sorority Row," *New Republic* 226, no. 4, Feb. 4, 2002.

4. Bob Ingram, "Siegelman Likely to Run for Governor," MA, Aug. 31, 1997.

5. Allusions to the musical group Alabama's "My Home's in Alabama" and a comment by Atticus Finch.

6. Michael Sznajderman, "Time to Dare Mighty Things," BN, Jan. 19, 1999.

7. Siegelman, "Inaugural Speech."

8. Siegelman, "Inaugural Speech."

9. "A New Day: Siegelman Must Deliver Progress," Editorial, MA, Oct. 4, 1998); Sznajderman, "'Time to Dare Mighty Things.'"

10. Sznajderman, "'Time to Dare Mighty Things'"; Bob Ingram, "Alabama Scene," GCD, Jan. 4, 2006; Kim Chandler, "Siegelman Adamant on Portables," MA, Nov. 12, 1998; Neil Probst, "Addition Subtracts Portables," MA, Nov. 5, 2001.

11. Bob Dotson, "Art of Politics Hitting New Low in Alabama," NBC News at Sunrise, Mar. 30, 1999; Marlon Manuel, "Feuding Alabama Senators," AJC, Mar. 31, 1999; David Firestone, "In Alabama, Senate Ends Bitter Rift over Leader," Mar. 31, 1999; n.a., "Alabama's Embarrassment," New Orleans Times-Picayune, Apr. 2, 1999.

12. Marlon Manuel, "Feuding Alabama Senators Finally Bury the Hatchet," AJC, Mar. 31, 1999.

13. David Firestone, "Religious Leaders Prevail as Alabama Shuns Lottery," NYT, Oct. 14, 1999; Jay Reeves, "Lottery Vote Sheds Light on James' Loss," AP, Oct. 14, 1999; Kim Chandler, "Lottery Passes," MA, Apr 15, 1999; Patrick R. Cotter and James G. Stovall, "Siegelman Brilliantly Blended Lottery and Education."

14. Debbie Elliott, "Tort Reform in Alabama," Weekend Edition, NPR, May 15, 1999; David Firestone, "Alabama Acts to Limit Huge Awards by Juries," NYT, June 2, 1999.

15. Linda Strange, "Alabamians Find Relief in Laughter," AJC, June 12, 1999.

16. Mike Cason, "$581 Million Verdict Puts Rural Family in Spotlight," MA, May 12, 1999; Kim Chandler, "Senate Passes Award Caps," MA, May 14, 1998; Elliott, "Tort Reform in Alabama"; Firestone, "Alabama Acts to Limit Huge Awards"; Samuel L. Webb and Margaret E. Armbrester, "Don Siegelman," 258–59; Bob Ingram, "Trial Lawyers Will Be Sorry," MA, May 4, 1997; "Republicans Win Majority on State Supreme Court," AP, MA, Nov. 5, 1998. Stuart Stevens, co-founder of the D.C. ad firm, was a native Mississippian tied closely to Haley Barbour. Tom Gordon, "The Ad Gurus Behind Riley Victory," BN, June 11, 2006; Phillip Rawls, "Presidential Aide Built Reputation in State Races," AP, Oct. 29, 2005.

17. Bob Johnson, "Siegelman's Hands-on Style Drives Session," MA, June 11, 1999; Mike Cason, "Siegelman Reinforces Pitch on Riley's Shortcomings," BN, May 16, 2006; "Siegelman's First Year," MA, Jan. 16, 2000.

18. David White, "Siegelman Wins Praise for Session," BN, June 13, 1999; Cason, "Siegelman Reinforces Pitch on Riley's Shortcomings."

19. Gary Palmer, "Lotteries Raid Poor to Benefit Middle Class Youngsters," MA, Aug. 3, 1997; Mike Cason, "Lottery Fight Cost $5 million, MA, Feb. 1, 2000; Jay Reeves, "Baptists to Work Against Lottery," MA, Nov. 17, 1998; Eddie Curran, "Alfa: Donation Never Meant for Lottery," MR, July 28, 2002; Tom Baxter, "Alabama Lottery May Rival

Georgia's, AJC, Aug. 31, 1999; David Wilson, "Alabama Must Help Poor Children Obtain College Educations," MA, Sept. 3, 2000.

20. Dewayne Key, "The Scholar as Activist," 198.

21. David White, "Year Later," BN, Jan. 16, 2000; Firestone, "Religious Leaders Prevail."

22. Seth Hammett, "Consequences Severe if Franchise Tax Not Replaced," MA, Nov. 14, 1999; Mike Cason, "Session to Tackle Tax Crisis," MA, Nov. 15, 1999; Bob Johnson, "Tax Gap a 'Catastrophe,'" MA, Nov. 16, 1999.

23. "For Siegelman, a Good Year," MA, Jan. 18, 2000. Alabama Education Association poll of registered and likely voters cited in Alvin Benn, "Education on Minds of Voters," MA, Feb. 2, 2000.

24. "Cities, States Brace for Hard Times," AP, Apr. 20, 2001; Ana Radelat, "Alabama Incomes Stagnate," MA, Apr. 26, 2001; Mike Cason, "Schools to Lose Millions," MA, Feb. 3, 2001; "Abridged Text of Proration Remarks," MA, Feb. 3, 2001; "Support for Bond Issue High," AP, May 28, 2001.

25. Jim Cargal, "Alabama Self-destructs Through Cuts," MA, Apr. 6, 2001.

26. Mike Cason, "No Support for Taxes, Forum Told," MA, Oct. 10, 2001; "Tax Loopholes Harm Schools," Editorial, MA, Oct. 5, 2001.

27. "Public Says Not Enough Spent on Schools," AP, Feb. 5, 2001.

28. Mike Cason, "Siegelman Vows 'Kids First,'" MA, Jan. 7, 2001.

29. William. V. Muse, "State Should Heed North Carolina's Example," MA, July 8, 2001. Muse left Auburn, where he had been president since 1992, to become chancellor of East Carolina University.

30. Brett J. Blackledge and Kim Chandler, "Firms Flourish under State's No-bid Edict," BN, Nov. 15, 2001; Eddie Curran, "State Paid Dearly for Discarded Web Deal," MR, Aug. 1, 2002; "A Bad Deal," Editorial, BN, Sept. 10, 2002.

31. Phillip Rawls, "Governor Battered by Issues," AP, Mar. 25, 2001.

32. Felicity Barringer, "Governors' Limits on Press Raise Concerns," NYT, Oct. 8, 2001; Jeb Schrenk "Governor's Staff Bars Interviews with Investigative News Reporter," MR, Sept. 22, 2001. Eddie Curran's extensive investigative reporting on Siegelman as governor is reprised and elaborated in his 2010 book *The Governor of Goat Hill.*

33. Bill Barrow, "Siegelman in Mobile to Raise Money for Reelection Campaign," MR, Dec. 4, 2001; Phillip Rawls, "Jobs Alter Legacy of Governor," AP, Aug. 11, 2002; Bob Ingram, "Alabama Scene," GCD, Aug. 22, 2001; "Alabamians in Poll Support Measured Response over War," AP, Oct. 14, 2001; Don Siegelman, "State Must Demand Fair Taxes from Businesses," Opinion Essay, MA, Nov. 18, 2001; Jeff Amy, Eddie Curran, and Sallie Owen, "Bailey Resigns Post with Siegelman Administration," MR, Nov. 22, 2001;

"Siegelman's Legacy May Prove to Include Corruption," Editorial, TN June 27, 2003; n.a., "Siegelman Says Earrings Not for Boys," MA, Aug. 22, 2001.

34. Brandt Ayers, "Favorable Tide Running in Alabama," MA, Aug. 14, 2001.

35. "Siegelman Stays Ahead of Challengers in Poll," AP, Nov. 5, 2001.

36. Kim Chandler, "Siegelman Touts Jobs, Education," BN, May 8, 2002; Manuel Roig-Franzia, "Governor Faces Tough Election Terrain," WP, June 22, 2002.

37. Thomas Noland, "The Dying Memory of Hugo Black," SC 1, no. 3 (1978): 20.

38. "Clay County," at http://en.wikipedia.org/wiki/Clay_County%2C_Alabama (accessed Aug. 17, 2006).

39. John Anderson, "GOP Rivals in Squabble over Gaming," HT, May 29, 2002; Bob Johnson, "Lawmaker Says Proration Should Not Affect Schools," AP, Aug. 18, 2001.

40. Bob Riley, "Alabama Should Honor President Reagan," *The Riley Report* (Washington, D.C.), Mar. 8, 2001. As governor, Riley would rename a section of Interstate 65 as the Ronald Reagan Memorial Highway, to, as he put it, "help remind all Alabamians, especially future generations, of the legacy of freedom President Reagan left us and the entire world." *Trucking News*, July 15, 2004, at http://www.truckflix.com/news_article.php?newsid=1377 (accessed Sept. 9, 2007).

41. "Early Entry Challenges Odds," AP, July 24, 2001; Bob Ingram, "Alabama Scene," GCD, July 25, 2001.

42. "Gubernatorial Debate," *For the Record*, APT, Aug. 5, 2002.

43. Matthew Korade, "Undeclared, Riley Can Raise Campaign Funds," AS, May 9, 2001; "One Bad Egg," Editorial, AS, Dec. 13, 2001.

44. Matthew Korade, "Bush Visits," AS, June 22, 2001; Mary Orndorff, "Bush Plans Campaign Visit for Riley," BN, June 15, 2002.

45. Thomas F. Schaller, *Whistling Past Dixie*, 207, 208.

46. Garry Mitchell, "Riley Makes Campaign Stop on Windom's Turf," AP, July 6, 2001; John Anderson, "Insider Onus Helped Beat Windom," HT, June 5, 2002.

47. Katherine Bouma, "Riley Garners Bachus Support," BN, Oct. 16, 2001; n.a., "Realtors Endorse Riley for Governor," AP, Sept. 4, 2001.

48. Thomas Spencer, "Bush Brings in Record $4.02 Million for Riley," BN, July 18, 2002.

49. Bouma, "Riley Garners Bachus Support"; n.a., "Realtors Endorse Riley for Governor."

50. Sallie Owen, "Gubernatorial Candidate Releases Policy Proposals," MR, Aug. 6, 2002; Bob Blalock, "Wasting Away While Awaiting End to Waste," BN, Aug. 9, 2002.

51. Mike Sherman, "New Challenges Await," MA, June 6, 2002.

52. Tom Gordon, Tom Spencer, and Kim Chandler, "Siegelman vs. Riley," BN, June 5, 2002.

53. See, for instance, the Alabama gubernatorial candidates debate of August 5, broadcast on c-span television on Aug. 16, 2002.

54. Kim Chandler, "Preparing for Life out of Office," BN, Jan. 12, 2003; Phillip Rawls, "Governor's Race Shaping Up as Must-see Politics," AP, Dec. 27, 2005.

55. Sallie Owen, "Republican Party Made New Gains Behind Rep. Riley," MR, Nov. 13, 2002.

56. "Gubernatorial Debate," FTR, Aug. 5, 2002.

57. Joey Kennedy, "Hayes Comes Home: That's Too Bad," BN, Jan. 4, 2002.

58. Exit polling reported in Jay Reeves, "Siegelman Not Taking Sides on Interracial Marriage Ban," AP, Nov. 10, 1998.

59. Hank Sanders, "Senate Sketches," GCD, May 10, 2006.

60. "Don Siegelman," Editorial, MA, May 17, 1998.

61. Harvey H. Jackson, "History and Don Siegelman: The Downfall of a Creature of the System," AS, Jan. 12, 2003.

62. "Siegelman Lax with Public Funds," MA, May 23, 2003; Eddie Curran, "Washington Law Firm Paid Siegelman Fees," MR, May 31, 2003.

63. "Lawyer: Former Siegelman Aide to Plead Guilty to Bribery Charges," AP, June 24, 2003; Phillip Rawls, "Ethics Probe Turns to Siegelman House Deal," MA, June 26, 2003; Robin DeMonia, "Indicting the Politics of Alabama," BN June 27, 2003; Kim Chandler, "Siegelman, Scrushy Deny Guilt," BN, Dec. 29, 2005; Eddie Curran, "Scrushy Gambled, Lost by Refusing Prosecutors' Offer," MPR, July 4, 2006.

64. Chandler, "Preparing for Life out of Office."

65. Eddie Curran, "New Twist on Old Words Coming for Siegelman," MR, May 8, 2006.

66. Chandler, "Preparing for Life out of Office."

67. Tavis Smiley Show, PBS television, Apr. 22, 2008.

68. Adam Nossiter, "Judges Uphold Bribery Conviction of a Former Alabama Governor," NYT, Mar. 7, 2009; Bob Johnson, "Siegelman, Scrushy Seek Dismissal of Charges," AP, Sept. 1, 2010.

69. Kim Chandler, "From the Top, What a View," BN, Jan. 19, 2003.

70. "Don Quixote Riley Prepared to Tilt at Alabama's Biggest Windmills," Editorial, BN, Jan. 31, 2003.

71. "Don Quixote Riley."

72. Kim Chandler, "Riley Eyes Special Budget Session," BN, Apr. 14, 2003.

73. NYT, June 4, 2003.

74. Mary Orndorff, "'Let Go of Vested Interests': Alabama Day Sermon at National Cathedral," BN, Mar. 27, 2003. Quotations from the sermon are taken from Rev. James L. Evans, "The Legacy of Our Ancestors," at Alabama Citizens for Constitutional Reform,

http://www.constitutionalreform.org/archive/speeches/speech_jle.html (accessed Mar. 28, 2009).

75. Evans, "The Legacy of our Ancestors."

76. Wayne Flynt, *Alabama in the Twentieth Century*, 18.

77. Bob Terry, "The Welfare of Alabama Is at Stake," *Alabama Baptist*, Apr. 10, 2003. And see Terry's "Time for Alabama Baptists to Step Up," *Alabama Baptist*, July 17, 2003.

78. "It's Time to Choose," Address to the People of Alabama on the Occasion of the Extraordinary Session of the Alabama Legislature, Office of Governor Bob Riley, Montgomery, Alabama, May 19, 2003.

79. David White, "Riley Signs Tax Package, BN, June 12, 2003.

80. Bill Barrow, "Survey Finds Voters Oppose Governor's $1.2 Billion Tax Plan," MR, June 15, 2003.

81. Luke Coppen, "The Governor of Alabama," *Times* (London), July 5, 2003; Greg Garrison, "Riley's Faith Guides Him on Tough State Issues," BN, May 25, 2003. Alabama welfare benefits have historically ranked among the nation's very lowest.

82. Riley, "It's Time to Choose."

83. See op-ed essay by ALFA president Jerry A. Newby, "Tax Package Far Exceeds Budget Gap," MA, Aug. 6, 2003.

84. Phillip Rawls, "Banker Bucks Tax Plan," AP, June 16, 2003; Sean Reilly, "Riley Plan May Be Spur to Broader Changes," MR, Aug. 4, 2003.

85. Malone, onetime Birmingham "Leader of the Future," John Archibald would write, "sold us out, moved to Florida and lost a bundle. Poetic justice." "Leadership Is More Than Your Photo in the Paper," BN, Feb. 3, 2009. In 2004 SouthTrust merged with Wachovia, which, in turn, was purchased in a government-forced sale by Wells Fargo during the national financial meltdown in 2008.

86. Citizens for a Sound Economy, "Dick Armey Comments on Governor Riley, Proposed Alabama Tax Increases," Press Release, Washington, D.C., June 20, 2003.

87. Bill Barrow, "Poll Finds Frail Support for Tax Plan," MR, Aug. 17, 2003.

88. Susan Parker, "A Matter of Trust," AS, Aug. 8, 2008.

89. Correspondence with Susan Pace Hamill, June 23, 2003. On Hamill's influence on Riley see, for example, "Is He the One?" Editorial, AS, Jan. 3, 2003; and John Fund, "'Too Damn Stupid': Alabamians Seem to Be a Lot Smarter Than Their Governor," WSJ, Aug. 28, 2003.

90. Susan Pace Hamill, "The Governor at Bat: A Single to Shallow Center Field," AS, May 25, 2003.

91. "Individuals claiming . . ." Quote from Susan Pace Hamill, "An Argument for Tax

Reform Based on Judeo-Christian Ethics." The "worst in the whole country" quote is from FTR, Aug. 19, 2002.

92. Hamill, "An Argument," 1, 80.

93. Hamill, "An Argument," 67.

94. Todd Kleffman, "Riley Taps Tax Sales Team," MA, June 22, 2003.

95. "Doing What's Right," Editorial, AS, May 28, 2003; "What Would Jesus Do?" *Economist*, Aug. 7, 2003. Some 1.6 million Southern Baptists (the state's dominant denomination) belonged to 3,200 Alabama churches as the twenty-first century began. Jannell McGrew, "Group Prays, Voices Needs," MA, Feb. 7, 2001.

96. "Shame on Alfa," Editorial, AS, Aug. 4, 2003. The Alabama Finance Department estimated that fewer than two thousand people or companies owned more than two thousand acres of timberland. "See Motivation of Opponents," MA, Aug. 6, 2003.

97. David White, "Riley Seeks Support by Black Clergy," BN, Aug. 1, 2003.

98. White, "Riley Seeks Support."

99. "What Would Jesus Tax?" Editorial, WSJ, Aug. 25, 2003.

100. Robin DeMonia, "'One Nation' Is Still a Country of Many Parts," *Newsday* (New York), Sept. 30, 2003.

101. John Fund, "'Too Damn Stupid.'"

102. Jack Kemp, "The Grinch Who Robbed the Internet," *San Diego Union-Tribune*, Nov. 18, 2003.

103. John Aloysius Farrell, "Tancredo Threatens Grand Plan," *Denver Post*, Nov. 9, 2003.

104. Russell Hubbard, "ThyssenKrupp Moving Ahead Despite Grim Economic News," BN, Nov. 28, 2009; Phillip Rawls, "Riley Delays Issuing New Car Tags for Two Years," AP, Mar. 22, 2004.

105. Paul Krugman, "Toyota, Moving Northward," NYT, July 25, 2005.

106. Bob Riley, "Inaugural Address," Montgomery, Office of the Governor, Jan. 21, 2003.

107. Bob Riley, "State of the State Address," MA, Feb. 3, 2009; Philip Rawls, "Riley Writes to Help State Students Read," AP, May 15, 2004.

108. "Living Proof," Editorial, BN, Mar. 8, 2004; "Alabama Reading Initiative, Frequently Asked Questions," Alabama Board of Education, at http://www.alsde .edu/html/sections/faqs.asp?section=50&footer=sections (accessed Aug. 14, 2009).

109. Markeshia Ricks, "Riley Praises State's AYP Progress," MA, Aug. 4, 2009.

110. Sam Dillon, "Federal Researchers Find Lower Standards in Schools," NYT, Oct. 30, 2009.

111. Mike Cason, "Riley Builds Cabinet," MA, Jan. 5, 2003.

112. Vivi Abrams, Benjamikn Niolet, and Mary Orndorff, "Alabamians Stand Behind Soldiers as Battle Unfolds," BN, Mar. 20, 2003.

113. Phillip Rawls, "Governor's Race Shaping Up as Must-see Politics," AP, Dec. 27, 2005. Similar expectations are expressed in Tom Baxter, "Social, Fiscal Division Emerge in Ala. GOP," AJC, Oct. 8, 2005.

114. Taylor Bright, "Riley Running, Touts Record," HT, Oct. 9, 2005.

115. FTR, Oct. 11, 2005.

116. Phillip Rawls, "Moore Makes 'Bama Governor's Race Official," AP, Oct. 3, 2005; Kim Chandler, "Roy Moore Announces Run for Governor," BN, Oct. 4, 2005; Phillip Rawls, "Alabama Governor to Seek Re-election," AP, Oct. 8, 2005; Robin DeMonia, "There's a New Matchup in Old Battle for Governor," BN, Oct. 9, 2005; James L. Evans, "Opinion," BN, Oct. 16, 2005.

117. Charles J. Dean, "Riley Sees Tax Cuts as Key to Plan 2010 for Progress," BN, Sept. 6, 2006.

118. "'Punt, Bama, Punt,'" Editorial, BN, Dec. 31, 2003.

119. Frank M. Johnson Jr., "The Alabama Punting Syndrome," 5, 54. Tony Freyer and Timothy Dixon, *Democracy and Judicial Independence.*

120. Glenn T. Eskew, "George Wallace," 254–55.

121. "'Punt, Bama, Punt.'"

122. Jonathan Walters, "Raising Alabama," *Governing Magazine*, Oct. 2000.

123. Jordan H. Weissmann, "Riley Tells Bankers State on Brink of 'Magnificence,'" BN, Aug. 12, 2006.

124. George Talbot, "Aero Notes," at http://blog.al.com/live/aerospace (accessed June 18, 2007).

125. Phillip Rawls, "Cost of Ending Alabama Discrimination Suit Tops $200 Million," AP, Jan. 7, 2007.

126. In 2006 the legislature raised the income tax threshold level for a family of four from $4,600 to $12,000. Phillip Rawls, "Plan Would Lift Sales Tax on Groceries," AP, Feb. 29, 2008. Riley continued his practice of not commuting death penalty convictions to life sentences; see Phillip Rawls, "Condemned Inmate Seeks Delay from Alabama Governor," AP, Aug. 20, 2007.

127. Guy Busby, "Riley Says State's Economy Is Better Than Most," MPR, Feb. 10, 2009.

128. Tony Allen-Mills, "Alabama Puts Bush Tax Cuts to Biblical Test," *Sunday Times* (London), June 15, 2003.

129. "Don Quixote Riley Prepared to Tilt at Alabama's Biggest Windmills," Editorial, BN, Jan. 31, 2003.

130. Bill Barrow, "Riley and Knight Huddle on Tax Plans," MR, Feb. 24, 2006.

131. Michael Tomberlin, "Riley Plans 'Radical Change' in Government Operations," BN, Mar. 2, 2003.

132. Roy L. Williams, "Alabama's Jobless Rate Hits 7.9 Percent," BN, Mar. 12, 2009.

133. David White, "Bill Authorizing $100 Million in Federal Aid to Jobless Alabamians a Step Closer to Passage," BN, Mar. 13, 2009; Sara Murray, "GOP Governors Face Fights on Stimulus," WSJ, Mar. 12, 2009; "While Mr. Perry and Mr. Jindal Fiddle," NYT, Mar. 21, 2009.

134. Slavoj Žižek, *On Belief*, 148.

135. David White, "Riley to Lead Southern Governors," BN, Aug. 24, 2009.

136. "Alabama Borrowing Millions to Pay Jobless Benefits," AP, Aug. 7, 2009.

137. Roy L. Williams, "Where Have All the Jobs Gone?" BN, Feb. 28, 2010.

138. "Alabama Jobless Rate up to 10.4 Percent in August," AP, Sept. 18, 2009.

139. "Alabama's Infant Mortality Rate Increases," AP, Mar. 10, 2010.

140. Desiree Hunter, "Stimulus Presents 'Glitches,'" AP, Mar. 27, 2009; Marie Leech, "Stimulus Money to Spare 3,800 Teacher Jobs in Alabama," BN, Mar. 24 2009.

141. Rahkia Nance, "Alabama's Rising Dropout Rate Could Slow State's Economic Recovery," BN, Feb. 11, 2009.

142. "Median Family Income in the Past 12 Months," U.S. Census, 2007 American Community Survey, at http://www.census.gov/hhes/www/income/statemedfaminc .html (accessed Aug. 15, 2009).

143. Steve Suitts and Lauren Veasey, *High School Dropouts: Alabama's Number One Education and Economic Problem*, 23.

144. George Altman, "While Others Launch Campaigns, Gov. Bob Riley Says There Is Still Much Work for Him to Do," MPR, Aug. 16, 2009.

145. Bronner repeated his warning in the winter of 2010. According to the U.S. Bureau of Economic Analysis, Alabama has the lowest personal and business taxes in the country, even when adjusted for household income. See Russell Hubbard, "Alabama Pensions Chief Bronner Sees State Financial Crash," BN, Feb. 25, 2010.

CHAPTER SIX. *Black Alabamas*

1. J. L. Chestnut, "The Hard Cold Truth," GCD, Aug. 29, 2001.

2. Ishmael Ahmad and Alvin Benn, "Thomas Hasn't Paid His Dues, Chestnut Says," MA, July 14, 1991. Some of the actors, possibilities, and limits of biracial politics in Alabama since the 1960s are sketched in Glen Browder with Artemesia Stanberry, *Stealth Reconstruction*.

3. J. L. Chestnut, *Black in Selma*, 313.

4. See Brian K. Landsberg's study of voting rights litigation and the U.S. Department of Justice's involvement in Perry, Sumter, and Elmore counties, *Free at Last to Vote*. The phrase quoted here is from page ix.

5. Michel E. Ruane, "Sheriff Made History Simply by Doing His Job," WP, Aug. 14, 2008. Amerson served as sheriff from 1967 to 1987.

6. Bill Plott, "Blacks Victorious in Key Greene Vote," TN, Nov. 4, 1970; "Greene County, Ala.: Change Comes to the Courthouse," *Time*, Feb. 1, 1971; Alvin Benn, "Civil Rights Pioneers Savor Legacy," MA, Aug. 5, 2005.

7. Alvin Benn, "Greene Celebrated 1968 Wins for Blacks," MA, July 31, 1996. Peter Kirksey had won a seat on the Greene County Board of Education in 1966. See Frye Gaillard's chapter "The Sheriff without a Gun," in *Cradle of Freedom*, 313–25. A detailed and insightful study of the struggle for racial justice and the contestation over voting rights in one Black Belt county is Hasan Kwame Jeffries, *Bloody Lowndes: Civil Rights and Black Power in Alabama's Black Belt*.

8. Landsberg, *Free at Last to Vote*, 228.

9. "Cutting the Turnip," Editorial, MA, Jan. 2, 1990.

10. "Alabama NAACP Supports Second Predominantly Black District," MA, June 14, 1993. According to Bob Ingram, the ADC's Joe Reed was instrumental in drawing the new congressional district's lines, although the federal panel was Republican-appointed; see Bob Ingram, "'Redistricting,'" MA, June 1, 1993; John D. Milazzo, "Redistricting Lawyers to Appeal Federal Judge's Ruling," MA, July 21, 1993.

11. Alvin Benn, "Winner in DA Race Makes History," MA, June 4, 1992.

12. Landsberg, *Free at Last to Vote*, 235.

13. The partnership begun by J. L. Chestnut and Rose and Hank Sanders became the state's largest black law firm. Alvin Benn, "Law Firm Celebrates Legacy," MA, July 13, 2002; John Zippert, "USDA and Lawyers Reach Settlement Agreement in Black Farmers Lawsuit," GCD, Feb. 24, 2010.

14. The folklife festival, held annually in Eutaw, was begun by Jane Sapp in 1975. "34th annual Black Belt Folk Roots Festival to be held August 22nd and 23rd," GCD, July 1, 2009.

15. Howell Raines, "Alabama Bound," *NYT Magazine*, June 3, 1990.

16. Iris Marion Young, *Justice and the Politics of Difference*, 249.

17. Jeffries, *Bloody Lowndes*, 245.

18. Young, *Justice and the Politics of Difference*, 249.

19. Blair Robertson, "Black AU Staffers Battle Prejudice," MA, Oct. 4, 1991.

20. Selena Roberts, "Auburn Trustee Boosts Everyone, Including the Chaplain," NYT, Jan. 3, 2005; Charles J. Dean, "AU Senate Wants Lowder to Consider Stepping Aside," BN, Mar. 31, 2006.

21. David Wilson, "Black Alabamian Says State Must Face Race, Poverty Issues," MA, June 15, 1997.

22. David Wilson, "Alabama Must Help Poor Obtain College Educations," MA, Sept. 3, 2000.

23. "Poor Unlikely to Attend College," AP, Aug. 13, 2000.

24. Thomas Spencer, "Wilson Leaving Auburn," BN, Dec. 10, 2005. E-mail correspondence from Wayne Flynt, Feb. 9, 2006. In 2009 Wilson accepted the presidency of Morgan State University. Childs Walker, "Wisconsin Administrator Is New Head of Morgan State," *Baltimore Sun*, Dec. 4, 2009.

25. Patricia Dedrick, "Riley Seeks Options to End DOT Discrimination Case," BN, Feb. 27, 2003.

26. Kyle Wingfield, "Suit Drains Millions from DOT," AP, Feb. 28, 2003; Mike Cason, "Riley Vows to Put End to Discrimination Case," MA, Mar. 1, 2003; "Agency's Hiring Suit Nears End," AP, May 24, 2003.

27. Phillip Rawls, "Cost of Ending Alabama Discrimination Suit Tops $200 Million," AP, Jan. 7, 2007.

28. This summary of the Golthy incident draws on the following: "One Man Dead after Shooting in State DOT Parking Lot in Grove Hill," AP, July 18, 2001; Patricia Dedrick, "High-profile Supremacist Attorney on Graves Case," BN, Aug. 8, 2001; "Lawyers Say White Client Was Beaten before Black Colleague Killed," AP, Mar. 19, 2002; Dedrick, "Victim Cried about Going Back," BN Aug. 1, 2001; Dedrick, "Graves Guilty in DOT Employee Golthy's Slaying," BN, Apr. 27, 2002; "Thomasville Man Sentenced to 25 Years in Racial Slaying," AP, June 5, 2002.

29. Bob Herbert, "In America: The Prom and the Principal," NYT, Mar. 16, 1994.

30. Rheta Grimsley Johnson, "Springtime Colored in Shades of '60s," *Rocky Mountain News*, Apr. 12, 1994. Of Randolph High's 600 students, 259 were black.

31. Larry Copeland, "Alabama Town Struggles with Stigma," *Philadelphia Inquirer*, Dec. 13, 1996; Tom Watson, "Prom-threatening Principal Denies He Burned His School," *USA Today*, Oct. 20, 1995.

32. J. L. Chestnut Jr., "The Hard, Cold Truth," GCD, Feb. 12, 1997.

33. This biographical sketch draws on Cynthia Tucker, "Confederacy Lives On," *San Francisco Chronicle*, Aug. 5, 1994, and "South Still May Not Be the Promised Land, but It's Far Better Than Before," AJC, Jan. 13, 1990.

34. Cynthia Tucker, "Our Opinion: Get Black Teens Back to Books," AJC, May 16, 2004; "New Editorial Board Has Opinion for You," AJC, Nov. 5, 2001.

35. Cynthia Tucker, "On Race, South Has Changed but Also Remains Predictable," AJC, Dec. 29, 1990.

36. Alvin Benn, "Black Belt Sees Mass Exodus," MA, Aug. 4, 1991.

37. Alvin Benn, "Greene Officials Express Relief," MA, Aug. 29, 1991.

38. Iris Marion Young, *Justice and the Politics of Difference*, 249.

39. See John Gaventa, *Power and Powerlessness*.

40. John Archibald and Jeff Hansen, "Life Is Short, Prosperity Is Long Gone," BN, May 12, 2002.

41. "Life After Cotton," *Economist*, Aug. 30, 2003. And see Ronald Smothers, "Old Racial Tensions Remind a New Selma of Goals Unmet," NYT, Feb. 20, 1999.

42. Jim Auchmutey and Priscilla Painton, "Black Belt: The Abandoned South, Part 1," AJC, Nov. 16, 1986. In a count of companies with more than fifty employees in the rural South, the AJC found that majority-black counties had roughly half as much industry as counties with less than a third black population.

43. Auchmutey and Painton, "Black Belt, Part 1."

44. Auchmutey and Painton, "Black Belt, Part 2," AJC, Nov. 17, 1986.

45. See a discussion of the series by writers John Archibald, Carla Crowder, and Jeff Hansen, "The Black Belt: Alabama's Third World Brought to Public Attention," *IRE Journal*, May 1, 2003.

46. Archibald and Hansen, "Life Is Short."

47. "Heart of Darkness," Editorial, BN, May 14, 2002.

48. John Archibald and Jeff Hansen, "Land Is Power, and Most Who Wield It Are Outsiders," BN, Oct. 13, 2002.

49. Archibald and Hansen, "Land Is Power."

50. "Senate Sketches," GCD, May 8, 2002.

51. Archibald, Crowder, and Hansen, "The Black Belt."

52. Hank Sanders, "Black Belt Action Commission Region's Best Chance," *Demopolis Times*, Nov. 17, 2005.

53. "Alabama's Black Belt," Editorial, *Decatur Daily*, AP, Nov. 29, 2002.

54. Hank Sanders, "Senate Sketches," GCD, July 19, 2000.

55. "ANSC Convention Inspired by Malika Sanders' Keynote Address," GCD, Nov. 16, 2005.

56. "Senate Sketches," GCD, Aug. 22, 2001, and "Hank Sanders Participates in Radio Talk Show," GCD, Dec. 21, 2005.

57. Tullos interview with Alabama state senator Hank Sanders, Selma, Aug. 6, 1991.

58. Peter Applebome, "In Alabama, Blacks Battle for the Authority to Govern," NYT, Jan. 31, 1992.

59. "Mayor Apologizes for 'Uppity' Remark," MA, Nov. 14, 2000.

60. Phillip Rawls, "Slavery Resolution Fuels Heated Debate," AP, Apr. 13, 2007.

61. Phillip Rawls, "Alabama House, Senate Approve Slavery Apologies," AP, Apr. 24, 2007.

62. Hank Sanders, "Senate Sketches," GCD, Apr. 18, 2007.

63. "Text of Slavery Apologies Approved in Alabama Legislature," AP, Apr. 24, 2007.

64. Phillip Rawls, "Slavery Resolution Fuels Heated Debate."

65. Phillip Rawls, "Slavery Apology Rewritten by Alabama Senate Committee," AP, Apr. 26, 2007; "Alabama House, Senate Approve Slavery Apologies," AP, Apr. 24, 2007.

66. "Senate Slavery Apology Vote," MPR, Apr. 25, 2007.

67. Hank Sanders, "Senate Sketches," GCD, July 4, 2007.

68. "Former Alabama Sen. E. B. McClain Gets Prison Term," Editorial, BN, May 20, 2009.

69. "Mobile Chosen for Alabama New South Coalition Convention," GCD, Apr. 23, 1986; Wayne Flynt, *Alabama in the Twentieth Century*, 368, 369. See the discussion of the ANSC in Richard Arrington, *There's Hope for the World*, 208–10.

70. John D. Milazzo, "ADC Remap Plan Wins Federal Favor," MA, July 24 1993.

71. Bob Ingram, "It's Figures," MA, May 9, 1995.

72. "Campaign for a New South," GCD, Apr. 24, 1985. The *Greene County Democrat* would be remarkable anywhere. Over the course of several decades, husband and wife John and Carol Zippert made this weekly paper in the town of Eutaw into the major African American voice in the Black Belt and a critical source of oppositional news and opinion ranging from local to international topics.

73. Gwen Ifill, *The Breakthrough*, 240.

74. See the discussion on Andrew Sullivan's *Daily Dish*, at http://andrewsullivan .theatlantic.com/the_daily_dish/2006/08/email_of_the_da_7.html (accessed May 20, 2009); Robin DeMonia, "Alvin Holmes' Grand Stand for Fairness," BN, Aug. 30, 2006.

75. Shaila Dewan, "Issues of Race and Sex Stir Up Alabama Election," NYT, Aug. 25, 2006.

76. Bob Ingram, "Alabama Scene," GCD, Sept. 6, 2006.

77. Phillip Rawls, "NEA Proposal Draws Alabama Legislator's Ire," AP, June 26, 2006.

78. An excellent summary of Davis's rise and ambitions is chapter 5 of Gwen Ifill's *The Breakthrough*.

79. Charles J. Dean, "The Rise and Stall of Politico Joe Reed," BN, June 22, 2008.

80. Joey Kennedy, "Finally, 'One Big City' Is a Real Possibility," BN, Apr. 1, 2009, at http://blog.al.com/jkennedy/2009/04/poster_odecko_suggested_that_a.html#more (accessed Apr. 2, 2009).

81. Eddie Lard, "The Joke's on Us If We Can't Think as One Region," BN, Apr. 5, 2009.

82. John Archibald, "Politicians Can Use Some Cross-culture," BN, May 26, 2009.

83. Russell Hubbard, "10 Years Ago, City Was Home to 6," BN, May 4, 2009.

84. Jerry Underwood, "Regions Financial Chief Forfeits $12.3 Million Gain on Shares," BN, Mar. 18, 2010.

85. Arrington writes that the JCCC began in 1975; see Richard Arrington, *There's Hope for the World*, 164, 197–210.

86. Wayne Flynt, *Alabama in the Twentieth Century*, 368.

87. Arrington, *There's Hope for the World*, 8.

88. Arrington, *There's Hope for the World*, 13.

89. That the AEA has often put teacher benefits before student progress is the gist of an op-ed essay by Bill Smith, Caroline Novak, and Cathy Gassenheimer, leaders of A+, an organization working to improve student learning. See "Put Kids First in the Education Debate," MA, Mar. 21, 2000.

90. Steve Suitts and Lauren Veasey, *High School Dropouts*, 17.

91. John Helyar, "Dr. James Andrews Still Works on the Cutting Edge," Sept. 20, 2007, at http://sports.espn.go.com/espn/news/story?id=3024046 (accessed Apr. 2, 2009).

92. "Universities Drive Economic Growth," Editorial MA, Sept. 28, 2001.

93. For a short history of the Civil Rights Institute, see Glenn Eskew, "The Birmingham Civil Rights Institute and the New Ideology of Tolerance," 28–66. See Arrington's account of the BCRI in *There's Hope for the World*, 169–78.

94. Jay Reeves, "Blount Sentenced to 52 Months in Prison for Bribery," AP, Feb. 27, 2010.

95. Shaila Dewan, "Birmingham Mayor Convicted," NYT, Oct. 29, 2009; Jay Reeves, "Mayor's Conviction Is Just One of the Problems Facing Birmingham," AP, Oct. 30, 2009.

96. John Archibald, "Jefferson County Not Just Broke, but Broken," BN, June 7, 2009.

97. David Pace, "Percentage of Blacks in Cities Up," AP, Feb. 9, 1991; "Birmingham, Alabama," at http://quickfacts.census.gov/qfd/states/01/0107000.html (accessed Aug. 26, 2009).

98. John Archibald, "City, Shelby Schools Near Crossroads," BN, Aug. 23, 2007.

99. "County Populations," Associate Press report of the U.S. Census figures, MA, Jan. 25, 1991; Phillip Rawls, "Alabamians Still Moving to Suburbs," MA, Jan. 25, 1991.

100. "Shelby County, Alabama," at http://en.wikipedia.org/wiki/Shelby_County ,_Alabama (accessed Aug. 26, 2009).

101. Nancy Wilstach, "Million-dollar Homes on the Rise," BN, Oct. 17, 2005.

102. Andrew Wiese, "African American Suburban Development in Atlanta," *Southern Spaces*, Sept. 29, 2006, at http://southernspaces.org/contents/2006/wiese/1a .htm (accessed Dec. 20, 2009).

103. For a discussion of the Metropolitan Area Projects Strategy (MAPS), see Arrington, *There's Hope for the World*, 7–12.

104. Iris Marion Young, *Inclusion and Democracy*, 8–9.

105. Guinier explores a variety of voting alternatives for the creation of a more inclusive democracy in *The Tyranny of the Majority*. The quote is from page 19. For Guinier's reflections on her Alabama experiences in the mid-1980s, see chapters 7 and 8 of her *Lift Every Voice*.

CHAPTER SEVEN. *Baghdad as Birmingham*

1. Ken Silverstein, "A Crude Likeness," *Harper's Magazine*, July 1, 2001.

2. Carla Marinucci, "Critics Knock Naming Oil Tanker Condoleezza," *San Francisco Chronicle*, Apr. 5, 2001.

3. Laura Flanders, "Beware the Bushwomen," *Nation*, Mar. 22, 2004; Mann, *Rise of the Vulcans*, 225–226; Carla Marinucci, "Chevron Redubs Ship Named for Bush Aide," *San Francisco Chronicle*, May 5, 2001.

4. Thomas Spencer, "Powell Crusades for Youth," BN, Oct. 19, 2000.

5. Bush received 9 percent of the black vote in 2000 and 11 percent in 2004. Roland Washington, "The Rise and Rise of Bush's Guru," *Times* (London), Nov. 17, 2004. On the GOP strategy for black votes, see David Reinhard, "Bush Courts the Black Vote," *Cleveland Plain Dealer*, Aug. 2, 2000, and "Rebuilding the Party of Lincoln," *Economist*, Apr. 23, 2005.

6. Patricia Williams, "From Birmingham to Baghdad," *Nation*, Dec. 13, 2004.

7. Derrick Z. Jackson, "For African-Americans, Folly of This War Hits Home," *Boston Globe*, May 9, 2007.

8. Sarah Abruzzese, "Iraq War Brings Drop in Black Enlistees," NYT, Aug. 22, 2007.

9. Dale Russakoff, "Lessons of Might and Right," *WP Magazine*, Sept. 9, 2001.

10. Louise Branson, "Rice Rises to the Occasion," *Straits Times* (Singapore), Aug. 20, 2000.

11. "Condoleezza Rice Delivers Remarks at Michigan State University Commencement," Federal Document Clearing House, May 7, 2004. See her commencement address to Boston College, June 6, 2006, at http://www.educatednation.com/2006/06/06/ secretary-condoleezza-rice-commencement-address-at-boston-college (accessed June 23, 2007).

12. For this background see Steven Hahn, *A Nation Under Our Feet: Black Political Struggles in the Rural South from Slavery to the Great Migration*.

13. Russakoff, "Lessons of Might and Right"; Marcus Mabry, *Twice as Good*, 24.

14. "Condoleezza Rice . . . from Preacher's Kid to National Security Advisor to President Bush," Bible Network News, Sept. 20, 2002, http://www.biblenetworknews.com/northamerica/092002_usa.html (accessed June 2, 2007).

15. Russakoff, "Lessons of Might and Right"; Condoleezza Rice, *Extraordinary, Ordinary People*, 88–103.

16. Diane McWhorter, *Carry Me Home*, 307–10, 359ff.

17. Russakoff, "Lessons of Might and Right."

18. Jonathan Tilove, "In Rice's Rise, Many See King's Dream Refracted," *New Orleans Times-Picayune*, Jan. 16, 2005; Marcus Mabry, *Twice as Good*, 40.

19. Jay Nordlinger, "Star-in-Waiting," *National Review*, Aug. 30, 1999.

20. Antonia Felix, "Condoleezza Rice at Stanford University: The Early Years," *Journal of Blacks in Higher Education* 38 (Winter 2002–03), 116–20.

21. Nicholas Lemann, "Without a Doubt," *New Yorker*, Oct. 14, 2002; Rice, *Extraordinary, Ordinary People*, 242–43.

22. Russakoff, "Lessons of Might and Right."

23. Mark Z. Barabak, "Condoleeza [*sic*] Rice at Stanford," *Los Angeles Times*, Jan. 16, 2005.

24. Lemann, "Without a Doubt."

25. See the discussion in Marcus Mabry, *Twice as Good*, 136–41.

26. Barabak, "Condoleeza [*sic*] Rice at Stanford"; Rice, *Extraordinary, Ordinary People*, 293–304.

27. Evan Thomas with John Barry, Richard Wolffe, Martha Brant, Daniel Klaidman, Nadine Joseph, "The Quiet Power of Condi Rice," *Newsweek*, Dec. 1, 2002.

28. Daniel Henninger, "George Shultz: Father of the Bush Doctrine," wsj, Apr. 29, 2006.

29. Glenn Kessler, *The Confidante*, 30.

30. James Mann, *Rise of the Vulcans*, ix–x. Vulcans listed by Mann include Rice, Rumsfeld, Cheney, Powell, Wolfowitz, Perle, as well as Richard Armitage, Scooter Libby, Stephen Hadley, Douglas Feith, Paula Dobrinansky, Dov Zakheim, Robert Blackwill, and Robert Zoellick, xiii–xvii, 251–52.

31. See Condoleezza Rice, "Campaign 2000: Promoting the National Interest," *Foreign Affairs*, Jan./Feb. 2000.

32. See "Vulcan," http://en.wikipedia.org/wiki/Vulcan_(Star_Trek) (accessed June 4, 2007).

33. Norman Mailer, "The White Man Unburdened," *New York Review of Books* 50:12, July 17, 2003.

34. See the discussion in Kessler, *The Confidante*, 18–19.

35. Fred Kaplan, "There Are Worse Things Than the Status Quo: Condi's Witless

Optimism about the Middle East," *Slate*, July 24, 2006, at http://www.slate.com/id/2146392 (accessed May 28, 2007).

36. R. Jeffrey Smith and Peter Finn, "Harsh Methods Approved as Early as Summer 2002," WP, Apr. 23, 2009.

37. "Rice, Cheney Approved Waterboarding," AP, Apr. 23, 2009.

38. Maureen Dowd, "How Character Corrodes," NYT, May 3, 2009.

39. Russakoff, "Lessons of Might and Right." For Rice's version of the post-9/11 world, see "Remarks as Prepared for Delivery by National Security Advisor Condoleezza Rice to the National Association of Black Journalists Annual Convention," Federal News Service, Aug. 7, 2003.

40. See Kevin Phillips, *American Dynasty*, 256–59. Rice sounds these themes in "Remarks As Prepared for Delivery by National Security Advisor Condoleezza Rice to the National Association of Black Journalists Annual Convention."

41. David M. Kennedy, "Bush's Place in the Pantheon," *Christian Science Monitor*, Jan. 20, 2004.

42. "The National Security Strategy of the United States of America," Washington, D.C.: The White House, Sept. 2002, http://www.globalsecurity.org/military/library/policy/national/nss-020920.pdf (accessed Apr. 4, 2010).

43. "The National Security Strategy."

44. "The American Thunderer," Interview, *American Spectator*, Mar.–Apr. 2003.

45. Glenn Kessler, *The Confidante*, 12.

46. Bonnie Greer, "Condoleezza Rice," *New Statesman*, Feb. 21, 2005.

47. John Lewis with Michael D'Orso, *Walking with the Wind*, 86–87, 472–73.

48. Judith Butler, "What Is Critique? An Essay on Foucault's Virtue (2000)," in *The Judith Butler Reader*, 321.

49. John Lewis, "Drums of War," Howard University Convocation, Sept. 27, 2002, reprinted in SC 24, no. 3–4 (2002); "Iraq War Resolution," http://en.wikipedia.org/wiki/Iraq_Resolution (accessed June 21, 2007).

50. "A Falling Star," *Economist*, Jan. 18, 2007.

51. "CNN Late Edition with Wolf Blitzer," Sep 8, 2002. See the United Nations Monitoring, Verification and Inspection Commission documents at http://www.unmovic.org (accessed May 24, 2007).

52. Patricia Williams, "From Birmingham to Baghdad," *Nation*, Dec. 13, 2004.

53. *When the Levees Broke*, DVD, directed by Spike Lee (HBO, 2006).

54. Marcus Mabry, *Twice as Good*, 268ff.

55. See video footage for Sep. 2 "Katrina Relief Benefit" at http://www.msnbc.msn.com/id/9147333/ (accessed June 21, 2009). West's comments are also found in Lee's *When the Levees Broke*.

56. Lee, *When the Levees Broke*. On Rice's shopping habits, see "Condi, Warrior Princess," *Irish Times*, Apr. 3, 2004.

57. Bonnie Greer, "Condoleezza Rice," *New Statesman*, Feb. 21, 2005.

58. David Charter, "The Condi Show," *Times* (London), Oct. 25, 2005.

59. Polling in early December 2005 showed that almost 60 percent of Alabamians thought that the Iraq War was going either "well" or "somewhat well." Phrased another way, however, the percentage of Alabamians who believed that the war was not worth fighting had increased from 26 percent in July to 44 percent in December. Dan Murtaugh, "Poll: Support for Iraq Efforts," MPR, Dec. 18, 2005.

60. Eugene Robinson, "What Rice Can't See," WP, Oct. 25, 2005. See also "Opening Statement by Dr. Condoleessa [*sic*] Rice," Senate Foreign Relations Committee Confirmation Hearing, *Congressional Quarterly*, Jan. 18, 2005.

61. J. L. Chestnut Jr., "The Hard Cold Truth," GCD, Nov. 16, 2005. On the life and times of Chestnut, see J. L. Chestnut Jr. and Julia Cass, *Black in Selma*.

62. George E. Curry, "Condoleezza Rice Pimps the Civil Rights Movement," GCD, Oct. 4, 2006.

63. "Remarks as Prepared for Delivery by National Security Advisor Condoleezza Rice to the National Association of Black Journalists Annual Convention," Federal News Service, Aug 7, 2003. On the Bush administration's and Rice's inconsistent views of the Iraqis' readiness for democracy, see Colbert I. King, "Baghdad, Birmingham and True Believers," WP, Sept. 20, 2003.

64. "Remarks as Prepared for Delivery by National Security Advisor Condoleezza Rice."

65. "Iraq Resolution," at http://en.wikipedia.org/wiki/Iraq_War_Resolution (accessed June 22, 2007). President Bush signed the Iraq War Resolution on October 16, 2007. All members of Alabama congressional delegation, including future governor Bob Riley, voted yes, except for Alabama's only African American member of Congress, Earl F. Hilliard.

66. In a memorable slip of the tongue, Rice almost made Bush into her "husband." See Mabry, *Twice as Good*, 209.

67. Russakoff, "Lessons of Might and Right."

68. Patricia Williams, "From Birmingham to Baghdad," *Nation*, Dec. 13, 2004.

CHAPTER EIGHT. *Invasions of Normalcy*

1. Slavoj Žižek, *The Fragile Absolute* (New York: Verso, 2000), 3.

2. Chet Fuller, *I Hear Them Calling My Name*, 159–60.

3. "The 1963 Inaugural Address of Governor George C. Wallace," Jan. 14, 1963,

Montgomery, Alabama. Alabama Governor, Inaugural addresses and programs, sp194, Alabama Department of Archives and History. Also found at http://www.archives.state .al.us/govs_list/inauguralspeech.html. That the speechwriter was Asa Carter is made clear in Dan T. Carter, "Legacy of Rage: George Wallace and the Transformation of American Politics," *Journal of Southern History* 62, no. 1 (1996), 7; Carter, *Politics of Rage*, 106–9.

4. Christopher Peterson, *Kindred Specters: Death, Mourning, and American Affinity*, 10.

5. Martin Fletcher, "Buchanan Plays on Old Prejudices in Southern Citadel," *Times* (London), Mar. 2, 1996.

6. Theodore Rosengarten, *All God's Dangers: The Life of Nate Shaw*, 223.

7. Bob Herbert, "Seeds of Destruction," NYT, May 10, 2008; Kathy Kiely and Jill Lawrence, "Clinton Makes Case for Wide Appeal," *USA Today*, May 8, 2008.

8. Avery F. Gordon, *Ghostly Matters*, 57, 202.

9. Russ Rymer, "The George Wallace We Forgot," Op-Ed, NYT, Oct. 24, 2008; "Rep. John Lewis: John McCain, Sarah Palin Are 'Sowing the Seeds of Hatred and Division,'" AP, Oct. 11, 2008.

10. Elisabeth Bumiller, "Congressman Rebukes McCain for Recent Rallies," NYT, Oct. 12, 2008; "U.S. Lawmaker Slams McCain Camp for Stoking Hatred," Agence France-Presse, Oct. 11, 2008; "On the Campaign Trail," *New Zealand Herald*, Oct. 13, 2008.

11. "Third Presidential Debate," Cable News Network, Hofstra University, Hempstead, New York, Oct. 15, 2008.

12. "John Lewis's Race Grenade," Editorial, WSJ, Oct. 14, 2008.

13. Eric Deggans, "Modern Media Need to Show a Little More Courage," *St. Petersburg Times*, Feb. 27, 2005.

14. Michael Jones and Robert Hofler, "H'W'D Rallying Cry," *Daily Variety*, Nov. 18, 2008.

15. Justin Phelps, "A Bad Legacy for Bush," *USA Today*, July 16, 2004.

16. Mike Williams, "For Good and for Ill, Wallace Legacy Lives On," AJC, Sept. 20, 1998.

17. Williams, "For Good and for Ill."

18. Ellis Henican, "DeLay Hammers Home His Heartless Influence on Terri," *Newsday*, Mar. 20, 2005.

19. Kay Hymowitz, "An Enduring Crisis for the Black Family," WP, Dec. 6, 2008.

20. Ellis Henican, "Long Lines Defy Jim Crow's Ghost," *Newsday*, Nov. 3, 2004.

21. Gwen Ifill, *The Breakthrough*, 17–18.

22. Frank Rich, "Even Glenn Beck Is Right Twice a Day," NYT, Sept. 20, 2009.

23. Scott Parrott and Katherine Lee, "UA Honors First Blacks to Integrate University," TN, June 12, 2003.

24. Parrott and Lee, "UA Honors First Blacks."

25. Žižek, Fragile Absolute, 4.

26. Sandeep Kaushik, "Two Battles over Gay Marriage, Two Different Outcomes," Boston Globe, July 26, 2004; see also Gene Johnson, "Gay Couples Sue for Right to Marry," AP, March 9, 2004.

27. Slavoj Žižek and Glyn Daly, Conversations with Žižek, 150, 151.

28. Patterson Hood, Drive-By Truckers, "The Three Great Alabama Icons," 2000, Southern Rock Opera, Soul Dump Records, 2001; rereleased 2002, Lost Highway Records.

29. The Muscle Shoals sound is surveyed in the "Alabama Bound" radio show in the American Routes series, available at http://americanroutes.publicradio.org/player/playlist/10100 (accessed Jan. 15, 2009).

30. Patterson Hood, Drive-By Truckers, "The Southern Thing," Southern Rock Opera.

31. Tullos interview with Patterson Hood and Jason Isbell, Athens, Georgia, Oct. 8, 2003.

32. Patterson Hood, Drive-By Truckers, "Wallace," 2000, Southern Rock Opera.

33. Gordon, Ghostly Matters, 182.

34. "The Challenges Ahead," Editorial, LAT, Dec. 29, 2008. "I've heard many Republican leaders in Congress say George Wallace was the father of the Contract with America," claimed one former Wallace aide who moved on to work in Congress. "James Reminiscent of Wallace," AP, June 6, 1995.

35. This concluding riff is indebted to Mike Cooley's "Women Without Whiskey," Southern Rock Opera.

36. "Injustice 5, Justice 4," Editorial, NYT, May 31, 2007.

37. Bill Evans, "Ala. Worker Testifies to Congress on Pay Discrimination," AP, June 12, 2007.

38. Judge Joel Dubina, appointed by G. H. W. Bush, and the bitterly contested William Pryor, by G. W. Bush.

39. Alison Grant, "Justices Restrict Job-bias Claims," Cleveland Plain Dealer, May 30, 2007; Linda Greenhouse, "Justices' Ruling Limits Lawsuits on Pay Disparity," NYT, May 29, 2007.

40. Linda Greenhouse, "Court Explores Complexities in Job Discrimination Case," NYT, Nov. 28, 2006; Steven Greenhouse, "Experts Say Decision on Pay Reorders Legal Landscape," NYT, May 30, 2007; "Supreme Court Guts Equal Pay Law," MA, June 13, 2007.

41. Sheryl Gay Stolberg, "Obama Signs Equal-Pay Legislation," NYT, Jan. 30, 2009; Phillip Rawls, "Ledbetter Endorses Davis for Ala. Governor," AP, Sept. 8, 2009.

42. Website of *Knight and Sims v. Alabama*, http://www.knightsims.com/index.html (accessed Mar. 14, 2007).

43. $200 million each to ASU and A&M, $100 million to the state's need-based financial aid program. "The End Is Here," Editorial, BN, Dec. 16, 2006.

44. Tom Gordon, "Desegregation Case Finally Pays Off for Students in State," BN, Aug. 28, 2005.

45. Thomas Spencer, "School Suit Lawyers Ask That Some Tax Laws Be Removed," BN, Jan. 9, 2004.

46. Bob Johnson, "Court Asked to Alter State Tax System," AP, Jan. 9, 2004.

47. Gordon, "Desegregation Case Finally Pays Off."

48. See http://www.knightsims.com/news.php. "Desegregation Suit Plaintiffs Want State's Tax Laws Overturned," AP, July 30, 2003. And see Spencer, "School Suit Lawyers."

49. "The Supreme Court's Ruling Claiming the State Constitution Wasn't Legally Ratified," Editorial, BN, Apr. 29, 2010.

50. Marie Leech, "State 47th to Graduate High School Students," BN, June 13, 2007.

51. Paul Gattis, "Fans Give Rousing 'Roll Tide' Welcome," HT, Jan. 4, 2007.

52. Rick Bragg, *All Over But the Shoutin'*, 137.

53. Thomas Murphy, "Mission Accomplished," MPR, Jan. 4, 2007.

54. Gattis, "Fans Give Rousing 'Roll Tide' Welcome."

55. Bob Johnson, "Study Says Education Struggling," AP, Jan. 4, 2007; Rena Havner, "Survey: Alabama Kids Face Long Odds," MPR, Jan. 4, 2007.

56. See http://www.edweek.org/ew/articles/2007/01/04/17execsum.h26.html (accessed Jan. 4, 2007).

57. Andrew Zimbalist, "Athletic Departments Are Turning Pro," NYT, Jan. 7, 2007.

58. See the National Association of State Student Grant and Aid Programs (NASS-GAP), at http://www.nassgap.org/viewrepository.aspx?categoryid=3 (accessed Jan. 20, 2007); Steve Suitts and Lauren Veasey, *High School Dropouts: Alabama's Number One Education and Economic Problem* (Atlanta: Southern Education Foundation, 2008), 19.

59. Bob Johnson, "Alabama Coach's $4 Million Salary Raises Questions in Poor State," AP, Jan. 4, 2007.

60. Bob Blalock, "A Football Coach, or 2 Million Meals for Hungry," BN, Jan. 7, 2007. A contrary view is "Saban Can Help Education," Editorial, MPR, Jan. 7, 2007.

61. Selena Roberts, "At Colleges, Money Doesn't Talk, It Screams," NYT, Sept. 30, 2007.

62. Russell Hubbard, "Saban Pay Too Steep, Says Ex-UA Trustee," BN, Jan. 4, 2007; Bob Johnson, "Alabama Coach's $4 Million Salary Raises Questions," AP, Jan. 4, 2007.

63. Warren St. John, "Keep the Faith: Turnarounds Can Happen," NYT, Dec. 13, 2009.

64. Joey Kennedy, "Old News Still News in Alabama," Opinion, BN, Jan. 10, 2003. Over twenty-five years after the *News* series, the regressive tax on food remained. Bob Blalock, "Prospects for Tax Fairness Next Year Are Iffy," BN, Nov. 22, 2009.

65. Howell Raines, "Alabama Bound," *NYT Magazine*, June 3, 1990.

66. Robin DeMonia, "'One Nation' Is Still a Country of Many Parts," *Newsday* (New York), Sept. 30, 2003.

67. Gita M. Smith, "Janie Shores: A New Constitution," MA, Jan. 19, 1992.

68. Don Logan, "Remedial Lesson," Opinion, BN, Feb. 1, 2003.

69. Eddie Lard, "Cuts Mean Poor Schools Get Poorer," BN, Oct. 24, 2003.

70. Kristen Campbell, "Poll: Alabama Rates Well in Biblical Literacy," MPR, Mar. 25, 2007; Gerrie Ferris and Gita M. Smith, compilers, "Bible-quoting Rivalry Leads to a Homicide," AJC, July 21, 1996.

71. "Measuring Progress," Editorial, BN, Aug. 24, 2003.

72. John Archibald, "Beat Goes On and Hurts Alabama's Children," BN, July 30, 2009.

73. David Firestone, "Bastion of Confederacy Finds Its Future May Hinge on Rejecting the Past," NYT, Dec. 4, 1999.

74. Alvin Benn, "Capital's Connection to History Fuels Local Tourism," MA, Mar. 4, 2000.

75. Rick Bragg, *The Prince of Frogtown*, 46.

76. Alvin Benn, "History Lives at Cemetery," MA, Apr. 29, 2002.

77. Alvin Benn, "Man Refuses to Surrender Civil War Re-enactment," MA, Apr. 12, 2009.

78. Diane McWhorter, "Clashing Symbols," *NYT Book Review*, Apr. 3, 2005, 20.

79. Barbara Knight, "Ceremonies Helping to Preserve Confederate History," MA, Apr. 25, 2000.

80. Letter from Lewis Regenstein, Atlanta, "Rebels with a Cause," *NYT Book Review*, Apr. 24, 2005. Also see Anne Ruisi, "Confederate Soldiers Honored for Defending Homes and Freedom," BN, Apr. 26, 2004.

81. "Students Say Blacks Ignored at Auburn," AP, Dec. 27, 1991.

82. Jim Yardley, "Diversity, 'Old South' Ways Collide," AC, Apr. 24, 1992; Tracey McCartney, "AU May Face Suit," MA, Nov. 26, 1991.

83. Blair Robertson, "Protest Disrupts Route of Auburn Old South Parade," MA, Apr. 25, 1992.

84. Blair Robertson, "Muse's Stance on Parade Ruffles Some Students," MA, Apr. 22, 1992.

85. Jay Reeves, "Fraternity Again Faces 'Old South' Complaints," AP, May 14, 2009. Kappa Alpha Order website, "Old South" http://www.auburn.edu/student_info/greeks/kappa_alpha_order/oldsouth.php (accessed Mar. 31, 2010). By fall 2001, blacks made up 7 percent of Auburn's students. "Auburn Enrollment Hits Record 22,469," AP, Sept. 20, 2001.

86. Diane Roberts, "Black, White and Greek," AJC, Nov. 29, 1998.

87. "UA President Seeks to Alleviate Segregation," MA, Apr. 21, 2000.

88. "University of Alabama Faculty Steering Committee Meeting Agenda," Dec. 15, 2001, at http://facultysenate.ua.edu/01-02/ag120401steering.html (accessed Mar. 15, 2009).

89. Jay Reeves, "Black Woman Doesn't Get Sorority Bid," MA, Sept. 11, 2001; "Sorority Rejects Black Student," AP, NYT, Sept. 12, 2001.

90. "University of Alabama," at http://www.upto11.net/generic_wiki.php?q=university_of_alabama (accessed Mar. 15, 2009).

91. "Diversity Comes to UA," Editorial, BN, Nov. 27, 2005.

92. Steve Reeves, "Witt Tackles Diversity, Enrollment," TN, Mar. 5, 2003.

93. George E. Curry, "A 'Complicated' Love Affair with the South," GCD, Jan. 4, 2006.

94. Alan Blinder, "Racism Still in UA Machine," BN, Mar. 15, 2009; Reeves, "Fraternity Again Faces 'Old South' Complaints"

95. Alvin Benn, "Country Club Chief Denies Racism Charge," MA, Sept. 11, 1999.

96. Amanda Peterson, "AKA Celebration Interrupted by Old South Parade," Crimson White, Apr. 27, 2009; "Black Sorority Protests 'Old South' Days," AP, Apr. 30, 2009.

97. "Kappa Alpha Fraternity, Inspired by Robert E. Lee, Bans Confederate Rebel Uniforms," AP, Apr. 22, 2010.

98. Peter Applebome, "New South Has New Face for Black Tourists," NYT, Sept. 10, 1990,

99. Alvin Benn, "Camden Debates Street Name," MA, July 16, 1991.

100. Alvin Benn, "Lawmakers to Address Marion Street Renaming," MA, Mar. 13, 1991.

101. Alvin Benn, "Highway Dedicated by 'King Caravan,'" MA, Apr. 5, 1992.

102. Alvin Benn, "New King Highway Markers Defaced, Stolen," MA, Apr. 15, 1992.

103. William Zinsser, "Deeds and Deaths That Made Things Better," Smithsonian 22, no. 6 (Sept. 1991), 32–43; Jeffrey C. Benton, "Civil Rights Monument One of a Kind," MA, Jan. 20, 1997.

104. Alvin Benn, "Proposal Would Make Voting Rights March Route National

Historic Trail," MA, Aug. 8, 1991; National Park Service, *Draft: Selma to Montgomery: Historic Trail Survey* (Washington, D.C.: U.S. Department of the Interior, 1993). See the trail website at http://www.nps.gov/semo/index.htm.

105. Alvin Benn, "Civil Rights Leaders Honor Woman Slain During Voting Rights Campaign," MA, Mar. 4, 1991.

106. "Denouncing Vandalism," photograph by Patricia Milik, MA, Feb. 2, 1997; "Monument Is Defaced in Alabama," NYT, Feb. 6, 1997.

107. Alvin Benn, "Mayor Opposes Change in Selma Seal," MA, Feb. 26, 1997; Benn, "Blacks Protest at Ceremony," MA, Oct. 8, 2000.

108. "Nathan Bedford Forrest," *Wikipedia*, at http://en.wikipedia.org/wiki/Nathan _bedford_forrest (accessed May 14, 2009).

109. Alvin Benn, "Blacks Protest at Ceremony," MA, Oct. 8, 2000.

110. Hank Sanders, "Senate Sketches," GCD, Jan. 24, 2001.

111. Iris Marion Young, *Inclusion and Democracy*, 50.

112. See Alvin Benn's reporting in the *Montgomery Advertiser:* "Statue Inspires Emotions," Jan. 17, 2001; "Marker Foe Calls for Fine," Jan. 22, 2001; "Statue Moved after Long Fight," Mar. 1, 2001; "Selma Council Votes to Move Forrest Statue," Feb. 27, 2001.

113. "Monument Action Hardly King Tribute," MA, Jan. 17, 2001.

114. Benn, "Statue Moved after Long Fight"; "Officials Debate Forrest Suit," AP, June 10, 2001; Benn, "Support, Anger Follow Final Vote," MA, Feb. 28, 2001.

115. On Gee's Bend, see J. R. Moehringer, "Crossing Over," at http://www.pulitzer .org/works/2000,Feature+Writing (accessed May 15, 2009).

116. See John Beardsley, William Arnett, Paul Arnett, and Jane Livingston, *The Quilts of Gee's Bend;* "Gee's Bend Quilts Are Commemorated with Stamps," GCD, Sept. 23, 2006.

117. Charles J. Dean, "In Black Belt, McCain Wins Hearts, Not Votes," BN, Apr. 22, 2008.

118. Phillip Rawls, "McCain Takes GOP Campaign into Rural Alabama Democratic Turf," AP, Apr. 21, 2008; Charles J. Dean, "McCain Visits Gee's Bend Quilters," BN, Apr. 21, 2008.

119. Elisabeth Bumiller, "On McCain Tour, a Promise to Find 'Forgotten' America," NYT, Apr. 22, 2008.

120. Useful in framing my discussion of the Pettus Bridge are Dolores Hayden, *The Power of Place*, and Georg Simmel, "Bridge and Door," 170–73.

121. Alvin Benn, "Historic Edmund Pettus Bridge Brings Fame, Fortune, to Selma," MA, Jan. 5, 1992.

122. Jannell McGrew, "Discrimination Still Alive, Jackson Says," MA, Mar. 10, 2003.

123. Alvin Benn, "Return to Selma," MA, Mar. 10, 2008.

124. Michelle Malkin, "Queen of Cringe," *New York Post*, Apr. 25, 2007; "The Big Story with John Gibson," Fox News Network, Mar. 5, 2007. And see "Hillary Quoting James Cleveland," at http://www.youtube.com/watch?v=DGDm4jkDbGQ (accessed Aug. 20, 2009).

125. Dahleen Glanton and Mike Dorning, "Clinton, Obama Commemorate Selma Anniversary," *Chicago Tribune*, Mar. 4, 2007.

126. For Toni Morrison's comment, see http://en.wikipedia.org/wiki/Toni _Morrison.

127. Robert George, "News and Notes," National Public Radio, Mar. 5, 2007.

128. Nedra Pickler, "In Selma, Obama Appeals to Black Voters," AP, Mar. 4, 2007; Tom Baldwin, "Quest for Black Vote Brings Obama and Clinton to Heart of Old South," *Times* (London), Mar. 5, 2007.

129. Glanton and Dorning, "Sen. Obama Delivers Remarks at a Selma Voting Rights March Commemoration," as released by the Obama Campaign, Mar. 4, 2007.

130. "Text of Democrat Barack Obama's Prepared Remarks for a Rally on Tuesday in St. Paul, Minn., as Released by His Campaign," Associated Press, June 4, 2008.

131. See the photographs of "The Children's Crusade" at "Veterans of the Civil Rights Movement," http://www.crmvet.org/images/imgbham.htm (accessed Jan. 22, 2010). Selma native Joanne Bland, later a cofounder and director of the National Voting Rights Museum, was eleven years old when she and her fourteen-year-old sister, Linda, participated in the Bloody Sunday events. See "Joanne Bland," at http://www.baylormag .com/story.php?story=004479, *Baylor Magazine* 2, no. 2, Sept.–Oct. 2003.

132. J. Mills Thornton III, *Dividing Lines*, 455–89.

133. My narrative of these incidents is drawn from Todd Kleffman, "Police Scandal Another Blemish," MA, Feb. 17, 2002.

134. Kleffman, "Police Scandal Another Blemish."

135. Dan Rather and Mark Strassman, "Police Suspended amid Brutality Scandal," *CBS Evening News*, Feb. 15, 2002.

136. http://www.youtube.com/results?search_query=birmingham+police+beat+un conscious+suspect&search_type=&aq=f (accessed May 22, 2009).

137. Robbie Brown, "Tape of Beating Leads to Firing of Five Officers," NYT, May 21, 2009; John Archibald, "Here Are the Questions: Who Knew What? And When?" BN, May 21, 2009; "Ala. Cops Fired for Beating of Suspect," *USA Today*, May 21, 2009.

138. John Archibald, "Birmingham Cannot Go Back," BN, May 24, 2009.

139. "Five Alabama Police Officers Fired After Camera Proves They Beat an Unconscious Man," NBC News, *Today*, May 21, 2009. The reaction to the police firings and to the statements by public officials and journalists touched off a storm on the

Birmingham News blogs, much of it vehemently supporting the officers' beating of the unconscious man.

140. "No Human Deserved the Beating an Unconscious Suspect Got from Birmingham Police," BN, Editorial, May 21, 2009.

141. "Alabama Gov. Bob Riley Condemns Beating by Police," BN, May 21, 2009.

142. John Archibald, "Birmingham Cannot Go Back," BN, May 24, 2009.

143. Patricia Dedrick, "Governor Vows State Will Lead Nation in Racial Unity," BN, Jan. 21, 2003.

144. "Race and Voting," Table, NYT, Apr. 28, 2009; "Election Results 2008," NYT, at http://elections.nytimes.com/2008/results/president/votes.html (accessed Dec. 14, 2008).

145. Phillip Rawls, "Whites Make Up Majority of Boards in Alabama," AP, July 7, 2009. Rawls notes: "The governor makes more appointments to state boards and commissions than anyone else."

146. Tom Gordon, Tom Spencer, and Kim Chandler, "Siegelman vs. Riley," BN, June 5, 2002; Markeshia Ricks, "Education Official Says Taxes not Enough," BN, Oct. 29, 2010.

147. "Election Center 2008: Exit Polls," Cable News Network, http://www.cnn.com/ELECTION/2008/results/polls/#val=ALP00p1 (accessed Dec. 14, 2008). Alabama's population in 2008 was 71 percent white, 26.5 percent black, and 2.5 percent other. Non-Hispanic population is 97.3 percent; Hispanic population 2.7 percent. Source: "2008 Election Coverage," *USA Today*, at http://www.usatoday.com/news/politics/election2008/al.htm (accessed Nov. 5, 2008).

148. Lydia Saad, "Political Ideology: 'Conservative' Label Prevails in the South," Gallup State of the States, Aug. 14, 2009, at http://www.gallup.com/poll/122333/Political-Ideology-Conservative-Label-Prevails-South.aspx (accessed Aug. 24, 2009). See also Schaller, *Whistling Past Dixie*.

149. Nicholas Dawidoff, "The Visible Man," *NYT Magazine*, Feb. 28, 2010.

150. Jay Reeves, "Artur Davis Seeks to Be Alabama's First Black Governor," AP, Feb. 6, 2009; "2004 African-American Percentage of Southern Population, Eligible Voters, Registrants, and Voters," Table 3.1, in Thomas F. Schaller, *Whistling Past Dixie*, 73.

151. Gwen Ifill, *The Breakthrough*, 104, 105.

152. "Final Results for Roll Call 165, Patient Protection and Affordable Care Act," at http://clerk.house.gov/evs/2010/roll165.xml (accessed Mar. 22, 2010); Mary Orndorff, "Rep. Artur Davis, Congressional Black Caucus Split on Health Care Bill," BN, Mar. 20, 2010. David Jarman; "The Ten Most Courageous (and Ten Most Cowardly) House Democrats," *Salon*, Mar. 21, 2010, at http://www.salon.com/news/the_numerologist/

2010/03/21/courageous_and_cowardly_democrats (accessed Mar. 22, 2010); John Archibald, "Picking Health Care's Winners and Losers," BN, Mar. 24, 2010.

153. Posted by rbn, March 21, 2010, at http://blog.al.com/sweethome/2010/03/alabama_house_delegation_unani.html (accessed Mar. 22, 2010).

154. Kim Chandler, "Artur Davis Says He Won't Seek Endorsements," BN, Apr. 14, 2010.

155. Hank Sanders, "Senate Sketches #1195," GCD, Apr. 28, 2010.

156. Sebastian Kitchen, "AEA May Be Helping PAC," MA, Apr. 20, 2010; Thomas Spencer, "AEA Is Hedging Its Bets," BN, May 2, 2010; "Byrne Says Untrue Attack about His Faith Is 'An Affront to All Believers,'" May 4, 2010, official Byrne campaign website, at http://byrneforalabama.com/news/byrne_says_untrue_attack_about_his_faith_is _an_affront_to_all_believe (accessed May 31, 2010); Gail Collins, "Alabama Goes Viral," NYT, May 29, 2010. On the eve of the primary vote, Collins pondered several egregious political ads from the Heart of Dixie.

157. Paul Krugman, "State of Paralysis," NYT, May 25, 2009.

158. Nicholas Confessore, "As Voter Disgust with Albany Rises, So Do Calls for a New Constitution," NYT, Aug. 24, 2009.

159. "California: The Ungovernable State," *Economist*, May 14, 2009.

160. "President Barack Obama's Prepared Remarks Before Congress, Sept. 9, 2009," *BusinessWeek.com*, Sept. 10, 2009 (accessed Sept. 11, 2009); Sean Reilly, "James Alleges Obama Plans Takeover of State's Health Care," MPR, Sept. 10, 2009; Charles J. Dean, "Candidates Get a Little Less Cordial," BN, Aug. 27, 2010.

161. "No Will and No Vision," Editorial, HT, May 10, 2009.

162. Sebastian Kitchen, "Senate Gets Early Start on Drama," MA, Feb. 15, 2009.

163. Phillip Rawls, "Alabama Ranks 49th in National Campaign Disclosure Study," AP, Oct. 17, 2007.

164. Nathan Koppel, "Ruling on 'Probable Bias' Spotlights Political Reality," WSJ, June 11, 2009; see also John Schwartz, "Effort Begun to Abolish the Election of Judges," NYT, Dec. 24, 2009.

165. Eric Velasco, "Ruling on Judges' Deciding Cases of Contributors Has Little Effect in Alabama," BN, June 9, 2009.

166. Steely Dan's reference to the Alabama Crimson Tide in "Deacon Blues," *Aja*, ABC 1006, 1977.

167. Roy L. Williams, "Execs: Ruben Lifts Birmingham Image," BN, May 23, 2003.

168. Kelefa Sanneh, "Laid-Back Love Ballads and Fervent Promises," NYT, Dec. 15, 2003.

169. "Bush Inauguration Jokes," *About.com: Political Humor*, at http://politicalhumor .about.com/od/bushinauguration/a/gwbinauguration_2.htm (accessed Aug. 9, 2007).

170. For a summary of Alabama's senatorial shift of increasing conservatism from the late 1950s to 2000, see Earl and Merle Black, *The Rise of Southern Republicans,* 126–28.

171. Bob Herbert's quotes in this and the following paragraph come from "Out of Touch," NYT, May 2, 2009.

172. "Stem Cell Vote: U.S. Senate Roll Call Votes 109th Congress–2nd Session," at http://www.senate.gov/legislative/LIS/roll_call_lists/roll_call_vote_cfm.cfm?congress =109&session=2&vote=00206 (accessed Aug. 31, 2007); Mary Orndorff, "Eight of Nine Delegates Vote No on Package," BN, Feb. 14, 2009.

173. Phillip Rawls, "Sen. Shelby Closes in on 'Free Ride' in 2010," AP, July 24, 2009.

174. Andrew Martin and Sewall Chan, "Autonomy of Consumer Watchdog Is in Dispute," NYT, Mar. 6, 2010.

175. Paul Krugman, "Punks and Plutocrats," NYT, Mar. 29, 2010.

176. Anna Velasco, "642,000 Alabamians without Health Insurance Would Be Able to Get Coverage," BN, Mar. 23, 2010.

177. Robert Pear, "Defying Bush, Senate Increases Child Care Funds for the Poor," NYT, Mar. 31, 2004; "Roll Call Results for the U.S. Senate Vote 'Welfare Reauthorization/Child Care Funding (in Sen.) HR4,' 108th Congress," *Congressional Quarterly,* at CQ Congress Collection, http://library.cqpress.com/congress/rollcall .php?id=rc2004-235-10328-663044 (accessed July 27, 2009).

178. Allen Tullos, "Voting Rights Activists Acquitted," *Nation,* 241, no. 3 (Aug. 3–10, 1985), 78–80. Hank Sanders recounts the "Black Belt Voter Persecution Cases" in his "Senate Sketches," GCD, Nov. 22, 1995.

179. Reporting and video clips presented on *The Rachel Maddow Show,* MSNBC-TV, May 4, 2009.

180. Sarah Wildman, *New Republic,* Dec. 30, 2002.

181. Mary Orndorff, "Sessions Splits with Shelby on Prisoner Abuse," BN, Oct. 7, 2005.

182. Both Senators Shelby and Sessions voted against Sotomayor in 1998, who was confirmed sixty-seven to twenty-nine as an appellate judge. Mary Orndorff, "U.S. Senator Jeff Sessions Opposed Sonia Sotomayor 11 Years Ago, But Now Says She Deserves a Fresh Review," BN, May 27, 2009.

183. Deborah Barfield Berry, "Sotomayor Nomination a 'Teaching Moment,'" MA, June 16, 2009; Mary Orndorff, "Sen. Jeff Sessions Issues First Direct Criticism of Supreme Court Nominee Sonia Sotomayor," BN, June 24, 2009.

184. Jeff Sessions, "Opposing View: Nominee Lacks Deep Convictions Needed to Resist Judicial Activism," *USA Today,* July 27, 2009; Sean Reilly, "Sessions Votes Against Sotomayor," MPR, July 29, 2009.

185. "Shelby to Oppose Sotomayor Confirmation," States News Service, July 28, 2009. Both senators also unsuccessfully opposed the nomination of Elena Kagan. See Mary Orndorff, "Sen. Richard Shelby to Oppose U.S. Supreme Court Nominee," BN, July 22, 2010.

186. Rodney Jones interviewed by Natasha Trethewey, Chicago, Ill., Feb. 13, 2009, SS, http://www.southernspaces.org/contents/2009/jones/1a.htm (accessed May 4, 2009).

187. Larry Lee, "Best and Brightest Leave State," MA, June 9, 1997.

188. Bob Lowry, "State Flunks Affordability Test for College," HT, Dec. 9, 2006.

189. Erin Stock, "Dropout Rate Seen as Threat to State Growth," BN, Apr. 30, 2008.

190. Iris Marion Young, *Inclusion and Democracy*, 50.

EPILOGUE

1. Jeff MacGregor, "The New Electoral Sex Symbol: NASCAR Dad," NYT, Jan. 15, 2004.

2. Al Levine, "Drivers, Fans Show True Colors at Talladega," AJC, Apr. 4, 2003; "Talladega's Grant Lynch Wins Governor's Award," *Birmingham Business Journal*, Apr. 23, 2004.

3. Chris Hedges, "Public Lives: Seeing the Pen Not as Mightier, but as More Honest," NYT, Feb. 6, 2003.

4. Kent Faulk, "State's First to Die in War Was Proud to Be a Soldier," BN, Mar. 27, 2003.

5. Joe Danborn, "Poll Finds Alabama Backs Bush but Worries over Missions," MR, July 20, 2003.

6. *Talladega Nights: The Ballad of Ricky Bobby*, Apatow Productions, 2006.

7. Rick Minter, "Waltrip Snaps Earnhardt's Streak," AJC, Sept. 28, 2003; Ryan Smithson, "Sadler Sent on Scary Tumble near Race's End," Turner Sports Interactive, Sept. 28, 2003.

8. Mark Inabinett, "Waltrip Denies Junior," MR, Sept. 29, 2003.

9. "Official Alabama Nut," at http://www.archives.state.al.us/Emblems/st_nut.html (accessed July 24, 2009).

SELECTED BIBLIOGRAPHY

BOOKS AND PERIODICALS

Akens, Helen Morgan, and Virginia Pounds Brown. *Alabama: Mounds to Missiles*. Rev. ed. Huntsville: Strode, 1966.

Arnesen, Eric. "Rethinking the Movement." *Nation*, December 2002. 28–33.

Arrington, Richard. *There's Hope for the World: The Memoir of Birmingham, Alabama's First African American Mayor*. Tuscaloosa: University of Alabama Press, 2008.

Atkins, Leah Rawls. "Creeks and Americans at War." In *Alabama: The History of a Deep South State*, by William Warren Rogers, Robert David Ward, Leah Rawls Atkins, and Wayne Flynt. Tuscaloosa: University of Alabama Press, 1994. 36–53.

———. *"Developed for the Service of Alabama": The Centennial History of the Alabama Power Company 1906–2006*. Birmingham: Alabama Power Company, 2006.

Ayers, Edward L. *Vengeance and Justice: Crime and Punishment in the 19th Century American South*. New York: Oxford University Press, 1984.

Baldwin, James. *The Price of the Ticket*. New York: St. Martin's, 1985.

Beardsley, John, William Arnett, Paul Arnett, and Jane Livingston. *The Quilts of Gee's Bend*. Atlanta: Tinwood, 2002.

Black, Earl, and Merle Black. *The Rise of Southern Republicans*. Cambridge: Belknap Press of Harvard University Press, 2002.

Blackmon, Douglas A. *Slavery by Another Name: The Re-enslavement of Black Americans from the Civil War to World War I*. New York: Doubleday, 2008.

Bond, Horace Mann. *Negro Education in Alabama: A Study in Cotton and Steel*. Washington, D.C.: Associated Publishers, 1939.

Bragg, Rick. *All Over but the Shoutin'*. New York: Pantheon, 1997.

———. *The Most They Ever Had*. San Francisco: MacAdam/Cage, 2009.

———. *The Prince of Frogtown*. New York: Knopf, 2008.

Brewer, Albert. Foreword to *Alabama Governors: A Political History of the State*, ed. Samuel L. Webb and Margaret E. Armbrester. Tuscaloosa: University of Alabama Press, 2001. ix–x.

Browder, Glen. *The South's New Racial Politics*. Montgomery: New South, 2009.

Browder, Glen, with Artemesia Stanberry. *Stealth Reconstruction: An Untold Story of Racial Politics in Recent Southern History.* Montgomery: New South, 2010.

Buck-Morss, Susan. *Dreamworld and Catastrophe: The Passing of Mass Utopia in East and West.* Cambridge: MIT Press, 2000.

Butler, Judith. *Giving an Account of Oneself.* New York: Fordham University Press, 2005.

———. *Undoing Gender.* New York: Routledge, 2004.

Carmer, Carl. *Stars Fell on Alabama.* New York: Literary Guild, 1934.

Carroll, Stephen J., and Emre Erkut. *The Benefits to Taxpayers from Increases in Students' Educational Attainment.* Santa Monica, California: Rand, 2009.

Carter, Dan T. "Legacy of Rage: George Wallace and the Transformation of American Politics." *Journal of Southern History* 62, no. 1 (1996): 3–26.

———. *The Politics of Rage: George Wallace, the Origins of the New Conservatism, and the Transformation of American Politics.* New York: Simon & Schuster, 1995.

Cason, Clarence. *Ninety Degrees in the Shade.* Chapel Hill: University of North Carolina Press, 1935.

Chabon, Michael. *The Amazing Adventures of Kavalier and Clay.* New York: Random House, 2000.

Chestnut, J. L., Jr., and Julia Cass. *Black in Selma.* New York: Farrar, Straus & Giroux, 1990.

Christgau, Robert. *Grown Up All Wrong: Seventy-five Great Rock and Pop Artists from Vaudeville to Techno.* Cambridge: Harvard University Press, 1998.

Coski, John M. *The Confederate Battle Flag: America's Most Embattled Emblem.* Cambridge: Belknap Press of Harvard University Press, 2005.

Cotter, Patrick R., and James Glen Stovall. *After Wallace: The 1986 Contest for Governor and Political Change in Alabama.* Tuscaloosa: University of Alabama Press, 2009.

Covington, Vicki. *Gathering Home.* New York: Simon & Schuster, 1988.

Crittenden, Ann. *The Price of Motherhood.* New York: Metropolitan, 2001.

Curran, Eddie. *The Governor of Goat Hill: Don Siegelman, the Reporter Who Exposed His Crimes, and the Hoax That Suckered Some of the Top Names in Journalism.* Bloomington, Ind.: iUniverse, 2010.

Curtin, Mary Ellen. *Black Prisoners and Their World, Alabama, 1865–1900.* Charlottesville: University Press of Virginia, 2000.

Daniels, Jonathan. *A Southerner Discovers the South.* New York: Macmillan, 1938.

Didion, Joan. *Political Fictions.* New York: Knopf, 2001.

———. *Where I Was From.* New York: Knopf, 2003.

Donovan, Gregory Donovan. "An Interview with Jake Adam York." *Blackbird* 4, no. 1

(2005). http://www.blackbird.vcu.edu/v4n1/features/york_ja_100105/interview_text
.htm (accessed May 7, 2008).

Durr, Virginia Foster. *Outside the Magic Circle: The Autobiography of Virginia Foster
Durr*. Tuscaloosa: University of Alabama Press, 1985.

Equal Justice Initiative. *Illegal Racial Discrimination in Jury Selection: A Continuing
Legacy*. Montgomery: Equal Justice Initiative, 2010.

Eskew, Glenn. "The Birmingham Civil Rights Institute and the New Ideology of
Tolerance." In *The Civil Rights Movement in American History*, ed. Renee C. Romano
and Leigh Raiford. Athens: University of Georgia Press, 2006. 28–66.

———. "George Wallace." In *Alabama Governors: A Political History of the State*, ed.
Samuel L. Webb and Margaret E. Armbrester. Tuscaloosa: University of Alabama
Press, 2001. 216–30.

Flynt, Wayne. *Alabama in the Twentieth Century*. Tuscaloosa: University of Alabama
Press, 2004.

———. "A Tragic Century: The Aftermath of the 1901 Constitution." In *A Century of
Controversy: Constitutional Reform in Alabama*, ed. Bailey Thomson. Tuscaloosa:
University of Alabama Press, 2002. 34–49.

Frederick, Jeff. "Divide and Conquer: Interest Groups and Political Culture in Alabama."
In *History and Hope in the Heart of Dixie: Scholarship, Activism, and Wayne Flynt in
the Modern South*, ed. Gordon E. Harvey, Richard D. Starnes, and Glenn Feldman.
Tuscaloosa: University of Alabama Press, 2006. 179–95.

———. *Stand Up for Alabama: Governor George Wallace*. Tuscaloosa: University of
Alabama Press, 2007.

Freyer, Tony, and Timothy Dixon. *Democracy and Judicial Independence: A History of
the Federal Courts of Alabama, 1820–1994*. Brooklyn: Carlson, 1995.

Fuller, Chet. *I Hear Them Calling My Name*. Boston: Houghton Mifflin, 1981.

Gaillard, Frye. *Cradle of Freedom: Alabama and the Movement That Changed America*.
Tuscaloosa: University of Alabama Press, 2004.

Gaventa, John. *Power and Powerlessness: Rebellion and Quiescence in an Appalachian
Valley*. Urbana: University of Illinois Press, 1980.

Gillespie, William L. "State Sentencing Policy." *Justice System Journal* 24, no. 2 (2003):
205–10.

Gopnik, Adam. "The Big One." *New Yorker*. August 23, 2004.

Gordon, Avery F. *Ghostly Matters: Haunting and the Sociological Imagination*.
Minneapolis: University of Minnesota Press, 1997.

Gottschalk, Marie. *The Prison and the Gallows*. New York: Cambridge University Press,
2006.

Grady, Dennis O., and Jonathan Kanipe. "Environmental Politics in the Tar Heel State." In *The New Politics of North Carolina*, ed. Christopher A. Cooper and H. Gibbs Knotts. Chapel Hill: University of North Carolina Press, 2008. 239–71.

Gray, Fred. *Bus Ride to Justice*. Montgomery: Black Belt, 1995.

Grooms, Anthony. *Bombingham*. New York: Free Press, 2001.

Guinier, Lani. *Lift Every Voice: Turning a Civil Rights Setback into a New Vision of Social Justice*. New York: Simon & Schuster, 1998.

———. *The Tyranny of the Majority: Fundamental Fairness in Representative Democracy*. New York: Free Press, 1994.

Hahn, Steven. *A Nation Under Our Feet: Black Political Struggles in the Rural South from Slavery to the Great Migration*. Cambridge: Harvard University Press, 2003.

Hall, Bob, and Mary Lee Kerr. *1991–1992 Green Index: A State-by-State Guide to the Nation's Environmental Health*. Washington, D.C.: Island, 1991.

Hamill, Susan Pace. "An Argument for Tax Reform Based on Judeo-Christian Ethics." *Alabama Law Review* 54, no. 1 (Fall 2002): 1–112.

———. *The Least of These: Fair Taxes and the Moral Duty of Christians*. Birmingham: Cliff Roads, 2003.

———. "Reform in Alabama? The Nation's Worst Constitution." *Southern Changes* 24, nos. 3–4 (2002): 10–11.

Harris, Eddy L. *South of Haunted Dreams: A Memoir*. New York: Simon & Schuster, 1993.

Harvey, Gordon E., Richard D. Starnes, and Glenn Feldman. *History and Hope in the Heart of Dixie: Scholarship, Activism, and Wayne Flynt in the Modern South*. Tuscaloosa: University of Alabama Press, 2006.

Hayden, Dolores. *The Power of Place: Urban Landscapes as Public History*. Cambridge: MIT Press, 1995.

Heaney, Seamus. *Opened Ground: Poems 1966–1996*. London: Faber & Faber, 1998.

Hemphill, Paul. *Leaving Birmingham: Notes of a Native Son*. New York: Viking Penguin, 1993.

Hobson, Fred. *But Now I See: The White Southern Racial Conversion Narrative*. Baton Rouge: Louisiana State University Press, 1999.

Hoffman, Roy. *Down Home: Journeys through Mobile*. Tuscaloosa: University of Alabama Press, 2001.

Hugo, Victor. *Les Misérables*. Ann Arbor: Borders Classics, 2006.

Ifill, Gwen. *The Breakthrough: Politics of Race in the Age of Obama*. New York: Doubleday, 2009.

Ingram, Bob. *That's the Way I Saw It*. Montgomery: B&E, 1986.

Ivins, Molly. *Molly Ivins Can't Say That, Can She?* New York: Random House, 1991.

Jackson, Harvey H., III. *Inside Alabama: A Personal History of My State.* Tuscaloosa: University of Alabama Press, 2004.

Jackson, Joshilyn. *Gods in Alabama.* New York: Warner, 2005.

Jeffries, Hasan Kwame. *Bloody Lowndes: Civil Rights and Black Power in Alabama's Black Belt.* New York: New York University Press, 2009.

Johnson, Frank M., Jr. "The Alabama Punting Syndrome." *Judges Journal* 18, no. 2 (Spring 1979): 5–7, 53–55.

Jones, Rodney. "A Half Mile of Road in North Alabama." In *The Remembered Gate: Memoirs by Alabama Writers*, ed. Jay Lama and Jeanie Thompson. Tuscaloosa: University of Alabama Press, 2002. 168–81.

———. *Salvation Blues.* New York: Houghton Mifflin, 2006.

Kelley, Robin D. G. *Hammer and Hoe: Alabama Communists during the Great Depression.* Chapel Hill: University of North Carolina Press, 1990.

———. *Race Rebels: Culture, Politics, and the Black Working Class.* New York: Free Press, 1994.

Kennedy, Renwick C. "Black Belt Aristocrats: The Old South Lives on in Alabama's Black Belt." *Social Forces* 13, no. 1 (Oct. 1934–May 1935): 80–85.

Kessler, Glenn. *The Confidante: Condoleezza Rice and the Creation of the Bush Legacy.* New York: St. Martin's, 2007.

Key, Dewayne. "Scholar as Activist." In *History and Hope in the Heart of Dixie: Scholarship, Activism, and Wayne Flynt in the Modern South*, ed. Gordon E. Harvey, Richard D. Starnes, and Glenn Feldman. Tuscaloosa: University of Alabama Press, 2006. 196–202.

Key, V. O., Jr. *Southern Politics in State and Nation.* New York: Vintage, 1949.

Knowles, Ralph. "Monitoring Committee on Prisons in Alabama Folds." *Journal of the National Prison Project* 20 (Summer 1989): 1–8.

Landsberg, Brian K. *Free at Last: The Alabama Origins of the 1965 Voting Rights Act.* Lawrence: University Press of Kansas, 2007.

Lassiter, Matthew D., and Joseph Crespino, eds. *The Myth of Southern Exceptionalism.* New York: Oxford University Press, 2010.

Lewis, Edna, and Scott Peacock. *The Gift of Southern Cooking.* New York: Knopf, 2003.

Lewis, John, with Michael D'Orso. *Walking with the Wind: A Memoir of the Movement.* New York: Simon & Schuster, 1998.

Lichtenstein, Alex. *Twice the Work of Free Labor: The Political Economy of Convict Labor in the New South.* New York: Verso, 1996.

Loury, Glenn C. *Race, Incarceration, and American Values.* Cambridge: MIT Press, 2008.

Mabry, Marcus. *Twice as Good: Condoleezza Rice and Her Path to Power*. New York: Modern Times, 2007.

Manley, Joey. *The Death of Donna-May Dean*. New York: St. Martin's, 1991.

Mann, James. *Rise of the Vulcans: The History of Bush's War Cabinet*. New York: Viking, 2004.

Mauer, Marc, and Tushar Kansal. *Barred for Life*. Washington, D.C.: Sentencing Project, 2005.

Mauer, Marc, and Ryan S. King. *Uneven Justice: State Rates of Incarceration by Race and Ethnicity*. Washington, D.C.: Sentencing Project, 2007.

McCarty, Clinton. *The Reins of Power: Racial Change and Challenge in a Southern County*. Tallahassee: Sentry, 1999.

McMillan, Malcolm Cook. *Constitutional Development in Alabama, 1798–1901: A Study in Politics, the Negro, and Sectionalism*. 1955. Reprint, Spartanburg: The Reprint Company, 1978.

——. *The Land Called Alabama*. Austin: Steck Vaughn, 1975.

McPherson, Tara. *Reconstructing Dixie: Race, Gender, and Nostalgia in the Imagined South*. Durham: Duke University Press, 2003.

McWhorter, Diane. *Carry Me Home*. New York: Simon & Schuster, 2001.

Melville, Herman. *The Confidence Man*. New York: Dix, Edwards, 1857.

Moore, Albert Burton. *History of Alabama*. University, Ala.: University Supply Store, 1934.

Moore, Roy, with John Perry. *So Help Me God: The Ten Commandments, Judicial Tyranny, and the Battle for Religious Freedom*. Nashville: Broadman and Holman, 2005.

Naipaul, V. S. *A Turn in the South*. London: Viking, 1989.

Permaloff, Anne, and Carl Grafton. *Political Power in Alabama: The More Things Change . . .* Athens: University of Georgia Press, 1995.

Peterson, Christopher. *Kindred Specters: Death, Mourning, and American Affinity*. Minneapolis: University of Minnesota Press, 2007.

Phillips, Kevin. *American Dynasty: Aristocracy, Fortune, and the Politics of Deceit in the House of Bush*. New York: Viking, 2004.

Pratt, Minnie Bruce. *Crime Against Nature*. Ithaca: Firebrand, 1990.

——. *The Dirt She Ate*. Pittsburgh: University of Pittsburgh Press, 2003.

——. *Rebellion: Essays, 1980–1991*. Ithaca: Firebrand, 1991.

Raines, Howell. *My Soul Is Rested: The Story of the Civil Rights Movement in the Deep South*. New York: Putnam's Sons, 1977.

Remington, W. Craig, and Thomas J. Kallsen, eds. *Historical Atlas of Alabama*. 2 vols.

Tuscaloosa: University of Alabama Department of Geography, College of Arts and Sciences, 1997–99.

Rice, Condoleezza. *Extraordinary, Ordinary People: A Memoir of Family*. New York: Crown, 2010.

Rich, Adrienne. Introduction to *My Mama's Dead Squirrel*, by Mab Segrest. Ithaca: Firebrand, 1985. 13–17.

Romano, Renee C. "Narratives of Redemption." In *The Civil Rights Movement in American Memory*, ed. Renee C. Romano and Leigh Raiford. Athens: University of Georgia Press, 2006. 96–133.

Rosengarten, Theodore. *All God's Dangers: The Life of Nate Shaw*. New York: Knopf, 1975.

Rushing, Wanda. *Memphis and the Paradox of Place: Globalization in the American South*. Chapel Hill: University of North Carolina Press, 2009.

Salih, Sara, ed., with Judith Butler. *The Judith Butler Reader*. Malden: Blackwell, 2004.

Schaller, Thomas F. *Whistling Past Dixie: How Democrats Can Win Without the South*. New York: Simon & Schuster, 2006.

Schulman, Bruce J. *From Cotton Belt to Sunbelt: Federal Policy, Economic Development, and the Transformation of the South, 1938–1980*. New York: Oxford University Press, 1991.

Segrest, Mab. *Memoir of a Race Traitor*. Boston: South End, 1994.

———. *My Mama's Dead Squirrel*. Ithaca: Firebrand, 1985.

Shafer, Byron E., and Richard Johnston. *The End of Southern Exceptionalism: Class, Race, and Partisan Change in the Postwar South*. Cambridge: Harvard University Press, 2006.

Shipler, David K. *A Country of Strangers: Blacks and Whites in America*. New York: Knopf, 1997.

Siddons, Anne Rivers. *Heartbreak Hotel*. New York: Simon & Schuster, 1976.

Simmel, Georg. "Bridge and Door." In *Simmel on Culture: Selected Writings*, ed. David Frisby and Mike Featherstone. London: SAGE, 1997. 170–73.

Spears, Ellen Griffith. *Toxic Knowledge: A Social History of Environmental Health in the New South's Model City, Anniston, Alabama, 1872–Present*. PhD diss., Emory University, 2007.

St. John, Warren. *Rammer Jammer Yellow Hammer*. New York: Crown, 2004.

Stevens, Kyes, ed. *Fold*. Auburn: Alabama Prison Arts and Education Project, 2006.

Stewart, William H. "Forrest ('Fob') James, Jr." In *Alabama Governors: A Political History of the State*, ed. Samuel L. Webb and Margaret E. Armbrester. Tuscaloosa: University of Alabama Press, 2001. 243–46.

———. "Guy Hunt." In *Alabama Governors: A Political History of the State*, ed. Samuel L. Webb and Margaret E. Armbrester. Tuscaloosa: University of Alabama Press, 2001. 249–53.

Suitts, Steve. *Hugo Black of Alabama*. Montgomery: New South, 2005.

Suitts, Steve, and Lauren Veasey. *High School Dropouts: Alabama's Number One Education and Economic Problem*. Atlanta: Southern Education Foundation, 2008.

Summersell, Charles Grayson. *Alabama History for Schools*. Northport, Alabama: American Southern, 1965.

Thompson, Anthony C. *Releasing Prisoners, Redeeming Communities: Reentry, Race, and Politics*. New York: New York University Press, 2008.

Thomson, Bailey. *A Century of Controversy: Constitutional Reform in Alabama*. Tuscaloosa: University of Alabama Press, 2002.

Thornton, J. Mills, III. *Dividing Line*. Tuscaloosa: University of Alabama Press, 2002.

———. Review of *The Politics of Rage: George Wallace, the Origins of the New Conservatism, and the Transformation of American Politics*, by Dan T. Carter. *Journal of Southern History* 62, no. 4 (Nov. 1996): 852–54.

Toobin, Jeffrey. "No More Mr. Nice Guy." *New Yorker*. May 25, 2009.

Tullos, Allen. "The Alabama Prison System: Recent History, Conditions, and Recommendations." Undergraduate honors thesis, University of Alabama at Tuscaloosa, 1972.

———. "Voting Rights Activists Acquitted." *Nation* 241, no. 3 (Aug. 3–10, 1985): 78–80.

Walton, Anthony. *Mississippi: An American Journey*. New York: Knopf, 1996.

Webb, Samuel L., and Margaret E. Armbrester, eds. *Alabama Governors: A Political History of the State*. Tuscaloosa: University of Alabama Press, 2001.

———. "Don Siegelman." In *Alabama Governors: A Political History of the State*, ed. Samuel L. Webb and Margaret E. Armbrester. Tuscaloosa: University of Alabama Press, 2001. 257–60.

Western, Bruce. *Punishment and Inequality in America*. New York: Russell Sage Foundation, 2006.

Wiegman, Robyn. "Whiteness Studies and the Paradox of Particularity." *boundary 2* 26, no. 3 (Autumn 1999): 115–50.

Williams, Horace Randall, and Christine Garrett, eds. *The Alabama Guide: Our People Resources, and Government*. Montgomery: Alabama Department of Archives and History, 2009.

Wilson, Charles Reagan. *The New Regionalism*. Jackson: University of Mississippi Press, 1998.

Wilson, Edward O. *Naturalist*. Washington, D.C.: Island, 1994.

Wilson, Walter. *Forced Labor in the United States*. New York: International, 1933.

Woodward, C. Vann. *Origins of the New South, 1877–1913*. Baton Rouge: LSU Press, 1951.

Yackle, Larry W. *Reform and Regret: The Story of Federal Judicial Involvement in the Alabama Prison System*. New York: Oxford University Press, 1989.

Yaeger, Patricia. *Dirt and Desire: Reconstructing Southern Women's Writing, 1930–1990*. Chicago: University of Chicago Press, 2000.

York, Jake Adam. "Leaving Alabama." In *Climbing Mt. Cheaha: Emerging Alabama Writers*, ed. Don Noble. Livingston: University of West Alabama, 2004. 251–52.

———. *Murder Ballads*. Denver: Elixir, 2005.

———. *A Murmuration of Starlings*. Carbondale: Crab Orchard Review and Southern Illinois University Press, 2008.

Young, Iris Marion. *Inclusion and Democracy*. New York: Oxford University Press, 2000.

———. *Justice and the Politics of Difference*. Princeton: Princeton University Press, 1990.

Younge, Gary. "Racism Rebooted: Philadelphia, Mississippi, Then and Now." *Nation*. July 14, 2005.

Žižek, Slavoj. *The Fragile Absolute*. New York: Verso, 2000.

———. *On Belief*. New York: Routledge, 2001.

Žižek, Slavoj, and Glyn Daly. *Conversations with Žižek*. Cambridge, England: Polity, 2004.

FILM AND VIDEO

Assault on Gay America: The Life and Death of Billy Jack, documentary film. Directed by Claudia Pryor Malis. A *Frontline* co-production with Turn of River Films. Alexandria, Va.: PBS Video, 2000.

Crisis: Behind a Presidential Commitment, documentary film. Directed by Robert Drew. New York: ABC News, 1963; New York: DocuRama, 2003.

Forrest Gump, feature film. Directed by Robert Zemeckis. Los Angeles, Calif.: Paramount Pictures, 1984.

Four Little Girls, documentary film. Directed by Spike Lee. New York: Forty Acres and a Mule Filmworks and HBO Video, 1997.

George Wallace: Settin' the Woods on Fire, documentary film. Directed by Daniel McCabe and Paul Stekler. A film in *The American Experience* series for the Public Broadcasting Service. Boston, Mass.: WGBH, 2000. Based in part on *The Politics of Rage*, by Dan T. Carter.

Heart of Dixie, feature film. Directed by Martin Davidson. Los Angeles, Calif.: MGM, 1989.

Lockup: Holman Extended Stay, five-part documentary series. First aired by MSNBC Television in December 2007. http://www.msnbc.msn.com/id/22083055/ (accessed April 17, 2009).

"No Easy Walk 1961–1963." Part 4 of *Eyes on the Prize: America's Civil Rights Years.* Alexandria, Va.: Blackside and PBS Home Video, 1986.

Sweet Home Alabama, feature film. Directed by Andy Tennant. Burbank, Calif.: Buena Vista Home Entertainment, 2003.

Talladega Nights: The Ballad of Ricky Bobby, feature film. Directed by Adam McKay. Los Angeles, Calif.: Apatow Productions, 2006.

When the Levees Broke, documentary film. Directed by Spike Lee. New York: Forty Acres and a Mule Filmworks and HBO Video, 2006.

INDEX

Abernathy, Ralph, 218

Acheson, Dean, 224

Adams, Henry, 41

Adams, Oscar, 118

Adkisson, David, 268

Advocate, 39, 41

affirmative action, 119, 189, 216

Afghanistan, 223

African Americans, 2, 60, 183–89, 194–95,
    197–98, 200–205; and death penalty,
    102–3; and Nathan Bedford Forrest,
    255; and Hurricane Katrina, 227; and
    Iraq War, 54–55, 59; in legislature, 205;
    and lottery vote, 150; opposition to
    Heart of Dixie, 7, 10; and prisons, 66,
    79; and Bob Riley, 158, 170; and Don
    Siegelman, 159; and statewide elective
    office, 203; as voters, 130, 170, 202, 214,
    263, 264; and voting rights, 89; and
    George Wallace, 120

Alabama A&M, 242, 243

Alabama Arise, 245, 247

Alabama Baptist, 165

Alabama Baptists, 150

Alabama Chamber of Commerce,
    5–6

Alabama Christian Movement for
    Human Rights, 217

Alabama Commission on Higher
    Education, 272

Alabama Cooperative Extension Service,
    189

Alabama Correctional Organization, 105

Alabama Day, 164, 165

Alabama Democratic Conference, 119,
    204–5, 206

Alabama Department of Archives and
    History, 5

Alabama Department of Corrections, 70,
    76, 78, 83–84, 87, 90; inaccurate infor-
    mation released to the public, 105

Alabama Department of Economic and
    Community Affairs (ADECA), 23, 160,
    197

Alabama Department of Environmental
    Management, 45, 50, 127

Alabama Education Association (AEA),
    126, 129, 205, 209, 265

Alabama Ethics Commission, 130

Alabama Fair Campaign Practices Act,
    161

Alabama Farm Bureau Insurance
    Company, 189

Alabama Farmers Federation (ALFA),
    150, 165, 189, 191; opposition to
    Amendment One, 167, 170

"Alabama Getaway" (Grateful Dead), 13,
    15

Alabama Highway Department, 191

Alabama Law Review, 168

Alabama National Guard, 56

Alabama New South Coalition (ANSC), 159, 201, 204, 205, 206; endorsement of Obama, 207

Alabama Power Company, 14, 50, 51–53, 141

Alabama Prison Project, 71

Alabama Public Television, 27, 35

Alabama Reading Initiative, 173

Alabama River, 53, 194, 256–58

Alabama Rivers Alliance, 50

Alabama Sentencing Commission, 92–93, 95, 100

Alabamastan, 2, 42

Alabama State University, 242, 243

Alabama Supreme Court, 267; ban on sex toys, 8; and education, 152; first female chief justice, 44; and prison system, 85; and Republican Party, 149

Alaska, 191

Alcoholic Beverage Control Board, 8

Allison, Davey, 275

Allison, Krista, 275

All Things Considered, 138

Al Qaeda, 221, 223

Alston, Philip, 99

Amendment One, 96, 165–72, 178

American Civil Liberties Union, 71, 73, 98, 139, 270

American Council for an Energy-Efficient Economy, 51

American Family Association, 38, 150

American Idol, 267

American Lung Association, 51

Americans for Tax Reform, 150

Amerson, Lucius, 186

Anderson, Minnie B., 255

Andrews, James, 210

Annie E. Casey Foundation, 248

Anniston Star, 56, 154, 156, 170

Applebome, Peter, 254

Archibald, John, 29, 208, 210, 211, 262, 263

Archie, Anita, 45

Argument for Tax Reform (Hamill), 169

Arkansas, 87

Armbrester, Margaret, 149

Armey, Dick, 167

Army, U.S., 274–75

Army Corps of Engineers, 3

Arrington, Richard, 143, 204, 208–9; on education, 209; and failed economic projects, 211; and police brutality, 263

Ashland, Ala., 156

Atlanta, Ga., 43, 195

Atlanta Journal-Constitution, 149, 195, 197, 237

Atlantic, 206

Auburn University, 31, 152, 189–91, 250–52, 271

auto industry, 14, 15

Ayers, Brandt, 56, 154

Azbell, David, 158

Bachus, Spencer, 157

Baggett, Agnes, 45

Baghdad, 57, 231–32

Bailey, Nick, 160

Baker, Jerry, 83

Baker, Pam, 46

Banerjee, Neela, 51

Barabak, Mark, 220

Barak, Gregg, 72

Barbour, Haley, 52, 178

Barnard, Bill, 129

Barnes, Roy, 143

Bartlett, Greg, 82

Bartley, Robert, 224

Bates, Jim, 148

Bauman, Christian: *The Ice Beneath You*, 274

Baxley, Bill, 70; gubernatorial campaigns, 115, 116, 117, 121, 122–23; loss of election, 124

Baxley, Lucy, 44, 159, 175

Bazzell, Mack, 59

Beasley, Jere, 115, 116–17

Beck, Glenn, 238

Bendolph, Mary Lee, 257

Benjamin, Rebecca, 48

Benn, Alvin, 256

Bevel, James, 218

Big Mules, 3, 9, 132

Birmingham, Ala.: city government, 207–12; Civil Rights cultural district, 14, 210; civil rights movement, 16, 34, 215, 217, 229–32, 260; corrections program, 92; corruption, 111; crime, 103; downtown, 210; drug laws, 91; fundraiser for Riley, 157; medical center, 23, 127, 209; in novel *Gathering Home*, 33; police brutality, 262, 263; pollution, 51, 52; racism, 218; and Condoleezza Rice, 213, 217, 229; and Ruben Studdard, 268; unemployment, 179; white-collar establishment, 127; white flight to suburbs, 211

Birmingham News: on Bill Baxley, 123; on Black Belt, 163, 196, 198–99; on Artur Davis, 264; on education, 4; on integrating sororities, 252; on Iraq War, 56; on lawsuits against state agencies, 84; letters to, 49; on police brutality,

262; on Bob Riley, 163; on Nick Saban, 245; on Don Siegelman, 153; on tax inequities, 246; on David Wilson, 191

Bishop, Charles, 203

Black, Hugo, 120, 155

Black, Lucius, 205

Black Alabama. *See* African Americans

Black Belt, 163, 184–88, 195–202; freedom movement, 187; health care, 47; mansions, 14; poverty, 196–97, 198–99; racism, 202; timberland, 199; unemployment, 3, 179

Black Belt Action Commission, 174, 200–201

Black in Selma (Chestnut and Cass), 184

Black Legislative Caucus, 94, 188

Blacksher, Jim, 243

Blanton, Thomas, 210

Blount, Bill, 146, 210

Blount, Winton, III, 142–43

Blount, Winton M., "Red," 136

Bond, Horace Mann, 3–4

Bonner, Jo, 59

Boortz, Neil, 42

Boston Globe, 139, 239

Bowen, Revonda, 193

Bracy, Mittie Marie, 48

Bradley, Tommy, 83

Bradley v. Haley, 83

Bragg, Rick: on chain gangs, 73; on Confederate monument, 249; on Emory Folmar, 120; on foodways, 49; on football, 244; on human dignity, 15; *The Prince of Frogtown*, 100, 249; on punishment, 101; on Wallace bumper stickers, 110

Branch, William McKinley, 186

Breakthrough, The, 206

Breaux, John, 131
Brecht, Bertolt, 273
Bremer, Arthur, 110, 113
Brewer, Albert: gubernatorial campaign, 115, 116; and states' rights, 25
Bright, Bobby, 261
Bright, Stephen, 99
Brinkley, Douglass, 227
Bronner, David, 14, 135, 141, 150, 180
Bronstein, Alvin, 73
Brown, Ron, 131
Bryant, Bear, 29–30, 133, 213, 244, 253
Bryant, Paul, Jr., 245
Buchanan, Pat, 234
Buffett, Jimmy, 146
Bullock County, 199
Bumiller, Elisabeth, 257
Burns, Ken, 249
Bush, George H. W., 131, 213, 219
Bush, George W.: appointment of judges, 42; Bush Doctrine, 223–24; foreign-policy team, 220–21, 223; and Hurricane Katrina, 228; and Iraq War, 55, 56, 59, 226; and Condoleezza Rice, 214, 220, 223; and Bob Riley, 156; and same-sex marriage, 236; torture policy, 222
Bush, Jeb, 178, 237
Business Council of Alabama, 45, 125, 128
Butler, Charles, 40–41
Butler, Judith: on alteration of the subject, 34; on formation of self, 226; on gender, 37; on habits of judgment, 8, 226; on linguistic horizon, 64; on relations to others, 27; on terrible parochialism, 33; on undoings, 35, 37–38

But Now I See (Hobson), 36
Byrd, James, 39
Byrne, Bradley, 265, 266

Cabaniss, Bill, 173
Caldwell, Antoine, 244
California, 265–66
Camden, Ala., 254
Campaign Disclosure Project, 266
Campbell, Donal, 86, 87
capital punishment. See death penalty
Carmichael, Ruth, 56
Carnes, Jim, 245
Carr, Jocelyn, 252
Carry Me Home (McWhorter), 16, 34, 232
Carter, Dan, 113, 120
Carter, Jimmy, 115, 219; The Politics of Rage, 113
Carter, Stephen L., 80
Carville, James, 21
Casey, Ron, 246
Casper, Gerhard, 219
chain gangs, 138
Chambliss, "Dynamite Bob," 116
ChemWaste, 126, 198
Cheney, Dick: and Haley Barbour, 52; and foreign policy, 223, 226; and interrogation methods, 222; and Bob Riley, 11
Cherry, Bobby Frank, 210
Chestnut, J. L., 200, 204; and Black Alabama, 183–84; on Black Belt, 185; Black in Selma, 184; on habitual-offender law, 90; on knee-jerk patriotism, 54; on Republican Party, 137; on Condoleezza Rice, 229; on southernness, 194
Chevron, 213–14

Children's Crusade, 260

Christian Coalition of Alabama, 4, 36, 142, 150, 155; opposition to Amendment One, 167, 170

Christian nationalism, 10

Christian Science Monitor, 21, 56

Chronicle of Higher Education, 245

Ciaramicoli, Arthur, 41

Civil Liberties Union of Alabama, 69, 70

civil rights, 14, 28

Civil Rights Act of 1964, 189, 218, 241, 260

Civil Rights Institute, 232

civil rights movement: in Birmingham, 16, 34, 217–18, 229–32; and Barack Obama, 259; and Condoleezza Rice, 214, 217, 229–31

Civil War, 249

Clark, Jimmy, 125

Clark Foundation, 72

Clay County, 56, 155–156

Clean Water Act, 45

Clemon, U. W., 82, 96

Clinton, Bill, 39, 77, 131; in Selma, 258, 259

Clinton, Hillary, 207, 235; in Selma, 257, 258–59

Clooney, George, 236

Cobb, Ned, 234

Cobb, Sue Bell, 44, 267

Coe, Tim, 194

Cole, David, 66

Coleman, Frances, 12

Collins, Gail, 265

Colson, Chuck, 92

Community Partnership for Recovery and Reentry, 95

Compassion in Action, 96

Confederate Battle Flag, The (Coski), 249

Confederate flag, 10, 192; atop the state capitol, 6, 23, 126, 130, 135, 248

Confederate Memorial Day, 250

Confidence Man, The (Melville), 25

Conley, Matt, 60–61

Conner, Roy Anne, 261

Connor, Bull, 25, 231

Connors, Marty, 89

constitution, of Alabama, 3–5, 110, 133, 162, 244; amendments, 111; and Fob James, 117; and Bob Riley, 163, 164, 178

convict lease, 67–68

Corrections Corporation of America, 86

Corts, Thomas, 247

Coski, John M.: *The Confederate Battle Flag*, 249

cotton, 185

Covington, Vicki, 33; *Gathering Home*, 33

Cramer, Bud, 55, 59

Crawford, Darrel, 251

Creeks (Native tribe), 24, 53–54

crime and crime rate, 72, 75, 77, 80, 89, 103

criminal justice system, 66, 101, 103. *See also* death penalty; prisons

Crimson Tide, 29–30, 244

Crisis, 110

Crittenden, Ann, 45; *The Price of Motherhood*, 45

Crowder, Carla, 79, 82, 90

Cummings Research Park, 23

Curran, Eddie, 153, 160

Curry, George E., 230, 253

Curtin, Mary Ellen, 67

Dale, Sam, 53

Dallas, Tex., 231

Daniels, Jonathan, 6

Davidson, Charles, 138

Davis, Artur, 44, 59, 207, 242, 264–65

Davis, Jefferson, 146–147, 234

Davis, Natalie, 173

Davis, Rosa, 85, 93

Death of Donna-May Dean, The
    (Manley), 30

death penalty, 66, 75, 90, 97–103; and
    racism, 102–3

Decatur Daily, 94, 201

Decoration Day, 33–34

Deggans, Eric, 236

Delay, Tom, 237

Delta Kappa Epsilon, 145–46, 159

DeMent, Ira, 140, 176

Democratic Party, 7, 126, 137, 143, 206,
    264; and African American voters,
    214; support in the South for, 28; and
    white supremacy, 28

DeMonia, Robin, 160, 247; on capital
    defense system, 97; on death penalty,
    100, 102–3; on punishment and jus-
    tice, 66; on tax reform, 171

desegregation, 118; of schools, 32, 48

diabetes, 49–50

Didion, Joan: *Where I Was From*, 16

disenfranchisement, 88

Djilas, Milovan, 106

Dobson, James, 142

Dodd, Christopher, 269

Donaldson Correctional Facility, 105

Dornan, John, 152

Doyle, Kevin, 99

Drake, Jack, 72, 137

Dream of Freedom, A (McWhorter),
    34

Drive-By Truckers, 239–40

Drummond Company, 13

Dunlap, Erika, 275–76

Dunn, Priscilla, 46

Durr, Virginia Foster, 31

Dyson, Michael Eric, 227

Earley, Mark, 92

Earnhardt, Dale, 274

Economic Development Association of
    Alabama, 141

Economic Development Partnership of
    Alabama, 141

Economist, 22, 132, 133, 266; on Black Belt,
    196–97; on prisons, 71

Edmund Pettus Bridge, 7, 10, 257–60;
    Bridge Crossing, 258

education, 4, 137, 150–52, 190, 195, 272;
    and Albert Brewer, 115; compared to
    football funding, 246; and Guy Hunt,
    126; poor record of, 245; as primary
    concern of voters, 143; and Bob Riley,
    11

Education Week, 245

Edwards, Bob, 138

Ellen, 38

Elliott, Debbie, 83, 138

Emelle, Ala., 198

environmental conditions and policies,
    50–53

Environmental Protection Agency,
    52

Equal Employment Opportunity
    Commission, 184

Equal Justice Initiative, 103

ethics commission, 111

Evans, Dwight, 51

Evans, James, 164, 165

evolution, 10, 139, 265

executions, 67. *See also* death penalty

Fair, Bryan, 42
Falwell, Jerry, 142
family, performance of, 33
Federal Emergency Management
Administration, 228
Federation of Child Care Centers of
Alabama, 47–48
Figures, Michael, 125, 204–6
Figures, Vivian, 55, 206
Fleming, John, 56
Florida, 77, 113, 137
Flynt, Wayne, 4; on Alabama Power,
53; on Richard Arrington, 209; on
education, 150–51; on Guy Hunt, 132;
on Fob James, 144; on Bobby Lowder,
189; on property taxes, 165; on school
prayer, 61; on Don Siegelman, 160; on
universities, 251; on George Wallace,
115
Folmar, Emory, 120, 131–32, 261
Folsom, Big Jim, 45, 133
Folsom, Jim, Jr., 132, 133–36, 157, 177;
cronyism, 135
foodways, 49
football, 29–30, 244, 246
Forbes, 50, 117, 214
Foreign Affairs, 221
Forrest, Nathan Bedford, 15; monument
in Selma, 255–56
For the Record, 27, 36
Foster, Autherine Lucy, 238
Fountain Correctional Center, 86,
91
franchise tax, 151
Frederick, Jeff, 121
French, Steve, 55
Friedman, Estelle, 220
Frontline, 39, 40

Frost, David, 39
Fuller, Chet, 25, 234

Gadsden, Ala., 16, 38
Gaither, Billy Jack, 39–42, 43
Gaither, Kathy, 41–42
Gaither, Marion, 41
Gaither, Ricky, 40
gambling, 11
Garner, Mary Texas Hurt, 45
Garrison, Carol, 46
Gathering Home (Covington), 33
Gaventa, John, 196
Gayle, John, 24
gay rights movement, 39
Gee's Bend quilters, 256
Gentle, Ed, 244
George, Roderick, 43
Georgia, 38, 77, 137; lottery, 150
Gibson, Larry, 91
Gilmore, Tom, 186
Ginsburg, Ruth Bader, 241
Glasgow, Kenneth, 89
globalization, 2, 3
Goat Hill, 110, 132, 156–57,
Goldberg, Arthur, 97
golfing, 14
Golthy, Freddie, 192–93
Golthy, Mary, 192
Gomillion v. Lightfoot, 176
Gonzales, Alberto, 222
Gordon, Avery, 65, 235, 240
Gordon, Tom, 63
Gottschalk, Marie: on capital punish-
ment, 97, 98; on incarceration rate, 80;
on prisoners' rights movement, 69; on
prison system, 66, 75, 77, 89; on social
justice, 86

Governing Magazine, 176

Graddick, Charles, 70, 71, 72, 122–23

Grafton, Carl, 136

Grateful Dead, 13, 15, 106

Graves, Daniel, 192

Graves, Marvin, 192, 193

Gray, Douglas Lamar, 90–91

Gray, Jerome, 264

Great Recession, 12, 15, 84, 179, 238, 265; and federal scrutiny of banks, 269; and work-release program, 105

Greco, Michael S., 98

Green, Robert, 77

Greene County Democrat, 205

Greenwood, Lee, 275

Greer, Bonnie, 228

Grenier, John E., 126, 188

Groundhog Day, 162

Grove Hill, Ala., 192

Guardian (London), 138

Guinier, Lani, 212

Gulf Restoration Network, 50

Gulf Shores, Ala., 14

Gulf States Paper, 167

Gulf War, 56

habitual-offender law, 90–91

Haley, Michael, 82

Hall, Laura, 138

Hall, Stuart, 224–25

Hamill, Susan Pace, 3, 168–69, 171, 178, 199; *Argument for Tax Reform*, 169

Hammett, Seth, 85

Hammond, James, 249

Harbour, Ron, 14

Harris, Art, 118

Harris, Eddy L., 22–23; *South of Haunted Dreams*, 22

Harris, Sophia Bracy, 47–48, 152

Harrison, James, 95

hate crimes, 43

health care, 26, 47–48, 266

health education, 47

HealthSouth, 85, 159

Heartbreak Hotel (Siddons), 31–32

Heart of Dixie, 1–2, 5–7, 36, 112, 138, 183, 232, 234, 248, 268

Heflin, Howell, 270

Henican, Ellis, 237

Herbert, Bob, 193, 268, 269

Herek, Gregory, 41

Hicks, Taylor, 267

high school dropout rate, 179–80, 272

Hilliard, Earl, 38, 55, 187, 207; on prisons, 87–88

Hobson, Fred, 31, 36, 37; *But Now I See*, 36

Holman Prison, 68, 86, 105

Holmes, Alvin, 6, 43, 184, 206; and Joe Reed, 207

homophobia, 37, 43

homosexuality, 35–43. *See also* same-sex marriage

Honda, 149, 272

Hood, James, 238

Hood, Patterson, 239–40

Hooper, Perry, 92

Hoover, Ala., 29, 51, 154, 207, 212, 262

Hopkins, Virginia, 52

Hopper, Joe, 74

Horn, Randolph, 174

Howard, Charles, 237

Hubbert, Paul, 126–30, 154, 206; and Alabama Education Association, 209

Hugo, Victor, 9

Hulett, John, 186–87, 188

Humphries, Hulond, 193, 194

Hunt, Guy, 2, 44, 125–26; felony conviction of, 132; gubernatorial campaigns, 123–24, 127, 128–30; and prisons, 72; second term as governor, 131

Huntsville, Ala.: manufacturing, 153; military personnel, 55, 58; science and research, 14, 23, 64, 177

Huntsville Times, 137, 157, 266

Hurricane Katrina, 227–28

Hussein, Saddam, 55, 58, 226, 231

Hyer, Marjorie, 117

Hyundai, 14, 153, 172, 272

I Am a Fugitive from a Georgia Chain Gang, 68

Ice Beneath You, The (Bauman), 274–75

Ifill, Gwen, 206, 238, 264

immigration, 63–64

incarceration rate, 66–67, 75, 77, 79, 80, 103. *See also* prisons

Independent (London), 132

infant mortality, 121, 179, 196

Ingram, Bob, 115, 135, 137, 145; on Mercedes-Benz plant, 134; on Bob Riley, 156; on Don Siegelman, 153

Inside Alabama (Jackson), 27–28

Institute for Southern Studies, 50

integration, 193; of fraternities and sororities, 252. *See also* desegregation

Internet, 7

Iraq War, 54–60, 221, 224, 226; and African Americans, 54–55, 215; and Alabamians, 275; and Condoleezza Rice, 214, 231; and Bob Riley, 11, 174; and Richard Shelby and Jeff Sessions, 26

Irish Times, 102

Isbell, Jason, 33, 60–61

Jackson, Andrew, 24, 53, 54

Jackson, Harold, 246

Jackson, Harvey, 27–28, 159–60; *Inside Alabama*, 27–28

Jackson, Jesse, 258

Jackson, Jimmie Lee, 260

Jacksonville, Ala., 15

jails, county, 81–82

James, Bobbie, 117, 142

James, Fob, 117–18, 136–43: and chain gangs, 73, 138; and education, 117; gubernatorial campaigns, 117, 136–37, 142–44; and image of Alabama, 26, 109; and prison system, 70, 74; and public prayer, 61, 140; on race, 190; and Ten Commandments, 139–40

James, Tim, 64, 266

James v. Wallace, 69, 84

Jefferson County, 29, 111, 208, 210

Jefferson County Citizens Coalition, 209

Jeffries, Hasan, 186, 188

Jim Crow, 4, 6, 21, 27, 29, 67, 80, 118, 185, 215, 232

Jindal, Bobby, 178

John, Elton, 39

Johnson, Alma, 214

Johnson, Bob, 105

Johnson, Frank M., 69, 70, 71, 175, 176; and Extension Service, 189

Johnson, Gerald, 150

Johnson, Howard, II, 275

Johnson, Howard, Sr., 275

Johnson, Pete, 94

Johnson, Rheta, 193

Johnson, Rhoda, 202

Jones, Rodney, 21, 109, 271
Jones, Ron, 73, 74
Jones, Vivian Malone, 238
Julia Tutwiler Prison, 78–79, 86

Kaminer, Wendy, 61
Kaplan, Fred, 222
Kappa Alpha, 251–53
Keller, Helen, 164
Kelly Ingram Park, 7, 201
Kemp, Jack, 171
Kennedy, David, 220, 223
Kennedy, Edward, 270
Kennedy, Joey, 158, 207, 246
Kentucky, 101
Kerry, John, 263
Kessler, Glenn, 224
Key, Dewayne, 144, 150
Keyes, Alan, 61, 140
Kilby Prison, 68
Kilgore, Mike, 165
King, Coretta Scott, 119, 254, 258
King, Martin Luther, III, 147, 261
King, Martin Luther, Jr., 147, 217, 240;
  "beloved community," 225; holiday
  in honor of, 257; jailing of, 218; and
  "normalcy," 233; streets named after,
  254–55
King, Troy, 78, 95, 99, 101–2
Kite, Hugh, 102
Kleffman, Todd, 261, 262
Knight, John, 242–43
Knight and Sims v. Alabama, 176, 242–43
Knighten, Brian, 91
Knowles, Ralph, 70, 72
Koppel, Nathan, 267
Korbel, Josef, 219
Krugman, Paul, 265, 269

Ku Klux Klan, 34, 122, 194, 255
Kung, Lisa, 78, 79

Land, Richard, 140
Landsberg, Brian, 186
Langford, Larry, 210
Lankster, Barron, 187
LaPierre, Al, 210
Lard, Eddie, 4, 208, 247
LCS Corrections Services, 79
Leavitt, David, 38
LeBlanc, Patrick, 79
Ledbetter, Lilly, 241–42
Lee, Larry, 271
Lee, Robert E., 147, 240
Lee, Spike: When the Levees Broke, 227
Lee v. Macon Board of Education, 176
Legal Defense Fund, 69, 98
Lemann, Nicholas, 219
Lennox, Tim, 27–28, 35–36
Levi, Ted, 14
Lewis, Anthony, 90
Lewis, John, 7, 225–26, 235, 258, 259; and
  definition of marriage, 38; on Iraq
  War, 57, 225; and John McCain, 236
Lichtenstein, Alex, 67, 86
Lilly Ledbetter Fair Pay Act, 242
Limestone Correctional Center, 82, 83, 87
Lin, Maya, 128, 255
Lind, Michael, 58
Liuzzo, Viola, 255
lobbyists, 111, 157
Lockup, 105
Logan, Don, 247
Los Angeles Times, 48, 240
Lost Language of Cranes, The, 38
lottery, 148, 150, 161, 190
Louisiana, 79

Loury, Glenn C., 88, 103
Love, Jay, 203
Lowder, Bobby, 189
Lowndes County, 186, 188, 199
Lowndes County Freedom Organization, 7
Lumpkin, Katharine Du Pre, 37
Lynch, Grant, 274
Lynch v. Alabama, 243
Lynyrd Skynyrd, 6
Lyons, Kirk, 192

Mabry, Marcus, 227
Macon County, 186, 199
Maher, Bill, 265
Mailer, Norman, 221
Malone, Wallace, 167
Manley, Joey, 21, 30; *The Death of Donna-May Dean*, 30
Mann, James, 221
marijuana laws, 93
Marion, Ala., 255
Marshall Space Flight Center, 59, 177
Maryland, 113, 204
Mathis, Karen, 242
Mathis, Nathan, 35–36, 38
Maxwell v. Bishop, 98
McCain, John, 235, 236, 256–57, 263, 264
McClammy, Thad, 151
McGregor, Milton, 136
McInnes, Joe, 192
McLester, Terry, 91
McMahon, John, 245
McMillan, George, 119
McNair, Denise, 218
McNatt, Norman, 56
McPherson, Tara, 37
McPherson, Vanzetta P., 46

McWhorter, Diane, 16, 34, 210, 232, 249; *Carry Me Home*, 16, 34, 232; *A Dream of Freedom*, 34
Melville, Herman: *The Confidence Man*, 25
Memoir of a Race Traitor (Segrest), 36
Memphis, Tenn., 3
Mercedes-Benz, 133–34, 135, 137, 272
Michigan, 113
military and militarism, 58–60
Miller, Zell, 146
Mississippi: at bottom of rankings, 12; as fattest state, 49; foreign-born population, 63; incarceration rate, 79; as object of jokes, 23; prisons in, 86
Missouri, 101
Mobile, Ala.: crime, 103; downtown, 2; military personnel, 58
Mobile Bay, 50–51, 127
Mobile Press-Register, 2, 51, 244
Mobile Register: on Islam, 57; on Fob James, 140; on prisons, 104; on Don Siegelman, 153
Moloney, Pat, 214
Monroeville, Ala., 194
Montgomery, Ala.: Black Belt and political power, 198; civil rights monument, 128; downtown, 2; police brutality, 261–62; political corruption, 120; prayer rally, 140; tourists, 248
Montgomery Advertiser: on Bama Day, 23; on congressional districts, 187; on Jim Folsom, 135; on Nathan Bedford Forrest monument, 256; on Paul Hubbert, 128; letters to, 24, 76; on Mercedes plant, 134; on prison commissioners, 74; on prison problems, 90; on UAB, 210

Moody's Investors Service, 111

Moore, Mal, 244

Moore, Mary, 203, 204

Moore, Roy: on health care reform, 266; and opposition to gay rights, 38–39, 42; and Ten Commandments, 26, 62, 139–40, 154, 173

Morgan, Charles, 186

Morrer, Frank, 118

Mountain Brook, Ala., 29, 207, 215, 217

Muhammad, Abdul-Malik, 215

Mullins, Steve, 40–41

Murder Ballads (York), 16

Murmuration of Starlings, A (York), 16

Murphy, Harold, 242, 243

Muse, William, 152–53

NAACP, 269

Nabers, Drayton, 173

Nachman, Roland, 69

NASCAR, 273–76

Nation, 22

National Democratic Party of Alabama, 186

National Governors' Association, 141

National Institute of Justice, 92

nationalism, 54

National Organization for Women, 43

National Prison Project, 69, 74

National Public Radio, 138

National Security Strategy, 223, 224

National Voting Rights Trail, 233, 255

National Women's Law Center, 46

Native Americans, 9, 24, 53–54

Nebraska, 100

Nelson, Josh, 56

New Jersey, 87

Newman v. Alabama, 68, 69, 72, 176

New Orleans, La., 227

New South, 128

New York, 265

New York Times: exit polling by, 263; on Ledbetter case, 241; on lottery, 148; on 1986 governor's election, 123; on Opelika schools, 49; on prisons, 82, 92; on Bob Riley, 163; on Ruben Studdard, 268

New York Times Magazine, 120

Nixon, Richard, 117

Norquist, Grover, 150, 171, 172

Norrell, Jeff, 26

North Carolina, 87, 137, 204

Norton, Eleanor Holmes, 264

Nossiter, Adam, 82

Nuckles, James, 261

Obama, Barack: appointment of surgeon general, 48; endorsement by ANSC, 207; and health care, 266; and Lilly Ledbetter Fair Pay Act, 242; presidential campaign, 235; in Selma, 257, 259; and voters, 263

obesity, 49–50

O'Brien, Conan, 268

Ohio, 102

Oklahoma, 44, 79

Ordinary People Society, 89

Orndorff, Mary, 165

Owen, Marie Bankhead, 24

Owens, Robby, 93

Paige, Satchel, 272

Palin, Sarah, 235

Parker, Susan, 168

parochialism, 33, 64

Paterson, Alexander, 95
patriotism, knee-jerk, 54–58, 174
Patterson, John, 112
Patton, Gwendolyn, 130
Peek, Michael, 91
Peeples, Melanie, 78
Perdue, Sonny, 178
Perkins, James, 256
Permaloff, Anne, 44, 136
Perry County, 199, 254
Peterson, Christopher, 234
Pew Research Center, 63
Phillips, Kevin, 28
Pickering, Charles, 270
police brutality, 261–62
Politics of Rage, The (Carter), 113
pollution, 50–52
Poole, Sibyl, 45
Powell, Adam Clayton, 133
Powell, Colin, 214, 226
Pratt, Minnie Bruce, 1, 19, 36, 37, 38;
    Rebellion: Essays, 1980–1991, 37
Pratt, Raleigh, 130
Price, Charles, 125
Price of Motherhood, The (Crittenden), 45
Prince of Frogtown, The (Bragg), 100, 249
prisons, 65–66, 68–90, 104–6; death rate
    in, 82–83; prison reform, 84; release of
    prisoners, 88–89, 95, 96
property taxes, 3–4, 153, 165, 169, 188,
    246; and Black Belt, 198; and *Lynch v.
    Alabama*, 243
Pryor, Bill, 42, 43, 241; and capital cases,
    99; and Christianity, 61–62, 140; and
    sentencing guidelines, 92
Public Affairs Research Council of
    Alabama (PARCA), 162, 178
public health, 52–53

public prayer, 61
Pugh v. Sullivan, 69, 84

Quiñones, John, 39

Race to Execution, 102
racism, 22, 36–37, 137; and death penalty,
    102; in politics, 125; and property
    taxes, 153; and George Wallace, 239
Radford, Bob, 249
Raines, Howell, 99, 109, 116; on Paul
    Hubbert, 127; on Guy Hunt, 126; on
    Fob James, 117, 138; on property taxes,
    246; on George Wallace, 113, 114,
    120–21
Rains, David, 94
Rammer Jammer Yellow Hammer (St.
    John), 29
Randolph County, 193–94
Rawls, Phillip, 174, 203
R. C. v. Hornsby, 176
Reagan, Ronald, 71, 121, 123, 155–56, 219,
    234, 269
Rebellion: Essays, 1980–1991 (Pratt), 37
Rector, Ricky Ray, 77
Redstone Arsenal, 58–59, 177
Reed, Joe, 119, 122; and Alabama
    Democratic Conference, 204–5,
    206–7; and Alabama Education
    Association, 209; as Paul Hubbert ally,
    129, 130; loss of city council seat, 207;
    relation to black voters, 130
Reed, Ralph, 61, 140, 142
Reed, Roy, 119
Reeves, Jay, 14
Regions Financial, 208
Reid, Mitch, 51
Reid, Randy, 91

Reilly, Sean, 51

Republican Party: business-first Republicans, 153; decades-long shift in, 137; as white people's party, 28, 126, 149, 264

Resource Renewal Institute, 50

Retirement Systems of Alabama, 2, 14, 135

Reynolds, Johnny, 191–92, 193

Reynolds v. Alabama, 191–92

Rice, Angelena, 217, 232

Rice, Condoleezza, 10, 184, 213–25, 226–32; and affirmative action, 216, 220; and George W. Bush administration, 220–26; and civil rights movement, 214, 217, 229–32; and Hurricane Katrina, 227–28; on torture, 222

Rice, John, 217, 218, 232

Rich, Adrienne, 22

Rich, Frank, 238

Richardson, Ed, 152

Riley, Bob, 154–58, 162–74, 177–80; and Amendment One, 165–72; and Black Belt Action Commission, 200; and constitution, 164; and death penalty, 101; and education, 171; election of, 10, 158; and Iraq War, 55–56, 58, 174; and "Opening Doors," 238; on police brutality, 262; and prisons, 86, 88, 89, 104; and proration, 264; on racial problems, 263; reelection campaign, 175, 177; and released inmates, 95, 96; and *Reynolds v. Alabama*, 192; and state's reputation, 11, 87; women in cabinet, 45

Ritter, Dowd, 208

Robert Trent Jones Golf Trail, 14, 80, 85

Roberts, Diane, 145, 252

Robertson, Blair, 251

Robertson, Pat, 142

Robinson, Eugene, 213, 228–29

Rogers, John, 8

Roper, A. C., 262

Rove, Karl, 85, 149, 161

Rumsfeld, Donald, 223, 226

Rushing, Wanda, 3

Russakoff, Dale, 114; and Condoleezza Rice, 215, 216, 217, 221, 223, 232

Saban, Nick, 244, 245, 246

Sabel, Cheryl, 43

Sack, Kevin, 42

Sadler, Elliott, 277

Safire, William, 140

same-sex marriage, 35–36, 42, 141, 207, 236, 239

Sanders, Hank, 184, 200–201, 202, 204; on Artur Davis, 265; and death penalty, 97; election to legislature, 205; on Nathan Bedford Forrest monument, 256; and Iraq War, 55; and naming of Hwy 14, 255; on senate fight, 8; on Don Siegelman, 159; on slavery, 203, 204

Sanders, Malika, 201

Sanders, Rose, 200–201, 204, 205, 255

Sanford, Mark, 178

Sanneh, Kelefa, 268

Schaeffer, Eric V., 51

Schiavo, Terri, 237

Schlafly, Phyllis, 142

Scowcroft, Brent, 219

Scrushy, Richard, 85, 159, 160

Second Chance Act, 96

segregation, 27–28, 119, 146, 218; and George Wallace, 234

Segrest, Mab, 32, 36–37, 38; *Memoir of a Race Traitor*, 36
Segrest, Marvin, 36, 37
Selma, Ala., 10, 170, 187, 257–60; and Civil War reenactment, 249; and Edmund Pettus Bridge, 257–59; and Nathan Bedford Forrest monument, 255–56; and Hank Sanders, 200; Voting Rights Hall of Fame, 259
sentencing guidelines, 92–94
September 11, 2001, 57, 221, 223
Sessions, Jeff, 36, 156, 206, 269–71; and chain gangs, 73; and image of Alabama, 26; and immigration, 63; and Iraq War, 58; and prosecution of voting rights activists, 212
Sewell, Terri, 44
Sharpless, Buddy, 82
Sharpton, Al, 258
Shashy, William, 81, 85
Sheehan, Miriam, 100
Shelby, Richard, 137; and Great Recession, 269; and image of Alabama, 26; and Iraq War, 55, 58; and Sonia Sotomayor, 271
Shelby County, 8, 51, 80, 119, 211
Shepard, Matthew, 39
Shivers, Lisa, 254
Shores, Janie, 247
Shultz, George, 220
Shuttlesworth, Fred, 34, 217, 229
Siddons, Anne Rivers: *Heartbreak Hotel*, 31–32
Siegelman, Don, 46, 145–55, 157, 159–61, 163; and Black Belt, 201; corruption conviction of, 85, 159, 160, 161; gubernatorial campaigns, 128, 143–44, 158, 175

Siegelman, Leslie Bouchet, 145–46
Sierra Club, 126
Sigler, Robert, 75
Signorile, Michelangelo, 39
Silverstein, Ken, 213
Sims, Ron, 239
Sixteenth Street Church bombing, 116, 210, 218, 230
60 Minutes, 230
slavery, 138, 203, 204, 250
Smiley, Tavis, 161
Smith, James, 189
Smith, Lillian, 36–37
Smitherman, Joe, 256
Snow, Donald, 57
social services, 46–48
Sorensen, Andrew, 252
Sosebee, Diane, 57
Sotomayor, Sonia, 270–71
South Carolina, 44
Southern Center for Human Rights, 78, 90, 105
Southern Company, 51–52
Southern Education Foundation, 179
Southern Exposure, 50
Southern Poverty Law Center, 69, 83
South of Haunted Dreams (Harris), 22
SouthTrust, 167
Sparks, Ron, 265
Spencer, Garria, 196
Spencer, Loretta, 203
Stanford University, 219, 220
"Stars Fell on Alabama," 6, 160,
Star Trek, 221
states' rights, 24
St. Clair Correctional Facility, 83, 87
Steele, Charles, 204
Stevens & Schriefer, 149

Stevenson, Bryan, 103

Steward, William, 63

St. John, Finis, IV, 245

St. John, Warren, 29–30, 246; *Rammer Jammer Yellow Hammer*, 29

Strain, Willie L., 189

Strange, Luther, 177

Straw, Jack, 228

streets, naming and renaming of, 254

Studdard, Ruben, 171, 267–68

Suellentrop, Chris, 77

Suitts, Steve, 70, 179

supreme court. *See* Alabama Supreme Court; U.S. Supreme Court

Survivor, 7

"Sweet Home Alabama," 6, 12

Tabet, Stephen, 83

Talladega Daily Home, 139

Tarver, Robert, 102–3

tax reform, 131, 132, 165, 168, 171; and Bob Riley, 163–71

tax structure, 3–4, 15, 169, 199, 246. *See also* property taxes; tax reform

Tedder, Robert, 105

Ten Commandments monument, 62, 139, 154

Tenet, George, 222

Tennessee, 77, 87, 137

Tennessee-Tombigbee Waterway, 3, 197–98

Tennessee Valley Authority, 50

Terry, Bob, 165

Texas: criminalization of homosexual acts, 42, 43; death row, 99, 102; incarceration rate, 79

Thomas, Clarence, 184

Thomas, Cleo, 245

Thompson, Bailey, 247

Thompson, Myron, 62, 78, 87, 191

Threadgill, Thomas L., 254

ThyssenKrupp, 23

Times (London), 167

Timmons, Bobby, 82

Titusville, Ala., 214–15, 217–18, 220, 224, 229, 232

Today Show, 62

Todd, Patricia, 43, 206, 210

tort reform, 148–49

Touré, Faya Rose, 257

tourism, 14

Tucker, Cynthia, 194–95

Tuscaloosa, Ala., 133, 145

Tuscaloosa News, 238

Tuskegee, Ala., 32

Tuskegee Civic Association, 186

Tutwiler, Julia, 78, 273

21st Century Youth Leadership Movement, 201–02

Twilley, Melody, 252

unemployment, 15, 179

United Nations, 63, 99

University of Alabama: at Birmingham, 64, 94, 127, 208–10, 277; at Tuscaloosa, 145, 146, 238, 252–53

Urban Dictionary, 23

USA Today, 73, 236, 271

U.S. Department of Agriculture, 187

U.S. Department of Justice, 79, 186

U.S. Public Interest Research Group, 51

U.S. Space and Rocket Center, 14

U.S. Supreme Court, 36, 140; on death penalty, 75, 97, 98, 101; on franchise tax, 151; on judges and campaign contributions, 267; on Ledbetter case, 241; *Reynolds v. Sims*, 186; *Roe v. Wade*, 62; on Texas "homosexual conduct" law, 42, 43

Varner, Robert, 71, 72
Vickery, Jim, 142
Viguerie, Richard, 115
Vines, Jerry, 58
Virginia, 204
Voting Rights Act, 123, 186, 257, 260
Vulcan, 220
Vulcans, 220–221, 231

Wacquant, Loïc, 104
Wade, Neal, 141
Wales, Jimbo, 23
Walker, Deloss, 117, 136
Walker, Sam, 258
Wallace, George, 109–16, 118–21, 231, 233–41; assassination attempt on, 113; and Confederate flag, 126; cronyism, 113, 135; fourth gubernatorial campaign, 118–19; image of, 233; legacy and specter of, 10, 121, 233–41; and media, 25; presidential campaign, 113, 115; and prison system, 69–70; racism of, 118, 120; on segregation, 234; and states' rights, 24
Wallace, George, Jr., 120, 137, 138
Wallace, Gerald, 113; tax evasion of, 113
Wallace, Lloyd, 105
Wallace, Lurleen, 44, 110, 115
Wallace, Rusty, 277
Wall Street Journal, 134, 171, 236
Washington Post, 222
Washington Post Magazine, 215

Waters, Jonathan, 176–77
Watkins, Suzanne, 46–47
Weaver, Scotty Joe, 43
Weaver, Vesla Mae, 70
Webb, Sam, 149
Webster, Gerald, 158
Wedowee, Ala., 193–94
Wells, H. Thomas, 267
Welsh, M. Cay, 49
West, Kanye, 228
Western, Bruce, 74–75, 79, 80, 89, 103
When the Levees Broke (Lee), 227
Where I Was From (Didion), 16
white fraternities and sororities, 252–53
white supremacy, 7, 28, 185, 271
Wiese, Andrew, 211
Wilcox County, 197, 254
Williams, Hank, 133
Williams, Jim, 111
Williams, Mike, 133, 237
Williams, Patricia, 101, 214, 227, 232
Williams, Randall, 122
Williamson, Donald, 49
Willing Workers for Freedom and Unity, 48
Wilson, David, 190–91
Wilson, John, 261
Windom, Steve, 85, 148, 157
Wingfield, Kyle, 64
Wiregrass, 35, 118, 205, 292
Witt, Robert, 252
women: and political power, 44–45; and social services, 45–46
Wood, Mary Williams, 237
Woodward, Vann, 67
Wright, Cathy, 46
Wright, Katie, 100
Wyatt v. Stickney, 68, 176

Yackle, Larry, 70, 71, 72, 84

Yancey, William Lowndes, 24, 110

Yardley, Jim, 251

York, Jake Adam, 16–17; *Murder Ballads*, 16; *A Murmuration of Starlings*, 16

Young, Iris Marion: on democratic struggle, 15; on democratization, 188, 196; on differentiated solidarity, 212; on disruption, 256; on inequality, 272; on scope of the polity, 211; on social equality, 3

Young, Neil, 15

Younge, Gary, 7, 109

Younger, Sammy, 36, 37

Žižek, Slavoj, 9, 179, 233

POLITICS AND CULTURE IN THE TWENTIETH-CENTURY SOUTH

A Common Thread: Labor, Politics, and Capital Mobility in the Textile Industry
by BETH ENGLISH

"Everybody Was Black Down There": Race and Industrial Change in the Alabama Coalfields
by ROBERT H. WOODRUM

Race, Reason, and Massive Resistance: The Diary of David J. Mays, 1954–1959
edited by JAMES R. SWEENEY

The Unemployed People's Movement: Leftists, Liberals, and Labor in Georgia, 1929–1941
by JAMES J. LORENCE

Liberalism, Black Power, and the Making of American Politics, 1965–1980
by DEVIN FERGUS

Guten Tag, Y'all: Globalization and the South Carolina Piedmont, 1950–2000
by MARKO MAUNULA

The Culture of Property: Race, Class, and Housing Landscapes in Atlanta, 1880–1950
by LEEANN LANDS

Marching in Step: Masculinity, Citizenship, and The Citadel in Post–World War II America
by ALEXANDER MACAULAY

Rabble Rousers: The American Far Right in the Civil Rights Era
by CLIVE WEBB

Who Gets a Childhood: Race and Juvenile Justice in Twentieth-Century Texas
by WILLIAM S. BUSH

Alabama Getaway: The Political Imaginary and the Heart of Dixie
by ALLEN TULLOS